HAMLYN
ORIENTAL COOKERY
COURSE

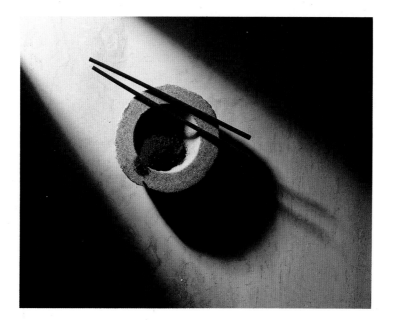

HAMLYN
ORIENTAL COOKERY
COURSE

Edited by

Suzy Powling

HAMLYN

This edition published in 1990 by the
Hamlyn Publishing Group Limited, a division
of the Octopus Publishing Group
Michelin House, 81 Fulham Road, London SW3 6RB

© 1990 The Hamlyn Publishing Group Limited

ISBN 0 600 57109 2

Produced by Mandarin Offset
Printed and bound in Hong Kong

CONTENTS

USEFUL FACTS

In this book quantities are given in metric and Imperial measures. Exact conversion from Imperial to metric measures does not usually give very convenient working quantities and so the metric measures have been rounded into units of 25 grams. The table shows the recommended equivalents.

Ounces	Approx g to nearest whole figure	Recommended conversion to nearest unit of 25	Ounces	Approx g to nearest whole figure	Recommended conversion to nearest unit of 25
1	28	25	11	312	300
2	57	50	12	340	350
3	85	75	13	368	375
4	113	100	14	396	400
5	142	150	15	425	425
6	170	175	16 (1 lb)	454	450
7	198	200	17	482	475
8	227	225	18	510	500
9	255	250	19	539	550
10	283	275	20 (1¼ lb)	567	575

Note: When converting quantities over 20 oz first add the appropriate figures in the centre column, then adjust to the nearest unit of 25. As a general guide, 1 kg (1000 g) equals 2.2 lb or about 2 lb 3 oz. This method of conversion gives good results in nearly all cases.

Liquid measures The millilitre has been used in this book and the following table gives a few examples.

Imperial	Approx ml to nearest whole figure	Recommended ml	Imperial	Approx ml to nearest whole figure	Recommended ml
¼ pint	142	150 ml	1 pint	567	600 ml
½ pint	283	300 ml	1½ pints	851	900 ml
¾ pint	425	450 ml	1¾ pints	992	1000 ml (1 litre)

Ingredients Many of the recipes in this book include ingredients which may be unfamiliar to you. The correct Oriental name is given first, with the English name in brackets afterwards. A brief description of these ethnic ingredients is given in the Ingredients section, pages 12–21). Many of these ingredients are now available in supermarkets, while specialist Oriental food stores should be able to supply those that supermarkets cannot.

Spoon measures All spoon measures given in this book are level.

Eggs Use size 2 or 3 eggs in all recipes that include eggs.

Oil temperatures Oil for deep-frying should be heated to the stated temperature, and that temperature should be maintained during the cooking process. At 180°C/350°F, a 2.5 cm (1 inch) cube of day-old bread browns in 30 seconds; at 160°C/325°F, it takes 45 seconds.

Servings The recipes in this book give a stated number of servings when presented as part of a complete meal.

Oven temperatures The table below gives recommended equivalents. All cooking times are for preheated ovens and grills.

	°C	°F	Gas Mark		°C	°F	Gas Mark
Very cool	110	225	$\frac{1}{4}$	Moderately hot	190	375	5
	120	250	$\frac{1}{2}$		200	400	6
Cool	140	275	1	Hot	220	425	7
	150	300	2		230	450	8
Moderate	160	325	3	Very hot	240	475	9
	180	350	4				

Measurements When making any of the recipes in this book, follow one set of measures only, as metric and Imperial measures are not interchangeable.

INTRODUCTION

'Oriental' means of the east, a word coined in medieval times to describe the lands where the sun rises. Even now it has a poetic ring to it, and although many Westerners have travelled eastwards, increased familiarity has not diminished the fascination of those exotic lands.

The wonderful food of the East is one of the features that continues to intrigue and delight us. In the vast continent of Asia there are many different peoples, with their own national cuisines. This book deals with the best known and major schools of China, India and Japan, as well as those which are fast acquiring new enthusiasts: Thailand, Vietnam, Indonesia, Malaysia, Burma and Korea.

China, the third largest country in the world, stretches from the arid plains of Mongolia in the north to the subtropical climate of Yunnan and Kwantung in the south (on the border with Vietnam). Peking, the capital, is in the north, where wheat, not rice, is the staple grain, from which noodles, steamed buns, dumplings and pancakes are made. In this rather bleak environment meat is something of a luxury. Mutton and lamb are popular, a relic of the invasion of the Mongols, though they are rarely eaten elsewhere in China. The Chinese cabbage, which can be stored over winter, is the most widely used vegetable. In contrast to this is the highly refined cooking developed at the Imperial Court of Peking, with such masterpieces as Peking Duck.

Eastern China lies on the great plain formed by the delta of the mighty Yangtse river, and is one of China's leading agricultural regions. Both wheat and rice are grown, as well as soy beans and an abundance of vegetables.

The southern province of Canton, with its mild, semi-tropical climate, grows produce in abundance all year round, and plentiful feed for livestock means a good supply of high-quality meat and poultry. The long coastline gives access to the rich fishing grounds of the South China Sea. It is little wonder that for centuries the Cantonese have been noted for their sophisticated cuisine, which is the best-known of the Chinese regional styles.

Szechuan, in the west, lies in a great basin ringed with mountains. With fertile soil and a warm, humid climate, crops can be grown all the year round, making this region one of the most prosperous. Fruit and vegetables grow in profusion, as well as spices such as chillies and the famous Szechuan peppercorns. Szechuan food is noted for being hot, spicy and strongly flavoured, using garlic and onions as well as chillies. Yunnan in the deep south-west is famous for its ham and game.

It was in Yunnan in the time of the Han Dynasty, almost 2,000 years ago, that tribes called T'ai settled along the border. These were the forerunners of the founders of Thailand; by the mid-fifteenth century they had moved south and created a great culture with fabulous cities in the middle of a large, fertile plain. Traders from India, Europe and China crossed paths here and exchanged goods – chillies from Mexico, spices from the East Indies – laying the foundation for a cuisine that is diverse and delicious. A monsoon climate ensures lush vegetation; paddy-fields of rice stretch for miles and the coast on the Gulf of Thailand yields great catches of fish and lobster. The Thais adopted many Chinese precepts about food as dictated by Confucius, and the Szechuan influence with spices is very clear. The effect of Indian cooking styles is also evident, in Thai curries, dishes of rice with a stew or sauce to add relish.

The population of India includes a number of races and creeds, all with their own dietary laws. Among the Hindus are 400 million strict vegetarians. South India is the Hindu stronghold; dishes here are based on vegetables in astonishing variety, a range of nourishing pulses, and rice. Curries are thin and fiery – the famous vindaloo comes from the south-western district of Goa. Gujarat, to the west, also has a distinctive vegetarian cuisine, here flavoured with red chillies, cumin and coriander. Parsi food combines the Gujarati love of sweet and sour flavours with Persian-style mixtures of meat and dried fruit.

Fish is of central importance in the eastern regions of Bihar, the birthplace of Buddha, and Bengal, close to the estuary of the Ganges. The mainly Hindu population celebrates many religious festivals, which may explain why some of the most popular Indian sweets, such as Cream Cheese Balls in Syrup (page 218), were invented here. The most elegant Indian food is found in the north, a legacy of the Mughal (Muslim) emperors and their splendid courts. The spicing of Kashmiri curries is subtle and sophisticated; there are some delicious recipes for game, and for meat and poultry. The rice grown here is the superb Basmati. Wheat is grown in the Punjab, which is famed for tandoori cooking.

South-east Asian countries have been involved in international trade for centuries, contributing to a cross-cultural exchange that continues to thrive. French influence has left its mark on Vietnamese cooking – delicate and delicious in its own right – in combinations of herbs and spices and the use of sauces. Some would say, of course, that nouvelle cuisine is very old in the East.

For many years, Japan deliberately kept visitors from other nations at arm's length. This self-enforced isolation of a country that is now a centre of world trade ensured that cultural traditions remained pure, and this is clearly evident in the preparation of food. Japanese food aims to satisfy the aesthetic sense as well as the physical appetite; its air of restraint derives as much from economy with scarce supplies (and cooking fuel) on the tiny islands as from cultivated tastes. Rice and fish are the most important ingredients, along with vegetables (and seaweed), chicken, beef, eggs and noodles, with sharp sauces and garnishes.

Diverse as they are, the cuisines of the East are united by a reliance on traditional ingredients and cooking methods that have proved their worth over centuries. These traditions are now seen to accord with the most modern ideas about food, its quality and presentation. In addition, the communal, relaxed atmosphere of Oriental meals makes them very attractive for Westerners.

In Part One, this book describes the skills necessary to practise classic Oriental cooking methods, as well as the ingredients and equipment required and authentic styles of presentation. Part Two presents the opportunity to practise these basic skills, with a collection of recipes from all corners of the East.

PART 1

This section introduces you to the basic techniques needed for the preparation of classic and everyday dishes in Oriental cuisine. To begin with, it is important to familiarize yourself with the variety of ingredients used in China, India, Japan and the rest of South-east Asia, some of which will become useful store-cupboard items as you add to the range of dishes in your own repertoire.

Important equipment is discussed next; distinctive though Oriental cooking methods certainly are, it is interesting to see that – with the exception of the invaluable wok – you do not have to invest in a great deal of expensive equipment to practise them. As you perfect your skills and enjoy the rewards they bring, you will probably want to buy one or two authentic pieces of equipment to further your progress.

The major part of this section is devoted to the cooking techniques special to oriental cooking; in each case the basic principles are explained and a master recipe given in simple steps to demonstrate how to achieve perfect results. Work through these, and if you like, move on to the suggested supplementary recipes, and you will have mastered all you need to know to cook any of the delicious recipes you will find in Part Two.

The way food is prepared for cooking is crucial to methods that are often fast and at high temperatures. Fish and poultry, both widely used in the East, need particularly careful preparation, as described on pages 50–57. This ensures not only perfect cooking, but the attractive appearance so crucial to Oriental meals. The section closes with a discussion of the importance of food presentation and gives some useful ideas on menu planning.

Left: Deep-fried fish and vegetables (page 37)

INGREDIENTS

The list below includes ingredients particular to Eastern cooking. Canned vegetables are a useful standby in the storecupboard. Flavourings sold in jars should be refrigerated after opening and used within 3 months. Buy spices in small quantities and store them in a cool, dark, dry place. Use within 6 months.

Abalone

A smooth-textured shellfish used in Chinese and Japanese cookery. It is available canned and is best steamed.

Aduki, azuki

Small red beans that can be prepared like lentils. In Japanese cookery canned sweetened beans are used in puddings.

Agar-Agar

An efficient setting agent, available in sticks, strands and powdered form, derived from a type of seaweed, but which has no flavour and is valued in hot countries because it does not melt in the heat and needs no refrigeration. A useful gelatine substitute for vegetarians. Called *kanten* in Japan.

Aromatic Salt

Aromatic salt – that is, salt enhanced by mixing in spices and other ingredients – is often used in the Middle East and is delicious sprinkled on many foods, including Indian dishes.

1 teaspoon coriander seeds
1 teaspoon white cumin seeds
½ teaspoon Szechuan pepper
½ teaspoon fennel seeds
½ teaspoon allspice
½ teaspoon sesame seeds
6–8 hazelnuts
75 g (3 oz) sea salt

Makes approx. 100 g (4 oz)

Akamiso

The Japanese name for red soy bean paste.

Aniseed

Small, grey-green, liquorice-flavoured seeds widely used in India in the preparation of confectionery and in sweet and hot chutneys.

Asafoetida

A pale yellow spice with a strong, distinctive flavour used in small quantities some Indian lentil and bean dishes as an enhancer of other flavours.

Ata

A type of finely ground wholemeal flour used to make chappati (recipe, page 199).

1. Roast the spices and nuts as described for garam masala (see page 16). Allow to cool, then grind them with the salt as finely or as coarsely as you prefer.

2. The mixture will keep indefinitely if stored in an airtight jar and kept in a cool, dry place.

Bamboo shoots

The tender young shoots which appear at the base of the bamboo are gathered at the end of the rainy season, parboiled and canned. Used extensively in Chinese and Japanese cookery, they are available sliced or unsliced.

Banh trang

Thin, brittle rice paper wrappers used for spring rolls and Vietnamese pancakes. Before use, they should be dipped in water to make them pliable.

Bean curd

Called *tofu* in China and Japan, this is made from puréed soy beans. It is soft and white, and has a cheese-like texture, which ranges from firm to 'silken'. Bean curd is high in protein and very low in fat, and is therefore highly nutritious. It has a bland flavour but combines well with other ingredients. Fresh bean curd, sold in cakes 6.5 cm (2½ inches) square and 1 cm (½ inch) thick, will keep fresh for several days if stored in the refrigerator. Dried bean curd is also sold in cake form. It can be cut into strips or slices, and braised or fried, generally with other ingredients. Dried bean curd skin is available in thin, stiff sheets. It must be soaked, preferably in warm water, for about 30 minutes before use, and is usually braised or stewed with meat and vegetables. See also Fermented bean curd.

Bean sprouts

These are the sprouts of small green mung beans which are available fresh and canned, and can also be easily grown at home. Rinse 2 tablespoons of mung beans in cold water and place in a large glass jar. Cover with muslin or a piece of greaseproof paper with a few airholes punched in. Place in a dark, fairly warm place until the beans germinate – probably overnight. Rinse the sprouting beans in clean water two or three times over the following day or two until the shoots are about 1 cm (½ inch) long. Use in crunchy Chinese vegetable mixtures, cooked very briefly to retain their crisp texture.

Beni-shoga

Sweet pickled ginger root traditionally used in Japan to garnish sushi dishes.

Besan

A very fine yellow flour used in Indian bread cookery. Made from ground chick peas, it should be sieved before use as it tends to form hard lumps during storage. It is low in gluten and very high in protein.

Bitter gourd

see Karela

Blachan

A strong-smelling, salty shrimp paste from South-east Asia, available in cans or packets.

Because it has a very pungent smell, keep it tightly sealed in the refrigerator after opening. Before use it must be well-fried, or wrapped in foil and roasted. Also called *trassi* (Malaysia), *kapi* (Thailand) and *nga pi* (Burma).

Black beans

Salted, fermented black beans with a strong, salty flavour, used in Chinese cooking. Soak for 5–10 minutes before use.

Black bean paste or sauce

Widely used in Chinese cookery instead of soy sauce when a thicker sauce is required, this paste is made from salted soy beans, ground and mixed with flour and spices. Sold in cans or jars, it should be refrigerated after opening.

Black jack

Dark brown, strong caramel colouring agent, available commercially prepared. Dark soy sauce may be used as a substitute, but is less sweet. Called *nuoc mau* in Vietnam. To make caramel at home, see Fish au caramel, page 94.

Bonito

see Katsuo-bushi

Brinjal pickle

Aubergines pickled in a spicy, curry sauce, this is a favourite condiment in India. (Recipe, page 207).

Candlenuts

Creamy white nuts used in Malaysia and Indonesia to thicken and sweeten curries. They are so oily they can be burned – hence the name – and must be cooked and ground before use (they are violently purgative in the raw state). Also called *kemiri nuts*. Use macadamia nuts as a substitute.

Cardamoms

Highly aromatic white or green pods used in Indian cookery. Black or brown cardamoms are large, less aromatic and cheaper. Used whole, cardamoms should not be eaten: remove them from the dish before serving if you wish. If a recipe calls for cardamom seeds, carefully remove them from the pods rather than buy them ready packed – they will have lost a lot of their potency.

Cassia bark

The bark of a tree similar to cinnamon but thicker. Can be used whole in Indian dishes like cinnamon sticks, and should be removed before serving.

Cayenne pepper

Powdered dried red chillies used to add fieriness to curries, soups and stir-fries. The strength varies from batch to batch and it should be used with caution.

Channa dal

See Dal, dhal

Chick pea flour

see Besan

Chillies

Chillies were introduced to South-east Asia in the early sixteenth century by Portuguese traders who brought them from central America. They are related to capsicums (sweet peppers) but are much hotter. Both red and green varieties are available fresh; red chillies are also available in dried form. Treat these little vegetables with care: do not touch your face or rub your eyes while handling, and wash your hands immediately afterwards. Discard the seeds for a less pungent effect. To do this, hold the chilli at the stalk end, pierce it

through the sides with a small sharp knife and slice lengthways from stem to tip. Scrape out the seeds with the point and back of the knife. Dried chillies may be deseeded by cutting off the base at the stem and rolling the pod between the thumb and fingers to loosen the seeds. These may be shaken out of the open end. Remember that the smallest chillies are the hottest. Store them wrapped in paper in a plastic box (to keep them well away from other foods) in the refrigerator.

Chilli oil

Vegetable oil flavoured with red chillies which can be used in stir-fried dishes to add pungency.

Chilli paste

Made from chillies, soy beans, salt, sugar and flour, this is added to curries, stir-fried and braised dishes to add pungency and thicken the sauce.

Chilli sauce

A reddish-orange sauce made from red chillies. Very hot, it has a consistency like tomato ketchup and is sometimes flavoured with garlic. Used in Chinese and South-east Asian cookery. See also Tabasco.

Chinese cabbage, napa cabbage

To the Chinese *Pe-tsai* is cabbage. Called *hakusai* in Japan, it looks like a tightly packed cos lettuce with white midribs and can be used in salads or lightly cooked. *Pak-choi* is Chinese mustard or mustard greens and the leaves do not form a heart. This is the variety which, as well as being used fresh, is fermented in salt to make pickled cabbage, sometimes called Chinese sauerkraut, which must be rinsed well before it is used in cooking.

Chinese wine

Rice wine is used to flavour many Chinese dishes. It is commonly called yellow wine because of its golden colour. A pale dry sherry makes an excellent substitute. See also Rice wine

Cilantro

see Coriander

Cinnamon

This spice comes from the bark of a tree, and is used in Indian sweet dishes. It can be used for savoury pilaus, but in India cassia bark is preferred.

Cloud ears

see Mushrooms

Cloves

An important spice used whole but with discretion to enrich some Indian meat and rice dishes – the flavour is very strong. The cloves themselves are not eaten but they are too small to be easily removed from the dish before serving.

Coconut

The coconut is one of the most important crops in South-east Asia, since it produces oil, sugar and fibre as well as the ingredients essential to many dishes, sweet and savoury. When choosing a fresh coconut, pick one that is heavy and free from mould, and shake it to make sure the juice inside has not dried up. To open the nut, pierce two of the eyes and drain the liquid into a cup (it cannot be used in cooking but is pleasant to drink). Hold the nut horizontally and crack a hammer against the ridges to open it. Prise off the flesh with a knife and peel off the skin with a potato peeler. Break up the flesh into pieces before grating it: it freezes beautifully and

Coconut Milk and Cream

In South-east Asia, coconut milk is produced by steeping the shredded flesh in boiling water and squeezing it to extract the liquid; in Malaysia there are special stalls where this is carried out. In the West the following method is more practicable.

225 g (8 oz) unsweetened desiccated coconut
600 ml (1 pint) boiling water

Makes 450 ml ($\frac{3}{4}$ pint)

1. Place the coconut in a food processor or blender, add 450 ml ($\frac{3}{4}$ pint) boiling water and process for 20–30 seconds.

2. Transfer the liquid to a large bowl and add the remaining water. Leave to cool.

3. Strain the cool coconut milk into a jug through a sieve lined with muslin, squeezing the coconut to extract the milk. Cover, and store in the refrigerator. The coconut cream will quickly rise to the surface and can be skimmed off for separate use if required. Store as fresh milk.

thaws fast. Desiccated coconut is the dried flesh and has good storage qualities. Coconut powder is the finely ground coconut flesh which when mixed with milk or water becomes a creamy paste.

Coconut milk, which is not the juice, but the liquid extracted from the flesh, is one of the most important ingredients in Thai and Indian cookery, savoury and sweet. (It is called *Nam Katee* in Thailand.) Instructions for preparing it are given above and it is also available in cans and cartons. Coconut cream can be used instead if preferred. This can be bought in blocks to which boiling water is added before use.

Coriander

The fresh leaves of this plant are of special importance to curries. They give a distinctive fragrant taste when added towards the end of cooking and are widely used to garnish Indian, Chinese and Thai dishes. In Thailand the chopped roots are also used, and fresh bunches are sold with the roots intact. Other names are *Chinese* or *Japanese parsley* or *cilantro*. Flat-leaved parsley can be used as an approximate substitute. Coriander seeds are an important spice, used whole or ground in meat and vegetable dishes, and essential to curries. The flavour is faintly redolent of oranges.

Cumin seeds

Called *jeera* in India, both black (*kala*) and white (*safed*) cumin seeds are available. They are botanically related to but in flavour quite distinct from caraway seeds. Of central importance in Indian cooking, the flavour combines well with coriander seeds, green lentils and spinach.

Curry leaves

The aromatic leaves of the neem tree are lemony in flavour. Usually available dried, but occasionally fresh, they are used in curry powder and to flavour rices dishes in India, Malaysia and Indonesia.

Curry powder

There is no single combination of spices that can rightfully claim to be the 'true' curry powder. There are certain

Mild Curry Powder

This powder will keep up to 18 months in a large screw-topped jar in a cool dark place. For a very mild powder, omit the chilli, mustard and pepper.

Mix together the following:

Ground spices	heaped teaspoons:
coriander	12
white cumin	6
gram flour (optional)	5
garlic powder	5
fenugreek seeds	4

with:

paprika	4
turmeric	4
garam masala (page 16)	4
curry leaves (optional)	1
asafoetida (optional)	1
ground ginger	1
mango powder (optional)	1
chilli powder	1
mustard powder	1
white pepper	1

Makes approx. 225 g (8 oz)

essential ingredients, but the proportions in which they are mixed and the variations on the basic formula are entirely at the cook's discretion. Malaysian and Thai curry powders are much less pungent than Indian; mild and aromatic, they may be bought in specialist Oriental food shops.

Commercially prepared curry powders vary enormously in strength and excellence. Making your own is not difficult, and makes it possible to devise a combination that suits your palate exactly, and which can be made hotter at will with a little extra chilli powder or cayenne pepper. The recipe above can be adjusted in this way to suit your own taste.

Daikon

Also called *Japanese radish* or *mooli*, the daikon is a long white radish with a crisp texture. It is used extensively as a garnish when grated, sliced and carved, and as a cooked vegetable.

Dal, dhal

The general name given to a variety of pulses grown in the Indian sub-continent. Along with rice, these pulses, split and sometimes skinned, form the staple diet of millions of people. There are several varieties – *moong* (from mung beans), *urhad* (from small round black beans), *channa* (from chick peas) and the dal which most people in the West are familiar with, the lentil. They are widely interchangeable, and the cooking methods are similar, requiring soaking in cold water and boiling before being incorporated in a cooked dish.

Dashi

Made with preflaked dried bonito flakes (*katsuo bushi*) and seaweed (*konbu*), dashi is the basic Japanese stock (recipe, page 69), and is used in many recipes. Dashi is easy to make but sachets of instant dashi mix, which sell under the name of *dashi-no-moto*, are available for the sake of convenience.

Dried mushrooms

see Mushrooms

Dried seaweed

see Konbu, Nori

Mild Curry Paste

It is well worth making up your own bottled curry paste, which will keep indefinitely providing all the water is evaporated during stir-frying.

225 g (8 oz) Mild Curry Powder (see left)
250 ml (8 fl oz) vinegar
250 ml (8 fl oz) sunflower oil

Makes approx. 425 g (14 oz)

1. Mix the curry powder with the vinegar and enough water to make a paste which is not too runny.

2. Heat the oil in a large frying pan or wok. Add the paste: it will splutter at first but will soon settle down. Stir-fry for 15 minutes or so until the water has completely evaporated to leave a creamy paste. The oil will rise to the surface when the paste is set aside. This means it is fully cooked.

3. Transfer the slightly cooled paste to a warm sterilized bottle or jar. Heat a little more oil and pour it on top of the paste to ensure that no mould develops. Cover tightly with a good-fitting lid.

Fenugreek

The bittersweet and powerful seed of the fenugreek plant, generally available in powder form. Used in Indian food, particularly in curry powders. Both seeds and powder should be used in moderation.

Fermented bean curd

Also called *bean curd cheese*, this is made by fermenting small cubes of bean curd in wine and salt. It is available in two forms – red and white. Both are very salty and strong-tasting and are normally used for seasoning meats and vegetables in Chinese cooking or as a condiment. For breakfast in China, very small quantities of fermented bean curd are sometimes eaten with copious amounts of rice gruel.

Fish sauce, fish gravy

Available in bottles, this very salty, thin, brown liquid is made by fermenting fish or shrimps with salt and soy and draining off the liquid. It is used in Indian cookery and very extensively in Malay and Thai cuisine, where it is called *nam pla* and in Vietnam, where it is called *nuoc mam*. It you cannot obtain it, use anchovy essence as a substitute.

Five-spice powder

This aromatic seasoning used in Chinese cookery is made from a selection of five ground spices: star anise, fennel, cloves, cinnamon and Szechuan pepper. It is normally used sparingly to season red-cooked or roasted meat and poultry. Store in an airtight container.

Flower flavourings and essences

Many Indian and Thai desserts and cakes are perfumed with such flower essences as rose- and orange-blossom water or jasmine oil. Screwpine (*kewra*) is sometimes used instead of rose-water as it is less expensive. A very few drops of these flavourings are needed as they are fairly powerful.

Food colourings

Yellow and red food colourings are used in some Indian foods, such as tandoori dishes, but make no contribution to the taste. If you are allergic to the tartrazine contained in these substances, use instead a little turmeric for yellow and mild paprika for red.

Curry Purée

In India, fresh garlic, ginger, onion, coriander and spices are 'wet ground' into a fine purée which is then fried at the beginning of many recipes. This is used to give a creamy texture and savoury taste to curry dishes. It is an important component in the making of a good curry and it is useful to make up one large batch and freeze most of it. This recipe makes a large quantity but the time and effort saved makes it worth doing. The quantities can be scaled down as required.

20 plump garlic cloves, peeled
225 g (8 oz) ghee or concentrated butter
1 × 50 g (2 oz) piece fresh root ginger, chopped
5 onions, coarsely chopped
1 × 125–175 g (4–6 oz) bunch coriander, finely chopped
225 g (8 oz) carrots, canned, frozen, or pre-cooked fresh
900 g (2 lb) canned tomatoes
1 × 425 g (14 oz) can Cream of Tomato Soup
7 heaped tablespoons Mild Curry Paste (see left)
salt

Makes approximately 4 litres (7 pints)

1. Place the garlic in a blender with a little water and process to a fine purée. Heat the ghee or butter in a 5.5. litre (10 pint) saucepan or use 2 smaller ones. Stir-fry the garlic purée for 5 minutes.

2. Place the ginger in the blender (there is no need to rinse the blender between processes) with a little water and work to a fine purée. Add the ginger to the frying garlic and stir-fry for 5 more minutes.

3. Meanwhile purée the onions and coriander with a little water, working in batches and adding each one to the pan as it is ready. Cover the pan and continue to cook for 30 minutes over a gentle heat, stirring occasionally.

4. Purée the carrots and tomatoes with their juices and add them to the pan. Cook the mixture for 5 minutes and add the tomato soup, curry paste and salt to taste. Simmer for a further 30 minutes. Add a little water if necessary to maintain a reasonably thick consistency.

Galangal

This light yellow root is a member of the ginger family, but it is stronger than ginger. Called *laos* in Indonesia and *ka* in Thailand, it is used sliced in a range of recipes. The powdered variety can be used instead if mixed with hot water. The old English name is galingale, dating from its – probably medicinal – use in the Middle Ages.

Garam masala

A blend of ground spices used in many savoury Indian dishes. It can be bought ready-made but tastes fresher if made at home. *Garam* = hot, *masala* = mixture, and the recipe given on page 16 is a fragrant blend mild enough to be used as a condiment.

Garlic

The garlic grown in the East is smaller than that of the West and the skin is much thinner, so they can be crushed together.

Garam Masala

There are almost as many recipes for garam masala as there are cooks in India. For this recipe, use green cardamoms. Measure the spices with teaspoons or tablespoons, depending on the quantity you wish to make. If stored in an airtight jar, garam masala should keep for 3–6 months.

1½ spoons cardamom pods
5 spoons coriander seeds
1 spoon cumin seeds
1½ spoons whole cloves
6 spoons whole black
    peppercorns

1. Remove the seeds from the cardamoms and place them on a baking tray with the remaining ingredients.

2. Bake in a preheated very hot oven (240°C, 475°F, Gas Mark 9) for 10 minutes, then leave to cool. Grind to a fine powder. Store in an airtight jar.

Variation:
For Fragrant Garam Masala, in a small pan separately dry-fry 3 × 7.5 cm (3 inch) cinnamon sticks, 2 teaspoons cardamom seeds, and 1 teaspoon whole cloves. When all are cool, grind together to a fine powder then add half a nutmeg, grated.

Our tough-skinned garlic needs to be peeled. Many meat, fish and poultry preparations need garlic (and/or ginger) paste so it is useful to prepare large quantities of each and store them. Both can be safely kept with or without refrigeration for 3–4 weeks without change in flavour. To make garlic paste, peel 100–175 g (4–6 oz) garlic cloves and grind with the minimum of water needed to make a fine paste. Add about ¼ teaspoon salt and mix well. Store wrapped in a polythene bag and placed in a sealed container away from other foods. Pickled garlic (see recipe, page 19) is sometimes used in Thailand as an addition to fried rice dishes, or as a condiment with Chinese sausages.

Ghee

Ghee is clarified butter. This can be heated to a higher temperature than butter and most oils without burning and is widely used in Indian cookery. For the best flavour, ghee is made from unsalted butter. Vegetable ghee is also available.
    Concentrated butter makes an acceptable substitute for ghee, but ordinary butter burns. You can buy ghee in some Indian stores, or make your own. To make 175 g (6 oz) ghee, melt 225 g (8 oz) butter in a saucepan over low heat. Slowly simmer the melted butter until it becomes clear and a whitish residue settles at the bottom. Remove the pan from the heat and spoon off any foam. Leave to cool slightly. Drain the clear oil from the top into a clean jar, pouring through a strainer lined with cheesecloth. Cover the jar. Ghee does not need to be refrigerated.

Ginger

Fresh root ginger, sometimes known as green ginger, is very widely used in Oriental cuisine. Before use, peel the root then slice, crush or chop finely. To keep ginger fresh, peel, then wash and place in a jar. Cover with pale dry sherry, seal and store in the refrigerator. Ground ginger is not an acceptable substitute, but dried root ginger may be used, in which case the quantity should be decreased as it is sharper in taste. Ginger paste can be made in the same way as garlic paste (see above), if the ginger is soaked overnight to soften it and chopped finely before being blended with water. See also Beni-shoga.

Ginkgo nuts

Used in Japan, these creamy nuts turn pale green when cooked and are included in savoury cup custards and other steamed dishes. Only the fresh nuts are worth using, although canned ones are available. To loosen the thin inner skin, drop the nuts in hot water.

Glutinous rice

see Rice, page 22.

Glutinous rice flour

Called mochiko in Japan, this flour is ground from glutinous rice and is used to make certain cakes and as a thickener for sauces.

Gobo

The edible roots of the burdock plant, used in Japanese cookery.

Goma-jio

Salted sesame seeds used as a condiment in Japan. Toast 2 tablespoons white sesame seeds in a dry frying pan until golden brown. Transfer to a small bowl and combine with 3–4 teaspoons salt. A simple dipping sauce is made from a combination of ground toasted sesame seeds, dark soy sauce and mirin from which the alcohol has been boiled off.

Gram flour

This flour, made from lentils, is used in India to thicken sauces, in curry powder and to make pakoras (recipe, page 199). Finely milled to a light gold colour, it has a distinctive taste. You can make your own substitute by grinding yellow split peas very finely.

Guava

This tropical fruit is yellow- or purple-skinned with pale green or pink flesh. Very high in vitamin C, guavas are available both fresh and canned in syrup and can be used in fruit salads or ice creams.

Hair seaweed

see Seaweed

Hakusai

Also called Napa cabbage. See Chinese cabbage.

Harusame

Japanese noodles, usually made from soy-bean flour, that are very fine and translucent. The name means 'spring rain'.

Hijiki

A brown algae seaweed used in Japanese cookery.

Hoisin sauce

This thick, brownish-red sauce is based on soy beans combined with sugar, flour, vinegar, salt, garlic, chilli and sesame seed oil. Used in China as a condiment and in cooked dishes, it will keep several months after opening if stored in the refrigerator.

Jaggery

Sugar from palm or cane that is dark and unrefined, used in India to flavour vegetarian curries and to sweeten hot milk. Sold in the market place in large sticky balls wrapped in leaves. Use molasses as a substitute.

Japanese radish

see Daikon

Kalonji

Small, tear-shaped black onion seeds used in India to add

piquancy to vegetable curries and certain breads.

Kampyo

Long, dried, ribbon-like strips from an edible gourd. Used in Japan for tying and securing foods. They can be cooked with vegetables or fish and should be soaked before use, kneaded with salt and washed again.

Kanten

see Agar-agar

Karela

The *bitter gourd* or *balsam pear* is a knobbly, yellow fruit often used in Indian vegetable curries and chutneys, roughly chopped and pre-soaked in salted water to remove excess bitterness. The young leaves can be cooked like spinach.

Kasu

The lees of rice wine, sold in large blocks in Oriental stores.

Katsuo bushi

The dried fillet of a bonito fish. When flaked, it is one of the essential ingredients of Japanese cookery, as it is used as the basic flavouring in dashi (Japanese stock, recipe page 69). It is also used as a garnish and is available pre-flaked.

Konbu

Dried kelp, a type of seaweed, is a basic ingredient in Japanese cooking, used not only to flavour dashi (Japanese stock, recipe page 69), but as a vegetable in its own right.

Laos

see Galangal

Lemon grass

A sub-tropical plant somewhat resembling a spring onion but which gives a delicious lemony flavour to South-east Asian dishes. The bulb may be ground in spice mixtures, the leaves bruised or sliced and cooked in sauces or used whole as an aromatic garnish. Called *takrai* in Thailand. Also known as *serah* or *serai*.

Lime leaves

Used in Indonesian, Thai and other South-east Asian cuisines, the glossy dark green leaves – *bai makrut* – of a particular variety of lime give an intense lemon aroma to curried dishes. They are also called *citrus leaf* or *kaffir lime leaves* and can be bought fresh. Refrigerated, they will keep for several weeks. The grated rind of the fresh fruit is also used, but is only available dried in the West. Add a quarter teaspoon to a dish with the grated rind of an ordinary lime.

Lotus

The lotus is an aquatic plant related to the waterlily. The parts commonly used in Oriental cookery are the edible roots (called *renkon* in Japan) and seeds, and the leaves. In China, fresh lotus root, which has a distinctive pattern when sliced, is sometimes eaten as a sweet, with an apricot sauce poured over. In the West, however, it is usually only available dried or canned, in which form it is best used as a constituent of a mixed vegetable dish – it tastes a little like artichokes. Dried lotus root should be soaked overnight before use. Lotus seeds are oval in shape and about 1 cm ($\frac{1}{2}$ inch) long. They are used in braised vegetable dishes, soups and savoury stuffings. Sugared lotus seeds are eaten as a festival sweet. Dried lotus leaves are used to wrap foods which are to be steamed. They impart a delicate flavour to the food, but the leaves themselves are not eaten. Soak in warm water for about 20 minutes before use.

Lychees, litchis

These Oriental fruits grow in bunches like cherries. They have a thin, hard pinky-brown shell that peels off easily to reveal white flesh with a delicate sweetly acid flavour. The fruits are sometimes dried like raisins and are sold as litchi 'nuts'.

Macadamia nuts

Ground or pounded with curry spices, macadamia nuts are used as thickening agents in the curries of Singapore and Malaysia. The flavour is rather sweet and they have a very high oil content.

Makrut

see Lime leaves

Mango powder

The ground powder of dried mangoes, which gives a sour flavour and a golden-brown colour to Indian curries. Use sparingly.

Matcha

The powdered green tea used for the traditional Japanese tea ceremony. It is made from the most tender leaves of the first spring picking, and is processed by a very expensive and laborious method.

Mirin

A sweet rice wine with a very low alcohol content. It is used in many Japanese dishes to add a subtle sweetness. If unavailable, use 1 teaspoon sugar for each tablespoon mirin.

Miso

A rich, savoury paste used in Japanese cooking. It is made from fermented soy beans, malt and salt, and has many applications, often being used in soups. There are several varieties available, of which white (or light) miso and red miso are the most common.

Mochigome

Glutinous rice: see page 22.

Mochiko

see Glutinous rice flour, page 16.

Monosodium glutamate (MSG)

This chemical compound is sometimes described as 'taste essence'. It is used in Chinese cookery to bring out the natural flavours in food, and is widely used in restaurants. However, it should be used sparingly at home – $\frac{1}{4}$ to $\frac{1}{2}$ teaspoon is ample in any recipe – or you may wish to omit it if you are allergic to such substances. It is obtainable in most Oriental stores.

Mooli

The Indian name for Japanese radish or daikon.

Mung beans

These tiny green beans, unlike other pulses or dal, are usually eaten as a whole grain (in India) or sprouted (in China) – they are the seeds of bean sprouts – rather than split. They cook quickly without prior soaking.

Mung bean threads

see Noodles

Mushrooms

Chinese mushrooms, called *shiitake* in Japan, are a beautiful pale gold colour when fresh, and have a pleasantly firm texture and a haunting flavour. They are widely available dried, and should be soaked before cooking. Other Oriental mushrooms used to give a contrasting texture to braised and stir-fried dishes are the little *straw mushrooms* and *tree ears*, both of which are available dried. The smooth, oval straw mushrooms are also available canned. Tree ears (also called *wood ears* or *cloud ears*) are a tree fungus, greyish-black in colour and unimpressive when dried, but they stretch out to gelatinous ear-shaped caps with a crunchy texture when soaked.

Mustard oil

This yellow oil made from mustard seeds is quite pungent when raw and amazingly sweet when heated to a slight haze. It is used in Bengal and Kashmir for cooking vegetables and fish. It is the favourite oil throughout India for pickling. Available only at Indian and Pakistani grocers. Groundnut/peanut oil may be used as a substitute.

Mustard seeds

These are tiny, round seeds which, though described as black, are really a reddish-brown colour, and used in Indian cookery. When scattered into hot oil they turn deliciously nutty.

Nam pla

see Fish sauce, fish gravy

Napa cabbage

see Chinese cabbage

Nga pi

see Blachan

Niboshi

Tiny dried sardines, sometimes used to make dashi (Japanese stock, see page 69).

Noodles

Noodles of various kinds occupy an important place in the daily diet in South-east Asia. The generic term *mien* is the Chinese word for the staple food of the northern provinces;

they are called *mee* in Thailand and Indonesia. Some are made from hard (durum) wheat, like Italian pasta, some from water and eggs, and are usually sold in dried form. Rice stick noodles (*sen mee* in Thailand) are white and brittle and should be soaked briefly before use, except when crisp-fried for *mee krob*, a famous Thai dish, in which the noodles puff up. They are delicious with fish. Mung bean threads (*woon sen* in Thailand, *saifun* in Japan), also called *cellophane* or *beanthread noodles*, are made from mung bean flour. Their Chinese name, *fun-see*, means 'powdered silk', which describes them well; very hard and fine, they must be soaked before cooking. Pea-starch transparent noodles are used in Chinese cooking primarily in soups, or to cook with and complement meat and vegetables. They are sometimes served with rice.

Japanese noodles come in a variety of types and sizes: *udon* noodles are broad white ribbons made from wheat, *soba* are made from buckwheat, *somen* are very thin wheat noodles and *shirataki* are gelatinous noodles made from yam flour. *Harusame* are fine soy bean noodles that can be used instead of mung bean threads.

Nori

The dried sheet form of 'laver' seaweed, used in Japan to roll around sushi (vinegared rice) and, when cut into slivers, as a garnish. The sheets of nori must be toasted briefly before use.

Nuoc mam

see Fish sauce, fish gravy

Nutmeg

A fragrant spice used in Indian cookery. Buy whole nutmegs and grate freshly for use on a special little nutmeg grater.

Oils for cooking

The cooking oil most widely used in China is peanut or ground nut oil. Peanut oil is high in monosaturated fatty acids, so although it contains nothing harmful it is of no particular benefit in the diet. Polyunsaturated oils which help to rid the body of cholesterol include sunflower oil, recommended in many of the recipes in this book, corn oil (which is very high in vitamin E) and rapeseed oil, which is the oil favoured by the Japanese. Olive oil is never used in Oriental cookery as the flavour is too pervasive. See also Sesame.

Onion flakes

Many Thai dishes are garnished with crisp-fried onion flakes, sold ready prepared in Thailand. They can be made from dried onion flakes fried quickly in a little oil and removed from the pan as soon as they begin to brown.

Oyster sauce

A dark brown sauce with a rich flavour made from extract of

oysters, salt and starch, used mainly in the south of China. Store in the refrigerator.

Palm sugar

see Jaggery

Panch phoran

A mixture of five whole spices used in Bengali cooking, especially in vegetable dishes. The most commonly used combination is equal parts of the seeds of white cumin, fennel, fenugreek, mustard and wild onion.

Paneer

A curd cheese used in India for both sweet and savoury dishes. See recipe, below.

Pe-tsai

see Chinese cabbage

Pickles, Chinese

Winter pickle (salted cabbage), which is brownish-green in colour, savoury and mildly salty, is sold in jars. Snow pickle (salted mustard greens), is greenish in colour and has a

Paneer

The cheese can be used after draining as it is (*chenna*) or compressed into a block that can be cut into squares (*paneer*).

1.2 litres (2 pints) full fat milk
2 tablespoons lemon juice

1. Bring the milk to the boil in a heavy saucepan. Reduce the heat and add the lemon juice. Stir gently and the milk will separate into curds and whey. Turn off the heat.

2. Pour the mixture into a colander lined with several squares of muslin. Bring up the corners of the muslin and tie them together. Twist gently to extract excess moisture, then hang the bag up to let the cheese drain. After about 1½ hours it should be sufficiently crumbly.

3. To make paneer place the cheese in its muslin bag on a clean work surface. Shape it into a cake or block with your hands, place a board on top and weight it down. Leave for 2 hours then cut into squares.

salty and mildly sour flavour, reminiscent of sauerkraut. Szechuan hot pickle (*Ja Chai*) is crunchy, yellowish-green in colour, hot and salty. These pickles are cooked with meat, and with vegetables which do not have a pronounced flavour. They should be rinsed thoroughly before use.

Plum sauce

A sweet, thick Chinese sauce available bottled from good supermarkets and Oriental shops.

Pomegranate seeds

Small, hard, black-red seeds used in Indian cookery to add a little sharpness to vegetarian dishes, and also included in some conserves and syrups.

Prawn ballichow

A relish made from prawns which is also used in cooking in South India, Burma and Thailand.

Red soy bean paste

A basic seasoning made from cooked soy beans, malt and salt.

Pickled Garlic

In Thailand pickled garlic is used as a condiment as well as being added to cooked dishes.

300 ml (½ pint) white vinegar
1.2 litres (2 pints) water
50 g (2 oz) sugar
1 tablespoon salt
6 heads of garlic, each clove peeled

1. Place the vinegar, water, sugar and salt in a saucepan. Bring to the boil, stirring to dissolve the sugar. Reduce the heat and simmer for 5 minutes.

It is often used instead of soy sauce when a thicker, sweeter sauce is required in stir-fry cooking, or as a dip, or to brush on to Mandarin pancakes with Peking Duck (see page 134). Called *akamiso* in Japan.

Renkon

see Lotus

Rice

see pages 22–23

Rice cakes

In Japan, boiled glutinous rice is pounded and formed into small chewy white cakes which are grilled and eaten with shoyu or added to soups.

Rice papers

see Banh trang

Rice vinegar

Known as *su* in Japan, this is light, delicately flavoured vinegar, used particularly for making sushi (vinegared rice, see page 23). Rice vinegar is distilled from white rice and is very aromatic. It is much milder

2. Add the garlic cloves to the pan and bring the liquid back to the boil. Boil for 1 minute. Remove the pan from the heat and leave to cool.

3. Transfer the pickled garlic to sterilized glass jars with screw tops. Store in the refrigerator for a minimum of 1 week before use. After opening, keep refrigerated and tightly covered.

than wine or cider vinegar. If unobtainable, substitute distilled white vinegar diluted with water. Seasoned rice vinegars, with sugar and monosodium glutamate added, are also available.

Rice wine

In China a number of wines varying in strength and sweetness are made from fermented rice. The most popular Chinese wine – 'yellow wine' – is very like medium-dry sherry (*amontillado*); in the recipes in this book they are interchangeable. Sake is the national drink of Japan, made by fermenting freshly steamed white rice. For cooking purposes, a very dry sherry makes a perfectly acceptable substitute.

Rose-water

see Flower flavourings and essences

Saffron

Saffron is used in India for its exquisite flavour and as a colouring agent for pilaus, biryanis, sweets, puddings and cakes. Gathered from the orange stamens of a type of crocus flower, thousands of fronds are needed to produce a very small amount. To make a solution of saffron for colouring, wrap the saffron fronds in a small polythene bag and crush with a rolling pin, or use a pestle and mortar. Transfer the saffron to a cup and pour the specified amount of hot water or milk over it. Leave it for 10 minutes and stir well with a spoon. For a large pinch of saffron fronds use 50–85 ml (2–3 fl oz) water or milk.

Saifun

The Japanese word for mung bean threads (made from mung bean flour). See Noodles.

Sake

see Rice wine

Salted black beans

The beans from which black bean sauce is made when ground and mixed with flour and spices. Gives richness and piquancy to vegetable dishes.

Sansho

Japanese fragrant pepper, made from the leaf of the prickly ash. Freshly ground black pepper may be substituted.

Seaweed

Purple seaweed (laver), hair seaweed and broad seaweed are the types most frequently used in Chinese cooking, mostly in conjunction with other vegetables in soups. They must be soaked in water for at least 20 minutes, but preferably overnight, before use, and should be rinsed thoroughly before and after soaking. In Japan the dried form of laver, called *nori*, is used to roll round sushi and, when cut into slivers, as a garnish. It is lightly toasted before use (in Japan it is waved over the flame of the gas hob until it just changes colour). Other seaweeds used in Japanese cooking are *hijiki*, *wakame* and *konbu*.

Sesame

Used in Oriental cooking as seeds to add flavour and texture (the taste is accentuated if the seeds are dry-fried). Sesame paste or sauce is made by pounding the seeds and is widely available under the name of *tahini*. Sesame seed oil is used as a finishing touch for its flavour, but not for cooking as it burns very easily.

Shichimi pepper

A mixture of seven ingredients used in Japanese cookery. Chilli,

Preparing shiitake mushrooms

Dry-frying Spices

Although fresh shiitake mushrooms are sometimes available, they are usually sold dried, and must be soaked before being incorporated in a recipe.

In India spices are cooked to bring out their distinctive aroma. A mixture (*masala*) of hot (*garam*) and fragrant spices is used as a condiment or as an ingredient added towards the end of the cooking time. This method can be used for any combination of spices.

50 g (2 oz) coriander seeds
50 g (2 oz) white cumin seeds
25 g (1 oz) cinnamon stick or cassia bark
25 g (1 oz) fennel seeds
10 g ($\frac{1}{4}$ oz) whole cloves
10 g ($\frac{1}{4}$ oz) brown or black cardamoms
10 g ($\frac{1}{4}$ oz) green cardamoms
10 g ($\frac{1}{4}$ oz) nutmeg

Makes approx. 200 g (7 oz)

1. Place the mushrooms in a bowl and pour over warm water to cover completely. Leave to stand for 20–30 minutes depending on quantity and size.

2. When the mushrooms are soft and plump, remove and discard the woody stems. Retain the liquid if it is to be used in the recipe. The mushroom caps may be used whole, shredded or quartered as required.

1. Place all the spices in an even layer in a dry frying pan set over a moderate heat. Stir-fry for 5 minutes until they are a shade or two darker and beginning to give off a delicious aroma.

2. Allow to cool. When cool, grind in a pestle and mortar (or a coffee grinder reserved for the purpose). Store in an airtight jar in a cool dark place. Keeps for up to 6 months.

black pepper, dried orange peel, sesame seeds, poppy seeds, nori and hemp seeds are ground to a spicy hot powder which is often used on noodles.

Shiitake mushrooms

see Mushrooms and Preparing shiitake mushrooms, above.

Shirataki

see Noodles

Shiromiso

Japanese white soy bean paste.

Shiso leaves

Used in Japanese cooking as a garnish and also as an ingredient of vegetable tempura. It is a member of the mint family. Fresh spearmint or basil may be substituted but the flavour is not quite the same.

Shoyu

Japanese soy sauce. Made from fermented soy beans, it is quite unlike the other soy sauces used in Oriental cookery, and when specified in a recipe there is no substitute.

Shrimp paste

see Blachan

Snow pickle

see Pickles

Soba

see Noodles

Somen

see Noodles

Soya bean products

The use of soya beans is one of the factors that most distinguishes Oriental cookery from that of the West. Soy sauce, which comes in various strengths and qualities, is well-known. Other products indispensable in the Oriental kitchen are the bean pastes, again of varying strength and colour, bean curd (*tofu*) and fermented bean curd (bean curd cheese). The value of soya beans to Oriental cooking, not only in terms of flavour and nutrition but also an indefinably satisfying quality which they impart to food, cannot be overestimated.

Soy sauce

Soy sauce is extracted from boiled soya beans fermented with an equal weight of barley or wheat, salted and fermented again. It is used in stewing, frying and to make sauces. It can be applied directly to food but as it is very salty care should be taken not to use it in excess. In cooking, soy sauce is best combined with other ingredients, such as wine, sugar and stock.

Star anise

This spice comes in the form of a dried, star-shaped seed pod. It is usually added to braised and simmered dishes in Chinese cookery to give a slight liquorice flavour.

Straw mushrooms

see Mushrooms

Su

see Rice vinegar

Sweet bean paste

see Red soy bean paste

Szechuan pepper

Despite its name this spice is not a species of pepper, though it does have a peppery taste. In China it is commonly ground and mixed with salt as a table condiment, as well as being added to sauces in cooking. Do not store longer than 6 months as the flavour deteriorates if allowed to get stale.

Szechuan pickles

see Pickles

Tabasco

A hot sauce made from chillies, which, though it originates in Mexico, like the chilli, is useful in Oriental cooking to add piquancy.

Tamarind

A fleshy fruit resembling a long date. It tastes sour and supplies a distinctive taste to the cooking of South India, Indonesia and Thailand. It is normally available in compressed blocks which are quite dry and do not deteriorate. To use, cut off part of the block; add it to 4 times its volume of water in a small pan. Bring the water to simmering point. Cool, and push the pulp through a sieve to give a thick liquid. Discard the pulp. Lemon juice or vinegar can be used as alternatives.

Tandoori masala

A mixture of spices used in marinade mixtures for Indian recipes. The flavour should be quite sour. A paste can be made by combining the spice mixture with vinegar and vegetable oil which is useful as it has excellent storage qualities. (See page 44 for recipe)

Tiger lily buds

Also known as *yellow flower* or *golden needles* in China, these are dried buds, golden-yellow in colour and crunchy in texture. To Western tastes the flavour is somewhat musty. They are used to garnish steamed fish and in some pork dishes, and must be soaked for 20 minutes before use.

Tofu

see Bean curd

Tonkatsu sauce

A commercially prepared sauce used in Japan. This thick brown sauce is made from fruit and vegetables combined with spices and seasonings. Soy sauce or ketchup may be used as substitutes.

Transparent noodles

Mung bean threads. See Noodles

Trassi

see Blachan

Tree ears

see Mushrooms

Tsukemono

Japanese pickled vegetables, which are traditionally served at every meal. They are available ready-made in vacuum packs and jars.

Turmeric

This spice is the ground root of a plant, used in India to give curries a yellowish colour. Used only in conjunction with other flavouring agents, turmeric has a slightly bitter, musty taste.

Udon

see Noodles

Urhad dal

One of the many pulses used widely in Indian cookery, these beans are small and dark. See Dal

Varak, vark

Silver foil made from silver dust compressed wafer-thin and used to decorate Indian puddings and sweetmeats. It is sold between two sheets of paper. Peel off the top sheet, then lift the silver foil with the bottom sheet of paper still attached and invert it over the dish. Gently peel away the paper. The varak is edible.

Wakame

A young seaweed with long green fronds and smooth texture. It is used in Japanese soups and salads.

Wasabi powder

Also known as *Japanese horseradish*, this powder is, in fact, the grated root of a riverside plant. It has a powerful flavour and is traditionally served with raw fish dishes. It is available in tubes or in powder form. It should be mixed with cold water before use.

Water chestnuts

A walnut-sized bulb with brown skin, and not a nut at all, but a tuber. Inside, the flesh is white and crisp. Used in many Chinese stir-fried dishes. Canned water chestnuts are ready-peeled. Once opened, and with regular changes of water, canned water chestnuts will keep in the refrigerator for up to 2 weeks. Water-chestnut flour is used in a number of Oriental cakes.

White radishes

These are used extensively in Oriental cooking, both as a garnish and as a cooked vegetable. They are long and thin, with a crisp texture and unique nutty flavour. See also Daikon, Mooli.

Winter pickle

see Pickles

Wonton skins

Made from wheat flour, egg and water, these wafer-thin wrappers are sold in 8 cm (3 inch) squares. In Chinese cooking they can be deep-fried on their own and served with a piquant dip sauce, or filled with a savoury mixture and then steamed, deep fried or boiled. Wonton wrappers can be stored in the freezer for up to 6 months, and thawed in 5–10 minutes.

Wood ears

see Mushrooms

RICE

In all the countries of the Orient, rice is a staple food of inestimable importance. Its crucial role in the survival of millions of people has ensured that rice has been given a place in myth and ritual as well as in the kitchen. In Japan, rice is synonymous with sustenance. In its uncooked state, the name is *okome*; but when cooked the honorific name *gohan* or *meshi* is bestowed upon it, which means 'food' or 'livelihood'. There are hundreds of different types of rice. As a general rule, the rice eaten in China, India, and as a staple in most of the countries of South-east Asia can be regarded as 'Indian', that is, a long-grain variety which when cooked is dry, separate and fluffy, and accords with Western tastes. Carolina rice from the USA falls into this category. Japanese rice is quite different: short-grained – like Italian risotto rice – moist and clinging together when cooked. This type of rice is also eaten in Northern Thailand, Burma and Cambodia. Glutinous rice, called *mochigome* in Japan, is a special short-grain type which becomes sweet and sticky when cooked.

In terms of nutrition, rice is high in carbohydrate, and contains some protein, some minerals (especially sodium), and an amount of vitamin B that varies according to the way it is processed. Most rice is grown in fields of standing water, giving two crops annually, but a small proportion is cultivated on dry land: this 'upland' rice has a rather higher nutritional content than paddy-field rice.

Of the long-grain varieties loosely termed 'Indian' but eaten in China, Thailand, Vietnam and elsewhere, the type most prized in India itself is Basmati rice, grown in the foothills of the Himalayas and called *jeera-sali* because the slender grains are slightly curved like *jeera* (cumin seeds). Basmati rice has a deliciously distinctive nutty aroma and fine flavour. It is more expensive than other long-grain varieties but it is well worth paying the little extra. Patna rice is another good variety; but other unnamed types are decidedly inferior and will not give satisfactory results. Basmati rice is carefully stored for up to a year before it is sold to perfect its flavour. Japanese rice, on the other hand, is prized for its freshness, and connoisseurs rush to buy *shinmai*, the 'new rice', when it becomes available, comparing the qualities of crops from different parts of the country – some say different sides of the same mountain! In accordance with a classical gourmet tradition, the cooking of rice is elevated to an art, and in the finest Japanese restaurants there is a chef whose sole task it is to prepare the day's rice to perfection.

There are various ways of cooking rice, and the chief methods used in the Orient are described here. Some recipes are appropriate to particular dishes, while others can be used as basic methods to be served as you prefer. It is misleading to give exact quantities of water and cooking times because different lots of rice will differ in their requirements, according to factors such as when and where it was harvested and how long it has been stored. Having said that, the general guidelines hold good, and once you have tried each of the methods you will easily find one that suits you and sense how to adjust it when necessary. One item that is indispensable is a heavy saucepan with a close-fitting lid.

Steamed Rice – Short-grain

Tsukiyo no kome nomeshi: 'moonlight and boiled rice' – so goes the Japanese proverb, meaning that rice is delicious to eat at any time of day or night. For this esteemed dish only short-grain rice is used in Japan. The method used for cooking, though it is called 'steamed' is similar to method 2 opposite, with some refinements. Broth or stock may be used instead of water if you wish to add flavour to the rice. The quantity of water is variable, but one rule observed in Japan is to increase the amount used if the rice is of American or European origin rather than home-grown, because it will not have been grown in wet fields. The quantities are expressed in volume rather than weight but approximate equivalents are given. The amount of water stated is for Oriental rice. When the rice is ready, the tradition is to bring it to the table in a cedarwood tub and transfer it to individual bowls with a wooden rice paddle.

2 cups (400 g/14 oz) Japanese short-grain rice
2½ cups (600 ml/1 pint) water

Preparation time: 10 minutes, plus straining
Cooking time: about 45 minutes
Serves 4

1. Place the rice in a large bowl and pour in cold water from the tap. Swish it around lightly and briefly until the water looks milky. Drain immediately and repeat this process 2 or 3 times until the water is almost clear.

2. Drain the rice into a colander and leave uncovered to drain for 1 hour.

3. Place the rice in a medium, heavy saucepan with the measured water, cover and set the pan over a moderately high heat until the water comes to the boil. Increase the heat, and as the water comes to a rolling boil the starch will bubble to the surface and escape from under the lid.

4. Reduce the heat to low and cook, covered, until all the liquid is absorbed by the rice – about 20 minutes.

5. Turn off the heat, but leave the pan on the hob and let it stand for 15–20 minutes for the rice to settle. Fluff it up with a fork (the Japanese use a rice paddle) and serve, or cover with a tea-towel and the lid of the pan until ready.

Boiled Rice – Long-grain (1)

This way of preparing long-grain rice is used in India, China and Thailand. Though not all cooks will pre-soak the rice, washing it in several rinsings of water is commonly done to remove excess starch. You may think that this is rendered unnecessary by modern methods of processing rice that involve 'polishing' it. Salt is rarely added to the cooking water (never in Thailand) since the dishes and relishes which it accompanies are strongly flavoured.

It is difficult to predict individual appetites for rice. The quantity given here is generous, but since leftover rice can be frozen or used as crispy rice (see below), it will not go to waste.

400 g (14 oz) Basmati rice
2 litres (3½ pints) water

Preparation time: 10 minutes, plus soaking
Cooking time: 10 minutes
Serves 4

1. Pick over the rice to make sure it is free of impurities. Leave it to soak in cold water for about 30 minutes. Drain and rinse several times in cold water until it runs clear. Drain again.

2. Bring the measured water to the boil in a large saucepan set on a high heat. Tip in the rice and cover the pan. After 1 minute, stir the rice to stop the grains sticking together. Replace the lid. When the water is at a full rolling boil, reduce the heat slightly and continue to cook for 7 minutes.

3. Test a few grains of rice to see if it is almost ready. It should have softened but still have some bite (overcooked mushy rice will stick together). Simmer for 1–2 minutes more.

4. Drain the rice thoroughly through a sieve. Transfer to a warmed serving dish and fluff it up with a fork to allow steam to escape. Serve hot. Alternatively, if you wish to keep the rice hot until you are ready to serve, return it to the pan, stretch a clean tea-towel over the top and replace the lid. The tea-towel will absorb any steam and the rice will keep perfectly for 15 minutes.

Boiled Rice – Long-grain (2)

Long-grain rice can also be prepared by the absorption method, also used in China and India. Because of the different qualities of different batches of rice, the quantity of water used and the time required may vary slightly.

400 g (14 oz) long-grain rice
½ teaspoon salt
about 450 ml (¾ pint) water

Preparation time: 5 minutes
Cooking time: about 30 minutes, plus standing
Serves 4

1. Wash and rinse the rice in cold water once, drain and place in a large heavy saucepan. Add sufficient fresh cold water to cover the rice by 2.5 cm (1 inch). Bring to the boil, add the salt, and stir to prevent the grains sticking together.

2. Reduce the heat to very low, cover the pan tightly and cook for 15–20 minutes. Turn off the heat and let the rice stand, covered, for 10–15 minutes.

3. Transfer to a warmed serving dish and fluff the rice up with a fork.

Vinegared Rice

Sumeshi

The term *sushi* is a corruption of *sumeshi*, which means vinegared rice and is used in all Japanese *sushi* dishes. Specially flavoured rice vinegar, called *sushi-su*, is available.

350 g (12 oz) Japanese short-grain rice
450 ml (¾ pint) water
50 ml (2 fl oz) rice vinegar
1½ tablespoons sugar
1 teaspoon salt

Preparation time: 15 minutes, plus draining
Cooking time: about 40 minutes
Serves 4

1. Wash and drain the rice as described in the recipe for Steamed Rice – short-grain.

2. Transfer the rice to a deep saucepan (the rice should not fill more than one-quarter of the pan). Add measured cold water and bring to the boil over high heat. Reduce the heat, cover and simmer gently for about 15 minutes, until all the water has been absorbed by the rice. Try not to remove the lid more than once during cooking to check whether the water has been absorbed. Remove the pan from the heat and leave it tightly covered for·10–15 minutes.

3. Put the rice vinegar, sugar and salt in a bowl and mix well until the sugar and salt have dissolved.

4. Transfer the rice to a large (non-metal) bowl and pour over the vinegar mixture. Using a wooden spatula or Japanese rice paddle, fold the vinegar into the rice; do not stir. Leave to cool at room temperature before using.

Crispy rice

When cooking rice the conventional way, do not discard any that has stuck to the bottom of the pan. In Japan this 'scorched' rice, *okoge*, is regarded as a delicious crunchy snack. Rice is sometimes deliberately scorched (not burnt!) to make Rice Balls, tasty mouthfuls of rice with a savoury morsel such as salted cod roe in the centre, wrapped in *nori* and eaten with the fingers. In China the same leftovers are used to make Crispy Rice. It is allowed to dry overnight, or dried off in a low oven, then deep-fried for 1 minute in hot oil so that it puffs up. When hot soup or food is poured over the rice it makes an appetizing sizzling sound. (See Sizzling Rice Soup, page 76).

Freezing cooked rice

Leftover rice can be refrigerated or frozen. To reheat, place the cold rice in an ovenproof bowl in a steamer. Cover and steam until fluffy and hot (about 10 minutes). Cooked rice used in fried rice dishes behaves better if it has been refrigerated.

Electric rice cooker

If you cook rice frequently, you may find it worth investing in an electric rice cooker (as many Oriental cooks have done). The cooker has a large covered pan set over an electric element. The rice and measured water are placed in the pan, which cooks the rice until the water is absorbed and then switches itself off.

24

EQUIPMENT AND UTENSILS

The kitchen equipment required for Oriental cooking methods, evolved over centuries to make best use of scarce fuels, is rather different from that required in Western kitchens. Even so, a good proportion of the equipment described in this chapter will already be in use in the average Western kitchen, in one form or another, and other, more specialized utensils are widely available in cook shops.

China

The cooking techniques of China are the inspiration behind the styles of Thailand and Vietnam and the rest of South-east Asia (though each has evolved in an individual way, and India has been an important influence). Broadly speaking the equipment needed for Chinese cooking can be used for these as well. This equipment is simple, made to designs that have hardly changed for centuries. In a typical domestic kitchen you would probably find the following:

chopping boards
bamboo whisk
cleaver
ladle
granite pestle and mortar
rice scoop
wok
wok rack
bamboo steamers
clay pots
bamboo baskets
cooking chopsticks
steaming rack
large deep saucepan
spatulas
scraper
fish slice
draining spoon
metal strainer

Preparation equipment:
Careful preparation of foods is central to success in Chinese cooking. Each item must be cut or sliced to the correct size for stir-frying or steaming, for example, and small enough to be eaten with chopsticks. For this cutting at least one thick,

solid *wooden chopping board* is essential, though it is useful to have two, one large and one small. Keep wooden boards immaculately clean, taking care to scrub and rinse them immediately after use. For hygiene reasons, many Western kitchens have plastic chopping boards, though plastic surfaces are not recommended for cutting: not only does the plastic blunt the blades of knives and cleavers very quickly, but synthetic boards may not always be heavy enough to support an efficient slicing action with a razor-sharp utensil.

The Chinese *cleaver* is a broad, square-edged chopper which can perform a number of cutting functions. The handle should be wooden, the blade tempered carbon steel. The front half of the blade is light enough for slicing and shredding, the heavier part near the handle used for chopping, pounding and tenderizing meat. The flat side of the blade is useful for lifting quantities of diced ingredients. In professional kitchens, the cleaver is often supplemented by three knives. Of these the *thin knife* is most used, for slicing, dicing, shredding and cutting into strips. A *heavy knife* is used for mincing – in practise the cook has a knife in each hand and chops the meat quickly as if beating a drum. Meat is not ground by machine as it would often be in the West, since the valuable juices are thought to be sacrificed in the process. The third knife is used for cutting through the bone, as

well as pushing through the joints of poultry, which is done far more frequently in Chinese cooking than in the West, and also for scoring large pieces of meat or fish.

Carbon steel blades must be kept clean and sharp. Wash and dry cleavers and knives immediately after use and keep them separately from other kitchen utensils – hanging up or on a knife rack. Sharpen both sides of the blade regularly.

A *pestle and mortar* is used in all Oriental countries for grinding spices and making pastes such as garlic paste. Freshly ground spices have a much richer aroma than those bought ready-prepared.

Cooking equipment: The *wok* is the most important piece of

equipment in the Chinese kitchen: for good stir-frying it is unbeatable, though a frying pan can be used if necessary. There are numerous other applications – steaming, braising, shallow-frying, for example – which make the wok indispensable. The traditional material is iron, because it conducts heat evenly and retains it more efficiently than other substances. The wok is cone-shaped with a rounded bottom, which encourages ingredients to return to the centre, however vigorously you stir them. A wok will fit on most gas burners, but you can obtain a special ring to keep it steady. Electric burners are generally less suitable because the heat cannot be controlled as easily. If you do a

Preparing a new wok

A new iron wok is coated with oil or a wax film to prevent it rusting. This must be removed before use. Heat the wok over high heat until it is very hot indeed, then scrub it in warm soapy water using a stiff brush. Rinse well. Place the cleaned wok over moderate heat to dry.

Now season the wok, to prevent it from rusting and to prevent food sticking. Wipe the entire surface with a pad of paper towels soaked in cooking oil. The wok is now ready to use.

After use, wash the wok in hot water, but do not use

washing-up liquid or other detergents as these will remove the seasoning. Should any food stick to the base of the wok, brush it off with a stiff brush or non-abrasive scourer. Repeat the seasoning process after use, so that the wok develops a smooth, shiny surface.

Cooking equipment and utensils typical of Chinese cooking

great deal of Oriental cooking it is worth buying two woks, a large double-handled one with a lid for deep-frying and steaming, and a smaller single-handled one for stir-frying. A *wok rack* fits on the rim to hold pieces of food during cooking. In Thai kitchens a large mesh frying basket, similar in shape to the wok, with a bamboo handle, is used to lower items into hot oil for deep-frying.

Bamboo steamers are round, lidded containers that stack one on top of the other. They are placed over boiling water so that steam filters through the holes in the bamboo and gently cooks food placed on heatproof plates within. Bamboo steamers are efficient, inexpensive and attractive.

A *large deep saucepan* is useful for boiling large joints of meat or for whole chickens. Clay pots called *sandpots* are used for clear-simmering, a long slow cooking process. A heavy-based flameproof casserole is a perfectly acceptable alternative.

Japan

The chief cooking methods of Japan are charcoal-grilling, steaming, simmering and deep-frying. A small *barbecue* is ideal for charcoal-grilling – *yakitori* dishes, for example – but the grill of a conventional oven can be used if set at the highest temperature.

Some of the utensils used in Chinese cooking are also used in Japan: *bamboo baskets*, for example, for draining and rinsing foods. After use, these should be washed and stored on an open shelf, not in a cupboard. *Chopsticks* are invariably used for stirring, beating and turning foods, as well as arranging them attractively on the serving platter. Two pairs, one long, one short, are convenient. The chopsticks are attached to each other by a string so they they

can be hung up for storage, but you can cut this off if you find it awkward. Long metal chopsticks with wooden grips are better for deep-frying than wood or bamboo, which get scorched.

Thick pots of iron or brass with short handles are used for deep-frying. Whatever deep pan you use, make sure it is heavy enough to keep the oil at a steady, high temperature.

The Japanese equivalent of the Chinese clay pot is the *donabe*, an earthenware casserole which can be used on a direct flame. These wonderful pots retain heat well and distribute it evenly. Again, a flameproof casserole can be used as a substitute.

Square *bamboo mats* are used for rolling *sushi*, but any woven mat will do as long as it is chemically neutral and colourfast. *Bamboo skewers* are essential for grilling Japanese-style (and in Vietnamese dishes) when foods are eaten directly from the skewer. They are

available in various lengths, are cheap and disposable. In Japan they are also used to test food to see if it is done. Stainless steel skewers for fish must be kept perfectly clean and with a sharp point.

Japanese cooks use two kinds of flat *grater*, one finer than the other – and both finer than Western graters – used for radish, horseradish and ginger. Tin-coated copper is the favoured material, but not available outside Japan; most homes have stainless steel or plastic graters. If you cannot obtain one, use the smallest hole on a multi-purpose Western grater.

Steamers are bamboo, just like those used in China, or metal and square in shape. These hold large quantities of food but are less efficient than bamboo as they lose heat too quickly. For steaming savoury custards and small quantities of food individual *lidded cups* with pretty designs, are used.

Japanese omelettes are rolled into an even cylinder as they cook; a *rectangular pan* has been developed for these. If you use a good, heavy round omelette pan you can slice off the ends of the rolled omelette for an authentic finish.

The fresh fish dishes of Japan are deservedly famous. They are served raw, but not without a good deal of care. A range of special knives is reserved for these and other dishes.

1. *Deba-bocho* A cleaver with a pointed end, the blade measuring from 18–30 cm (7–12 inches). Relatively heavy but versatile, For fish, chicken, meat.
2. *Nakiri-bocho* A large round-ended vegetable chopper that looks like a cleaver but is much lighter. There is no exact Western equivalent of this invaluable utensil.
3. *Sashimi-bocho* A long, thin-bladed knife developed to cut boned fish fillets. The end may be pointed (*yanagi-ba*) or blunt. The blunt version, used in

Tokyo, is called *tako biki*, 'octopus-cutter'. The blades may be 18–39 cm (7–15 inches) long.

It is possible to buy similar Western knives in good stores, which will be of great value in all cooking. Choose high-quality, hard carbon steel, keep the knives honed and clean and dry them thoroughly after washing.

India

The traditional cooking of India is distinguished in many ways from the other styles described in this book; a unique feature is the use of an oven, making it possible to bake meat and fish and to cook *naan*, a delicious unleavened bread. This oven is made of clay, shaped like a beehive, and is called a *tandoor*. It is fired by charcoal which is lit 3 hours before cooking begins. The temperature is very hot and food cooks quickly; *naan* is cooked on the walls of the oven. While it is possible to buy a

tandoor in the West, the most practical way to cook tandoori dishes is to part-cook the marinated food in a conventional oven and finish it off over a charcoal grill. (*Naan*, for instance, can be baked with satisfactory results in a conventional oven.)

The Indian equivalent to the Chinese wok is the *karhi*, a large cast-iron pan with its base rounded to sit snugly in a charcoal fire. *Karhis* with flattened bottoms are available for use on a hob; but use your wok, as the heat will be better distributed and the food will cook more evenly.

Cast-iron frying pans are best for dry-frying spices and for breads. A small (13 cm/5 inch) pan is useful for spices, with a larger one for breads as an alternative to the traditional *tawa*, a dome-shaped disc heated over an open fire. If you have a griddle, it would be nice to use it for *chappati*, but it is not necessary to buy one specially.

Modern equipment

Chopping and pounding foods can be hard work. A number of labour-saving devices can be used to save time on certain tasks. For example, an electric coffee-grinder (reserved for the purpose) is very useful for grinding spices. If you cook large quantities of rice, you will probably find an electric rice cooker a blessing. Food processors should be used with restraint – the Chinese would not use them for grinding meat, for example, because of the loss of vital juices. There is also the intangible element of the cook's relationship with the ingredients of a meal, which traditionalists would say depends upon preparation by hand. Having said that, for making garlic or ginger paste or chopping onions finely, a food processor is invaluable. A deep-frying cooker is an efficient and safe method for cooking batter-covered foods like tempura and similar dishes.

A selection of equipment and utensils used in Indian cookery

COOKING TECHNIQUES

The cooking techniques described in this chapter cover the broad spectrum of Oriental cooking, from the stir-frying, steaming and braising basic to Chinese cooking, to the unique tandoor oven used in India. Also covered are the barbecuing techniques used on the open charcoal stoves common throughout South-east Asia.

The Chinese characters for 'cooking' translate as 'fire control', but under this broad umbrella at least 40 different methods of applying heat to food can be distinguished. Like the Japanese, the Chinese are very economical in their use of precious cooking fuel. Most Oriental cooking techniques have evolved not only with the aim of producing food that is pure in flavour and beautiful to look at, but also with an underlying need to observe economy. Indeed, in the restraint typical of Japanese cooking it is possible to detect a note of asceticism. Indian food, by contrast, is unmistakably sensuous, prepared in order to

derive maximum flavour from imaginative combinations of spices. This has given rise to meat dishes that are wonderfully flavourful and succulent, as well as a range of vegetarian dishes that are the best in the world. In the rest of South-east Asia there are styles of cooking that have drawn on the best of the major influences while adding unmistakeably individual characteristics. Certain techniques are common to all.

Broadly speaking, Oriental cooking techniques can be divided into those using water – simmering, boiling, and steaming; those using oil – for deep-frying, shallow-frying and quick stir-frying; baking in an

oven – an exclusively Indian method – and grilling over direct heat, which is particularly important in Japan. (The most important category of food in Japan is not cooked at all – this is *sashimi*, raw fish which is expertly sliced and served with piquant sauces and garnishes.) In China many dishes are produced by a combination of methods: 'cross-cooking', as it is known, enables the cook to achieve a delectable variety of textures and flavours.

In Western restaurants, we are accustomed to tell the chef how well-cooked we like our food; in the East, this is left to the cook, who is best qualified to judge what will bring out the

best in a particular cut of meat or freshly caught fish. This instinct for the best is passed on from generation to generation: in China there are no 'classic cookbooks' and in the households of large extended families in India favourite recipes are learnt in the kitchen from aunts and sisters bustling over sizzling pans and steaming bowls.

Oriental cooking is not 'cooking to formula', it is an art, one that is a pleasure to learn and which gives delicious rewards. Practise the recipes in this section and you will be on your way to mastering the basic techniques necessary to all the legendary cooking of the East.

COOKING IN WATER

Water is a versatile and economical cooking medium, two virtues much appreciated by the Oriental cook, who cooks not only *in* water – boiling, simmering and poaching – but over it too, with open and closed steaming. By skilfully adjusting the temperature and varying the cooking time, which may be extremely lengthy or very brief, all kinds of foods can be cooked to perfection, whether large joints of meat, delicate fish or fresh vegetables.

BOILING

In Chinese cooking there are six main methods of cooking food in boiling water, no less than 15 in Japan. The main difference between the two styles is that in Japan the food to be cooked is always cut into small portions, which reduces the cooking time considerably. Often the water is flavoured with seasonings such as dashi, sake, shoyu (Japanese soy sauce) and mirin.

White-cooked Chicken

Chicken cooked by this Chinese method must be fresh and of very high quality. In China, the food is cooked for a short time in boiling water on the stove – no more than a minute at a rolling boil – then the heat is turned off and the remainder of the cooking is achieved by the receding heat. Modern cookers do not retain heat to the same extent, but a similar effect can be obtained by reducing the heat after the initial period of boiling and simmering very gently for a short period before removing the pan from the heat.

2.5 litres (4½ pints) water
4 slices fresh root ginger
1 × 1.5 kg (3 lb) chicken
Dips:
1 tablespoon shredded fresh root ginger
1 tablespoon shredded spring onion
1 tablespoon sunflower oil
2 tablespoons soy sauce
1 tablespoon chilli sauce
2 tablespoons coarse sea salt
1 tablespoon coarsely crushed black peppercorns

Preparation time: 15 minutes, plus cooling
Cooking time: 35 minutes
Serves 6

1. Place the water in a large saucepan with the slices of ginger and bring to the boil. When the water is boiling, immerse the chicken and boil for 2 minutes.

2. Reduce the heat to very low, cover the pan and simmer for 20 minutes. Remove the pan from the heat and leave the chicken to cool in the water.

3. When the chicken is cold, drain off the liquid and place the chicken on a chopping board. Using a cleaver, chop the chicken, through the skin and bones, into bite-sized pieces.

4. Arrange the pieces of chicken on a serving dish and serve with dips: combine the shredded ginger with the spring onion and sunflower oil; mix the soy and chilli sauces together; combine the salt and peppercorns.

White-cooked Pork

A variation on white-cooking used successfully with belly of pork requires the meat to be alternately boiled and left to rest 3 times. Because belly pork is well endowed with fat, the result is tender and tasty.

2.5 litres (4½ pints) water
1 × 1.5 kg (3 lb) piece belly pork, off the bone
Dips:
4 garlic cloves, crushed
2 tablespoons sesame seed oil
2 tablespoons soy sauce
1 tablespoon shredded root ginger
2 tablespoons hoisin sauce
chilli flowers, to garnish (see page 62)

1. Place the water in a large saucepan and bring to the boil. Add the pork, reduce the heat slightly and slowly bring the water back to the boil. Skim the surface.

2. Boil steadily for 10 minutes, then turn off the heat and leave to stand for 10 minutes. Repeat this process twice more. Let the pork cool in the water.

3. When the pork is cold, drain, and place on a chopping board. Cut across the grain (so that each slice shows fat and lean) into thin slices. Arrange on a serving dish and garnish.

4. To make the dips, put the garlic and sesame seed oil in one bowl, the soy sauce and ginger in another, and the hoisin sauce in a third bowl.

Twice-cooked Pork

In this example of cross-cooking, rapid boiling is followed by long slow cooking in water and finally deep-frying for a golden finish. The cooking liquid is not wasted, but used as the basis of a nourishing soup, such as Egg Drop Soup, right.

2.25 litres (4 pints) water
1 × 2 kg (4½ lb) piece belly pork, off the bone
3 slices fresh root ginger
oil for deep-frying
Dips:
2 tablespoons soy sauce
2 tablespoons chopped spring onions
4 tablespoons wine vinegar
1 tablespoon shredded fresh root ginger
4 garlic cloves, crushed
2 tablespoons sesame seed oil

Preparation time: 15 minutes, plus cooling
Cooking time: 3 hours
Serves 6–8

1. Bring the water to the boil in a large pan. Add the pork and ginger and bring back to the boil, skimming off any scum that rises to the surface. Reduce the heat, cover the pan and simmer for 2½ hours.

2. Drain the pork and allow to cool, reserving the cooking liquid to make soup. Discard the ginger. When the pork is cold, cut it into 4 equal pieces across the grain.

3. Prepare the dips. Combine the soy sauce and spring onions in one bowl, the vinegar and ginger in another, and mix the garlic with the oil in a third dish.

4. Heat the oil in a wok to 180°C/350°F or until a cube of bread browns in 30 seconds. Deep-fry the pieces of pork 2 at a time for 4–5 minutes.

5. Drain the fried pork well and cut each piece again into 5 mm (¼ inch) slices across the lean and fat. Serve hot, accompanied by the dips.

Egg Drop Soup

4–5 dried shiitake mushrooms, soaked for 20 minutes in warm water
reserved cooking liquid from Twice-Cooked Pork.
2 eggs, beaten
chopped spring onions, to garnish

Preparation time: 10 minutes
Cooking time: 10 minutes
Serves 6–8

1. Drain the mushrooms, remove and discard the stems and shred the caps.

2. Place the cooking liquid in a clean saucepan and add the mushrooms. Simmer over gentle heat for 5–6 minutes.

3. Stir the soup with chopsticks, gently pouring in the beaten egg over the chopsticks and trailing the egg over the surface of the soup.

4. As soon as the eggs have set, pour the soup into individual bowls and scatter chopped spring onions liberally on top. Serve hot.

Shabu-shabu

Quick-boiling or quick-poaching in broth or water kept at a rolling boil is a favourite form of cooking and serving food in northern China in the winter. Although the cooking is plain and simple, the flavouring can be varied with dips. A typical example of this type of cooking is Mongolian Hot Pot or Mohammedan Fire Kettle (page 153), cooked at the table in fondue style. This is the Japanese version; the name comes from the swishing sound made as the slices of beef are wafted in the steaming liquid. It is a good idea for a dinner party as the kettle is a conversation piece in itself. Again, nothing is wasted: the liquid, which becomes progressively richer as the meal continues, is finally served as a soup.

900 g (2 lb) prime quality beef (sirloin), well-marbled with fat
12 open cap mushrooms
10 spring onions
6 leaves Chinese cabbage
1 bunch watercress
2 cakes bean curd
225 g (8 oz) canned bamboo shoots
100 g (4 oz) transparent noodles
Stock:
2.25 litres (4 pints) water
6 leaves Chinese cabbage, shredded
1 carrot, peeled and finely sliced
2 open cap mushrooms, quartered
To garnish:
175 g (6 oz) grated daikon (giant white radish)
75 g (3 oz) finely chopped spring onion
Dips:
Sesame Sauce (see below)
juice of 2 lemons, strained
shoyu (Japanese soy sauce)
rice vinegar

Preparation time: 1 hour
Cooking time: see method
Serves 6

1. Cut the beef into paper-thin slices. This is easier if it is partially frozen.

2. Make the court bouillon: place the water in a saucepan with the Chinese cabbage, carrot slices and quartered mushrooms. Bring to the boil slowly, reduce the heat and simmer gently while you prepare the vegetables.

3. Cut decorative crosses into the mushroom caps. Slice the spring onions diagonally into 4 cm (1½ inch) lengths. Wash the Chinese cabbage and plunge into boiling water for 2–4 minutes or until just tender. Drain, salt lightly, and pat dry. Pick over the watercress, wash, drain and pat dry. Cut the bean curd into 4 cm (1½ inch) squares. Drain the bamboo shoots, cook for 3 minutes in boiling water, and drain again. Cut into half-moon shapes about 5 mm (½ inch) thick.

4. Drop the noodles into boiling water, leave to stand for 30 seconds and drain.

Sesame Sauce

75 g (3 oz) white sesame seeds
175 ml (6 fl oz) dashi
6 tablespoons dark soy sauce
2 tablespoons mirin
1 tablespoon sugar
1–2 tablespoons sake

1. Place the sesame seeds in a small heavy frying pan without oil and dry-fry over moderate heat until golden brown. Grind in a pestle and mortar until flaky.

2. Gradually add all the other ingredients, combining well after each addition. Transfer to a screwtop jar and shake well before use.

5. Arrange the noodles and vegetables attractively on a platter. Place the dips into shallow saucers and the garnish in bowls. On another platter, arrange the slices of beef. Preheat the fire kettle and pour the hot stock into the moat.

6. Using chopsticks, each guest helps himself to a slice of beef and cooks it in the hot stock, adding vegetables and noodles as required, and dips the food into condiments of his choice to cool it before eating, adding garnishes for contrast of texture.

7. When all the meat has been eaten, the remaining vegetables and noodles are placed in the stock and cooked for 3–4 minutes and served as soup.

CLEAR SIMMERING

In China the technique of clear-simmering is most frequently used to cook meat, fish and clear soups in an earthenware pot (called a sandpot) over a low charcoal heat. In the West, it can be achieved by cooking in a heavy flameproof casserole over a very low heat or in a cool oven. Few flavouring ingredients are used during cooking; any additional ingredients are added during the last few minutes of cooking.

Clear-simmered Beef

In this typical clear-simmering recipe spicy dips are usually served at the table to counteract the blandness of food cooked in this way. Many people prefer this to heavy flavouring effected during cooking, as they can then flavour their portion to taste. This is a good way of cooking less expensive cuts of meat, and again, the liquid is used as a broth, served over rice, which is very filling.

1.25 kg (2½ lb) stewing beef
1.75 litres (3 pints) water
3 slices fresh root ginger
2 teaspoons salt
450 g (1 lb) spinach leaves, roughly chopped
1 tablespoon chopped coriander
Dips:
4 tablespoons soy sauce
1 tablespoon shredded root ginger
2 tablespoons hoisin sauce
2 tablespoons English mustard
1 tablespoon chilli oil
1 teaspoon chilli sauce or Tabasco

Preparation time: 15 minutes
Cooking time: about 3 hours
Serves 6

1. Using a Chinese cleaver or a sharp knife, cut the beef into 5 cm (2 inch) cubes and trim away any excess fat.

2. Place the beef in a large pan with the water, ginger and salt. Bring to the boil and boil for 5 minutes. Skim off any scum that rises to the surface.

3. Reduce the heat, cover the pan and simmer very gently for 2½–3 hours.

4. Meanwhile, make the dips. Mix 2 tablespoons soy sauce with the ginger and place in a bowl. Put the hoisin sauce in a second dish, the mustard in a third, and mix the chilli oil, chilli sauce or Tabasco and the remaining soy sauce in a fourth dish.

5. Just before the end of the cooking time, add the spinach to the pan and simmer gently for 2 minutes. Sprinkle with the chopped coriander.

6. Serve in individual soup bowls. To eat this semi-soup, each diner lifts the meat out of the broth with chopsticks and flavours it with the dips. Serve boiled rice in separate bowls. When the meat has been eaten the broth is spooned or poured into the rice bowls and eaten with the rice.

STEAMING

Steaming as a cooking method has many advantages: as well as preserving all of the natural flavour of the food to be cooked, it keeps it tender and retains vitamins efficiently. Quick-steaming is particularly successful with delicate fish, breast of chicken, vegetables and the famous Japanese savoury cup custard *Chawan Mushi* (see page 72). The food is either placed in an open plate inside the steamer or in small lidded bowls or special custard cups. Steaming is not much used in Indian cookery, but greatly valued in Japan and China and other South-east Asian countries. The easiest way to steam is in a bamboo steamer set over a wok of boiling water; stacking metal steamers are also available. For some recipes, such as *Chawan Mushi*, it is possible to steam in an oven using a bain marie. Whatever method you use, the golden rule is that the water should be boiling merrily *before* you put the food in its container over it.

Flounder in the Woodpile

450 g (1 lb) flounder or plaice
    fillets
salt
8 open cup mushrooms, cut into
    matchstick strips
1 × 5 cm (2 inch) piece carrot,
    cut into matchstick strips
100 g (4 oz) green beans, cut
    into matchstick strips
1 egg white, lightly beaten
sake
To garnish:
2 tablespoons finly grated
    daikon (Japanese white
    radish)
1 teaspoon finely grated wasabi
    (Japanese horseradish)

Preparation time: 15 minutes, plus salting
Cooking time: 10 minutes
Serves 4

1. Lightly salt the fish fillets and set aside 10 minutes.

2. Remove the skin from the fillets and cut them across into 4 pieces.

3. Place all the vegetables in a bowl, sprinkle them lightly with salt and toss lightly. Coat the vegetables with beaten egg white.

4. Place the fish fillets in the bottom of individual heatproof bowls and sprinkle them with sake. Arrange the vegetables on top radiating out from the centre. Cover tightly with foil (and with a lid if using traditional Japanese bowls).

Silver Sauce

350 ml (12 fl oz) Japanese
    stock (dashi)
pinch of salt
1 teaspoon light soy sauce
1½ tablespoons cornflour
juice of 1 lemon (optional)

Preparation time: 2 minutes
Cooking time: 7 minutes
Makes 350 ml (12 fl oz)

1. Place the stock in a saucepan with the salt and soy sauce. Cook, stirring occasionally, over a moderate heat until simmering point is reached.

2. Blend the cornflour with 1½ tablespoons of water to make a thin paste. Gradually add this paste to the stock, stirring until thickened. Add lemon juice if liked and serve hot.

5. Have the water ready boiling in the wok. Place the bowls in a steamer set over the water, cover and cook for 10 minutes.

6. To serve, remove the foil and arrange mounds of grated daikon and wasabi on top of each bowl. Serve hot, with Silver Sauce (see left) handed separately.

Long-steamed Beef

Long-steaming gives a result similar to long-simmering, with the advantage that the temperature can be maintained steadily and evenly all round, instead of just underneath. In this recipe the beef is marinated briefly before cooking for added flavour and to prevent it drying out in the long cooking period. The finished dish is served directly from the cooking pot, and as it does not move during cooking, it is nice to know that the careful arrangement of meat and vegetables you make when preparing the casserole will look just the same when it is ready.

1 teaspoon salt
2½ tablespoons soy sauce
2 tablespoons Chinese wine or dry sherry
1 tablespoon hoisin sauce
1 slice fresh root ginger
2 teaspoons cornflour
1 kg (2¼ lb) lean rump beef, cut into 4 cm (1½ inch) cubes
1½ tablespoons sunflower oil
6 shiitake mushrooms, soaked in warm water for 20 minutes
100 g (4 oz) canned bamboo shoots, cut into cubes
the green part of 3 spring onions, cut into 5 cm (2½ inch) lengths
2 sprigs parsley, finely chopped
1 teaspoon sesame seed oil

Preparation time: 15 minutes, plus marinating
Cooking time: 2 hours
Serves 6

1. Mix the first six ingredients together to make a marinade and marinate the cubes of beef for 30 minutes. Trickle the sunflower oil on top and stir.

2. Drain the mushrooms, reserving 4 tablespoons of the liquid.

3. Place the bamboo shoots in a layer on the base of a heatproof casserole. Pack the meat in its marinade on top. Pour over the reserved mushroom liquid.

4. Arange the mushrooms and spring onions attractively on top of the beef. Cover with foil and then the lid.

Steamed Scallops in Black Bean Sauce

The southern Chinese province of Canton has a long coastline, giving access to the rich fishing grounds of the South China Sea and there are many sophisticated ways of presenting seafood in Cantonese cuisine. This easily prepared dish makes an unusual starter.

12 scallops, on their shells
2 tablespoons sunflower oil
2 tablespoons salted black beans, soaked, drained and crushed
1 chilli, seeded and finely chopped
1 garlic clove, crushed
2 spring onions, finely chopped
2 tablespoons soy sauce
2 teaspoons sugar
3 tablespoons chicken stock
2 teaspoons cornflour

Preparation time: 5 minutes
Cooking time: 8 minutes
Serves 4

1. Clean the scallops (see page 55) and replace them on their shells with the corals. Place in a bamboo steamer set over a saucepan or wok of boiling water and steam gently for 5–6 minutes.

2. Heat the oil in a wok and add the black beans, chilli, garlic and spring onions. Stir-fry for 1 minute and add the soy sauce and sugar.

3. Blend the chicken stock with the cornflour and add it to the sauce. Cook, stirring continuously, until the sauce has thickened.

4. Arrange the scallops on a serving dish and pour the hot sauce over. Serve immediately.

Illustrated on page 66

5. Use a wok with a trivet or inverted plate in the bottom. Stand the casserole on the plate and pour in enough boiling water to come one third up the side of the casserole. Place the lid on the wok and set over gentle heat to steam for 2 hours. Add more boiling water from time to time to keep the level up.

6. Serve the beef in the casserole, sprinkled with parsley and sesame seed oil.

COOKING IN OIL

Oriental cooking employs oil much more frequently than in the West, yet in most cases it is fairer to describe the technique as 'cooking with oil' rather than 'cooking in oil' as the quantity of oil used is minimal. A complete meal may be prepared by the quick stir-frying method; deep-frying may be used for foods wrapped in paper, coated in batter, or as the last stage of a more complex cooking process. Shallow-frying is a gentler technique suitable for fish.

STIR-FRYING

This method is widely used all over South-east Asia and has been readily adopted by Western cooks. The food is cooked quickly over intense heat in a wok in oil, with seasonings and optional stock, wine and sauces. A great variety of foods can be prepared with great success in this way – meat, offal, poultry, seafood, vegetables, rice, noodles and so on – either singly or in combination, making a delicious meal in a very short time. The wok is the ideal utensil for stir-frying. Western cooks sometimes find it difficult to manipulate the wok with one hand and the spatula with the other (in professional Chinese kitchens the cook operates the gas flame with a switch at knee level to leave both hands free) – a stand to keep the wok steady over the hob is invaluable, or you could use a large frying pan instead.

Successful stir-frying depends on a number of factors. First, because, the cooking time is extremely brief, the food must be cut into pieces of similar size and shape, so that it cooks evenly. Second, the wok must be preheated before the cooking oil is added (use a good quality light oil such as sunflower oil); heat the oil until it is smoking, then let it cool slightly –until it is sizzling – before adding the food. Keep the heat high, to keep the cooking time brief. This releases the juices from the food to make a natural gravy (as well as any stock or sauce you may be adding). Ingredients requiring longer cooking time should be added first.

The most important thing is to stir the food vigorously and continuously with chopsticks or a spatula, keping it on the move all the time as it cooks. Never overcook stir-fried food – it must be tender but still just crisp and with a fresh appetizing colour – and serve it as soon as it is ready.

Fried Vermicelli with Crabmeat

Mien Xao Cua

Because stir-frying is a quick cooking method, it is essential that each item of food is correctly prepared before being thrown into the wok. Usually, in the case of meat or vegetables, this means careful chopping and slicing, but for rice vermicelli – a type of very fine noodles much used in Vietnam – it entails soaking and drying the noodles so that they will soften and cook until soft but *al dente* in the hot oil.

100g (4 oz) transparent rice vermicelli
5–7 tablespoons sunflower oil
3 spring onions, roughly chopped
100 g (4 oz) fresh or canned crabmeat, picked over and flaked
3–4 tablespoons chicken stock
1 teaspoon salt
2 tablespoons nuoc mam (fish gravy)
$\frac{1}{4}$ teaspoon monosodium glutamate (optional)
To serve:
freshly ground black pepper
sprigs of fresh coriander

Preparation time: 10 minutes, plus soaking and drying
Cooking time: 12 minutes
Serves 4

1. Soak the transparent rice vermicelli in warm water for 15 minutes. Drain thoroughly in a colander, then spread out and allow to dry for 15 minutes.

2. Heat 5 tablespoons of oil in a large non-stick frying pan or wok over low to moderate heat. Add the spring onions and stir-fry for 3–5 minutes until the white portions are lightly coloured.

3. Stir in the crabmeat and vermicelli, adding more oil if necessary, and stir-fry for 2 minutes more. If the mixture is very dry, moisten it with the chicken stock and cook, still stirring, for about 5 minutes or until the vermicelli are soft and all the strands are separate.

4. Season with salt and nuoc mam, adding the monosodium glutamate, if using.

5. Serve immediately, sprinkled with pepper and garnished with sprigs of coriander.

Right: Fried vermicelli with crabmeat

Quick-fried Beef Ribbons with Ginger, Carrots and Spring Onions

Use good-quality beef for this dish, which has a delicious flavour and is a favourite in both Chinese homes and restaurants.

600 g (1¼ lb) lean beef (rump, fillet or topside)
2 tablespoons dark soy sauce
2 tablespoons hoisin sauce
¾ teaspoon sugar
1 tablespoon Chinese wine or dry sherry
a pinch of freshly ground black pepper
2 spring onions, trimmed and chopped
4 tablespoons sunflower oil
3 slices fresh root ginger, shredded
1 young carrot, shredded

Preparation time: 15 minutes, plus marinating
Cooking time: 5 minutes
Serves 4

1. Using a very sharp knife, cut the beef into thin slices, then into double matchstick-size ribbons. Place the beef in a large bowl. Add half the soy and hoisin sauces, the sugar, wine or sherry and pepper. Stir together well and leave the beef to marinate in the mixture for 15 minutes.

2. Cut the spring onions diagonally into 5 cm (2 inch) pieces.

3. Heat the oil in a wok. When hot, add the shredded ginger and carrot. Spread them out evenly over the pan and stir-fry over high heat for 1 minute.

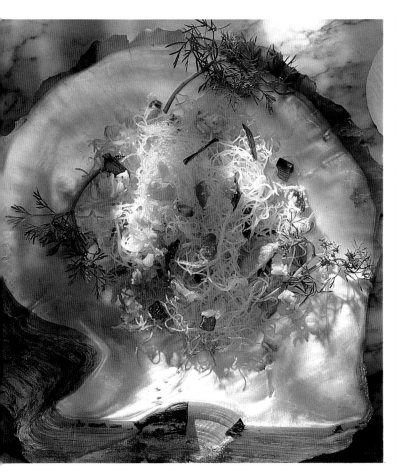

4. Add the marinated beef and stir-fry briskly with the ginger and carrot for 1½ minutes.

5. Add the remaining sauces, with any remaining marinade. Continue to stir-fry briskly for a further 30 seconds still over high heat.

6. Add the spring onion, stir and turn once more and serve immediately.

Variation:
For a hotter dish, add 2 fresh green chillies and 1 dried red chilli, with the seeds removed. (See page 13, Chillies, for a note on how to seed chillies). Chop finely and add to the wok with the ginger and carrot, before adding the beef.

DEEP-FRYING

Deep-frying is used in Chinese cooking in the same way as it is in the West, to produce crisp-textured food. Occasionally, as in the recipe below, it is used as the final stage in a cross-cooking process, which as well as giving a pleasing contrast of textures between the crisp skin of the duck and the tender flesh, gives it an appetizing appearance. The duckling is first boiled in water, then simmered in a master sauce and finally deep-fried. The master sauce can be re-used in another dish.

Crispy Duckling

1 × 1.75 kg (4 lb) duckling
sunflower oil for deep-frying
Sauce:
1.2 litres (2 pints) rich stock
600 ml (1 pint) Chinese wine
  or dry sherry
7 tablespoons light soy sauce
4 tablespoons soy bean paste
4 tablespoons hoisin sauce
4 onions, sliced
6 slices fresh root ginger
1½ tablespoons sugar
6 garlic cloves, crushed
1 chicken stock cube
1 teaspoon five-spice powder
900 g (2 lb) pork bones
450 g (1 lb) shin of beef, cubed
To serve:
10–12 Mandarin pancakes (see
  page 134)
5 tablespoons hoisin sauce
2 cucumbers, peeled and sliced
  lengthwise
5 spring onions, shredded

Preparation time: 25 minutes
Cooking time: about 2½ hours,
plus cooling
Serves 6

1. Plunge the duckling into a wok or pan of boiling water. Boil for 10 minutes, then drain.

2. Combine all the ingredients for the sauce in a large wok or saucepan. Bring to the boil, cover and simmer for 30 minutes. Discard the bones.

3. Add the duckling to the sauce and coat it thoroughly. Bring to the boil, cover and simmer gently for 1½ hours, turning the duckling a few times during the cooking period.

4. Lift the duckling out of the sauce and transfer to a wire rack to drain thoroughly while cooling.

5. When the duckling is thoroughly dry, heat the oil in a wok to 180°C/350°F or until a cube of bread browns in 30 seconds.

6. Lower the duckling into the oil and deep-fry for 8–10 minutes, spooning the oil over the exposed surface of the duckling.

7. Drain and transfer to a heated serving dish. Serve hot with accompaniments as for Peking Duck (see page 134).

Deep-fried Fish and Vegetables

Tempura

When the Japanese adopt a cooking technique from another country – in the case of deep-frying from China or from Europeans – they are not content until it has been refined to suit their standards of perfection. The airy lightness of tempura is legendary, and is achieved first by taking great care over the temperature of the oil and then by blending the batter in a very particular way. To Western eyes the combination of egg, water and flour correctly mixed for tempura looks as if it could do with a good beating – but that is as it should be. As each piece of food is dipped into the batter it is coated first in egg, then in water, then in flour, the three ingredients held together in a fragile suspension that works brilliantly.

Specially blended tempura oil is available in Japan. Good substitutes are corn, safflower or peanut oil. Never use animal fats or olive oil, as the flavour is much too strong. Once you have got the oil to the recommended temperature, do not let it cool down but keep it at that temperature throughout the cooking time.

8 headless uncooked fresh prawns
1 medium squid, cleaned (see page 54)
1 large red pepper
8 button mushrooms, halved
1 large carrot, peeled
100 g (4 oz) French beans, trimmed
1 small aubergine, trimmed and sliced
100 g (4 oz) mangetout, trimmed
vegetable oil for deep-frying
plain flour for coating
Batter:
1 egg
75 g (3 oz) plain flour
25 g (1 oz) cornflour
Tentsuyu sauce:
200 ml (7 fl oz) Japanese stock (see page 69)
50 ml (2 fl oz) shoyu (Japanese soy sauce)
50 ml (2 fl oz) mirin (sweet rice wine)
Accompaniments:
2.5 cm (1 inch) piece fresh root ginger, peeled and grated
5 cm (2 inch) piece daikon (Japanese radish), peeled and grated
1 lime, cut into wedges

Preparation time: 40 minutes
Cooking time: about 15 minutes
Serves 4

Illustrated on page 10

1. Wash and shell the prawns, retaining the tail shell. Remove the black vein from along the back of the prawns then make a slit along the belly to prevent them curling during cooking.

2. Cut the squid into 5 × 4 cm (2 × 1½ inch) pieces.

3. Prepare the vegetables. Cut the pepper lengthways into quarters; remove the seeds, then halve each piece to make 8 bite-sized pieces. Halve the mushrooms. Cut the carrot into 5 cm (2 inch) pieces, then cut these into decorative triangles (see page 62).

4. Make the batter immediately before frying – do not let it stand. Mix the egg and 100 ml (3½ fl oz) ice-cold water in a bowl, then sift in the plain flour and cornflour.

5. Mix very briefly, using chopsticks (when you are practised hold a pair of chopsticks in each hand). Do not overmix – there should still be lumps in the flour.

6. If you do not have a draining rack for your wok, put a wire rack over a roasting tin by the side of the hob. Heat the oil in the wok or a deep-fat frier to about 160°C/325°F or until a cube of bread browns in 45 seconds. Using chopsticks, dip the pieces of pepper in the batter so that only the inside is coated, then deep-fry skin side up for about 30 seconds; drain on the rack. Repeat with the other vegetables.

7. Increase the temperature of the oil to 180°C/350°F. With chopsticks, hold the prawns by their tails and dip them into the batter one at a time (do not batter the tail shell). Deep-fry for about 1 minute, remove and drain.

8. Coat the squid pieces with flour, dip them in the batter and deep-fry in the hot oil for 1 minute. Drain.

9. Make the Tentsuyu Sauce (see page 160), then pour it into four small bowls.

10. Arrange the fish and vegetables on a dish with the grated ginger and daikon. Garnish with lime and serve with the bowls of sauce. Each person mixes ginger and daikon to taste with some of the sauce, then dips the tempura into the sauce.

Deep-fried Paper-wrapped Chicken

Jee Bow Ghuy

Wrapping food that is to be deep-fried in paper prevents it from absorbing oil, while sealing in the flavour. In China cellophane wrapping used to be used, which is attractive, but non-stick parchment is easier to work with and just as efficient. Rice paper is sometimes used, which has the benefit of being edible, but it does not prevent the absorption of oil. Other suitable fillings for the envelopes are fish (see page 107) and marinated shredded beef with ginger and onions.

Preparation time: 30 minutes, plus marinating
Cooking time: 3 minutes
Serves 4

1 × 1.5 kg (3 lb) roasting chicken
3 tablespoons Chinese wine or dry sherry
2 tablespoons sunflower oil
3 tablespoons soy sauce
a generous pinch of salt
4 spring onions, finely chopped
1 × 5 cm (2 inch) piece fresh root ginger, peeled and grated
22 pieces non-stick baking parchment or greaseproof paper, 12.5 cm (5 inches) square
sunflower oil for deep-frying
Accompaniments:
cucumber slices
Chinese leaves, shredded radish rose (see page 61)

1. Take all the chicken meat from the bones and cut it into small thin slivers (see page 57, Boning poultry). Mix the meat in a bowl with the wine or sherry, oil, soy sauce, salt, spring onions and ginger. Leave to marinate for 2 hours at room temperature.

2. To make the paper parcels, put about 1 tablespoon of the chicken towards one corner of the piece of greaseproof paper (see diagram). Fold over the nearest corner (A), then the two sides (B, C) and continue to fold from the opposite corner (D). Tuck in the final corner (E) to seal the parcel tightly.

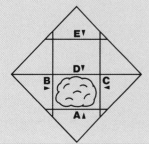

3. Heat the oil in a wok to 180°C/350°F or until a cube of bread browns in 30 seconds. Deep-fry the parcels 4 or 5 at a time for 3 minutes. Drain on a rack while you fry the remainder.

4. When all the parcels have been fried, return them to the hot oil and fry for a further 1 minute to heat through. Drain thoroughly. Serve hot with salad vegetables. Each diner takes a parcel from the serving dish and opens the paper with chopsticks.

SHALLOW FRYING

Shallow-frying is a comparative term: the amount of oil used is not inconsiderable, but after the first cooking most of it is poured off from the pan and sauces or seasonings added.

Soft-fried Sole Fillets in Wine Sauce

The shallow-frying technique is especially suited to delicate fish like sole. In this recipe the fish is not overpowered, but rather complemented by the delicious sauce. The method also ensures that the separate ingredients retain their distinctive flavours.

750 g (1½ lb) sole fillets, cut into
  small triangles
1½ teaspoons salt
1 tablespoon cornflour
2 egg whites, lightly beaten
300 ml (½ pint) sunflower oil or
  corn oil
2–3 tablespoons dried wood
  ears, soaked for 20 minutes,
  drained and stemmed
2 garlic cloves, crushed
Sauce:
2 slices fresh root ginger,
  crushed to extract the juice
4 tablespoons dry white wine
4 tablespoons chicken stock
1 teaspoon sugar
1 tablespoon cornflour
a few spring onions, chopped, to
  garnish

Preparation time: 15 minutes
Cooking time: about 10 minutes
Serves 6

Above: Soft-fried sole fillets in wine sauce

1. Sprinkle the fish pieces with salt and coat with the cornflour. Mix the egg whites with 1½ teaspoons of the oil in a bowl. Dip the fish into this mixture.

2. Heat the remaining oil in a wok over a moderate heat. When the oil is hot, fry the fish pieces a few at a time, for about 2 minutes until crisp and golden. Lift the fish out of the oil, drain and keep warm while cooking the remainder.

3. Pour away all but 1 tablespoon of oil from the wok. Add the wood ears and crushed garlic to the wok and stir-fry for a few seconds.

4. To make the sauce, combine the ginger juice, wine, stock and sugar. Mix the cornflour with 3 tablespoons of cold water to make a thin paste and add to the wine and stock mixture. Pour the sauce into the wok and cook, stirring, for about 1½ minutes until thickened.

5. Return the fish to the wok, a piece at a time. When the sauce returns to the boil, reduce the heat and simmer for 45 seconds. Serve hot, garnished with chopped spring onions.

GRILLING

If stir-frying and red-cooking (see page 43) are the quintessence of Chinese cooking, grilling takes pride of place as the technique perfected by the Japanese. In its basic form a primitive method – our earliest ancestors must have stuck pieces of meat on twigs to cook them over an open fire – in Japan charcoal-grilling is typically refined. The choice of particular cuts of meat or fillets of fish is made with great care; delicious sauces ensure that the food stays moist and flavoursome while exposed to very high temperatures, and the cooking medium itself is unique to Japan. The traditional charcoal used there is called *binchō* and is made from oak. Hard and shiny, it burns without smoke or smell: the characteristic 'char-broiled' flavour we are fond of in the West is too coarse for cultivated Japanese tastes; but *binchō* is very expensive, so a standard quality charcoal, more closely resembling the kind available in the West, is often used. The crucial factor is that good charcoal reaches a very high temperature and stays hot for hours, a condition which is very difficult to achieve with gas or electricity.

Nevertheless, a gas or electric grill preheated to high can give satisfactory results, and has the advantage of not interfering with the flavour of the food. When using charcoal, light the fire at least 1½ hours before cooking, so that the coals are red when the food is placed over them. Place the skewered food at the correct distance from the heat, taking into account its size. For example, a whole fish should be further away from the coals than cubes of beef. Remove food from the fire *before* it is completely cooked, since retained heat will continue to cook it for a few minutes afterwards.

Grilled food is delicious and attractive enough to feature at formal dinners, but is ideal for more casual occasions. In Japanese restaurants specializing in grilled foods, diners choose what they want to eat and sit at the bar with a drink to watch it being cooked – a very relaxed affair.

Grilled Skewered Chicken

Yakitori

The Japanese word for 'grilled things' is *yakimono*, and under this heading are to be found some of the tastiest mouthfuls in Oriental cuisine. In Japan, of course, standards are set for the correct degree of 'doneness', so that while pork must be cooked through, beef should be well-done on the outside but very rare in the centre; the outside of prawns must be crisp, the middle moist. Vegetables such as mushrooms and aubergines are done till slightly charred, and cubes of tofu to the same degree.

The chicken kebabs described here are perfect barbecue food, not only because they can be prepared in advance and cooked when you are ready, but also because they are easy to eat at an informal gathering (in Japanese cities there are corner stalls selling yakitori skewers to workers who stop off for a quick bite and a beer on their way home).

The best part of the chicken for kebabs is juicy leg or thigh. Substitute squares of green pepper or whole button mushrooms for the leeks if you wish. The kebabs should be at least three-quarters done before dipping them in the sauce for the first time. Use bamboo skewers which have been soaked in water for 30 minutes before use.

2 chicken legs
2 thin leeks, white part only, or
    2 large spring onions
Tare sauce:
65 ml (2½ fl oz) shoyu
    (Japanese soy sauce)
65 ml (2½ fl oz) mirin (sweet
    rice wine) or cooking sake
2 tablespoons sugar
2 teaspoons plain flour

Preparation time: 30 minutes
Cooking time: 25–30 minutes
Serves 4

1. Bone the chicken legs (see page 57), and cut the meat, with the skin on, into 24 bite-sized pieces. Cut the leeks or spring onion into 16 pieces.

2. To make the Tare Sauce, place the shoyu, mirin, sugar and flour in a small pan and bring to the boil, stirring constantly (this will burn off the alcohol, which is necessary to make the sauce digestible). Reduce the heat and simmer for 10 minutes, until the sauce is reduced to about two-thirds its original volume. Transfer the sauce to a shallow dish.

3. Thread the pre-soaked skewers, each with 3 pieces of chicken and 2 pieces of leek or onion, arranged alternately and with spaces between each piece.

4. Grill the kebabs over charcoal until browned all over.

5. Dip the three-quarters cooked kebabs into the sauce and return them to the grill. Cook for a few more minutes until the chicken is cooked (it should be just done, still moist inside).

6. Dip the kebabs in sauce once more, grill again briefly, and serve.

Grilled Langoustines

Tom Cang Nuong

In this recipe the langoustines are briefly deep-fried before being placed over the coals, and brushed with aromatic oil during grilling. As pretty as any Japanese dish, but with a certain French influence, the dish is unmistakeably Vietnamese, and eaten in typically informal fashion, each guest combining the ingredients in individual rolls at the table.

oil for deep-frying
12 large langoustines
225 g (8 oz) boiled fat pork, cut into 32 cubes
2 tablespoons chopped shallots
2 tablespoons chopped spring onion tops
24 sheets banh trang (rice paper)
1 iceberg lettuce, shredded
½ cucumber, thinly sliced
1 tablespoon fresh mint leaves
1 tablespoon freshly chopped coriander leaves
Nuoc mam giam sauce (see Transparent Spring Rolls, page 92)

Preparation time: 15 minutes
Cooking time: 30 minutes
Serves 4

1. Heat the oil in a wok or deep fat fryer, add the langoustines and cook for 30 to 45 seconds. Remove the langoustines with a slotted spoon and drain on paper towels. Reduce the heat to low.

2. When the langoustines are cool enough to handle, shell and devein them. Cut each langoustine in half lengthways.

3. Thread 3 langoustine halves and 4 pork fat cubes alternately on to 8 metal skewers, beginning and ending with pork.

4. Place the chopped shallots and spring onion tops in a small bowl. Using a soup ladle, scoop up a little of the hot oil in which the langoustines were cooked and add this to the bowl. Mix well.

5. Arrange the langoustine kebabs on a grid over medium to hot coals, or under a preheated medium grill, and brush liberally with the aromatic oil mixture. Cook for 5–8 minutes, turning frequently and brushing several times with the aromatic oil.

6. Meanwhile, prepare the banh trang by soaking them in tepid water for 1 minute. Shake off excess water, roll the banh trang loosely and arrange on a large platter with the lettuce, cucumber, mint and coriander leaves. Place the nuoc mam giam sauce in a bowl.

7. When the langoustines and pork cubes are cooked, slide them off the skewers on to a second platter and serve. Guests make their own rice paper rolls, using a half langoustine, one or two pork cubes and a selection of vegetables as the filling for each roll, and dipping the rolls in the Nuoc mam giam sauce.

Using skewers

For food to be cooked evenly over charcoal it should be correctly threaded on to skewers, and in such a way that it looks attractive when arranged on a plate. This is particularly important with fish, and the Japanese have evolved a number of methods for retaining the shape while cooking.

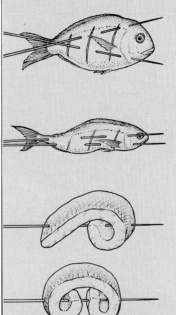

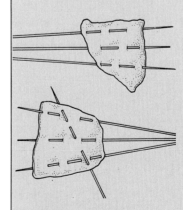

● **Whole fish**
Slash the skin lightly once or twice to prevent it shrinking. Use 2 skewers for larger fish, 1 for smaller varieties, threading through one side only so that the other is unblemished. The body of the fish curves slightly, giving rise to the name 'wave-skewering', because it looks as if the fish is swimming.

● **Fish fillets**
In order to slow down the cooking and keep the fish moist, fillets are curled in place on the skewers in one of two possible arrangements. When removed, they keep their pretty shape.

An alternative with round fish such as mackerel is flat-skewering. Place the fattest parts to the centre so the fish cooks evenly.

● **Squid or octopus**
Flesh from the body of squid or octopus tends to curl when grilled unless several skewers are used to keep it flat. Again, only one side should be pierced.

● **Small fish**
Sardines, for example, can be grilled together on a fan arrangement of skewers, which makes turning the fish simplicity itself and keeps the shape perfectly.

COOKING IN SAUCE

Every major cuisine has its equivalent of the stew, a tasty, nourishing dish that is as comforting as it is filling. China's version is exemplified by 'red-cooking', cooking in a rich gravy of which soy sauce is an essential ingredient. Two examples are given opposite, one for beef and one for fish.

In the West, Indian curries are perhaps the best known of Oriental 'casseroles'. The blanket use of the term curries is misleading, since it conceals the marvellous variety of Indian cooking, which differs from region to region and in which the subtle use of spices is unsurpassed. In the following recipe the meat is sealed on all sides before being combined with a mild but aromatic sauce and simmered until tender. The use of yoghurt to both tenderize the meat and sweeten the spices is distinctively Indian.

Lamb with Double Onions

Gosht Dopiaza

The Hindu word for onion is *piaz* and the word for two is *do* (pronounced as dough), so Gosht Dopiaza means 'meat with double onions'. Onions form a crucial part of virtually all Indian curry dishes and, in fact, many Indians regard onions as vegetables in themselves.

675 g (1½ lb) boneless shoulder of lamb
5 large onions, peeled
100 g (4 oz) ghee or concentrated butter
6 cloves garlic, peeled and thinly sliced
1 × 7.5 cm (3 inch) piece fresh root ginger, peeled and thinly sliced
1 tablespoon chilli powder
2 teaspoons ground coriander
2 teaspoons ground cumin

2 teaspoons freshly ground black pepper
1½ teaspoons turmeric
2 teaspoons salt
350 g (12 oz) natural yoghurt
300 ml (½ pint) beef stock
6 fresh green chillies, cored and chopped into 5 mm (¼ inch) pieces
1 tablespoon fenugreek seeds
2 tablespoons freshly chopped mint leaves

Preparation time: 30 minutes
Cooking time: about 1 hour 15 minutes
Oven: 180°C/350°F/Gas Mark 4
Serves 4–6

1. Cut the lamb into 4 cm (1½ inch) cubes, trimming off excess fat and gristle. Purée 1 onion to a paste, and thinly slice the remaining 4 onions. Add the lamb to the puréed onion in a bowl and mix well together.

2. Melt the ghee in a large heavy-based saucepan. Add the lamb and brown the pieces on all sides. Remove the lamb with a perforated spoon and set aside.

3. Place the sliced onions in the pan with the garlic and ginger. Fry gently for 4–5 minutes until soft. Mix the ground spices and salt with the yoghurt and add this to the pan.

4. Increase the heat and add the lamb, combining the ingredients well. Add the stock, stir well, and bring to the boil.

5. Transfer the mixture to a casserole, cover and place in a preheated oven for 40 minutes.

6. Add the fresh chillies, fenugreek seeds and chopped mint and return the casserole to the oven for a further 5–10 minutes or until the meat is tender. Serve hot.

Red-cooking

Red cooking is a method unique to China. It is a variation on braising characterized by the use of soy sauce, which gives the food a delicious flavour as well as the distinctively rich colour denoted by the name. It is traditionally used for larger cuts of meat and whole chicken or duck, but the method is equally effective with cubed beef such as shin, a rather tough meat, which benefits from the tenderizing effect of long cooking or oily fish with a strong flavour such as mackerel.

Red-cooked Fish

Red-cooking is here adapted for a full-flavoured carp. The soy sauce imparts a rich flavour and a reddish-brown colour to the food. The recipe can also be used for mackerel, sea bass or mullet. If the whole fish weighs more than 900 g (2 lb), cut it into 2 or 3 pieces before cooking.

1 × 900 g (2 lb) carp
1 teaspoon salt
2 garlic cloves
2 slices root ginger, peeled
4 spring onions
250 ml (8 fl oz) vegetable oil
2 tablespoons soy sauce
1 tablespoon sherry
1½ teaspoons sugar
300 ml (½ pint) Chinese Clear Stock (see page 68), or water
1 teaspoon cornflour
1 teaspoon sesame seed oil

Preparation time: about 20 minutes
Cooking time: 30 minutes
Serves 6

1. Scale and clean the carp. Slash both sides of the fish diagonally, as far as the bone, at intervals of about 1 cm (½ inch). Dry it thoroughly and rub on the salt both on the inside and outside of the fish.

2. Crush the garlic, thinly slice the root ginger and cut the spring onions into 2.5 cm (1 inch) lengths.

3. Heat the oil in a wok or frying pan to 160°C/350°F or until cube of bread browns in 45 seconds. Place the fish in the wok and fry for 2 minutes on each side. Lift the fish out of the wok with a slotted spoon and drain on paper towels. Set it aside to keep warm.

4. Pour most of the oil out of the wok, leaving about 1 tablespoon in the bottom. Add the garlic, ginger and spring onions and fry for a few seconds only.

5. Combine the soy sauce, sherry, sugar and stock or water in a bowl. Replace the fish in the wok and pour over this mixture. Leave to simmer for 10–15 minutes.

6. Mix the cornflour with a little cold water to make a thin paste. Add to the pan, stirring constantly, until the sauce is thickened and the fish heated through.

7. Transfer the fish to a heated platter. Sprinkle the sesame seed oil on top and serve immediately.

Red-cooked Beef with Tomatoes

Red-cooked beef is the Chinese version of the international stew. Tomatoes are often included in north China where they are plentiful. Long slow cooking turns the muscles of the shin of beef into delicious jelly, giving the finished dish a beautifully smooth texture.

1.5 kg (3 lb) shin of beef
3 tablespoons sunflower oil
2 large onions, sliced thinly
2 slices fresh root ginger, peeled and shredded
2 garlic cloves, crushed
1 piece dried tangerine peel, soaked for 20 minutes and drained
1 teaspoon salt
5 tablespoons soy sauce
450 g (1 lb) tomatoes, skinned and chopped
1 tablespoon sugar
6 tablespoons Chinese rice wine or dry sherry
½ tablespoon hoisin sauce
To garnish:
tomato slices
1 tablespoon finely chopped chives

Preparation time: 15 minutes
Cooking time: about 3½ hours
Serves 6–8

1. Put the beef in a saucepan with enough water to cover. Bring the water to the boil and boil for 10 minutes. Drain the beef, reserving the liquid, and cut it into 4 cm (1½ inch) cubes. Measure the cooking liquid. If necessary, make it up to 750 ml (1½ pints) with hot water.

2. Heat the oil in a heavy flameproof casserole set over high heat. Stir-fry the pieces of beef for 5–6 minutes. Remove the meat from the pan with a slotted spoon and drain on paper towels.

3. Add the onions, ginger and garlic to the casserole and stir-fry over medium heat for 3–4 minutes. Add the measured liquid and stir in the tangerine peel, salt and 2 tablespoons of soy sauce. Bring to the boil and add the cubes of beef. Bring the liquid back to the boil, reduce the heat to very low, cover and simmer gently for 2 hours.

4. Add the skinned and chopped tomatoes to the casserole with the remaining soy sauce, the sugar, rice wine or sherry and hoisin sauce. Stir well, cover and continue cooking over a very low heat for 1 hour more.

5. Transfer to a heated platter, garnish with sliced tomatoes and chopped chives and serve immediately.

COOKING IN A TANDOOR OVEN

In most Oriental countries cooking is done in a pot or wok over a flame or over charcoal. Oven-baking is almost unknown, with one notable exception. The Tandoor oven of the Punjab in northern India is a clay structure shaped like a beehive, fired from below by charcoal which reaches very high temperatures. Pieces of meat to be cooked in the oven must first be marinated (see page 58) to keep them tender and succulent. They are then placed on a skewer and inserted vertically into the oven where they cook very quickly in the fierce, dry heat. The smooth sides of the oven are used for baking bread: the Punjab is an important wheat-growing area. Naan is the local bread (see page 196).

Tandoori Chicken

Tandoori Murgh

This is India's version of barbecued chicken. The secret is the marinade: the longer the chicken is left in it, the more authentic the finished dish will be. This recipe has been adapted so that the dish can be made successfully in a conventional oven.

1 × 1.5 kg (3 lb) chicken, cut
 into 4 pieces
juice of 2 lemons
4 teaspoons salt
2 garlic cloves, sliced
1 large onion, sliced
1 teaspoon ground coriander
1 tablespoon red paprika
½ teaspoon chilli powder
2 teaspoons grated fresh ginger
150 ml (¼ pint) natural yoghurt
To garnish:
1 lettuce
1–2 tomatoes, sliced
½ onion, sliced into rings
few wedges of lemon

Preparation time: 20 minutes plus marinating
Cooking time: 1 hr 20 minutes
Oven: 180°C, 350°F, Gas Mark 4; then 200°C, 400°F, Gas Mark 6
Serves 4

1. Make 3 deep cuts in each piece of chicken with a sharp knife. Rub the flesh all over with half the lemon juice, then rub in the salt.

2. Blend the remaining ingredients to a paste with the remaining lemon juice, using a liquidizer, if available.

3. Put the chicken in a baking dish lined with foil, then pour over the marinade. Cover and leave to marinate for at least 12 hours.

4. Put in the preheated moderate oven and roast for 1 hour, or until tender, basting occasionally. Then increase the oven temperature to hot and roast for a further 15–20 minutes until the chicken is browned on top.

5. Serve hot on a bed of lettuce, garnished with onion rings and lemon wedges.

Tandoori Masala

Like garam masala, Tandoori masala is a mixture made with variations by different cooks. This blend is particularly rich and subtle. Combine heaped teaspoons of the following spices well, and transfer them to an airtight tin or jar.

	heaped teaspoons
ground coriander	6
ground white cumin	6
garlic powder	6
paprika powder	6
garam masala	4
mango powder (optional)	3
ground ginger	3
dried mint	3
chilli powder	2

Makes approx. 200 g (7 oz)

Tandoori Marinade

*75 ml (3 fl oz) natural
   yoghurt*
75 ml (3 fl oz) milk
*2 tablespoons Tandoori
   Masala (see page 44)*
*1 tablespoon Mild Curry
   Powder or Paste (see
   pages 14 and 15)*
*2 teaspoons garam masala
   (see page 16)*

*½–4 teaspoons chilli powder
   (optional)*
*1 tablespoon freshly
   chopped mint*
*1 tablespoon chopped
   coriander*
2 teaspoons garlic purée
*1 × 2.5 cm (1 inch) piece
   fresh root ginger, finely
   chopped*

*1 teaspoon white cumin
   seeds, roasted and
   ground*
2 tablespoons lemon juice

Combine all the ingredients
thoroughly in a large bowl
and use to coat items of
food such as chicken or fish
before baking.

Tandoori Paste

This paste is particularly useful
to incorporate in sauces for
grilled or baked foods.

*200 g (7 oz) Tandoori Masala
   (see opposite)*
250 ml (8 fl oz) vinegar
250 ml (8 fl oz) vegetable oil

Preparation time: 5 minutes,
plus cooling
Cooking time: approximately
15 minutes
Makes approx. 375 g (12 oz)

1. Mix the tandoori masala with
the vinegar and enough water to
make a paste.

2. Heat the oil in a deep frying-
pan or wok. Add the paste. It
will splutter at first but soon
subside. Stir-fry for about 15
minutes until the liquid has
evaporated to leave a creamy,
smooth paste. Set the pan aside
to cool. The oil will rise to the
surface if the paste is fully
cooked.

3. Transfer the paste to a warm
sterilized jar and fill it to the top
with a little more warm oil to
prevent mould developing.
Cover the bottle tightly and
store in a cool dark place. It will
keep indefinitely as long as all
the liquid has evaporated.

Tandoori chicken

ROASTING

Roasting is used to a lesser extent in Oriental cooking than in the West because the average kitchen is not equipped with an oven. In restaurant kitchens, however, it is a popular method, particularly in Peking and Canton, giving rise to such famous dishes as Peking Duck (page 134) which can be very successfully prepared by Western cooks. The Chinese method of roasting involves hanging the meat or poultry on a rotisserie, or a hook in the oven.

Whole Spiced Baked Chicken

Murgh Mussalam

In this Indian recipe roasting is used as the last stage of a cooking process in which a whole chicken is oven baked at a moderate temperature for 1 hour – relatively quick by Western standards but much gentler than Cantonese Cha Shao (page 48). In both cases marinating the meat helps to keep it moist and tender. Skinning the chicken helps the marinade to penetrate the meat. Skinning is not difficult, but ask your butcher to do it for you if you are uncertain how to set about it.

1 tablespoon coriander seeds
1 tablespoon cumin seeds
2 bay leaves
1.5 kg (3 lb) roasting chicken
100 g (4 oz) thick natural yoghurt
1 medium onion, roughly chopped
3 cloves garlic, roughly chopped
3 fresh green chillies, cored, seeded and roughly chopped
Roasting mixture:
100 g (4 oz) ghee
1 large onion, thinly sliced
2 cloves garlic, thinly sliced
7.5 cm (3 inch) piece fresh root ginger, peeled and thinly sliced
5 cm (2 inch) cinnamon stick
10 cloves
10 cardamoms
2 teaspoons black peppercorns
2 teaspoons salt
150 ml ($\frac{1}{4}$ pint) chicken stock
2 teaspoons garam masala (see page 16)
To garnish:
fresh coriander leaves
lemon wedges

Preparation time: 35 minutes plus marinating
Cooking time: about 2 hours
Oven: 200°C/400°F/Gas Mark 6, then 190°C/375°F/Gas Mark 5, then 230°C/450°F/Gas Mark 8.
Serves 4

1. Spread the coriander seeds, cumin seeds and bay leaves on a baking tray. Roast in a preheated oven (200°C/400°F, Gas Mark 6) for 10–15 minutes, until the bay leaves are crisp.

2. Meanwhile, skin the chicken and wash it well. Pat the chicken dry with paper towels, then make deep slashes in the leg and breast meat with a sharp knife.

3. Put the yoghurt, onion, garlic and fresh chillies in a blender or food processor and purée until smooth. Grind the roasted seeds and bay leaves together with a pestle and mortar and add to the yoghurt mixture. Rub this mixture over the chicken, and leave it to marinate in a cool place for 24 hours, basting the chicken from time to time with the yoghurt mixture.

4. When ready to cook the chicken, make the roasting mixture: melt the ghee in a flameproof casserole with a close-fitting lid. Add the onion, garlic and ginger and fry gently for 4–5 minutes until soft. Gently pound the cinnamon, cloves, cardamoms and peppercorns with a pestle and mortar and add to the casserole. Sprinkle in the salt, then add the chicken stock and bring to the boil. Add the garam masala, stirring well, then add the chicken together with the marinade. Cover tightly, increase the heat on the stove and shake the casserole continuously for 2 minutes.

5. Transfer the casserole to a preheated moderately hot oven and cook for 1 hour. Remove the casserole from the oven and increase the oven temperature to hot.

6. Remove the bird from the casserole and place it in a roasting tin. Baste with some of the sauce from the casserole, then roast in the oven for about 30 minutes, or until the outside of the chicken is crisp and the juices run clear when the thickest part of a thigh is pierced with the point of a sharp knife.

7. When the remaining juices from the casserole have cooled slightly, pour them into a blender or food processor and purée until smooth, then reheat. Serve the chicken hot, garnished with coriander and lemon wedges. Serve the juices as a sauce in a separate bowl.

Right: Whole spiced baked chicken

Cha Shao Quick-roast Beef

Cha Shao is a method of quick-roasting meat or poultry at a high temperature for a short time. The meat is seasoned and marinated before roasting. The high temperature causes the marinade to become encrusted on to the meat, forming a highly seasoned crisp outer layer while the inside of the meat stays tender and juicy and very rare. Compare this with the Indian recipe for Spiced Leg of Lamb (page 148), which has an equally delicious crust but takes much longer to cook. Only tender cuts are suitable for Cha Shao roasting.

1 kg (2¼ lb) fillet of beef
4 cloves garlic, crushed
3 slices fresh root ginger, shredded
Marinade:
3 tablespoons soy sauce
1½ teaspoons red bean curd cheese (fermented bean curd)
1 tablespoon soy bean paste
1½ teaspoons brown sugar
1 tablespoon sunflower oil
Dips:
1 tablespoon English mustard
2 tablespoons chilli sauce
3 tablespoons plum sauce

Preparation time: 20 minutes, plus marinating
Cooking time: 10–12 minutes
Oven: 230°C/450°F/Gas Mark 8
Serves 6–8

1. Place the beef in a shallow dish and sprinkle with the garlic and ginger. Combine the marinade ingredients and pour over the meat, basting it well. Leave to marinate for 2 hours, turning the beef every 20 minutes.

2. Prepare the dips while the meat is marinating. Spoon the mustard and chilli sauce into one dish and place the plum sauce in another.

3. Put the beef on a rack in a roasting pan and baste with the marinade. Roast in the top of a preheated oven for 10–12 minutes, turning the beef and basting it with the marinade halfway during cooking.

4. Remove the beef from the oven and cut it across the grain into 1 cm (½ inch) thick slices. Arrange on a serving dish and serve hot or cold, accompanied by the dips.

PREPARATION TECHNIQUES

The preparation of food often takes longer than the actual cooking processes in the Oriental kitchen, with the cook spending much time preparing food, perhaps as a prelude to marinating some of it for several hours, before cooking it all very quickly in a carefully planned sequence. This chapter explains the importance of this careful preparation in Oriental cooking.

It is possible to distinguish over 40 separate cooking methods in China alone, covering every possible refinement of the basic techniques of boiling, frying and so on. Food that is to be cooked with such attention necessarily needs to be prepared with equal care, not only so that it will taste delicious but also so that it will look beautiful when served and be easy to eat with chopsticks. The first rule is to buy produce of high quality that is absolutely fresh – the Oriental cook goes to market every day and hand-picks his or her raw materials.

Chinese dishes and those derived from them often consist of a combination of different ingredients cooked together to give a harmonious contrast of flavour and texture. These separate ingredients must be cut into similar shapes – diced meat with diced vegetables, for example, or shredded meat with shredded vegetables or

beansprouts – and of such a size that, cooked in the correct sequence, each will be ready at the same moment. Other traditional shapes are chunks, slices, strips and grains (a fine mince). Strips of meat or vegetables should be used to accompany noodles. To cut meat, fish or vegetables ready for cooking, use a heavy chopping board and a Chinese cleaver or thin knife. Meat is easier to cut, whether into paper thin slices or small dice, if it is slightly frozen (though it must be allowed to thaw completely before marinating and cooking). Beef is usually cut across the grain, but cuts in pork and chicken are made with the grain, otherwise it would soon fall apart in the cooking. The exception is diced pork or chicken, which is cooked so fast that it does not have time to disintegrate, so the direction of the cut does not matter. Some

vegetables are cut with a perpendicular slice – that is, at right angles to the board – for example, onions, shallots and mushrooms. Root vegetables and coarse cabbages, once cleaned, are sliced diagonally in order to expose a larger area to the heat of cooking. Vegetables such as ginger or cloves of garlic that threaten to slip off the board can be lightly crushed with the flat of the cleaver blade to make them sit more steadily.

The preparation of fish in Oriental cookery is described on pages 50–52. Fish is the foundation of Japanese cookery, in which, if anything, cutting and slicing are more important than in other Oriental cuisines. In Japanese dishes each item remains separate and makes an individual contribution to the success of the finished dish.

Many Chinese, Indian and other Oriental dishes are cooked very quickly, but always

smoothly and without fuss, because of adequate preparation. The work surface should ideally be large enough to hold whatever basic ingredients you need, such as soy sauce, spices, cooking oil, salt, pepper, sugar and cornflour, as well as specific ingredients for the recipe you are following. Bowls and saucers are needed to hold the prepared items. When these are laid out, food preparation begins. Meat is usually prepared first, as it generally requires marinating, even if only for a short time. Then each vegetable is chopped in turn and stacked neatly in individual saucers. Have to hand not only the cooking pots and implements you need, but also the serving dishes appropriate for the meal. Organize the kitchen so that once you have begun to cook, you can proceed without interruption to the end.

FISH PREPARATION

When choosing fish, look for plump freshness, indicated by bright eyes, red gills and firm flesh. If fish smells even faintly unpleasant, reject it. The only permissible odour is a breath of the sea. Take your fish home and prepare it with speed.

While a good fishmonger will scale, gut and fillet your purchase for you, it is useful to know how to do it yourself, especially if you have freshly caught fish at your disposal occasionally.

Scaling

Many fish have scales, though some are so small as to be insignificant. In other cases, they must be removed. In Japan – where the preparation of fish is almost an art form – the preferred method is to place the fish on a wetted wooden board with the head away from you. Grasp the fish by the tail and lift it up slightly. Using a firm knife (or a clean scallop shell), scrape the scales away in short strokes from tail to head. Be careful not to damage the skin or flesh. When the first side is completely free of scales, rinse the board, turn the fish over and scale the other side.

Removing gills

If the fish is to be served whole, head and tail intact, the gills should be removed.

1. Open the mouth of the fish to open the gill flaps. Sever the bone under the lower jaw of the fish to free the gills.

2. With one hand, hold the opening wide. Insert the tip of a knife and cut the base of the gills where they are attached to the bone. Scrape around the edges of the cavity. Pull out gills with knife tip.

3. Hold down the part of the gills which has come free with the knife tip. Lift up the fish and gills should come away.

Gutting

Round fish: in Japan small round fish such as horse-mackerel (scad) are often cleaned through the mouth. Two chopsticks are inserted into the body cavity, twisted round two or three times and pulled out with the innards attached. The advantage of this method is that the fish keeps its shape well when cooked, and the gills come away with the rest. This method only works well with fish that is super-fresh.

The more common method of cleaning fish is the same everywhere. Make a slit along the underside of the belly. Pull out and discard the innards, without damaging the liver or roe, which are delicacies. Puncture pockets of blood with the point of the knife and wash the cavity thoroughly with cold water.

Flatfish: to preserve the shape of flatfish, remove the innards through an incision made behind the gills on the underside (the pale side).

Filleting

Japanese methods of filleting are similar to those used in the West, but the stages of preparation are more clearly defined. Fillets produced this way are perfect for all Oriental methods of cooking.

Two-piece Cutting

Nimai Oroshi

Suitable for round fish such as mackerel, this method produces one piece free of bones and a second still attached to the backbone to preserve its shape while grilling.

Clean the fish and cut off its head. Place on a dampened board. Use a sharp carving knife (e.g. *deba-bocho*, page 96.)

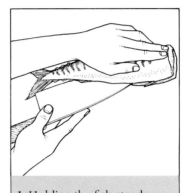

1. Holding the fish steady with one hand, slice from the belly to the tail with a single smooth action. The knife point should reach the centre of the spine, with the blade at an angle when cutting to the tail. Lift the filleted half up and out of the way as it comes free.

2. Turn the fish round. Cut from tail to head as above.

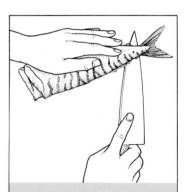

3. Turn the blade and make a second cut from head to tail; the blade should just reach the spine.

4. Insert the knife point at the tail end and slice toward the head. Lift the fillet free to give 2 pieces.

Three-piece Cutting

Sanmai Oroshi

This method is a continuation of two-piece cutting in order to obtain a second fillet.

Place the fish piece which still has the bone belly-down on the board and repeat steps 1–4 above. The backbone with a little flesh adhering to it is the third piece.

Variation

When filleting fish such as sea bass to obtain two or three pieces, the fillets must be pulled from the bones rather than removed by cutting. As before, the fish should be cleaned and its head removed.

1. Cut from below the cavity to the tail, slicing just above the bones.

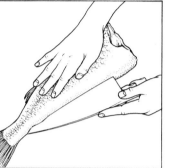

2. Turn the fish round. Slicing just above the bones, cut from tail to head as far as the spine.

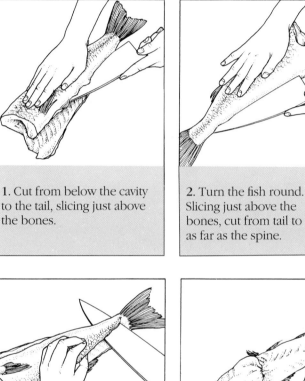

3. Lift up the fillet with one hand and make a horizontal cut to free it at the tail end.

4. Hold the fillet at the tail end and pull it away from the skeleton. Remove any small bones with tweezers. Turn the fish over and repeat the process to remove the second fillet.

Five piece cutting

Gomai Oroshi

This technique is for flatfish such as sole, plaice or flounder, and closely resembles the method commonly used in Western kitchens. It produces four fillets and the skeleton. Leave the head on before you start. In Japan the skin is removed after the fish has been filleted, in contrast to the Western method of skinning first. Do whatever you find easiest.

1. Make one cut across the fish at an angle behind the head and a second, short straight cut at the tail. Draw the point of the knife in a line along the centre spine, through to the bone, from cut to cut.

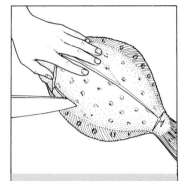

2. Turn the fish round and reverse the knife blade. Make a shallow cut from head to tail, skimming the fins closely. Turn the fish round again and make a similar cut on the other side, this time working from tail to head.

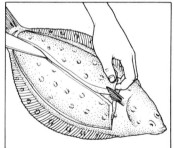

3. Insert the point of the knife into the left-hand side of the fish where the central and head incisions meet. Make a shallow cut as close to the bones as possible, freeing the fillet as you work.

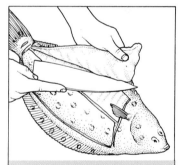

4. Lift the fillet and make a second cut to free it completely. Remove the second fillet in the same way, turning the fish round for ease of cutting. Turn it over to remove the remaining two fillets. The strip of fish remaining at the outer edges is particularly sweet: in Japan it is used in *sashimi*.

Skinning

To remove the skin from a flatfish in Western style, start with the whole fish. On one side, make an incision across the tail, then gently ease a thumb under the skin. Run your thumb along the fin edges to free the skin. Holding the tail end of the fish down firmly on the board, pull the skin from the tail to the head end to remove it completely. Repeat with the other side.

In the Japanese method, the skin is cut away after filleting. Place the fillet skin side down on a wetted board, holding it by the tail. Using a long-bladed knife, make a cut close to the tail end. With the knife blade close to the skin, pull it towards you, cutting the flesh away as closely as you can. Soft-fleshed fish break up if skinned in this way and the skin is simply sliced off with a very sharp *sashimi* knife.

Salting

Once prepared, fish should be sprinkled lightly with salt and placed in the coldest part of your refrigerator until you are ready to cook. Use good sea salt. In Japan fish is allowed to rest in salt for 40 minutes–1 hour to extract moisture and any odour. The most common method is to sprinkle 2–3 tablespoons salt on a board, place the fillet skin side down on the board and scatter more salt liberally on top. For fish which is to be served raw, paper-salting is used. When the board has been salted, place a paper towel on top, then the fish, a second paper towel, and finally more salt. Leave to stand for up to 1 hour.

Sashimi

The essential features of a dish of sashimi – Japanese sliced raw fish – are first that it should consist of perfectly fresh fish in season, and second that the arrangement of the fish should be aesthetically pleasing (see page 106). The most common shapes are rectangular ('domino') slices, paper-thin slices and cubes. Good sharp knives are essential; wipe the blade on a clean cloth occasionally as you work. Have a chilled serving dish ready before you start.

For 'domino' slices, prepare fillets as shown on page 51. The skin of mackerel can be left on, just the outer membrane stripped off. Coarser, less attractive skins should be removed. Trim the fillets to make sure they are of almost even thickness. Slices should be between 0.5–1.5 cm ($\frac{1}{8}$–$\frac{1}{2}$ inch), depending on the type of fish. The firmer fleshed fish can be sliced more finely – paper-thin once you are practised.

1. Hold the trimmed fillet skin side up on a board. Cut the first slice with a smooth action of the knife, drawing it through the fish from the base . . .

2.. . . to the tip. Lay the slice on its side.

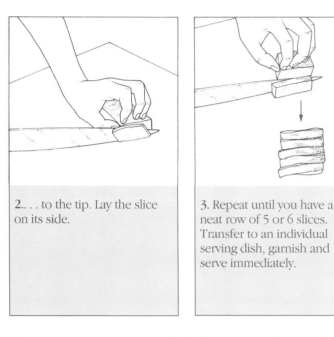

3. Repeat until you have a neat row of 5 or 6 slices. Transfer to an individual serving dish, garnish and serve immediately.

Firm, white-fleshed fish can be sliced paper-thin – no more than 0.25 cm ($\frac{1}{16}$ inch). Each slice should be transferred to the serving dish as soon as it is cut. Overlap the slices in a fan shape.

Tuna is one of the most popular fish in Japan, with thick but soft fillets that can be cut into cubes. First cut the fillets lengthwise into strips. Without separating the strips, cut straight across them all at once, to form a series of identical 2 cm ($\frac{3}{4}$ inch) cubes.

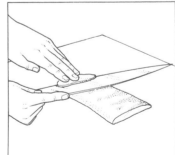

1. Place fillet on board skin side up, with the thinnest part at your left (if you are right-handed). With the knife almost horizontal, start to cut with the bottom of the blade and draw it through.

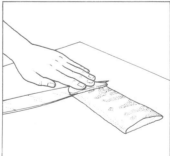

2. As the point of the knife slices through the fish, hold the slice with your free hand. Lift it up on the knife blade and transfer to the serving dish.

SHELLFISH PREPARATION

Lobster, crab, scallops and prawns and other shellfish figure prominently in much South-east Asian cooking. To ensure freshness and flavour, it is best to choose live shellfish where appropriate and kill and cook them yourself. Lobsters and crabs should be lively and the lobster's tail should curve under its body. Both are often sold cooked, however, and if you prefer to buy them this way look for dry, bright shells, and specimens which are heavy for their size. Cooked shrimps and prawns should be bright pink and smell fresh and pleasant. Whether live or cooked, buy all shellfish on the day it is to be eaten.

How to prepare a lobster

Avoid lobster with white blemishes on the shell – this is a sign of age. Lobsters are dark blue-black when alive, and cook to a bright red. Female ('hen') lobsters have finer flesh, and the body contains the highly prized coral (bright orange when cooked) which is used as a garnish or in sauces. The female is larger than the male but with smaller claws. The best weigh between 3 and 3.5 kg (1½–2 lb). Buy lobster in season, from spring to late summer; frozen lobsters lack texture and should be avoided.

There are two methods of killing lobster: one is to pierce its head with a strong sharp knife at the well-defined cross. This kills it instantly and it is ready for boiling or for cleaning prior to deep frying and braising in the Cantonese style, for example. The second method is described in the steps illustrated on this page.

1. Tie the claws together with string or a rubber band.

2. Place the lobster in a large pan of salted water. Place a weight on the lid and slowly bring the water to the boil. Simmer for 15 minutes for the first 500 g (1 lb) and 10 minutes per 500 g (1 lb) thereafter, or until the shell turns bright red.

3. Leave the lobster to cool in the cooking liquor.

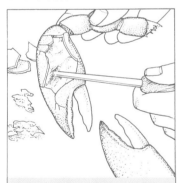

4. Twist off the claws and remove the legs. Using a hammer or shellfish crackers, crack the claws and pull out the meat.

5. Cut away the thin undershell of the tail section, using sharp scissors, and carefully pull out the flesh.

6. Place the lobster on a board and cut it in half along its length with a sharp knife.

7. Remove the thin grey vein of intestine running along its length. Split the head and discard the stomach sac and gills.

8. Scrape out the red coral, if present, and reserve.

9. If liked, add the grey-green liver to the flesh. This is situated near the head, and is delicious.

10. Pick out the flesh and any remaining liver and roe from the head.

11. Wash the shell and dry it well. Both the head and tail sections can be used to hold and serve the meat if the recipe is suitable.

How to prepare a crab

In many Chinese recipes crabs are served in the shell, and part of the pleasure of the meal is cracking open the claws to extract the delicious meat. There are a number of Thai recipes for crab which call for it to be extracted from the shell in the way we would do in the West for dressed crab. Live crabs should be cooked like lobster and for the same time, according to weight, and left to cool in the liquid.

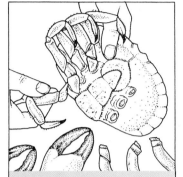

1. Rinse the cold crab under cold water. Place it shell down on a large board with the legs uppermost.

2. Twist off the legs and claws at the joint with the body.

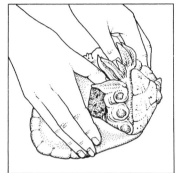

3. With the tail flap facing you, hold the crab firmly with both hands and, using your thumbs, push and prise the body section or 'apron' upwards so that the whole body section is released from the hard back shell.

4. Pull away and discard the greyish-white stomach sac (just behind the mouth) and the long white pointed gills known as 'dead men's fingers'. These are very obvious and should be removed.

5. Using a small spoon, scoop out all the meat from both shells, keeping the white and brown meats in separate bowls. Reach in carefully to all the crevices with a lobster pick or metal skewer and be careful to remove all pieces of shell.

6. Crack the claws, using a hammer or shellfish crackers, and remove the white meat. Break the legs at the joints and extract the meat. Use as directed in the recipe. If you wish to use the empty shell to serve the meat, tap it to remove the thin undershell. Wash and dry the shell before use.

Preparing squid and octopus

The squid is a relative of the octopus and the cuttlefish. From the squid's large head ten tentacles extend and on its body are two fins. The edible parts are the body and tentacles, and the ink sac can be used to colour a sauce if you wish. The flesh is sweet and tender but needs gentle cooking or it becomes rubbery. The head and inner part of the body must be removed and discarded. The body is usually cut into rings for cooking, but with larger specimens, up to 15–20 cm (6–8 inches) in length, it can be stuffed and stewed. The tentacles are chopped into 2 cm ($\frac{3}{4}$ inch) pieces.

Prepare octopus the same way, but the body flesh should be beaten before cooking to tenderize it.

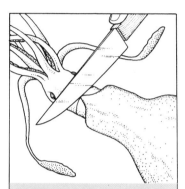

1. Hold the squid in one hand and pull the head and tentacles away sharply from the body with the other. This will bring most of the innards with it.

2. Pull out the thin hard transparent backbone – the 'pen' – from the body and scoop out any remaining innards.

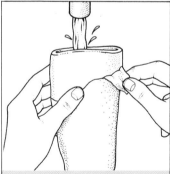

3. Peel the thin purplish skin from the body part and discard it. This is easily done by scraping gently with a sharp knife. Rinse the body cavity well, to ensure that all the matter inside has been rinsed away. Drain and pat dry.

4. Cut the body into rings or chunks.

5. Cut the tentacles off the head. Remove the ink sac from the head if you wish to use it. Discard the head. Scrape the tentacles free of skin if they are large. Wash well, pat dry and cut into pieces.

How to prepare scallops

Scallops are among the most delicious of shellfish, looking beautiful on their curved shells. They are easy to cook, whether poached, grilled or fried, and combine well with hot and spicy flavourings. Frozen scallops are available, but fresh ones in the shell, in season in the winter months, are far superior.

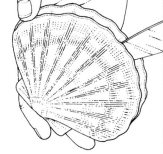

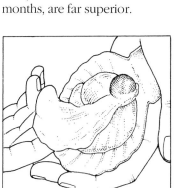

1. Scallops are sometimes sold with the shells closed. To open, insert a knife into the shell and twist. Detach the rounded shell and reserve for serving.

2. The white flesh is attached to the flat half of the shell. Discard the greyish fringe surrounding it. Separate the coral and set aside to be used according to the recipe.

3. Ease the scallop from the shell.

4. Slice the white flesh horizontally in two. Remove and discard the black intestinal thread.

How to prepare prawns

In the West we are used to buying prawns and shrimps ready-cooked, bright pink and needing only to be shelled and cleaned before use. In this state they should only be cooked for as long as it takes to heat them through or they become tough.

In South-east Asia prawns are often sold raw, and are increasingly available in this state in other parts of the world. They are blue-grey in colour before cooking, and are delicious grilled or stir-fried.

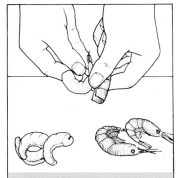

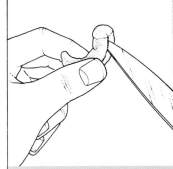

1. Remove the head and legs and carefully peel away the shell on the body, working from the head end to the tail. Some recipes require the shell to be left on the tail.

2. Devein the prawns by removing the black thread running along the back. This is easier if you run the point of a knife along the back and open it out slightly.

Langoustines are a delicious species of prawn resembling a lobster, but only about 10 cm (4 inches) in length. Pale pink when live, they deepen in colour when cooked. Only the tail section is eaten; to prepare for cooking remove the head and claws. They can be boiled for 10–12 minutes or quick stir-fried before grilling.

POULTRY

Since chickens for the table were first bred in South-east Asia, Oriental cooks have centuries of experience to draw on in cooking poultry of all kinds. They have invented an extraordinary range of dishes, from the spicy stir-fries of Szechuan to the creamy curries of northern India and the classic Peking duck. While some recipes use the whole bird, it is often jointed first when faster cooking methods are used and to facilitate marinating.

JOINTING A CHICKEN

For a recipe such as Drunken Chicken (page 130), in which the bird is simply chopped into bite-sized pieces, all you need is a sharp cleaver and a good eye. For innumerable other Oriental recipes, however, it is necessary to joint a chicken correctly, not only because cooking smaller sections takes less time, but also because specific parts of the bird will be necessary to a particular recipe. The Japanese favour the leg and thigh, and use the inner breast almost raw in sashimi, for example, while in Thailand and China boned chicken wings, filled with a delicate stuffing, are a deep-fried delicacy.

The art of jointing lies in the cutting through the tendons and cartilages rather than hacking through bones, and although it takes time and care, is not especially difficult. This method can also be used for duck or small birds like poussin. A pair of poultry shears or small sharp scissors can be useful.

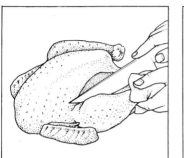

1. Place the chicken on a chopping board with the legs facing you and pull one leg away from the body. With a strong, sharp knife cut through the skin down to where the thigh joins the body. Bend the leg outwards to expose the ball and socket joint and cut down between the ball and socket to free the leg. Repeat with the other leg.

2. To separate the drumstick and thigh, pull them apart to expose the joint and cut through cleanly. Press down through the shoulder joint attaching the wing to the body (illustrated above). Pull the wing away from the body and cut down through the skin at the base of the wing. Repeat with the other wing.

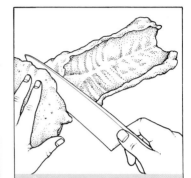

3. Place the knife inside the carcass and carefully slit along the ribs on both sides, to separate the breast from the lower carcass. Pull the breast away from the back to expose the shoulder bones and cut down to detach the breast. Keep the lower carcass for stock.

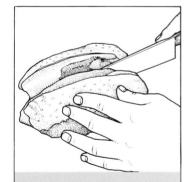

4. Place the breast section skin side up on the board. Cut down on either side of the breast bone to give two breasts. With larger birds the breast portions can then be cut widthways to give 4 or 6 portions.

5. The sasami breast fillets used in Japanese sashimi are those snugly attached to the upper breast bone (not those next to the wing). To separate them from the bone, snip through the tendons holding them at each end and slide your fingers underneath the length of the fillet to ease it free. If the tendon clings to the meat, scrape it off with the point of the knife.

BONING POULTRY

Once boned, a chicken or duck is simplicity itself to carve, and can be the basis of elegant dishes such as Boneless Duck with Eight Precious Stuffing (page 132). Before starting, trim off the wing tips at the second joint, remove the parson's nose – as this can impart a bitter flavour to the finished dish – and cut off the scaly part of the legs at the first drumstick joint.

Scrape rather than cut the flesh away from the bones, using the point of the knife. Take great care not to cut or pierce the skin of the bird otherwise the appearance of the finished dish will be spoiled. Use a cloth or paper towel if it helps you get a firmer grip when breaking the joints.

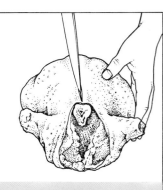

1. Place the chicken, breast side down, on a flat surface, then using a very sharp, small knife, make a deep cut right down the centre of the backbone, cutting down to the bone.

2. Cut the flesh away from one side of the chicken by carefully cutting it away from the bones, working down over the rib cage to the tip of the breast bone. Keep the knife very close to the bones all the time. As you work down the rib cage you will come to the ball and socket joint, where the leg is attached to the body. Simply work the knife under the joint to free it.

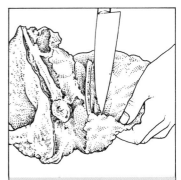

3. Continue working down the rib cage until you come to the joint that connects the wing. Once again, slip the knife under the joint to cut it free. (On small game birds such as quail, leave the wings in place.) As you work down the rib cage, the joints will become exposed automatically.

4. Having removed the flesh from one side of the rib cage, repeat with the other side. Cut along the top edge of the breast bone to free the entire rib cage completely. Reserve this and the other bones to make stock.

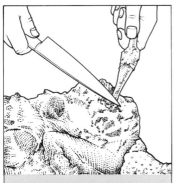

5. Remove the bones from the legs and wings. Hold each exposed bone in turn, scraping the flesh away from the bones and keeping the knife as close to the bones as possible. As each bone comes free, the flesh will be pulled inside out.

6. When all of the bones have been removed, remove as many of the white sinews from the breast and legs as is possible, by scraping the flesh away from each one.

BONING CHICKEN WINGS

This is a laborious task patiently undertaken by Oriental cooks for such rewards as *Peek Gai Yod Sai*, a Thai dish of chicken wings stuffed with shrimps, prawns, onions and spices, coated in batter and deep-fried.

1. Bend the two wing joints backwards to loosen them.

2. With a sharp, small knife, make an incision around the top of the large bone (the one that was next to the body of the chicken). Cut into this ring a second time.

3. With the knife blade, ease the flesh and skin down the bone towards the first joint. Use a scraping action, and as you work fold back the skin so that it is inside out.

4. When the joint is exposed, break off the larger bone from the two smaller ones.

5. With your finger, separate the skin from the flesh and very carefully roll it back. Try not to puncture the skin. Peel back the flesh to that you can see where

the two smaller bones are joined together; cut them apart.

6. Roll the skin back further, scraping the flesh carefully away from the two small bones. When you have almost reached the wing tip, break the bones off from the skin, without puncturing it. Turn the skin right side out. The wing is ready for stuffing.

MARINATING

For centuries cooks have experimented with ways of making food tasty and succulent. One method with a long and successful history is marinating, soaking raw meat, game or fish in a flavoured liquid for a length of time before being cooked. The most important ingredient of any marinade is the acid one that tenderizes the raw food by breaking down the muscle structure. In Western cookery this tends to be wine, vinegar or lemon juice. Because this process ultimately tends to dry out the raw food, a second ingredient, such as olive oil, has to be added to keep it moist and soft during cooking. The soaking time also provides a good opportunity to imbue the food with flavour, and herbs and spices are usually added for this purpose.

Marinating is used much more frequently in Oriental cooking than in the West. One of the reasons is that fast cooking methods such as charcoal-grilling or quick stir-frying tend to toughen all but the best cuts. Furthermore, a shorter cooking time limits the opportunity of marrying flavours together, so food benefits from being seasoned before being subjected to heat. Finally, a marinade acts as a short-term preservative, a quality that is useful in hot countries.

In Oriental cooking the food may be marinated for as short a time as 30 minutes. This will still be effective because it is either cut into small chunks or, if in one piece, deeply scored all over to provide maximum surface area to be penetrated by the seasoned liquid. A simple and typical Japanese marinade for both meat and fish is sake and mirin, for acidity and sweetness, and soy sauce for flavour. A good Chinese combination for beef is a blend of hoisin and soy sauces with freshly grated ginger. Thin slices of beef are left to stand in the mixture for 1 hour before being coated in batter and deep-fried. Pork that is to be roasted can be sliced first and marinated for up to 3 hours in a blend of yellow bean and soy sauces with brandy, sugar and a little chicken stock. For white fish, cut into cubes and marinate in Chinese wine (or sherry) with freshly grated ginger, soy sauce, finely chopped spring onions, garlic, five-spice powder and sugar. Leave to stand for 1 hour before deep-frying. Marinades used for foods that are to be grilled can be used to baste them as they cook and intensify the flavour.

The tandoori style of cooking unique to India (see pages 44–45) has generated one of the most popular and inspired marinades. To prepare for marinating, a whole or jointed chicken is first slashed to the bone and rubbed with salt and lemon juice. After 20 minutes it is immersed in the classic mixture. While there are variations, the basic ingredients are yoghurt, which miraculously both tenderizes the meat and keeps it moist when subjected to the fierce heat of the tandoor, plus for flavour onion, garlic, ginger, chilli and garam masala. (Food colouring is traditional but optional – it does not contribute to the effect of the marinade.) The chicken can be left from 6 to 24 hours, at the end of which time it is wonderfully tender. Chicken joints prepared in this way can be cooked to perfection in only 25 minutes.

In the recipes in this book you will find a great variety of ideas for marinades, and once you have discovered how effective they can be you will be certain to invent your own variations on the basic theme.

Baked Spiced Fish

Masala Dum Macchi

This Indian method of preparing fish works best with whole fish such as bream, snapper or flounder. Mackerel can also be used very successfully if the amount of vinegar is increased to 2 tablespoons to offset the natural oiliness of the fish. Cod steaks can also be used if preferred.

250 ml (8 fl oz) natural yoghurt
1 medium onion, chopped
1 garlic clove, chopped
1 teaspoon grated fresh root ginger
1 tablespoon vinegar
1½ teaspoons ground cumin
a pinch of chilli powder
1 × 1 kg (2 lb) whole fish, cleaned, or 750 g (1½ lb) fish fillets
juice of 1 lemon
1 teaspoon salt
To garnish:
slices of lemon
coriander leaves

Preparation time: 10 minutes, plus marinating overnight
Cooking time: 30 minutes
Oven: 180°C, 350°F, Gas Mark 4
Serves 4

1. Place a quarter of the yoghurt in a liquidizer with the chopped onion and garlic, grated ginger, vinegar, cumin and chilli powder. Blend to a smooth sauce. Combine this sauce evenly with the remaining yoghurt.

2. Score the fish and place in an ovenproof dish. Rub with the lemon juice and sprinkle with the salt. Pour over the yoghurt mixture, cover and leave to marinate in the refrigerator overnight.

3. Cover the fish with foil and bake in a preheated moderate oven for 30 minutes. Transfer to a heated platter to serve, garnished with slices of lemon and coriander leaves.

Beef Satay

Indonesian satay is popular over a vast area, from Java to Hong Kong, and is served at every occasion from elegant buffets to casual barbecues.

1 tablespoon blanched almonds
1 slice fresh root ginger, peeled
1 teaspoon coriander seeds
1 teaspoon turmeric
300 ml (½ pint) coconut milk (see page 14)
450 g (1 lb) lean steak (rump, fillet or sirloin)
salt
freshly ground black pepper
1 teaspoon brown sugar

Preparation time: 20 minutes, plus marinating
Cooking time: 8–10 minutes
Serves 4

1. Using a pestle and mortar, pound the almonds, ginger, coriander seeds and turmeric to a paste. Gradually dilute this mixture with the coconut milk.

2. Cut the beef into bite-sized cubes, season to taste with salt and pepper and place in the spiced coconut milk. Leave to marinate for 2 hours.

3. Drain the beef, retaining the marinade, and thread the pieces on to bamboo skewers. Do not crowd them together. Sprinkle the beef with a little brown sugar and grill under a preheated grill or over hot coals, turning to brown evenly and brushing frequently with the coconut marinade.

4. Serve hot or warm with Satay Sauce (see page 208).

Above: Beef satay

THE PRESENTATION OF FOOD

In presenting food with exquisite style, the Oriental cook is observing long-followed traditions and rituals, all aiming at a harmony of appearance and content. This chapter looks at how this harmony is achieved, and provides a guide to the preparation of the garnishes which add the essential finishing touch to many Oriental dishes.

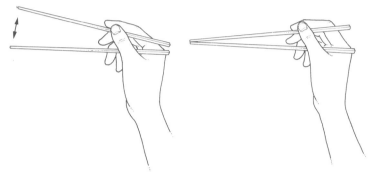

In the Orient, the strong influences of tradition, history and religion are obvious in many aspects of life. Because, of all things, food is crucial to survival, these traditions have become deeply ingrained in the rituals of cooking and eating. The Oriental cook observes these rituals in his creations, aiming for the harmony which the ancient philosophers decreed lay at the heart of a happy life.

Good cooks all over the world know how important it is for food to look attractive in order to stimulate the appetite. A Chinese meal, exquisitely prepared as it is, is a visual as well as a gastronomic feast; unlike formal Western meals or Japanese banquets, all the dishes are placed upon the table simultaneously in a dazzling array. A round table is the ideal shape for such a meal, with the dishes arranged so that guests can easily help themselves – a central revolving tray is useful. Porcelain bowls rather than flat plates are used; food stays hot longer and is easier to eat with chopsticks. The Chinese have no qualms about lifting a bowl to their lips to shorten the chopsticks' journey or to drink soup after all the solid morsels have been picked out. Pretty porcelain spoons are also used for soups and probably accord better with Western ideas about table manners.

Thai food is served in bowls or on flat plates depending on the consistency of the food. Individual flat rattan trays are often used, lined with the ubiquitous and multi-purpose banana leaf, to hold a bowl of soup, noodles or curry, with colourful vegetables, raw or lightly steamed, arranged around it. Whether you use chopsticks, or a spoon and fork, as in Malaysia and Indonesia, a bowl of water and iced towels will be offered first to refresh the hands before eating. If food is to be eaten with the fingers – barbecued spare ribs, for example – fingerbowls and napkins should be provided for each guest.

In India the bowls of food which comprise the meal – meat or fish, vegetables, rice and side dishes – are given to each guest on a *thali*, a large, rimmed metal plate. Food is eaten with the right hand, using a piece of bread as a scoop – in the East eating is a serious, sensuous business.

The origin of chopsticks is unknown, though certainly ancient. Their use was endorsed by Confucius, who was offended by the idea of instruments of slaughter on the table. (Tiny bamboo forks are permitted in Japan for the consumption of fruit.) Lacquered chopsticks with beautiful designs are in everyday use in China and Japan, with elegant cedarwood chopsticks for special occasions. Pairs of plastic chopsticks wrapped in paper envelopes are widely available. These are attractive and sensible if you only cook Oriental-style from time to time. Each guest uses the same pair throughout the meal, turning them round and using the handles to select items from the main serving dish, although you may prefer to place serving spoons on the table in Western fashion. When not required the chopsticks are laid on little china rests. Most food is bite-sized or tender enough to be 'cut' with a chopstick – larger pieces should be picked up with the chopsticks and held while two or three bites are taken. It is ill-mannered to gesture with chopsticks. Japanese tradition has it that chopsticks should never be left standing upright in a bowl of rice, nor should a piece of food be handed from one person's chopsticks to another's: these restrictions are connected with funerary rites.

Chopsticks are not difficult to use – in fact, millions of people never use anything else! The important thing, once you have got them in the right position as shown above, is to relax your hand. Practise on a stock cube.

The classic cooking of Japan is a highly refined art, in which every bit as much attention is paid to the presentation of food as to its choice and preparation. Family meals are as relaxed as in any other part of the world, but still influenced by the high standards set by traditional banquets, at which as many as 14 separate dishes may be served in sequence. Each of these dishes is exceptionally delicate and refined, its individual appearance heightened by its separateness from the rest. The Japanese cook places great value on fresh foods in season. This appropriateness to season is reflected not only in the choice of bowls and platters, but also in the use of other materials such as a polished wooden board to hold a whole steamed fish, a frosted glass bowl for chilled soup, a lined bamboo basket for rice balls or a shiny black lacquer tray for sushi. The dining table would not be complete without a restrained arrangement of suitable flowers: irises, mimosa, chrysanthemums or wisteria blossom, for example. While striving for aesthetic and gastronomic harmony reaches its peak in the Japanese style, all Oriental food is prepared and presented with this noble objective in view.

Garnishes

In Chinese cooking and those styles which derive from it, food is arranged on the serving dish with an expert hand. Garnishes are simple but charming, and some of the most frequently used are described here. Many familiar herbs are used to add colour, contrast and freshness to a dish, especially in combination with slices or wedges of lime or lemon. Variegated herbs such as purple basil, golden thyme or marjoram are ideal for enhancing Oriental dishes, as are edible flowers such as nasturtium or pot marigold.

Lemon and cucumber slices

1. Holding a canelle knife firmly, use the notch to remove strips of skin at regular intervals down the cucumber or round a lemon.

2. Cut into even slices (remove any lemon pips). Use as soon as possible.

Spring onion tassels

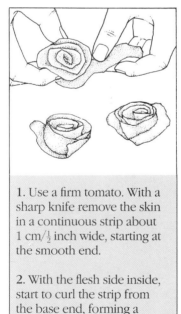

1. Remove the root from the spring onions and trim to about 7.5 cm (3 inches). Cut lengthwise through the green stalk several times to within 4 cm (1½ inches) of the end. Place in iced water for about 1 hour to open out.

Radish rose

1. For a radish rose, remove the stalk and with the pointed end of small sharp knife cut a row of petal shapes round the radish, keeping them joined at the base.

2. Cut a second row of petal shapes in between and above the first row and continue cutting rows of petals until the top of the radish is reached.

3. Place the radish rose in iced water for several hours to open out.

Radish water-lily

1. For a radish water-lily, remove the stalk and with a small sharp knife cut through 4–6 times, keeping the radish joined at the base.

2. Place the radish water-lily in iced water for several hours to open out.

Celery curls

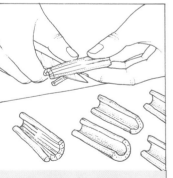

1. Cut the celery into even lengths and cut down each end several times and in each direction, keeping the celery joined in the middle. Place in iced water for about 1 hour to open out.

Tomato water-lily

1. Hold the tomato between thumb and forefinger; with a sharp knife, make zig-zag cuts around the middle.

2. Carefully separate the two halves and place a small sprig of parsley in the centre of each.

Tomato rose

1. Use a firm tomato. With a sharp knife remove the skin in a continuous strip about 1 cm/½ inch wide, starting at the smooth end.

2. With the flesh side inside, start to curl the strip from the base end, forming a bud shape.

3. Continue winding the strip of skin into a rose.

Carrot flowers

1. Take a washed and scrubbed carrot, trim the ends, and make 'V' cuts along the carrot with a sharp knife.

2. Cut across the carrot into slices

Turnip chrysanthemum

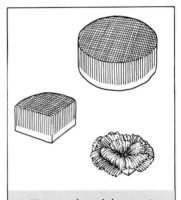

1. Trim and peel the turnip and cut the top off flat. Turn the turnip over and rest it on a board between two chopsticks (these prevent the knife from cutting right through the turnip).

Carrot triangles

1. Cut a carrot into slices lengthways then cut the slices into rectangles about 5 × 2.5 cm (2 × 1 inch).

2. Starting from the right-hand edge of each rectangle, make a horizontal cut three-quarters of the way across and about one-third of the way down.

3. From at the left-hand edge, make a similar cut about two-thirds of the way down. Gently twist the 3 sections into a triangle.

2. With a very sharp knife, make thin parallel slices to within the chopstick width from the base of the turnip. Make a second series of very thin slices at right angles to the first.

3. Cut the turnip in quarters and leave to soak in salted water for 20 minutes. Remove, drain and squeeze gently. Place in a bowl and cover with rice vinegar to which a little sugar has been added. Refrigerate overnight.

4. Drain the turnip quarters and separate the petals gently with a chopstick. Place a tiny square of red pepper in the centre of the flower.

Thai vegetable sculpture

In Thailand the carving of fruits and vegetables into intricate shapes has been elevated to an art form, an adaptation from the Japanese magic art of transformation – from carrot to rose, from turnip to a spray of leaves, from daikon to fish – the fantasy is part of the pleasure. The most ornate of these sculptures are impossible to do at home, but some ideas can be adopted. Use a sharp knife and have a bowl of iced water to hand in which to store the carved vegetables until required.

Cucumber leaves

1. Peel away a large section of skin from a cucumber with a vegetable peeler. Cut the skin into rectangles measuring 5 × 2.5 cm (2 × 1 inch).

2. With the point of the knife, cut out a leaf shape from each rectangle. Make a shallow incision from top to bottom to represent the central rib of the leaf.

3. Make incisions from the central 'rib' to the edge.

4. Carefully cut serrations all round the leaf. Use to float on soups or to garnish fish dishes.

Chilli flowers

This is one of the most popular decorative elements in Thai cooking. Remember when handling chillies not to touch your eyes or lips, and wash your hands immediately afterwards.

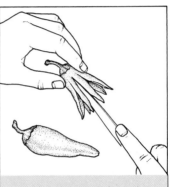

1. On a chopping board, hold the chilli by the stem. Insert the point of the knife near the stem and slice straight down through to the tip.

2. Give the chilli a half turn and make a second cut at right angles to the first. Ease out the seeds. You now have 4 pointed slivers attached to the stem. If you wish, you can repeat the process to give 8 or even 16 points. Drop the chilli in iced water and the slivers will curve outwards to form petals.

MENU PLANNING

Oriental cuisine offers plenty of scope for many different kinds of entertaining, from quickly prepared and served impromptu suppers, to elaborate dinner parties which can take days to prepare. Using recipes from this book, the menu planner in this chapter offers a guide to creating perfectly balanced, delicious meals to suit all occasions.

In China, as in India, Thailand and all over South-east Asia, people 'snack' all day long: an incredible array of tasty mouthfuls are sold by street vendors and at corner stalls to satisfy the customers who eat on the move. When it is time to settle down to the main meal of the day in the evening, it is not surprising that 'starters' as we think of them in the West are largely overlooked in preference to a selection of more satisfying dishes. Having said that, in one of Thailand's traditional restaurants you may be offered a bronze tray covered with minuscule hors d'oeuvre to eat with drinks before your meal; in India, tiny samosas or pakoras with a refreshing sherbert may be served, though always at least 45 minutes before dinner, so as not to dull the appetite. Traditional Japanese banquets are formal affairs based on a style of cooking called *Kaiseki*

ryori. Food is presented in a particular order determined by the cooking method, and the four seasons dictate the selection of ingredients to be served. The courses follow one another in a set order: clear soup, appetizer, simmered dish, grilled dish, meat dish, vegetables, large fried dish, boiled rice and finally *sunomono* (vinegared vegetables), *miso* soup and green tea. Nowadays, *kaiseki* dishes are only served in first-class Japanese restaurants called *ryotei*, although at special parties and on ceremonial occasions, meals at home will be served with a little more formality.

For family dinners and entertaining at home, at Oriental meals all the dishes are placed on the table at the same time and everyone helps themselves – indeed many favourite dishes

are either cooked or assembled at the table, such as Mongolian Hot Pot (page 153) or Grilled Langoustines (page 41). Such meals are enjoyable, communal occasions. Orientals take their food seriously, however, and behind the apparently effortless ease and evident enjoyment is the observance of certain rules. These rules are designed with the aim of achieving harmony and balance. Epitomized by Japanese *kaiseki ryori*, in everyday terms this means choosing a selection of dishes which complement each other, but give contrast in flavour, texture and colour. A meal composed of three main dishes and one soup will provide adequate contrast and will be sufficient for four to six people, while four main dishes will be enough for six to eight people, and so on. The cooked dishes form one part of a meal; rice or

wheat – cooked either as dumplings, noodles or bread – the other. Balance between meat, fish and vegetables should be matched by a variety of cooking methods – one fried dish, one steamed and another grilled or baked, for example. The Thai principle of balancing the essential five flavours – bitter, salt, sour, hot and sweet – is a good standard to aim for. The menu suggestions overleaf demonstrate how Oriental ideas about harmony at mealtimes can be put into practice.

Oriental meals do not normally finish with a dessert (most sweet dishes are served as snacks), but with fresh fruit. If you like to bring a meal to a close with dessert, you will find some suggestions in the desserts and sweets chapter in Part Two, but a simple salad or compôte of exotic fruits will suffice.

DRINKS

In China, people drink tea all day long; but at meals soup is served to wash down the savoury foods. At more formal occasions, alcohol is always served, whether beer, wine or spirits according to preference: many Chinese people drink whisky or brandy with their meals. There is no reason why Westerners should deny themselves a glass of favourite wine when enjoying Chinese, Vietnamese and Thai foods. Try

a Beaujolais or Macon, a red from the Loire, California or Italy, or a Spanish Rioja. If you prefer, chilled beer is equally acceptable, and is certainly to be recommended with Indian meals. In India sweet and milky tea is taken throughout the day. Lassi (see right) is a drink based on yoghurt, which is a refreshing accompaniment to hot and spicy curries, whether Indian, Thai or Malaysian.

Almond Lassi

If you chill the glass tumblers for 30 minutes before filling them with lassi it will help to keep the drink cool and the glasses will have an attractive frosted appearance.

300 ml (½ pint) natural yoghurt
2–3 tablespoons caster sugar
600 ml (1 pint) ice-cold water
8 ice-cubes, crushed
4 teaspoons flaked almonds

Preparation time: 5 minutes
Serves 2

1. Place all the ingredients except the almonds in a blender and blend until well mixed and frothy.

2. Pour into tumblers and sprinkle with the almonds. Serve immediately.

Milk and Saffron Sherbet

Thandai

Also known as *kesher doodh*, this is a very popular Indian refreshment and can be made with hot milk, too. In many parts of India, a little alcohol is added, and the sherbet is drunk during festivals such as Holi (festival of spring). The mixture may be prepared in a large quantity and stored in a sealed jar.

15 g ($\frac{1}{2}$ oz) blanched almonds
15 g ($\frac{1}{2}$ oz) pistachio nuts
10–12 small green cardamoms, shelled
a pinch of saffron fronds
50 g (2 oz) caster sugar (to taste)
2 pints milk, chilled
$\frac{1}{4}$ teaspoon ground turmeric
$\frac{1}{4}$ teaspoon ground nutmeg
crushed ice (optional)

Preparation time: 15 minutes
Serves 6

1. Finely grind the almonds, pistachio nuts, cardamoms and saffron fronds with a pestle and mortar.

2. Dissolve the sugar in the milk by stirring thoroughly. Add the turmeric, nutmeg and the ground mixture. Stir well and serve, adding crushed ice if liked.

Menu Suggestions

The following menu ideas are composed entirely of Oriental dishes, but there is no reason why, if you are a beginner at Oriental cooking styles, you should not start by introducing one dish into a Western menu – perhaps a starter, or a main dish with plain vegetables – before progressing to a complete meal made up of recipes from this book.

Japanese Lunch

Rolled Rice Wrapped in Nori (page 80)
Chicken with Prawns and Vegetables (page 116)
Steamed Pink Rice with Beans (page 187)
Marinated Mackerel (page 98)
Tangerine Baskets (page 216)

Chinese Dinner Party

Quail's Eggs on Toast with Mashed Shrimps (page 90)
Fish in Vinegar Sauce (page 108)
East-River Salt-buried Chicken (page 132)
Crispy 'Seaweed' (page 175)
Boiled Rice (page 23)
Lychee Sorbet (page 212)

Indian Vegetarian Feast

Chick Pea Fritters (page 199)
Lime Rice (page 189)
Rajma Lobia Curry (page 166)
Onion Salad (page 202)
Spiced Okra (page 162)
Dry-fried Spinach (page 164)
Spiced Aubergines and Tomatoes (page 164)
Indian Salad (page 168)
Almond Lassi (page 63)
Spiced Semolina Dessert (page 218)

South-east Asian Family Supper

Thai Spicy Chicken Soup (page 77)
Indonesian Mee Goreng (page 180)
Fish Bergedel (page 100)
Indonesian Festive Vegetable Achar (page 170)
Thai Caramelized Banana Slices (page 218)

GLOSSARY

This brief list explains some of the most common names used to describe cooking techniques and equipment, and alternative names for some widely used ingredients. See pages 12–21 for A–Z of specialist ingredients; equipment is discussed on pages 24–26.

Aemono (*Japan*) salad
Agemono (*Japan*) a fried dish, especially tempura
Aloo (*India*) potatoes

Baghaar (*India*) small amounts of spices heated in hot oil
Bhindi (*India*) okra, or ladies' fingers
Bhoona (*India*) dry-frying
Biryani (*India*) casserole of meat layered with rice

Blachan (*Malaysia*) shrimp paste
Brinjal, baigan (*India*) aubergines
Bun (*Vietnam*) rice vermicelli

Cha (*China*) deep-frying
Chai (*India*) tea; *masala chai* = spiced tea
Cha-Shoa (*China*) quick roasting
Ch'eng (*China*) open steaming
Chien (*China*) shallow-frying
Chow, ch'ao (*China*) simple stir-frying
Curry (*India*) stewing with liquid and spices to form a sauce. Derived either from *kari*, a Tamil word for sauce, or from *karhai*, a cooking vessel.
Cu cai trang (*Vietnam*) Japanese white radish or daikon

Dashi (*Japan*) basic stock (see page 69)
Dahi (*India*) plain yoghurt
Daikon (*Japan*) white radish

Dim sum (*China*) savoury snacks served at tea houses in the afternoon. A Cantonese speciality.
Donabe (*Japan*) an earthenware casserole
Dua chua (*Vietnam*) pickled vegetables

Gajar (*India*) carrots
Gohan (*Japan*) rice; food; *gohan-mono*, rice dishes
Gosht (*India*) meat, especially lamb

Hashi (*Japan*) chopsticks
He hou (*China*) heat or fire control, hence 'cooking'

Kaiseki ryori (*Japan*) formal meals deriving from traditional tea ceremonies, now only served in special restaurants
Kapi (*Thailand*) shrimp paste
Kulfi (*India*) ice cream

Macchi (*India*) fish
Masala (*India*) mixture of spices
Matar (*India*) peas
Matcha (*Japan*) powdered tea for tea ceremony
Mee (*Thailand*) noodles
Mien (*China*) noodles
Miso (*Japan*) soybean paste, the basis of a traditional soup
Murgh (*India*) chicken
Mushimono (*Japan*) steamed dish

Nam dong co (*Vietnam*) dried Chinese mushrooms

Nam pla (*Thailand*) fish sauce
Nga pi (*Burma*) shrimp paste
Nimono (*Japan*) simmered dish
Nuoc mam (*Vietnam*) fish sauce

Ocha (*Japan*) green tea
Otoshi-busha (*Japan*) wooden drop lid, used in simmering; smaller in diameter than the pot, it sits on the food, submerging it and ensuring even cooking. A circle of paper *larger* than the diameter of the pot can be used instead, pushed down over the food.

Paan (*India*) served at the end of the meal, a heart-shaped leaf spread with lime paste and stuffed with chopped betel nuts, then folded into a triangle and secured with a clove.

Ruou de (*Vietnam*) rice alcohol, drunk like sake or used in cooking

Saag (*India*) spinach
Sake (*Japan*) rice wine
Sashimi (*Japan*) raw fish, delicately sliced
Satay (*Indonesia, Thailand*) finely sliced or minced meat barbecued or grilled on skewers and served with peanut sauce
Shiitake (*Japan*) Chinese mushrooms

Shoyu Japanese soy sauce
Sukiyaki (*Japan*) dish of beef sliced very thin and cooked on a hotplate at the table
Suimono (*Japan*) clear soup
Sunomono (*Japan*) vinegared vegetables
Sushi (*Japan*) vinegared rice

Tandoor (*India*) small clay oven fired by charcoal
Tava (*India*) a round, concave cast-iron plate used to cook breads
Teppan-yaki (*Japan*) hot-plate cooking
Tempura (*Japan*) battered, deep-fried foods
Thali (*India*) individual round metal tray on which food is served
Tofu (*Japan, China*) bean curd
Tsukemono (*Japan*) pickles
Tun (*China*) closed steaming

Vindaloo (*India*) hot curries from Goa, which may be made from pork as the population is Christian rather than Hindu. The name is thought to come from the Portuguese meaning 'with wine and garlic'.

Xa (*Vietnam*) lemon grass

Yakimono (*Japan*) grilled or pan-fried dish
Yakitori (*Japan*) chicken skewered and grilled with a dipping sauce

Zensai (*Japan*) hors d'oeuvres

PART 2

In this part of the book you will find an array of recipes
from the Orient for all tastes and occasions. Some are quick
and easy to prepare, ideal for family meals; others are more
complex and demanding, set pieces for dinner parties and
special occasions. All are based on the cooking techniques
described in Part One.

The first chapter is made up of a range of soups, from the
light and elegant Spring Rain Soup of Japan to Thai Spicy
Chicken Soup, almost a meal in itself. This is followed by a
chapter devoted to starters and snacks. Oriental cuisine
boasts more ideas for little savouries than any other: you
could make a complete meal from Japanese sushi, India
samosas or Chinese dumplings.

The waters of the Indian Ocean and the South China Sea
produce fish and shellfish in abundance. Chapter 3 includes
a varied selection of the recipes that make the most of this
bounty, with mouthwatering ideas such as Bream with
Lemon Grass from Vietnam and Indonesia's Fish Bergedel.
There are as many delicious recipes for poultry following,
from the classic Peking Duck to the intriguing Stewed
Chicken with Chestnuts.

Oriental cooks have a great respect for meat, preparing it
with care and economy. The results, as shown in Chapter 5,
are irresistible, from India's rich curries to the stir-fried
dishes of China and Vietnam. Chapter 6 draws together from
all over the Orient imaginative vegetable recipes that are as
delicious as they are nutritious. Chapter 7 gives recipes for
rice and noodles, the staple foods of the Orient and
increasingly popular in the West. Breads and pancakes come
next, then a selection of ideas for the colourful
accompaniments without which no Oriental meal is
complete. Part Two ends with a collection of desserts, many
based on fruit, with some exotic specialities like Indian Ice
Cream and Vietnamese Banana Cake.

*Left: Ginger and spring onion crab (page 112); Steamed scallops
in black bean sauce (page 33)*

SOUPS AND STOCKS

*The range of soups found in Oriental cuisine defies imagination.
The delicious combinations of ingredients are always good to
look at, whether served throughout the meal, as in China and
Thailand, or forming a distinct course in a long menu, as in Japan.
Good stock is vital to the success not only of soups but sauces and stews.*

Chinese Clear Stock or Broth

Qing Tang

Although described as a soup in Chinese, this is the basic stock which is the first thing a cook prepares at the beginning of the day in the kitchen. It is used for cooking throughout the day and is the basis for most soups. On its own, with the addition of seasonings, it can be served as a clear soup. For every 600 ml (1 pint) add 1 tablespoon light soy sauce and 1 teaspoon salt, with 2 teaspoons finely chopped spring onions if liked.

1 kg (2–2¼ lb) chicken pieces
750 g (1½ lb) pork spareribs
450 g (1 lb) ham, bacon or beef
  bones
2 teaspoons dried shrimps
  (optional)
50 g (2 oz) fresh root ginger,
  unpeeled and cut into large
  chunks
4–5 spring onions, trimmed
2.75 litres (5 pints) water
50 ml (2 fl oz) Chinese wine or
  dry sherry (optional)

Preparation time: 25 minutes,
plus cooling
Cooking time: about 2½ hours

1. Trim off the excess fat from the chicken and pork, and place in a large saucepan with the bones, the dried shrimps (if using), the ginger and spring onions. Cover with the water and bring to the boil. Skim off the scum that rises to the surface.

2. Reduce the heat to a rolling boil and cook, partly covered, for at least 1½–2 hours, skimming off scum from time to time.

3. Leave to cool. When cold, use a perforated spoon to skim any fat from the surface.

4. Strain the stock and return it to a clean saucepan. Add the rice wine or sherry (if using) and bring back to the boil. Simmer for 5 minutes or so before using. Any leftover stock should be stored in a covered container in the refrigerator, where it will keep for up to 4–5 days.

*Left: Chinese clear stock or broth
Far right: Pepper water*

Japanese Stock

Dashi

Dashi provides Japanese cooking with its characteristic flavour, and the ultimate success of a dish is determined by the quality of the dashi that seasons it. The best-tasting dashi is made with bonito flakes shaved immediately prior to use. Since this takes time, skill and practice, many cooks use commercially prepared flakes. Instant stock, or *dashi-no-moto*, can be used for convenience, but is less subtle than home-made dashi.

25 g (1 oz) konbu (dried kelp)
1.2 litres (2 pints) water
25 g (1 oz) katsuo-bushi (dried bonito flakes)

Preparation time: 10 minutes, plus standing
Cooking time: 15 minutes

1. Place the konbu in a medium saucepan with the water. Bring slowly to the boil. Just before the water reaches boiling point, remove the konbu.

2. Immediately add the katsuo-bushi and bring to a rapid boil. As soon as the water comes to the boil, remove the pan from the heat. Leave to stand for a few minutes, until the katsuo-bushi settles at the bottom.

3. Strain the dashi through a sieve lined with muslin and use as required.

Saffron Soup with Chicken

Safuran Sumashi

The addition of saffron gives this Japanese soup a delicate yellow colour which contrasts beautifully with the white of the chicken.

100 g (4 oz) boneless chicken breast, skinned
a little cornflour, to coat
600 ml (1 pint) chicken stock
1 whole bone from a flat white fish
a pinch of saffron threads
salt
freshly ground black pepper
4 sprigs watercress, to garnish

Preparation time: 10 minutes
Cooking time: about 10 minutes
Serves 4

1. Cut the chicken breast into 2.5 cm (1 inch) squares. Coat lightly with cornflour. Plunge into a saucepan of boiling water for 5 minutes, or until cooked.

2. In a separate saucepan, bring the chicken stock to the boil. Add the fish bone and boil gently for 5 minutes. Remove the bone and discard. Add the saffron to the stock, and season with salt and pepper to taste.

3. Drain the chicken pieces and divide them equally among 4 warmed individual soup bowls. Pour over the saffron-coloured soup, garnish with watercress and serve.

Pepper Water

Mulligatawny

Pepper water can be mouth-scorching in south India, where this soup originates. As a variation, a little coconut cream can be blended in just before serving to lower the temperature.

2 tablespoons ghee
2 teaspoons Mild Curry Powder (see page 14)
1 teaspoon celery seeds
1 teaspoon black mustard seeds
1 teaspoon black peppercorns
1 garlic clove, finely chopped
1 onion, chopped
2–3 green chillies, chopped finely
900 ml (1½ pints) vegetable or chicken stock or water
1 tablespoon red lentils
1 tablespoon Basmati rice
1 small carrot, grated coarsely
3–4 tablespoons lemon juice, strained
salt

Preparation time: 10 minutes
Cooking time: 15–20 minutes
Serves 4

1. Heat the ghee in a 2.5 litre (4 pint) saucepan. Add the curry powder, celery seeds, mustard seeds and peppercorns and stir-fry for 1 minute. Add the garlic and onion and stir-fry until soft.

2. Add all the remaining ingredients, bring to the boil and simmer for 10–15 minutes. Serve very hot.

Spring Rain Soup

Harusame

Japanese clear soups must always be served piping hot. The ideal bowls are the traditional lacquer bowls but porcelain ones are fine: the important thing is that each one should have a lid, not only to keep the liquid hot, but to preserve as much of its delicate aroma as possible.

2–3 dried shiitake mushrooms
100 g (4 oz) dehydrated mung bean threads, or harusame (soy bean noodles), soaked in boiling water for 30 minutes
1 litre (1¾ pints) Japanese Stock (see page 69) or chicken stock
1 tablespoon sake (rice wine)
salt

100 g (4 oz) peeled prawns
6–8 mangetout
1 gobo (burdock root), parboiled (optional)
4–6 spring onions
2 carrots, peeled
a few cucumber strips
100 g (4 oz) napa (Chinese cabbage)
a few young spinach leaves
To garnish:
1 teaspoon grated freshly ground ginger
1 spring onion, shredded finely
2 teaspoons puréed daikon (Japanese radish)

Preparation time: 15 minutes, plus soaking
Cooking time: 6–7 minutes
Serves 4

1. Place the shiitake mushrooms in a bowl, cover with boiling water and leave to soak for 20 minutes.

2. Drain the mung bean threads or harusame and cut into 5 cm (2 inch) lengths.

3. Drain the mushrooms, reserving the liquid, and discard the stems.

4. Place the stock in a medium saucepan. Carefully pour in the reserved mushroom liquid, leaving any sandy sediment at the bottom – this should be discarded. Bring the stock to the boil, reduce the heat and simmer for about 2 minutes. Add the sake and season with salt to taste.

5. Divide the stock among 4 warmed individual soup bowls.

6. Place the mung bean threads or harusame in the centre of a serving dish and arrange the mushrooms on top with a few spinach leaves. Arrange the prawns and vegetables in clusters around the edge. Serve the garnishes in separate dishes. Each guest helps himself to the vegetables and garnish of his choice.

Bird's Nest Soup

Ghuy Yoong Yien Waw

The chief ingredient for this famous Chinese soup comes from a species of sea swallow native to the South Seas. The 'nests' are the high-protein food left by the swallows for their young, mostly fish and seaweed, dried and purified and sold in nestlets or chips called 'dragon's teeth'.

100 g (4 oz) dried bird's nest, soaked overnight and drained (see method)
1.5 litres (2½ pints) Chinese Broth (see page 68)
100 g (4 oz) cooked chicken meat, chopped
1 tablespoon dry sherry
10 pigeon or quail eggs, boiled and peeled
1 tablespoon cornflour dissolved in 1 tablespoon water
½ teaspoon salt
pepper
2 egg whites
To garnish:
2 tablespoons shredded cooked ham
2 tablespoons freshly chopped parsley

Preparation time: 15 minutes, plus soaking
Cooking time: about 1 hour
Serves 4

1. Remove any loose feathers from the bird's nest with tweezers. Place in a saucepan, cover with water and boil for 15 minutes; drain and rinse. Cover with fresh cold water and soak for 3 hours. Reboil for 5 minutes. Drain and soak in fresh water overnight.

2. The next day, drain the bird's nest, which will have separated into chips like transparent noodles. Place in a saucepan with half the broth and bring to the boil. Cover and simmer for 30 minutes. Drain, discarding the stock.

3. Place the remaining broth in the saucepan and bring to the boil. Add the chicken, bird's nest chips, sherry and eggs. When the soup comes to the boil, add the cornflour mixture and simmer, stirring, until thickened. Season with the salt and pepper to taste.

4. Beat the egg whites until they are stiff, then fold into the soup. To serve, pour into warmed soup bowls and garnish with shredded ham and chopped parsley.

Left: Spring rain soup is a perfect example of the delicacy of touch important in Japanese cooking. The bright fresh colours of the vegetables retain their clarity in the pale liquid, which must be served in white porcelain bowls.

Thick Egg soup

Chawan Mushi

In Japan, custard soups like this one are traditionally served in straight-sided porcelain cups, so shaped that the egg sets evenly. Chawan Mushi sets come in many beautiful designs, but the soup can just as easily be made in straight-sided coffee mugs.

100 g (4 oz) boneless chicken breast, skinned
4 teaspoons sake (rice wine)
1½ teaspoons shoyu (Japanese soy sauce)
8 uncooked prawns, defrosted if frozen
salt
4 mangetout
500 ml (18 fl oz) Japanese Stock (see page 69)
1 teaspoon mirin (sweet rice wine)
3 eggs, beaten
8 small button mushrooms, wiped

Preparation time: 20 minutes
Cooking time: 30 minutes
Serves 4

1. Thinly slice the chicken, and sprinkle it with 1 teaspoon of the sake and ½ teaspoon of the shoyu.

2. Wash and shell the prawns and remove the black vein from the back. Sprinkle with the remaining sake and a pinch of salt.

3. Bring a saucepan of lightly salted water to the boil. Plunge the mangetout into the boiling water for 1 minute, then drain.

4. Bring the stock to the boil in a medium saucepan. Add ½ teaspoon of salt, the mirin and the remaining shoyu. Remove from the heat and leave to cool for 5 minutes.

5. Whisk a little of the stock into the beaten eggs. Pour this mixture into the stock, whisking all the time.

6. Divide the chicken equally among 4 Chawan Mushi cups and pour in the egg soup. Add 2 mushrooms, 2 prawns and 1 mangetout to each cup.

7. Place the cups in a steamer and steam vigorously for 2 minutes. Reduce the heat and steam for a further 12–14 minutes or until the juice runs clear when the thickened soup is pierced with a skewer. If you do not have a steamer, put the cups in a shallow baking dish half-filled with hot water. Cover with foil and cook in a preheated hot oven (220°C, 425°F, Gas Mark 7) for 5 minutes, then reduce the heat to moderate (180°C, 350°F, Gas Mark 4) for 20–25 minutes.

8. Serve the soup the moment it is ready, garnished if liked with extra prawns, mangetout or mushrooms.

Clear Soup with Prawns

Sumashi-jiru

Light as this Japanese soup is, the noodles make it a satisfying addition to the meal.

4 headless, uncooked prawns, defrosted if frozen
1 teaspoon salt
a little cornflour, to coat
40 g (1½ oz) somen (fine noodles)
600 ml (1 pint) Japanese stock (see page 69)
½ teaspoon shoyu (Japanese soy sauce)
4 sprigs watercress, to garnish

Preparation time: 10 minutes
Cooking time: 8–10 minutes
Serves 4

1. Wash and shell the prawns, retaining the shell on the end of the tail. Remove the black vein from the back of the prawns. Pat dry with a little of the salt, then dust with cornflour. Plunge the prawns into a saucepan of boiling water, then drain and set aside.

2. Bring a large saucepan of water to the boil. Throw in the noodles and cook for 3 minutes. Drain, rinse in cold water, and drain again.

3. Bring the stock to the boil in a medium saucepan. Season with the shoyu and remaining salt.

4. Divide the prawns and noodles equally among 4 warmed soup bowls and pour over the stock. Garnish with sprigs of watercress and serve.

Three Shredded and Five Ingredients Soup

This simple soup is typical of Chinese clear soups that are quick to prepare, based on a high-quality chicken stock and vegetables that are cooked quickly to retain flavour and 'bite'.

1.5 litres (2½ pints) chicken stock
15 g (½ oz) root ginger, peeled and chopped
2 garlic cloves, crushed
25 g (1 oz) onion, chopped
25 g (1 oz) dried shiitake mushrooms, soaked for 20 minutes
25 g (1 oz) dried shrimps, soaked for 20 minutes
2 spring onions, shredded
3 large peeled prawns, shredded
100 g (4 oz) Chinese cabbage, finely shredded
1 teaspoon sesame seed oil

Preparation time: 10 minutes, plus soaking
Cooking time: 20 minutes
Serves 6

1. Heat the stock in a wok or large saucepan and bring to the boil. Add the ginger, garlic and onion. Drain the mushrooms, discard the stems and chop the caps. Drain and chop the shrimps. Add the mushrooms and shrimps to the stock. Simmer for 5 minutes.

2. Add the shredded spring onions, prawns and cabbage and simmer for a further 2 minutes.

3. To serve, pour into warmed soup bowls and sprinkle sesame seed oil on top.

Left: Thick egg soup; Clear soup with prawns
Below: Three shredded and five ingredients soup

Bean Soup

Miso-shiru

Miso (soy bean paste) soups are traditional for family meals in Japan, mainly because they are so nutritious and filling. They also feature at the end of formal *kaiseki* meals with the traditional green tea and *sunomono* (vinegared vegetables).

25 g (1 oz) niboshi (dried small whole sardines)
1–2 packets wakame (dried young seaweed)
4 tablespoons miso (soy bean paste)
50 g (2 oz) firm tofu (bean curd)
2 spring onions, finely chopped

Preparation time: 20 minutes, plus soaking
Cooking time: 25 minutes
Serves 4

1. To make the stock, put the niboshi in a saucepan, add 600 ml (1 pint) water and place over high heat. Bring quickly to the boil and simmer for 5–10 minutes, depending on the strength of flavour required. Remove the pan from the heat and strain the liquid through a clean teatowel. Return the liquid to the rinsed-out pan. Discard the niboshi.

2. Place the wakame in a bowl and cover with cold water. Leave to soak for 5–10 minutes or until fully expanded and soft. Drain the wakame and set it aside.

3. Place the miso in a small bowl and dilute it with a few spoonfuls of the stock.

4. Place the saucepan of stock over a moderate heat. Just before boiling point is reached, add the diluted miso and reduce the heat so that the stock does not boil.

5. Cut the tofu into small cubes and add them to the pan with the wakame. Bring to the boil, then remove the pan from the heat and add the finely chopped spring onions. Serve hot, in warmed individual soup bowls.

Shark's Fin Soup

Yu Chi Tang

Shark's fin is an expensive delicacy; thread-like, transparent and rich in vitamins and calcium, it takes a week to prepare. Trim the fin, wash it, then place in a saucepan. Cover with water, boil for 2 hours, and drain. Cover with cold water and leave to soak overnight. Repeat this for 5 days. Shark's fin can be obtained with the rough outer skin removed; this form requires less preparation. Canned shark's fin is also available.

225 g (8 oz) shark's fin, soaked
1.75 litres (3 pints) Chinese Broth (see page 68)
2 spring onions
3 slices fresh root ginger
2 tablespoons sunflower oil
225 g (8 oz) chicken meat or lean pork, shredded
65 g (2½ oz) canned bamboo shoot, drained and shredded
50 g (2 oz) mushrooms, shredded
100 g (4 oz) cooked ham, shredded
1 tablespoon dry sherry
2 tablespoons light soy sauce
1 tablespoon red wine vinegar
½ teaspoon sugar
½ teaspoon salt
3 tablespoons cornflour dissolved in 3 tablespoons water
spring onions, cut into strips, to garnish

Preparation time: see recipe introduction
Cooking time: see recipe introduction
Serves 4–6

1. Rinse the soaked shark's fin under cold running water for 10 minutes. Drain. Place in a saucepan and add 750 ml (1¼ pints) of the broth, the spring onions and ginger. Bring to the boil, cover and boil for 15 minutes. Drain the shark's fin, discarding the broth.

2. Heat the oil in a clean saucepan. Add the meat and stir-fry until it takes colour. Stir in the remaining broth and bring to the boil.

3. Add the bamboo shoot, mushrooms, ham, sherry, soy sauce, vinegar, sugar, salt and shark's fin and simmer for 15–20 minutes.

4. Add the cornflour mixture and simmer, stirring, until the soup is thickened.

5. Serve hot in warmed soup bowls, garnished with strips of spring onion.

Beef and Tomato Soup

Ngow Fan Keh Tang

Most Chinese recipes using beef are from Szechuan, where oxen are used as beasts of burden. The addition of hot pickles gives this soup the spicy flavour typical of the region.

100 g (4 oz) beef steak, thinly
*   sliced*
1 teaspoon salt
freshly ground black pepper
50 g (2 oz) Szechuan pickle,
*   chopped*
1 tablespoon cornflour
600 ml (1 pint) beef stock
225 g (8 oz) tomatoes, skinned
*   and roughly chopped*
spring onions, sliced, to garnish

Preparation time: 5 minutes
Cooking time: 2 minutes
Serves 4

1. Dust the beef with a little of the salt and the pepper. Mix with the pickle and toss in the cornflour.

2. Place the stock in a saucepan and bring to a rolling boil. Add the beef and pickle, tomatoes and remaining salt and let it boil for 1 minute. Serve immediately in warmed soup bowls, with spring onions scattered on top.

Pork, Ham and Bamboo Shoot Soup

Siu Jook Sun Tang

This clear soup from China is typically light but satisfying. Dredging the slices of meat in flour before cooking gives them a smooth texture and keeps them tender.

50 g (2 oz) pork fillet
cornflour, for dredging
2 teaspoons light soy sauce
600 ml (1 pint) Chinese Broth
*   (see page 68)*
50 g (2 oz) cooked ham,
*   shredded*
50 g (2 oz) bamboo shoots,
*   shredded*
1 teaspoon salt
1 teaspoon sherry

Preparation time: about 20 minutes
Cooking time: 10 minutes
Serves 4

1. Slice the pork very thinly and mix it with the soy sauce. Dust with cornflour.

2. Place the broth in a large saucepan and bring to the boil. Put in the pork, ham and bamboo shoots. When the soup comes back to the boil, add the salt and sherry.

3. Transfer to warmed soup bowls and serve immediately.

Beef and tomato soup (top); Pork, ham
and bamboo shoot soup

Hot and Sour Soup

Suan ba Tang

This thick soup is more popular in north China than the south. Chinese dried mushrooms are an essential ingredient, and bean curd is almost always used, but for the pork given here other meat, fish, crab or shrimp could be substituted. In the classic Chinese version, solidified chicken blood is included.

1.2 litres (2 pints) Chinese Broth (see page 68)
100 g (4 oz) lean pork, shredded
50 g (2 oz) canned bamboo shoot, drained and shredded
3 dried Chinese mushrooms, soaked for 20 minutes
1 cake bean curd, shredded
1 tablespoon dry sherry
2 tablespoons red wine vinegar
½ teaspoon salt
pepper
2 teaspoons light soy sauce
2 tablespoons cornflour dissolved in 4 tablespoons water
1 egg, beaten
a few drops of sesame seed oil
1 spring onion, shredded

Preparation time: 15 minutes
Cooking time: 25 minutes
Serves 4–6

1. Place the broth in a saucepan and bring to the boil. Add the pork and bamboo shoot. Drain the mushrooms, remove the stems and shred the caps. Add the mushrooms to the broth. Cover and simmer for 10 minutes.

2. Add the bean curd, sherry, vinegar, salt, a generous pinch of pepper and the soy sauce. When the soup returns to the boil, add the cornflour mixture. Simmer, stirring continuously, until thickened.

3. Reduce the heat. Slowly pour the beaten egg through a strainer into the soup, stirring gently.

4. To serve, pour the soup into warmed soup bowls and sprinkle sesame seed oil and shredded spring onion on top.

Right: Spicy chicken soup; Stuffed squid soup

Sizzling Rice Soup

Guopa Tang

In China the rice for this soup is dried in the sun. Prepare it by spreading an even layer of freshly cooked rice on a baking sheet, pressing it down firmly. Place in a very slow oven until it is brittle. Alternatively, use the rice stuck to the bottom of the pan.

1.2 litres (2 pints) Chinese Broth (see page 68) or water
225 g (8 oz) prawns, shelled and deveined
100 g (4 oz) mushrooms, halved
½ teaspoon salt
1 tablespoon soy sauce
1 tablespoon dry sherry
pinch of pepper
sunflower oil for deep-frying
150 g (5 oz) crisped rice, broken into 7.5 cm (3 inch) pieces

Preparation time: 15 minutes
Cooking time: 20 minutes
Serves 4–6

1. Bring the stock or water to the boil in a saucepan. Add the prawns, mushrooms, salt, soy sauce, sherry and pepper and stir well. Cover and simmer until the ingredients are heated through, then pour into a warmed soup tureen. Keep hot while preparing the rice.

2. Heat the oil in a heavy saucepan to 180°C/350°F, or until a cube of bread browns in 30 seconds. Deep-fry the pieces of rice for about 30 seconds until crisp but not brown. Drain on paper towels and keep on a warmed plate until all the pieces are cooked.

3. To serve, place the rice in individual bowls and, at the table, ladle the stock mixture over the rice. The resulting sizzling gives the dish its name.

Sweetcorn and Crab Soup

Sook Muy Daai Haah Tong

In Canton, soups based on sweetcorn, with fish or chicken, are often served at banquets. In the West the combination of sweetcorn and crab has become a great favourite.

1 teaspoon finely chopped fresh root ginger
100 g (4 oz) crab meat, flaked
2 teaspoons Chinese wine or sherry
1 egg white
3 teaspoons cornflour
600 ml (1 pint) Chinese Clear Stock (page 68)
1 teaspoon salt
100 g (4 oz) sweetcorn kernels
1 spring onion, finely chopped, to garnish

Preparation time: 15 minutes
Cooking time: 15 minutes
Serves 4

1. Combine the finely chopped ginger with the crab meat and wine or sherry.

2. In a bowl, lightly whisk the egg white.

3. Combine the cornflour with 2 tablespoons of cold water to make a thin paste.

4. Place the stock in a saucepan set over moderate heat and bring to the boil. Add the salt, sweetcorn kernels and crab meat mixture. When the liquid comes back to the boil, stir in the cornflour paste and cook, stirring constantly, until the soup is smooth and thickened.

5. Blend in the egg white. Transfer the soup to individual bowls and serve hot, garnished with chopped spring onion.

Spicy Chicken Soup

Tom Yam Kai

This economical soup from Thailand is typical of South-east Asian recipes that can be adapted to suit whatever your kitchen can offer in the way of leftover meat.

3 tablespoons sunflower oil
½ large onion, sliced thinly
2 garlic cloves, crushed
1 teaspoon chopped ginger
½ teaspoon freshly ground black pepper
a pinch of turmeric
175 g (6 oz) cooked chicken
1 tablespoon light soy sauce
1 litre (1¾ pints) chicken stock
a handful of beanthread noodles, soaked till soft
75 g (3 oz) bean sprouts
spring onions, to garnish

Preparation time: 15–20 minutes
Cooking time: 15 minutes
Serves 4

1. In a medium saucepan heat the oil and fry the onion, garlic and ginger until the onion is soft. Add the pepper, turmeric and chicken meat and stir for 30 seconds.

2. Add the soy sauce and stock and bring to the boil. Adjust the seasoning if necessary. Reduce the heat slightly and cook for 5 minutes.

3. Drain the noodles. Divide them equally with the bean sprouts among 4 warmed soup bowls and pour the soup on top. To serve, garnish with chopped spring onions.

Stuffed Squid Soup

Muek Tian Nam

This soup comes from Singapore, where an amazing variety of seafood is harvested at night, with huge nets marked out with hurricane lamps to attract the fish.

8 medium squid
175 g (6 oz) minced pork
1 stalk spring onion, chopped
1 teaspoon salt
½ teaspoon pepper
1 teaspoon cornflour
500 ml (18 fl oz) water
1 tablespoon light soy sauce
1 tablespoon sesame oil
spring onions, chopped, to garnish

Preparation time: 20 minutes
Cooking time: 10 minutes
Serves 4

1. Clean the squid as described on page 54, retaining the tentacles.

2. Mix the minced pork with the spring onion, salt, pepper and cornflour. Stuff the squid with a little of the pork mixture and secure the tentacles to each one with a half cocktail stick. Set aside any leftover mixture.

3. Bring the water to the boil and add the soy sauce and sesame oil. Add the stuffed squids and cook for 3 minutes.

4. Stir in any leftover pork mixture to give the soup 'body'. Adjust the seasoning. To serve, place 2 squid in each of 4 individual soup bowls, removing the cocktail sticks. Pour over the soup and garnish with chopped spring onion.

SNACKS AND STARTERS

Oriental cuisine can be characterized by the multiplicity of savoury snacks invented to punctuate the day. These little mouthfuls are deliciously versatile – make a selection for an informal supper, serve them as part of a complete menu, or to accompany drinks before dinner. Whatever the occasion, they are irresistible.

Sushi

In Japan, restaurants tend to specialize in one kind of dish. Sushi bars are popular at lunchtime, when the raw fish which is an important component of these recipes is at its freshest. Making elegant sushi takes practice and skill, but the results are exquisite. There can be few hors d'oeuvres as tempting as a beautifully arranged tray of sushi.

The essential ingredient of sushi is vinegared rice (see page 23). To this is added absolutely fresh fish in season and a saucer of shoyu (Japanese soy sauce) with grated wasabe. Sheets of nori are used to make sushi rolls or thinly sliced as a garnish.

Vinegared rice or pickled ginger is served to refresh the palate. The only accompaniment is an omelette roll sliced into rounds.

Mackerel Sushi

Saba Zushi

1 large fresh mackerel, filleted
salt
rice vinegar
vinegared rice (see page 23), made with 350 g (12 oz) rice and 450 ml (¾ pint) water
To garnish:
beni-shoga (pickled ginger roots)
shredded chives

Preparation time: 30 minutes, plus salting and chilling
Serves 4

1. Place the mackerel fillets on a bed of salt, then pour over more salt to cover the fish completely. Leave for several hours. Remove the fillets from the salt and rub the salt off roughly with paper towels. Wash the remaining salt away with rice vinegar. Using your fingers and working from the tail end, remove the transparent skin from each fillet, leaving the silver pattern intact. Carefully remove all bones hidden in the mackerel fillets.

2. Put the fillets, skin side down, on a wooden board. Using a sharp knife, slice off the thick flesh from the centre to make the fillets even in thickness. Reserve these slices of flesh.

3. Place one of the fillets, skin side down, on the base of a wooden mould or loaf tin lined with waxed paper or cling film. Fill any gaps with some of the reserved slices of thick flesh.

4. Press the vinegared rice down firmly in an even layer on top of the fish with your hands. Place the remaining mackerel fillet on top, skin side up, and fill in any gaps with the remaining slice of thick flesh.

5. Place the wooden lid on top of the mould (or fold over the sheet of cling film) and put a weight on top. Leave in a cool place for 1 hour.

6. Turn out the loaf and remove the cling film or waxed paper. Slice into fingers. Garnish with beni-shoga and shredded chives and serve immediately.

Sushi with Five Ingredients

Gomoku Zushi

This dish is a variation on *chirashi-zushi* or 'scattered sushi' which is the easiest to assemble at home. *Gomoku* means 'five kinds'.

1 small mackerel, filleted
salt
rice vinegar
3 dried shiitake mushrooms
1 medium carrot, peeled and
    shredded
5 tablespoons sugar
3 tablespoons shoyu (Japanese
    soy sauce)
2 tablespoons mirin (sweet rice
    wine)
50 g (2 oz) mangetout, cooked
2 eggs
1 tablespoon sunflower oil
vinegared rice (see page 23),
    made with 350 g (12 oz) rice
    and 450 ml (¾ pint) water
beni-shoga (pickled ginger
    roots), shredded
1 sheet nori (optional)

Preparation time: 30 minutes,
plus salting
Cooking time: 5 minutes (for 1
omelette)
Serves 4

1. Sprinkle the mackerel fillets
with salt and leave for 3–4
hours. Wash the salt away with
rice vinegar.

2. Using your fingers and
working from the tail end,
remove the transparent skin
from each fillet, leaving the
silver pattern intact. Remove all
the bones which are hidden in
the mackerel fillets. Slice the
flesh into thin strips, cover and
set aside.

3. Soak the mushrooms in warm
water for 25 minutes, then
drain, reserving 120 ml (4 fl oz)
of the liquid. Squeeze the
mushrooms dry, discard the
hard stalks, and finely shred the
caps. Place in a saucepan with
the carrot. Add 3 tablespoons
sugar, the shoyu and mirin.
Simmer until all the juice has
been absorbed. Cut the
mangetout into thin strips.

4. Beat the eggs in a small bowl,
add the remaining sugar and a
pinch of salt. Heat the oil in a
heavy-based frying pan. Pour in
half of the egg mixture, tilting
the pan so that it spreads evenly
over the base. Fry over the
lowest possible heat for 30
seconds, or until the surface of
the mixture is just set. Do not
overcook. Turn the omelette on
to a board and leave to cool.
Repeat with the remaining
mixture. Cut the 2 omelettes
into thin strips 5 cm (2 inches)
long.

5. Put the vinegared rice into a
large porcelain bowl (a metallic
bowl will taint the flavour). Add
the mushrooms, carrot,
mangetout, mackerel and
shredded beni-shoga. Using a
wooden spatula, gently fold the
ingredients into the rice; do not
stir. Garnish with the omelette
strips.

6. If using nori, grill it under the
lowest possible heat for only a
second until crisp (a Japanese
cook toasts the nori by passing
the shiny side over a high flame
until the colour changes). Shred
the sheet of nori into 4 cm
(1½ inch) strips with a sharp
knife. Arrange on top of the rice.
Serve cold.

Above: Sushi with five ingredients

Rolled Rice Wrapped in Nori

Nori-maki

In this recipe, sumeshi (vinegared rice) is mixed with kampyo, omelette strips, fish flakes, mushrooms, carrots and spinach to make Nori-maki (*maki* means 'rolling'). You can use almost any ingredient you wish as long as it looks attractive: any colour goes well with the brilliant white of sumeshi. Slices of cucumber look good, or strips of raw tuna, smoked cod's roe, ham, cheese and tsuke-mono (Japanese pickled vegetables); you can even use canned sardines, tuna, salmon or anchovies.

25 g (1 oz) packet kampyo (dried shaved gourd strings), cut into 15 cm (6 inch) lengths
salt
6 tablespoons sugar
6 tablespoons shoyu (Japanese soy sauce)
5–6 sheets of nori (dried lava paper)
3 dried shiitake mushrooms
1 medium carrot, peeled and shredded
2 tablespoons mirin (sweet rice wine)
100 g (4 oz) fresh spinach leaves, washed and trimmed
vinegared rice (see page 23), made with 500 g (1 lb 2 oz) rice and 685 ml (23 fl oz) water
beni-shoga (pickled ginger roots), shredded, to garnish (optional)
Thick egg omelette:
2 eggs
3 tablespoons Japanese Stock (see page 69)
2 tablespoons sugar
1 tablespoon vegetable oil
Fish flakes:
1 white fish fillet (e.g. cod, haddock or whiting)
1½ tablespoons sake (rice wine)
1½ tablespoons sugar
red food colouring

Preparation time: 1 hour, plus soaking
Cooking time: 20 minutes
Serves 4

1. Put the kampyo in a saucepan, add 1 teaspoon salt and a few drops of water, then squeeze with your fingers. Rinse the salt away, then add enough water to cover and soak for 20 minutes. Place the pan over a moderate heat and bring to the boil. Boil until the kampyo becomes soft enough to break if pinched between the fingers, then drain. Add half of the sugar and shoyu, and simmer until all the juice disappears. Remove from the heat and set aside.

2. Grill the nori sheets lightly on both sides, placing them on the lowest possible grill position. This brings out their flavour and makes them crisp. Remove from the heat and set aside.

3. Make the omelette. Beat the eggs in a bowl, add the stock, sugar and ¼ teaspoon salt and beat well to mix. Heat the oil in a heavy-based (preferably square) frying pan. Pour in one-third of the egg mixture, cook until it is set, then fold in half. Grease the empty half of the pan with a wad of paper towels dipped in oil. Pour the remaining egg mixture into the empty half of the pan and cook until set. Fold on to the previously cooked half, then remove this omelette 'sandwich' from the pan. Leave to cool, then cut into long strips about 5 mm (¼ inch) thick.

4. Make the fish flakes. Put the fish fillet in a saucepan, add just enough water to cover and bring to the boil. Drain thoroughly. Using 2 pairs of hashi (chopsticks) or a fork, mash the fish to make flakes.

5. Put the sake in a shallow frying pan with the sugar, ¼ teaspoon salt and enough food colouring diluted with a little water to turn the mixture pink. Add the fish flakes, place over very low heat and cook for 2 minutes, stirring all the time. Remove from the heat and leave to cool.

6. Soak the mushrooms in warm water for 25 minutes, then drain and reserve 120 ml (4 fl oz) of the soaking liquid. Squeeze the mushrooms dry, discard the hard stalks, and finely shred the mushroom caps. Place the mushrooms and carrot in a saucepan with the remaining sugar and shoyu, the mirin and the reserved soaking liquid from the mushrooms. Simmer over very low heat until all the juice has been absorbed.

7. Blanch the spinach in lightly salted water for 1 minute. Drain, then squeeze out the water with your hands.

8. Place a sheet of nori, shortest side closest to you, on a makisu (bamboo mat). Put half a sheet of nori crossways in the centre on top (this is not strictly necessary, but it does help to prevent the wrapper splitting). Spread 200–225 g (7–8 oz) vinegared rice over the nori, leaving a 1 cm (½ inch) margin on the side nearest to you and on the opposite side. Using your fingers, press the rice to the nori. Place one-quarter of the kampyo and one-third of the omelette strips, fish flakes, mushrooms, carrots and spinach crossways to within 5 cm (2 inches) of the side furthest from you. Roll up the makisu from the side nearest to you so that the ingredients are in the centre of the vinegared rice. Lightly press the rolled makisu with your fingers. Repeat with more nori and the same filling ingredients to make 3 thick nori-maki altogether.

9. Use the remaining vinegared rice, kampyo and nori to make thinner nori-maki: place half a sheet of nori on a makisu, with the longest side nearest to you. Put a handful of rice on the nori, then spread it with your fingers and press it to the nori, leaving a 5 mm (¼ inch) margin on the side nearest to you and 1 cm (½ inch) on the opposite side. Put 1–2 kampyo strips crossways in the centre and roll the makisu from the side nearest to you.

10. To serve, cut the thick nori-maki into 6–8 rings and the thinner ones into 4–6 pieces. Arrange them on a wooden or bamboo dish, or on a serving platter, then garnish with shredded beni-shoga. Serve cold.

Right: A beautiful arrangement of nori-maki makes a colourful start to a Japanese dinner. These little mouthfuls of Rice wrapped in nori are substantial enough to take the edge off the appetite while refreshing the palate in preparation for the next course.

Mustard-pickled Aubergine

Nasu no Karashi

This spicy Japanese pickle will add zest to any dinner. It is an unusual way to blend ingredients.

1 medium aubergine, or 6 small Japanese elongated aubergines
750 ml (1¼ pints) water
1 tablespoon salt
Dressing:
1 teaspoon dry mustard
3 tablespoons shoyu (Japanese soy sauce)
3 tablespoons mirin (sweet rice wine)
3 tablespoons sugar

Preparation time: 15 minutes, plus soaking
Serves 4

1. Cut the aubergine crossways into slices about 3 mm (⅛ inch) thick, then cut the slices into quarters. Soak in the water, with the salt added, for 1 hour.

2. Meanwhile, make the dressing: put all the ingredients in a bowl and stir well.

3. Drain the aubergine and pat dry with paper towels. Arrange in a glass serving bowl and pour over the dressing.

4. Cover with plastic wrap and chill in the refrigerator for several hours or overnight before serving, to allow the flavours to develop.

Cabbage Pickles

Nappa no Tsukemono

Pickles appear on every Japanese menu; they go especially well with the blandness of the rice and tea; and they also help to clear the palate of lingering tastes such as fish. Many methods of preserving vegetables are used, including brine, rice bran, soy bean paste and mustard.

This recipe, using brine, is one of the simplest ways of preserving. If kept in the brine in the refrigerator, the napa will keep for about 1 week.

1 large head of napa (Chinese cabbage), quartered
3 tablespoons coarse salt
4 tablespoons seedless raisins or stoned prunes
250 ml (8 fl oz) water
3 dried chillies

Preparation time: 15 minutes, plus marinating
Serves 4–6

1. Put the napa in a glass bowl, sprinkling the layers with the salt. Add the remaining ingredients and mix well until the salt has dissolved.

2. Place a saucer on top of the cabbage, put a heavy weight on top, then leave to marinate for 12 hours.

3. Discard the raisins or prunes and chillies and wash the cabbage quickly. Squeeze out the excess moisture, then slice the cabbage into bite-sized pieces. Serve cold.

Vinegared Cucumber

Sunomono

This classic Japanese vinegared salad of finely sliced cucumber and soft wakame can be served as an hors d'oeuvre or as a refreshing accompaniment to a main meal.

1 large or 2 small cucumbers
1 teaspoon salt
15 g (½ oz) wakame (dried young seaweed)
2.5–4 cm (1–1½ inch) piece of fresh root ginger
Saubaizu sauce:
3 tablespoons rice vinegar
1 tablespoon shoyu (Japanese soy sauce)
1 tablespoon sugar
¼–½ teaspoon salt

Preparation time: 20 minutes
Serves 4

1. Halve the cucumber(s) lengthways; remove the seeds with a sharp-edged teaspoon. Slice the cucumber very thinly and sprinkle with the salt. Using your hands, squeeze the cucumber slices a few times, then rinse under cold running water in a bamboo strainer or sieve.

2. Put the wakame in a bowl and cover with cold water. Leave to soak for 5–10 minutes or until it becomes fully expanded and soft. Drain in a sieve, rinse with boiling water, then rinse under cold running water. Drain well and squeeze out any excess water with your hands. Cut the wakame into 2.5 cm (1 inch) lengths, if it is not already chopped.

3. Peel and shred the ginger, then place in a bowl of ice-cold water to crisp it up.

4. Put all the ingredients for the sauce in a bowl. Mix well together and add the sliced cucumber and wakame. Toss well to mix.

5. Transfer the salad to individual bowls, shaping it into neat mounds. Drain the shredded ginger and sprinkle it over the top. Serve cold.

Meat Samosa

Keema Samosa

This Indian dish is a snack which can be eaten hot or cold. It is good served at parties, with drinks, for tea or picnics. It is popular throughout Asia.

Pastry:
125 g (4 oz) plain flour
¼ teaspoon salt
25 g (1 oz) ghee
2–3 tablespoons water
Filling:
1 tablespoon sunflower oil
1 small onion, minced
1 garlic clove, crushed
1 green chilli, minced
½ teaspoon chilli powder
250 g (8 oz) minced beef
125 g (4 oz) tomatoes, skinned
 and chopped
1 tablespoon freshly chopped
 coriander
salt
oil for deep frying

Preparation time: 1 hour
Cooking time: 30 minutes
Serves 4

1. To make the pastry, sift the flour and salt into a mixing bowl. Rub in the ghee until the mixture resembles breadcrumbs. Add the water and knead thoroughly to a very smooth dough. Cover and chill while preparing the filling.

2. Heat the oil in a frying pan, add the onion and garlic and fry until golden. Add the chilli and chilli powder and fry for 3 minutes. Stir in the meat and cook until well-browned. Add the tomato, coriander and salt to taste and simmer gently for 20 minutes, until the meat is tender and the mixture dry; skim off any fat. Stir well and cool slightly.

3. Divide the pastry into 8 pieces. Dust with flour and roll each piece into a thin round. Cut each round in half. Fold each half into a cone and brush the seam with water to seal.

4. Fill the cone with a spoonful of filling – do not overfill – dampen the top edge and seal firmly. Cover the prepared samosas with a damp cloth, keeping them separated from each other.

5. Heat the oil in a deep pan to 180°C/350°F, or until a cube of bread browns in 30 seconds. Slide 4 samosas at a time into the oil. Reduce the heat a little and fry the samosas until they are light brown on both sides. Take care when turning them over that the filling does not escape.

6. Remove the cooked samosas from the pan and drain them on paper towels.

Meat samosa

Vegetable Samosa

Aloo Samosa

Pastry:
125 g (4 oz) plain flour
¼ teaspoon salt
25 g (1 oz) ghee
2–3 tablespoons water
Filling:
1 tablespoon sunflower oil
1 teaspoon mustard seeds
1 small onion, minced
2 green chillies, minced
¼ teaspoon turmeric
1 teaspoon finely chopped
 ginger
salt
125 g (4 oz) frozen peas
125 g (4 oz) cooked potatoes,
 diced
½ tablespoon freshly chopped
 coriander
1 tablespoon lemon juice
oil for deep-frying

Preparation time: 1 hour
Cooking time: 30 minutes
Serves 4

1. Make the pastry as for Meat Samosa (above). Chill while preparing the filling.

2. Heat the oil in a pan and add the mustard seeds. Leave for a few seconds until they start to pop, then add the onion and fry until golden. Add the chillies, turmeric, ginger, and salt to taste and fry for 3 minutes. If it starts sticking to the pan add ½ tablespoon water and stir well.

3. Add the peas, stir well and cook for 2 minutes. Add the potatoes and coriander, stir well and cook for 1 minute. Stir in the lemon juice. Cool slightly.

4. Divide the pastry into 8 pieces. Shape and deep-fry as for Meat Samosas (above).

Channa chaat (top), Potato chaat (centre) and Chicken chaat (bottom) are served as snacks in India. Tasty and filling, chaat dishes make a good basis for a light meal served with Indian salad (page 168), Cucumber raita (page 202) and chutney.

Channa Chaat

Throughout India savoury snacks are tremendously popular. They are sold by street vendors and are also available at special *chaat* shops which usually open in the early evening.

250 g (8 oz) chick peas
2 tablespoons sunflower oil
1 onion, sliced
1 teaspoon white cumin seeds
1 teaspoon black mustard seeds
⅓ teaspoon fenugreek seeds
2 teaspoons Mild Curry Paste (see page 15)
1 tablespoon tomato purée
4 small tomatoes, quartered
1 tablespoon vinegar
1 teaspoon dried mint
1 tablespoon freshly chopped coriander
salt
mint sprigs, to garnish

Preparation time: 10 minutes, plus soaking
Cooking time: 15–20 minutes
Serves 4

1. Carefully pick over the chick peas to remove any grit. Soak them overnight in a large pan with 1.25 litres (2 pints) water. Rinse the chick peas and return them to the pan with 1.25 litres (2 pints) of fresh water. Bring to the boil and cook for 45 minutes until cooked but not mushy. Strain and set aside.

2. Heat the oil in a large frying pan or wok and fry the onion until soft and transparent. Add the cumin, mustard and fenugreek seeds and stir-fry for 1 minute.

3. Add the curry paste, tomato purée, tomatoes, vinegar and enough water to prevent them sticking to the pan. Stir-fry for 3–5 minutes then add the mint, coriander and chick peas. Season with salt to taste.

4. Serve hot or cold, garnished with mint and accompanied by a salad.

Chicken Chaat

Murghi Chaat

To save time, substitute 1 × 425 g (15 oz) can of chick peas for the dried chick peas.

125 g (4 oz) chick peas
250 g (8 oz) boneless, skinless chicken breast
3–4 tablespoons lemon juice
2 tablespoons sunflower oil
1 onion, sliced
1 teaspoon white cumin seeds
1 teaspoon black mustard seeds
½ teaspoon fenugreek seeds
2 teaspoons Mild Curry Powder or Paste (see pages 14 or 15)
1 tablespoon tomato purée
4 small tomatoes, skinned and quartered
1 tablespoon vinegar
1 teaspoon dried mint
1 tablespoon freshly chopped coriander
salt
coriander sprigs, to garnish

Preparation time: 10–15 minutes, plus marinating
Cooking time: 20–25 minutes
Serves 4

1. Prepare the chick peas as described for Channa Chaat (left) or use canned chick peas.

2. Cut the chicken into 5 cm × 5 mm (2 × ¼ inch) strips and rub with lemon juice. Leave to marinate for 1–2 hours.

3. Heat the oil in a large frying pan or wok and stir-fry the chicken for 5 minutes until it goes white. Remove the chicken and set aside.

4. Set the frying pan or wok over a moderate heat and fry the onion until soft and transparent. Add the cumin, mustard and fenugreek seeds and stir-fry for 1 minute.

5. Add the curry powder or paste, tomato purée, tomatoes, vinegar and enough water to prevent them sticking to the pan. Stir-fry for 3–5 minutes then add the mint, chicken, chick peas and coriander. Season with salt and cook gently until heated through.

6. Serve hot, garnished with coriander.

Onion Fritters

Piaz Bhajis

A standby for *chaat* shops in eastern India, these savoury mouthfuls have become popular starters in Indian restaurants everywhere.

1 medium onion, cut into fine strips 2.5 cm (1 inch) long
oil for deep-frying
Batter:
6 tablespoons plain flour
3 tablespoons rice flour
1 teaspoon turmeric
1 teaspoon ground cumin
¼ teaspoon garam masala (see page 16)
salt
85 ml (3 fl oz) water
coriander sprigs, to garnish

Preparation time: 10 minutes
Cooking time: 30 minutes
Makes about 10

1. To make the batter, thoroughly mix the flours, turmeric, cumin, garam masala and salt in a large bowl. Stir in the water to make a batter that has a very thick consistency.

2. Combine the onion strips with the batter until they are completely coated.

3. Heat the oil in a deep pan to 180°C/350°F or until a cube of bread browns in 30 seconds. Take a spoonful of the onion mixture and shape it with your fingers to a ball 4 cm (1½ inches) in diameter. Using a slotted spoon, gently lower it into the hot oil. Allow 30 seconds for the bhaji to firm up, then shape another ball and lower it into the oil. Prepare each bhaji in this way until the onion mixture is used up. Cook each for 3 minutes, turning frequently, until the bhajis are golden brown.

4. Remove from the oil and drain on paper towels. Serve immediately, garnished with coriander.

Potato Chaat

Aloo Chaat

In the Indian *chaat* shop the customer is supplied with a range of spices to sprinkle over his hot snack, such as pounded red chillies, garam masala and ground, roasted cumin seeds. Serve them in tiny saucers so that your guests can mix them up to individual taste.

450 g (1 lb) potatoes
2 tablespoons sunflower or mustard blend oil
1 onion, sliced
1 teaspoon white cumin seeds
1 teaspoon black mustard seeds
½ teaspoon fenugreek seeds
2 teaspoons Mild Curry Powder or Paste (see pages 14 or 15)
1 tablespoon tomato purée
4 small tomatoes, quartered
1 tablespoon vinegar
1 teaspoon dried mint
1 tablespoon freshly chopped coriander
salt

Preparation time: 10 minutes
Cooking time: 30 minutes
Serves 4

1. Peel and dice the potatoes if they are large. If they are small and new leave whole with the skins on. Boil them until almost cooked, strain and set aside.

2. Heat the oil in a large frying pan or wok and stir-fry the onion until soft and transparent. Add the cumin, mustard and fenugreek seeds and stir-fry for 1 minute.

3. Add the curry powder or paste, tomato purée, tomatoes, vinegar and enough water to prevent them from sticking to the pan. Stir-fry for 3–5 minutes then add the mint, potatoes and coriander. Season with salt to taste.

4. Serve hot or cold, with a salad.

Pan-fried Meat Dumplings

Jaah Ngow Gow Jee

These little dumplings are a Korean variation on the ever-popular Chinese wonton. The wonton skins are pinched into decorative shapes, or the edges pulled down and twisted together to form a shape like a hat with a brim (like the Italian *cappelletti*). Serve hot as part of a main meal, or cold as part of assorted hors d'oeuvre.

*225 g (8 oz) topside of beef,
    minced*
½ teaspoon sesame seeds
1 teaspoon sesame oil
*2 teaspoons chopped spring
    onion*
1 teaspoon crushed garlic
½ teaspoon salt
100 g (4 oz) wonton skins
4 tablespoons sunflower oil
To garnish:
*turnip chrysanthemums (see
    page 62) (optional)*
parsley sprigs (optional)

Preparation time: 20 minutes
Cooking time: 15 minutes
Makes 30

1. Put all the ingredients except the wonton skins and sunflower oil into a bowl. Mix well. Put a small teaspoon of the mixture in the centre of each wonton skin. Fold the skin over and pinch together to form a semi-circle or triangle.

2. Bring a large saucepan of water to the boil. Drop the dumplings into the water and boil for 3 minutes. (Cook them in batches if necessary.) Remove the dumplings from the water with a slotted spoon and drain well on paper towels.

3. Heat the sunflower oil in a wok and stir-fry the dumplings until they are golden, turning them constantly. Remove from the wok with a strainer and drain.

4. To serve, arrange the dumplings on a heated serving dish. Garnish, if liked, with flower shapes cut from turnip and with sprigs of parsley, accompanied by Korean soy sauce as a dip.

Savoury-coated Courgettes

Fan Gwa Cha Dan

Tasty little mouthfuls like these would be served as part of.an extensive menu in Asia, but they make excellent finger foods for a buffet or with pre-dinner drinks.

*400 g (14 oz) large courgettes,
    thinly sliced*
salt
100 g (4 oz) bean curd
*100 g (4 oz) topside of
    beef, minced*
2 teaspoons sesame seeds
2 teaspoons sesame oil
*1 tablespoon chopped spring
    onion*
1 teaspoon crushed garlic
*½ teaspoon freshly ground black
    pepper*
100 g (4 oz) plain flour
2 eggs, beaten
4 tablespoons sunflower oil
To garnish:
carrot flowers (see page 62)
*spring onion tassels (see page
    61)*
parsley sprigs

Preparation time: 25 minutes
Cooking time: 10 minutes
Serves 4

1. Put the courgette slices in a single layer on a plate or board. Sprinkle with salt, then set aside.

2. Mash the bean curd. Squeeze out the water with your hands until the bean curd is dry. Place in a bowl with the beef, sesame seeds, sesame oil, spring onion, garlic, pepper and salt to taste. Mix well.

3. Rinse the courgettes in cold water and drain thoroughly. Dip one side of each slice in flour. Spread a little beef mixture on the floured side, pressing down well and spreading it out to cover. Dip both sides of each courgette slice in more flour, then in the beaten egg.

4. Heat the oil in a wok set over a moderate heat. Add the courgette slices, meat side down, and fry for 2–3 minutes until brown. Turn the slices over and fry until the underside is golden. Remove with a slotted spoon or strainer and drain on paper towels.

5. Arrange on a heated serving dish. Garnish with carrot flower shapes, spring onion tassels and parsley sprigs. Serve with Korean soy sauce as a dip (recipe on page 87).

Steamed Siu Mai

These Cantonese dim sum are full of flavour, with a soft texture achieved by steaming.

6 dried shiitake mushrooms
450 g (1 lb) minced pork
5 cm (2 inch) piece canned
    bamboo shoot, drained and
    finely chopped
100 g (4 oz) peeled prawns,
    finely chopped
2 eggs, lightly beaten
½ teaspoon salt
1 spring onion, finely chopped
a pinch of freshly ground white
    pepper
½ teaspoon sugar
2 tablespoons cornflour
2 tablespoons sunflower oil
1 teaspoon sesame oil
100 g (4 oz) wonton skins

Preparation time: 20 minutes
Cooking time: 10 minutes
Serves 4

1. Place the dried mushrooms in water to soak for 20 minutes. When they are ready, drain the mushrooms, remove the stems and chop the caps finely.

2. In a bowl, mix together the pork, bamboo shoot, prawns and eggs. Add the finely chopped mushrooms. To this mixture add the salt, spring onion, white pepper, sugar, cornflour and oils. Beat the ingredients together well.

3. Place about 1 teaspoon of the mixture in the centre of each wonton skin, then pull the edges up and twist to close tightly.

4. Place the wontons in a bamboo steamer set over a wok or saucepan of boiling water and steam gently for 10 minutes. Serve hot.

Illustrated on page 89

Korean Soy Sauce

This is a basic soy sauce enhanced with additional ingredients and served in individual bowls as a dip.

3 tablespoons soy sauce
1 tablespoon chopped spring
    onion
1 teaspoon sesame seeds
1 teaspoon sesame oil
1 teaspoon crushed garlic
½ teaspoon sugar
1 teaspoon vinegar
a pinch of chilli powder

Preparation time: 5 minutes

1. Mix all the ingredients together, blending them well. Serve immediately, divided equally between 4 small shallow dishes.

Pan-fried meat dumplings and Savoury-coated courgettes are typical of dim sum, *dainty morsels served in small but satisfying amounts to satisfy a yearning appetite.* Dim sum *means 'touch the heart' (or perhaps the stomach!); they are eaten at mid-morning or during the afternoon with tea rather than before a main meal. Korean soy sauce makes a cooling but piquant dip.*

Sauté Dumplings

Gow Jee Pien

These delicious dumplings demonstrate effectively how Chinese cooks use 'cross-cooking' – two different cooking methods in the preparation of one dish – to achieve delectable results.

450 g (1 lb) plain flour
175 ml (6 fl oz) boiling water
120 ml (6 fl oz) cold water
450 g (1 lb) minced pork
450 g (1 lb) peeled shrimps, minced
100 g (4 oz) finely chopped spring onion
1 tablespoon shredded root ginger
1 tablespoon light soy sauce
1½ teaspoons salt
freshly ground black pepper
1 bunch watercress, coarsely chopped
5½ tablespoons sunflower oil
Dip:
2 tablespoons wine vinegar
2 tablespoons soy sauce

Preparation time: 30 minutes
Cooking time: 10 minutes
Serves 4–6

1. To make the dough, place the flour in a bowl with the boiling water. Beat well until smooth. Leave to rest for 2–3 minutes. Add the cold water and knead well.

2. To make the filling, mix together the pork, shrimps, spring onion, ginger, soy sauce, salt and pepper. Add the chopped watercress and 1 tablespoon of the oil. Blend well together.

3. Roll the dough into a long sausage shape 4 cm (1½ inches) thick. Divide into 3 cm (1¼ inch) lengths. Roll each one flat to make small pancake shapes. Place 1 tablespoon of stuffing on each pancake then fold in half. Pinch the edges together to close firmly.

4. Heat a wok and place 3 tablespoons of oil in it. Tilt the wok several times until the surface is evenly oiled. Arrange the dumplings evenly over the surface of the pan. Turn the heat to high and shallow-fry for 2–3 minutes to brown the underside of the dumplings.

5. Add 120 ml (4 fl oz) water to the wok and cover. Steam the dumplings over high heat until almost all the water has evaporated. Remove the cover and pour in 1½ tablespoons of hot oil from the side. Reduce the heat and cook until all the liquid has evaporated.

6. Mix the wine vinegar and soy sauce together to make a dipping sauce.

7. Use a fish slice to loosen the dumplings from the wok. Place a large serving dish upside down over the wok, and invert the wok so that the dumplings sit on the dish browned side upwards. Serve hot, with the dipping sauce.

Crispy Wonton with Sweet and Sour Sauce

Wun Tun Cha Tiem Shun

Wonton are usually served as part of an assortment of *dim sum*, teatime snacks, in Chinese teahouses. Present them on trays of mixed hors d'oeuvres with the Steamed Siu Mai, Peking Dumplings and Sauté Dumplings.

175 g (6 oz) finely minced pork
50 g (2 oz) peeled shrimps, minced
1 teaspoon salt
pinch of freshly ground white pepper
1 tablespoon soy sauce
100 g (4 oz) wonton skins
600 ml (1 pint) sunflower oil
Sauce:
1 tablespoon cornflour
4 tablespoons water
1 tablespoon tomato purée
2 tablespoons wine vinegar
2 tablespoons orange juice
2 teaspoons light soy sauce
1½ tablespoons sugar
2 teaspoons sunflower oil

Preparation time: 30 minutes
Cooking time: 7–8 minutes
Serves 4

1. To make the stuffing, place the pork, minced shrimps, salt, pepper and soy sauce in a bowl and beat together until well blended. Place 1 teaspoon of stuffing in the centre of each wonton skin, gather up the corners and twist to enclose.

2. Heat the oil in a wok to 180°C/350°F or until a cube of bread browns in 30 seconds. Add the wonton and deep-fry for 2½ minutes, then remove and drain on paper towels. Keep the wonton hot.

3. Blend the cornflour with the water then place in a pan with the rest of the sauce ingredients. Stir together over medium heat for 3–4 minutes then pour into a bowl and serve with the wonton. Each guest dips the wonton into the sauce.

Peking Dumplings

Gow Jee Beijing

450 g (1 lb) plain flour
175 ml (6 fl oz) boiling water
120 ml (4 fl oz) cold water, plus 1 tablespoon
450 g (1 lb) minced pork
100 g (4 oz) peeled shrimps, minced
1 tablespoon finely chopped spring onion
1 tablespoon shredded root ginger
1 tablespoon light soy sauce
1½ teaspoons salt
1 teaspoon sugar
450 g (1 lb) Chinese cabbage, finely shredded and blanched
a pinch of freshly ground black pepper

Preparation time: 20 minutes
Cooking time: 20 minutes
Serves 4

1. To make the dough, place the flour in a bowl with the boiling water. Beat well until smooth. Leave to stand for a few minutes, then add 120 ml (4 fl oz) cold water. Knead well.

2. To make the filling, mix together the pork, shrimps, onion, ginger, soy sauce, salt, sugar and remaining water. Blend well, then add the cabbage and mix into a paste. Season with pepper to taste.

3. Roll the dough into a long sausage shape 4 cm (1½ inch) thick. Divide this into 3 cm (1¼ inch) lengths. Roll each one flat into a small pancake shape. Place 1 tablespoon of the stuffing on each pancake and fold the pancake in half. Pinch together to close, crimping the edges attractively.

4. Place the dumplings in a bamboo steamer set over a wok or saucepan of boiling water. Cook for 20 minutes and serve piping hot.

Clockwise from top left: Steamed siu mai (page 87); Peking dumplings; Sauté dumplings; Crispy wonton with sweet and sour sauce

Quail's Eggs on Toast with Mashed Shrimps

This elegant starter from the southern Chinese province of Canton can be eaten with the fingers.

750 g (1½ lb) peeled shrimps,
   mashed to a paste
50 g (2 oz) pork fat, minced
1 teaspoon minced root ginger
1 spring onion, finely chopped
1 egg white, lightly beaten
pinch of freshly ground white
   pepper
2 teaspoons salt
½ teaspoon sesame oil
1 tablespoon Chinese wine or
   dry sherry
1½ teaspoons cornflour
2 sprigs of parsley, finely
   chopped
1 slice cooked ham, finely
   chopped
8 thin slices white bread, crusts
   removed and cut in half
16 quail's eggs, hard-boiled and
   shelled
600 ml (1 pint) sunflower oil

Preparation time: 10 minutes
Cooking time: 5 minutes
Serves 6

1. In a bowl, mix together the shrimps, pork fat, ginger, spring onion, egg white, white pepper, salt, sesame oil, wine and cornflour. Beat all together until thoroughly blended.

2. Mix together the parsley and ham.

3. Divide the shrimp mixture between the 16 pieces of bread. Spread on in an even layer and place a quail's egg firmly in the centre of each. Sprinkle on the ham and parsley and press into the filling.

Quail's eggs on toast with mashed shrimps

4. Heat the oil in a wok to 180°C/350°F or until a cube of bread browns in 30 seconds. Gently place the bread slices, filling side down, in the oil. Fry until golden brown on both sides. Carefully remove from the oil with a slotted spoon. Drain on paper towels and serve hot.

Deep-fried Aubergine Cake

Keh Yung Juh Yook

In the Szechuan province of China this substantial starter would be served with a 'dip' of salt mixed with crushed Szechuan peppercorns.

25 g (1 oz) dried shrimps
3 aubergines, cut into 2.5 cm
   (1 inch) thick slices
75 g (3 oz) minced pork
½ teaspoon salt
2 spring onions, finely chopped
1 tablespoon soy sauce
1 tablespoon sesame oil
1 tablespoon shredded root
   ginger
125 g (5 oz) plain flour
50 g (2 oz) cornflour
1 egg, beaten
2 tablespoons water
600 ml (1 pint) sunflower oil

Preparation time: 10 minutes
Cooking time: 5 minutes
Serves 4–6

1. Soak the shrimps in water for 20 minutes. Drain, discard the water, and chop the shrimps finely.

2. Dust the aubergine slices with salt and leave for 10 minutes. Rinse in cold water and pat dry with paper towels. Cut a slit in each aubergine deep enough to hold the stuffing.

3. Mix together the minced pork, shrimps, salt, spring onions, soy sauce, sesame oil and ginger. Beat well together. Stuff each aubergine slice with ½ teaspoon of filling. Dust each slice with a little plain flour.

4. To make the batter, mix the remaining flour with the cornflour, egg and water to form a smooth paste. Dip each slice of aubergine in the batter to coat well.

5. Heat the oil in a wok to 180°C/350°F or until a cube of bread browns in 30 seconds. Deep-fry each aubergine slice until bright yellow. Cook in batches without crowding the pan. Lift out and drain on paper towels. Serve hot.

Chicken Spring Rolls

Spring rolls are the most popular dish in Vietnamese cuisine, for both rich and poor. They are usually filled with pork and crab, but a combination of any meat or seafood may be used. Serve as an appetizer with a bowl of Tangy Chilli Sauce (see right) or as a main course accompanied by a green salad. Serve the sauce separately in individual bowls as a dip.

Filling:
50 g (2 oz) cellophane noodles
2 tablespoons dried shiitake mushrooms
450 g (1 lb) chicken breast meat, skinned and cut into thin strips
3 garlic cloves, finely chopped
3 shallots, finely chopped
225 g (8 oz) crabmeat, canned or fresh
½ teaspoon freshly ground black pepper

Wrappers:
4 eggs, beaten
20 banh trang (rice papers)
450 ml (¾ pint) oil for deep frying
shredded spring onion, to garnish

Preparation time: 25 minutes, plus soaking
Cooking time: 15–20 minutes
Makes 20 rolls

1. Soak the cellophane noodles in water for 10 minutes. Drain, and cut into 2.5 cm (1 inch) pieces.

2. Soak the mushrooms in warm water for 25 minutes, drain, and discard the stalks. Slice the caps.

3. To make the filling, put all the ingredients in a bowl and mix well by hand. Divide the mixture into 20 portions and shape into small cylinders.

4. To assemble each spring roll, brush beaten egg over the entire surface of each piece of rice paper. Leave for a few seconds until soft and flexible. Place the prepared filling along the curved edge of the paper, roll once, then fold over the sides to enclose the filling and continue rolling. (The beaten egg holds the wrapper together.)

5. Heat the oil in a wok to 180°C/350°F or until a cube of bread browns in 30 seconds. Deep-fry about one-third of the spring rolls over moderate heat until golden brown. Remove with a slotted spoon and drain on paper towels. Fry the remaining spring rolls in the same way.

6. Serve hot or warm, garnished with shredded spring onion.

Tangy Chilli Sauce

This Vietnamese sauce is a hot dressing for cooked foods that can also be incorporated into many recipes. Combine 2 cloves of garlic with fresh or dried chillies (quantity to taste) and pound to a paste with 5 teaspoons of sugar. Squeeze in the juice of a lime quarter, then scrape out the flesh and add it to the bowl. Mix in 4 tablespoons of nam pla (fish gravy) and 5 tablespoons of water, stirring well. Use immediately. Alternatively, make a larger quantity, transfer to a tightly stoppered glass jar and store in the refrigerator for up to 1 week.

Vietnamese Crab Rolls

Not unlike the Chinese spring roll, this crisp delicacy has pork and crab as one of its favourite Vietnamese fillings. Serve with a bowl of Tangy Chilli Sauce (see box, above right).

Filling:
50 g (2 oz) cellophane noodles
6 dried shiitake mushrooms
1 tablespoon sunflower oil
450 g (1 lb) lean minced pork
8–10 spring onions, finely chopped
350 g (12 oz) crabmeat, canned or fresh
4 egg yolks, lightly beaten
1 teaspoon salt
½ teaspoon white pepper
Wrappers:
4 eggs, beaten
16 banh trang (rice papers)
450 ml (¾ pint) oil for deep frying
shredded spring onion, to garnish

Preparation time: 30 minutes, plus soaking
Cooking time: 20 minutes
Makes 16 rolls

1. Soak the cellophane noodles in warm water for 10 minutes. Drain, and cut into 2.5 cm (1 inch) pieces.

2. Soak the mushrooms in warm water for 25 minutes. Drain, discard the stalks and slice the caps.

3. To make the filling, combine the noodles with the mushrooms. Heat the oil in a wok and add the pork, mashing it constantly with the back of a spoon to break up any lumps. Cook for about 2 minutes. Remove from the heat and add the chopped spring onions, crabmeat, noodles and mushrooms, stirring constantly, then the egg yolks and

seasoning. Mix well. Divide into 16 portions and pat each into the shape of a cylinder, about a finger's length.

4. To assemble each crab roll, brush the beaten egg over the entire surface of each piece of rice paper. Leave for a few seconds until soft and flexible. Place the filling diagonally across the wrapper, roll over once, fold over the sides and roll once. Brush the exposed wrapper with beaten egg and roll into a neat package. (The beaten egg will seal the wrapper and keep the roll intact.) Place the crab rolls on a plate. Refrigerate the rolls, covered with cling film if liked until ready to fry.

5. Heat the oil in a wok to 180°C/350°F or until a cube of bread browns in 30 seconds. Deep-fry the crab rolls, 3 or 4 at a time, turning them with a slotted spoon, for about 4–5 minutes or until golden brown and crispy. Drain on paper towels and keep warm while frying the remaining rolls.

6. Serve the crab rolls hot, garnished with a few shredded spring onions.

Prawn Balls

Chao Tom

These irresistible little Vietnamese snacks can be served with drinks.

450 g (1 lb) raw prawns, shelled and deveined
2 teaspoons salt
50 g (2 oz) boiled fat pork, diced
1 small onion, finely chopped
4 garlic cloves, crushed
⅓ teaspoon baking powder
⅓ teaspoon white pepper
oil for deep-frying
lettuce leaves
fresh coriander leaves
ground roasted peanuts

Preparation time: 15 minutes, plus drying
Cooking time: 20 minutes
Serves 4

1. Prepare the prawn paste. Place the prawns in a large bowl with the salt. Using clean hands, scoop up the prawns, pressing and squeezing them to remove excess liquid. Transfer to a colander and rinse under cold water. Pat dry with paper towels or spread the mixture out and allow to dry naturally for 1 hour.

2. Spoon the prawns into a food processor or blender, add the fat pork and grind to a smooth paste. Scrape the paste into a bowl and add the remaining ingredients (except the oil).

3. Taking about 1 heaped teaspoon of the prawn paste at a time, roll it between well-oiled hands to form small balls about the size of shallots. Set aside.

4. Heat the oil in a wok or deep-fat fryer and cook the balls, a few at a time, until golden brown. Remove with a slotted spoon and drain on paper towels. Serve with lettuce and coriander leaves and a selection of purchased sauces, such as barbecue and plum sauce, sprinkled with roasted peanuts.

Transparent Spring Rolls

Goi Cuon

These spring rolls from Vietnam differ from their crispy counterparts (recipe on page 91) because the wrappers are uncooked and transparent, allowing the filling to be seen.

225 g (8 oz) pork fillet
50 g (2 oz) transparent rice vermicelli
100 g (4 oz) prawns, shelled, deveined and cut in half lengthways then cooked (see page 55)
50 g (2 oz) bean sprouts
12 sheets banh trang (rice paper)
1 small round lettuce, shredded
2 tablespoons shredded fresh mint leaves
3 tablespoons ground roasted peanuts
Nuoc mam giam sauce:
1 garlic clove, roughly chopped
1 fresh red chilli, chopped
1 tablespoon nuoc mam (fish gravy)
1 teaspoon lemon juice or vinegar
1 tablespoon tepid water
1 tablespoon sugar

Preparation time: 25 minutes
Cooking time: 25 minutes
Serves 4

1. Place the pork in a saucepan with water or vegetable stock to cover. Bring to the boil, lower the heat and simmer for 15–20 minutes or until the pork is cooked. Set aside and, when cold, cut into thin strips.

2. Bring a large saucepan of water to the boil, add the vermicelli and cook for 2 to 3 minutes or until tender. Drain in a colander, rinse well under cold water, then drain again. Place in a large bowl with the pork, prawns and bean sprouts. Mix gently.

3. Dip the sheets of banh trang in cold water, carefully shake off excess water, and lay the sheets on a clean work surface. Divide the filling between them, piling it along one end of each sheet, about 2.5 cm (1 inch) from the end and a similar distance from the sides.

4. Add lettuce, mint and peanuts to each filling, turn in the sides and roll up the banh trang. Arrange on a platter and serve with Nuoc mam giam sauce.

5. To make the sauce, grind the garlic and chilli together in a blender or food processor, or pound in a mortar and pestle. Transfer to a small bowl and stir in the remaining ingredients.

Sweet and Sour Spare Ribs

Pi Gwut Tiem Shun

This Cantonese version of spare ribs has become one of the most popular Chinese dishes in the West, and makes an excellent starter. Provide your guests with finger bowls and hot towels to clean their hands.

750 g (1½ lb) spare ribs, cut into 5 cm (2 inch) pieces (ask the butcher to do this for you)
4 tablespoons Chinese wine or dry sherry
4 tablespoons soy sauce
3½ tablespoons cornflour
600 ml (1 pint) vegetable oil
2 teaspoons chopped spring onion
2 teaspoons chopped root ginger
1 garlic clove, crushed
3 tablespoons sugar
3 tablespoons wine vinegar
2 tablespoons tomato ketchup
4–5 tablespoons water

Preparation time: 20 minutes, plus marinating
Cooking time: 10 minutes
Serves 4–6

1. Place the spare ribs in a bowl with the wine and 3 tablespoons soy sauce and leave to marinate for 20 minutes.

2. Toss the marinated spare ribs in 3 tablespoons cornflour. Heat the oil in a wok, put in the spare ribs and cook over medium heat for 2 minutes. Remove and drain on paper towels. Reheat the oil until it is smoking. Return the spare ribs to the wok and deep-fry again for 5 seconds. Remove and drain on paper towels.

3. Pour off all but 2 tablespoons of the oil from the wok and reheat. Add the remaining marinade, chopped spring onion, ginger and garlic and stir-fry for 1 minute. Add the sugar, vinegar, remaining soy sauce, tomato ketchup, remaining cornflour and water and bring to the boil. Place the spare ribs in this sauce and mix well. Serve immediately.

Spare Ribs with Black Bean Sauce

Pi Gwut Jeung Dow See

This version of spare ribs comes from Peking. It takes longer to cook than the Cantonese method, but the flavour is richer and the sauce more subtle.

5 tablespoons vegetable oil
750 g (1½ lb) spare ribs, cut into 5 cm (2 inch) lengths
3 tablespoons black bean paste
2 spring onions, finely chopped
2 thin slices root ginger, peeled and finely chopped
1 garlic clove, crushed
2 dried chillies, finely chopped
1 tablespoon Chinese wine or dry sherry
2 tablespoons soy sauce
1½ teaspoons sugar
2 teaspoons cornflour
1 tablespoon water

Preparation time: 15 minutes
Cooking time: about 1 hour 10 minutes
Serves 6

1. Heat the oil in a wok until it is smoking and add the spare ribs. Stir-fry for about 2 minutes, then transfer the ribs to a heatproof bowl.

2. Pour off most of the oil, leaving about 1 tablespoon, and reheat the wok. Put in the black bean paste, half the spring onions, the ginger, garlic and chillies. Stir-fry together for 30 seconds, then add the wine, soy sauce and sugar. Mix together, then stir into the bowl with the spare ribs. Place the bowl in a steamer and steam for 1 hour.

3. Pour off the liquid from the bowl into a pan and bring to the boil. Blend the cornflour with the water, and stir into the pan to make a smooth sauce.

4. Transfer the spare ribs to a warmed serving dish and sprinkle on the remaining spring onions. Pour over the hot sauce and serve immediately.

Far left: Transparent spring rolls, Prawn balls
Below: Sesame prawn toasts

Sesame Prawn Toasts

These fingers of toast with a crunchy topping from northern China are often served as a snack or hors d'oeuvre.

25 g (1 oz) pork fat, minced
125 g (5 oz) peeled prawns, minced
1 egg white, lightly beaten
pinch of salt
pinch of freshly ground white pepper
3 teaspoons cornflour
2 thin slices of white bread, crusts removed
75 g (3 oz) sesame seeds
600 ml (1 pint) vegetable oil

Preparation time: 15 minutes
Cooking time: 5 minutes
Serves 6

1. Mix together in a bowl the pork fat, prawns, egg white, salt, pepper and cornflour. Spread this mixture on to the bread slices.

2. Place the sesame seeds on a flat plate, then press on the bread slices, prawn side down, until thickly coated with the seeds.

3. Heat the oil in a wok to 180°C/350°F or until a cube of bread browns in 30 seconds. Carefully lower in the prawn toasts, spread side down, and deep-fry for 5 minutes, keeping them well immersed. Lift out and drain on paper towels. Cut each slice into 4 fingers.

FISH AND SHELLFISH

The quantity and variety of seafood and freshwater fish available in South-east Asia are unrivalled, and the range of recipes devised to present fish at its best is the most imaginative in the world. In Japan it may be delicately steamed, in China deep-fried, in India baked in a spicy sauce, always moist and full of flavour.

Charcoal-grilled Fish

Tandoori Macchi

Cooking in a *tandoor* or clay oven is a speciality of the Punjab in northern India. The food to be cooked is first marinated then baked over charcoal, and the flavour is incomparable. Fish is often rubbed with spices and wrapped in a banana leaf, then cooked in the ashes. This process keeps the fish beautifully moist.

1–1.5 kg (2–3½ lb) halibut,
  cleaned and washed
juice of 1 lemon
2 teaspoons salt
1½ teaspoons freshly ground
  pepper
Masala:
1 large onion
1 garlic clove
1 tablespoon freshly chopped
  coriander leaves
4 teaspoons natural yoghurt
2 teaspoons garam masala
  (see page 16)
1 teaspoon chilli powder
1 teaspoon ground coriander
1 teaspoon ground cumin
1 teaspoon ground fenugreek

Preparation time: 15 minutes, plus marinating
Cooking time: 25 minutes
Oven: 160°C, 325°F, Gas Mark 3
Serves 4

1. Select a baking dish which is large enough to take the whole fish, and line it with a sheet of foil 2½ times the size of the fish itself.

2. Make 4 or 5 deep cuts in both sides of the fish. Rub the lemon juice on the fish and sprinkle with the salt and pepper. Place the fish on the foil and set aside.

3. To make the masala, place the onion and garlic in a blender or food processor and chop finely. Place in a bowl with the remaining masala ingredients. Mix together well, and smear the mixture over the fish, inside the cuts and the cavity. Draw up the sides of the foil to make a tent shape, fold over and seal. Leave to marinate in a cool place for at least 4 hours.

4. Bake the fish in a preheated moderate oven for 20 minutes. Carefully remove the fish from the foil, place it on a wire mesh and finish cooking over a charcoal barbecue. Care is obviously needed at this stage: if the fish is already over-cooked, there is a risk that it will break up when transferred to the barbecue.

5. When the outside of the fish has taken colour and crisped up, carefully transfer it to a serving dish and serve immediately.

Fish au Caramel

Ca Bho

This Vietnamese recipe is particularly good with oily fish as these best withstand the long cooking time and contribute to the smoothness of the sauce. Black jack can be replaced by home-made caramel. To prepare this, heat 1 tablespoon sugar in a heavy-bottomed pan until it darkens. Remove the pan from the heat and carefully stir in 2 tablespoons cold water, protecting your hands with oven gloves as the mixture may spit.

450 g (1 lb) firm-fleshed fish,
  such as salmon, bass or
  mackerel, cleaned and
  filleted
5 tablespoons sunflower oil
2 shallots, thinly sliced
2 Chinese white carrots, scraped
  and thinly sliced
1 piece of root ginger or
  rhizome, shredded
2 tablespoons nuoc mam (fish
  gravy)
1 teaspoon black jack
½ teaspoon freshly ground black
  pepper

Preparation time: 15 minutes
Cooking time: 1 hour 15 minutes
Serves 4

1. Cut the cleaned and filleted fish into large pieces at least 5 cm (2 inches) thick.

2. Heat the oil in a large saucepan. Add the shallots and fry until soft but not coloured: this will take about 2–3 minutes. Arrange the pieces of fish on top of the softened shallots, tucking the thinly sliced carrots and shredded ginger between them.

3. Mix the nuoc mam, black jack and pepper in a small bowl. Stir in 4 tablespoons water. Pour this mixture over the fish, adding extra water to just cover the fish.

4. Bring the liquid to the boil, reduce the heat and simmer very gently, uncovered, for 1 hour, carefully turning the fish over several times. The cooking liquid should gradually reduce to a thick, flavoursome sauce.

5. Serve hot or cold with boiled rice.

Right: Steamed sea bass (top); Fish au caramel

Steamed Sea Bass

Ca Hap

Following the Chinese tradition, this Vietnamese version of a classic Asian fish dish presents the fish whole on a large serving dish, brought to the table steaming and succulent. Fresh bass combines beautifully with the sharp flavourings in this recipe, which can also be used for cod cutlets.

25 g (1 oz) transparent rice vermicelli
4 dried shiitake mushrooms
4 slices root ginger, cut into small strips
½ teaspoon ground salted black beans
½ white onion, sliced and separated into rings
1 teaspoon sugar
120 ml (4 fl oz) water
1 × 1.5 kg (3 lb) sea bass, gutted and cleaned
To garnish:
freshly chopped coriander
basil leaves

Preparation time: 15 minutes
Cooking time: about 30 minutes
Serves 4

1. Place the vermicelli in a bowl. Add warm water to cover and set aside to soak and swell for 15 minutes.

2. Place the dried mushrooms in a bowl and set aside to soak in warm water for 15 minutes. When both vermicelli and mushrooms are soft, drain both thoroughly. Cut the vermicelli into short lengths. Discard the mushroom stalks and chop the caps roughly.

3. Combine the vermicelli and mushrooms in a bowl with the ginger, black beans, onion, sugar and water. Mix well.

4. Place the sea bass in a shallow ovenproof dish that will fit inside a steamer. Pour the vermicelli mixture over the fish and steam for 10 minutes per 450 g (1 lb) or until the fish flakes easily when tested.

5. Transfer the fish and rice vermicelli mixture to a heated platter, sprinkle with fresh coriander and basil leaves and serve immediately.

Fried Octopus with Celery and Tomato

Muc Xao Can Tay Voi Ca Chua

In China, fish dishes are never enhanced with fish flavourings. Otherwise reminiscent of Mediterranean cooking, this Vietnamese recipe uses chicken stock to poach the octopus.

450 g (1 lb) octopus
250 ml (8 fl oz) corn oil
5 sticks celery, sliced diagonally
*   into 1 cm (½ inch) lengths*
1–2 garlic cloves, crushed
250 ml (8 fl oz) chicken stock
½ teaspoon salt
½ teaspoon sugar
3 tomatoes, skinned and
*   quartered*
½ teaspoon cornflour
3 tablespoons water
To garnish:
fresh coriander leaves
freshly ground white pepper

Preparation time: 15 minutes
Cooking time: about 30 minutes
Serves 4

1. Clean and prepare the octopus (see page 54). Score the flesh and cut it neatly into large thin slices. Unless the octopus is very young, it may be necessary to tenderize the slices with a meat mallet.

2. Heat the oil in a large frying pan, add the octopus and fry gently for 10 minutes. Using a slotted spoon, remove the octopus slices to a plate and set aside.

3. Add the celery to the oil remaining in the frying pan and cook for 10 seconds. Remove with a slotted spoon and set aside.

4. Drain all but 5 tablespoons of oil from the frying pan. To the oil remaining add the crushed garlic with the reserved octopus. Stir-fry for 30 seconds, then stir in the chicken stock, salt and sugar. Reduce the heat and cook for 10–15 minutes, or until the octopus is tender. Add the celery and tomatoes and cook for a further 2 minutes.

5. Combine the cornflour and water in a cup and mix to a cream. Add to the octopus mixture and cook, stirring constantly until the sauce thickens.

6. Transfer the mixture to a serving dish, sprinkle with coriander leaves and white pepper and serve immediately.

Bream with Lemon Grass

Ca Muoi Xa Ot

Many of the best recipes for sea bream come from Asia. This Vietnamese dish is simple but brings out the best flavour.

1 × 1.75 g (4 lb) sea bream or
  haddock, cleaned and scaled,
  but with head and tail intact
salt
2 tablespoons finely chopped
  lemon grass
6 tablespoons corn oil
½ teaspoon freshly ground black
  pepper

Preparation time: 15 minutes,
plus standing
Cooking time: 10–15 minutes
Serves 4

Left: Bream with lemon grass, Fried octopus with celery and tomato

1. Rub the skin of the bream with salt and rinse thoroughly inside and out with cold running water. Drain and set aside to dry.

2. Meanwhile, combine the lemon grass, 2 tablespoons of the oil, ½ teaspoon salt and pepper in a small bowl and mix well.

3. Score the skin on the back of the fish in several places to allow the sauce to be absorbed while cooking. Rub the lemon grass mixture into the fish, pressing it firmly into the incisions on the back. Place the fish in a shallow dish and set aside for 15 minutes.

4. Heat the remaining oil in a large frying pan and carefully slide the fish into it. Fry over moderate heat for 10–15 minutes, turning carefully once, until the flesh of the fish flakes easily when tested with a fork.

5. To serve, transfer the fish to a large heated platter and serve immediately with rice, pickled vegetables and Nuoc mam giam sauce (see page 92).

Prawns in Batter

While there are many imaginative Oriental recipes for prawns, plump Pacific specimens are just as delicious simply deep-fried. Use uncooked prawns and, after cleaning, open them out slightly to form a butterfly shape. Make a batter: sift 40 g (1½ oz) self-raising flour with 1 tablespoon plain flour and a pinch of salt. Add 2 teaspoons vegetable oil and 350 ml (12 fl oz) water and beat until smooth. Fold in 1 beaten egg white. Holding them by the tail, dip the prawns in the batter and deep-fry until golden in hot oil. Drain and serve hot with quartered lemons.

Spiced Prawns in Coconut Milk

Jhinga Pathia

This dish is popular in southern India, where coconuts and large orange-coloured prawns are plentiful.

3 tablespoons ghee
1 medium onion, sliced
3 garlic cloves, sliced
2 teaspoons ground coriander
1 teaspoon turmeric
1 teaspoon chilli powder
½ teaspoon salt
½ teaspoon freshly ground black
  pepper
1 teaspoon grated fresh ginger
2 tablespoons vinegar
250 ml (8 fl oz) coconut milk
  (see page 14)
450 g (1 lb) peeled cooked
  prawns
2 tablespoons tomato purée

Preparation time: 10 minutes
Cooking time: 25 minutes
Serves 4

1. Melt the ghee in a heavy pan, add the onion and garlic and fry gently until soft.

2. Mix the spices and seasonings to a paste with the vinegar. Add this mixture to the pan and fry for a further 3 minutes, stirring continuously.

3. Stir in the coconut milk, and simmer, stirring, for 5 minutes. Add the prawns and tomato purée and simmer for 2 minutes until the prawns are well coated in the sauce. Transfer to a heated serving dish and serve immediately.

Madras Dry Prawn Curry

Jhinga Kari Madrasi

Some of the best curries of India are 'dry', that is not swimming in sauce. From Madras come superb seafood dishes like this one, in which the mixture of spices is relatively mild.

3 tablespoons ghee
1 small onion, sliced
2 garlic cloves, sliced
½ teaspoon freshly grated ginger
1 teaspoon ground coriander
½ teaspoon turmeric
½ teaspoon ground cumin
½ teaspoon salt
450 g (1 lb) peeled cooked
  prawns
1 tablespoon vinegar
a pinch of chilli powder, to
  garnish

Preparation time: 5 minutes
Cooking time: 10–12 minutes
Serves 4

1. Melt the ghee in a heavy pan. Add the onion, garlic and ginger and fry gently until soft. Add the spices and salt and fry for a further 3 minutes, stirring the mixture constantly.

2. Reduce the heat to very low. Add the prawns and toss lightly for 1 minute until they are coated with the spices. Stir in the vinegar, then increase the heat and cook for 30 seconds.

3. Transfer to a heated serving dish, sprinkle with chilli powder and serve immediately.

Prawns and Spinach

Saag Jhinga

The combination of spinach and prawns in this Indian dish is unusual, yet the two flavours complement each other very well. Quick stir-frying ensures that the flavour is fresh and the texture has 'bite'.

450 g (1 lb) spinach
3 tablespoons ghee
1 large onion, sliced
2 garlic cloves, sliced
1 tablespoon tomato purée
½ teaspoon garam masala (see page 16)
1½ teaspoons ground coriander
½ teaspoon turmeric
½ teaspoon chilli powder
½ teaspoon ground ginger
1 teaspoon salt
450 g (1 lb) peeled cooked prawns

Preparation time: 10 minutes
Cooking time: 20 minutes
Serves 4

1. Wash the spinach in several changes of cold water. Remove the thick stalks and chop the leaves roughly.

2. Melt the ghee in a heavy pan, add the onion and garlic and fry gently until soft. Stir in the tomato purée and fry, stirring, for 1 minute. Add the spices and salt and fry for a further 5 minutes, stirring constantly.

3. Add the chopped spinach to the pan and toss with a wooden spoon. Cook until the spinach has softened, stirring frequently.

4. Add the prawns and cook for a further 5 minutes, turning the prawns gently to coat them with the spinach. Transfer to a heated dish and serve immediately.

White Fish in Coconut

Mach Tarki

This recipe comes from Orissa near the Bay of Bengal in north-eastern India, and is good with any firm white fish.

4 tablespoons sunflower or mustard blend oil
1 teaspoon black mustard seeds
½ teaspoon turmeric
1 onion, chopped very finely
1 tablespoon Mild Curry Paste (see page 15)
flesh of ½ fresh coconut plus its milk or 2 tablespoons desiccated coconut
300 ml (½ pint) milk
4 haddock fillets, about 175 g (6 oz) each
1 tablespoon chopped coriander
salt
To garnish:
2 tablespoons shredded fresh coconut
sprigs of coriander

Preparation time: 15 minutes
Cooking time: 25 minutes
Serves 4

1. Heat the oil in a large flat frying pan and stir-fry the mustard seeds and turmeric for 1 minute. Add the onion and continue to stir-fry for 3 minutes. Stir in the curry paste. Let the mixture simmer.

2. If using fresh coconut, purée the white flesh with the coconut milk in a food processor or blender. Alternatively, mix the desiccated coconut with enough water to make a paste. Add the purée or paste to the frying pan and stir-fry to simmering point. Stir in the milk.

3. Place the fish fillets in the pan so that the sauce just covers them. Simmer gently for 10 minutes. Test the fish with a fork to see if it is cooked through. It should be almost ready, depending on thickness. Add the chopped coriander and season with salt to taste. Continue to simmer for 2–3 minutes until the fish is completely cooked.

4. Transfer the fish and sauce carefully to a heated serving dish and serve immediately, garnished with coconut and coriander sprigs.

Marinated Mackerel

Tatsuta-age

Tatsuta-age is a Japanese method of frying. In this recipe the fish is marinated before frying to give it extra flavour. To obtain ginger juice, grate fresh root ginger, then squeeze out the juice.

2 medium mackerel, total weight about 750 g (1½ lb), filleted
4 tablespoons shoyu (Japanese soy sauce)
2 tablespoons sake (rice wine)
1 teaspoon ginger juice
50 g (2 oz) cornflour
vegetable oil for deep-frying
8 small button mushrooms, wiped and trimmed

To garnish:
4 lemon wedges
1 × 5 cm (2 inch) piece daikon (Japanese radish), peeled and grated

Preparation time: 15 minutes, plus marinating
Cooking time: 6 minutes
Serves 4

1. Using tweezers, remove all the bones from the centre of the mackerel fillets. Place the fillets skin side down on a board and cut slightly on the diagonal into slices about 2.5 cm (1 inch) thick.

2. Put the shoyu in a shallow dish with the sake and ginger juice and mix well. Add the mackerel slices, cover, and leave to marinate for about 10 minutes, stirring occasionally to ensure the slices of fish are evenly coated.

3. Drain the mackerel thoroughly. Coat the slices in some of the cornflour.

4. Heat the oil in a deep-fat frier or deep frying pan to 160°C/325°F or until a cube of bread browns in 45 seconds. Deep-fry the mackerel slices until golden brown. Remove from the oil with a perforated spoon and drain on paper towels. Keep hot.

5. Coat the mushrooms in the remaining cornflour. Add to the hot oil and deep-fry for 1 minute. Remove and drain as for the mackerel slices.

6. Arrange a few slices of mackerel and 2 mushrooms on each of 2 warmed individual plates. Garnish each serving with a lemon wedge, and some of the grated daikon. Serve immediately.

Each mouthful of Devilled Sri Lankan squid (top) is a delicious combination of tender fish and crisp spicy batter. By contrast, White fish in coconut (bottom) is a mild and succulent dish, excellent for a family dinner served with Lime rice (page 189) and Dry-fried spinach (page 164).

Devilled Sri Lankan Squid

Serve this dish with Indian Salad (see page 168) and Cucumber Raita (see page 202).

375 g (12 oz) squid
2 teaspoons Mild Curry Powder (see page 14)
1 teaspoon garam masala (see page 16)
1 teaspoon mango powder (optional)

50 g (2 oz) plain flour
50 g (2 oz) semolina
2 eggs, beaten
corn oil for frying
To garnish:
lemon slices, quartered
coriander leaves

Preparation time: 15 minutes
Cooking time: 8 minutes
Serves 2

1. Clean and prepare the squid (see page 54). Slice it into rings.

2. Combine the curry powder, garam masala, mango powder (if using), flour and semolina on a flat plate. Dip the slices of squid into the beaten egg and coat with the flour mixture.

3. In a large saucepan heat the oil to 180°C/350°F or until a cube of bread browns in 30 seconds. Carefully place the squid in the hot oil and deep-fry for 5–8 minutes, depending on thickness, until they are crisp and golden. (Shallow-fry the squid if you prefer.) Lift out the squid with a slotted spoon and drain well on paper towels.

4. Transfer to a heated serving dish and garnish with lemon quarters and coriander leaves before serving.

Fish Bergedel

When the Dutch and Portuguese brought their potato-eating habit to South-east Asia, it rubbed off on the natives: bergedel is a rendering of the Dutch *frikadeller*, a potato and meat ball. Bergedel are often used as dumplings in spicy soups.

175 g (6 oz) cod
450 g (1 lb) mashed potatoes
4 tablespoons soft white
 breadcrumbs
1 tablespoon ground coriander
½ teaspoon pepper
2 teaspoons salt
1 tablespoon chopped onion
1 egg, lightly beaten
400 ml (14 fl oz) corn oil

Preparation time: 20 minutes, plus cooling
Cooking time: 20 minutes
Serves 4

1. Place the cod in a saucepan and just cover with cold water. Set the pan over a moderate heat. When the water comes to the boil, reduce the heat and poach the fish for 5 minutes, covered. Drain, leave to cool, and flake the fish.

2. Place the fish in a large bowl with the mashed potato, breadcrumbs, ground coriander, pepper, salt and chopped onion. Combine well and stir in the beaten egg to bind the mixture.

3. Using floured hands, shape the mixture into balls, each the size of a plum but slightly flattened.

4. Heat the oil in a deep pan to 180°C/350°F or until a cube of bread browns in 30 seconds. Deep-fry the bergedel in batches of 3 or 4 at a time until they are golden brown. Lift from the oil with a slotted spoon and drain on paper towels. Serve hot or cold with sliced cucumber or Festive Vegetable Achar (see page 170).

Vietnamese green salad (page 167);
Thai-style shallow-fried fish

Tamarind Fish Curry

Pla Mak Kam Gaeng Ped

The range of spicy seafood dishes belonging to South-east Asian cooking is wide and varied. Many have a liquid base of coconut milk; the other common liquid base is the sour but fruity juice of the tamarind. If you cannot obtain tamarind paste, use 1 tablespoon of lemon juice for 1 tablespoon tamarind paste and the same amount of water.

2 tablespoons tamarind paste
500 ml (18 fl oz) water
350 g (12 oz) halibut
1 stalk lemon grass, sliced from
 5 cm (2 inches) of thick end
½ large onion, quartered
1 teaspoon turmeric powder
2 red chillies
1 teaspoon blachan
4 tablespoons vegetable oil
1 tablespoon light soy sauce
1 teaspoon sugar
1 stalk lemon grass, bruised
1 tomato, quartered

Preparation time: 15 minutes, plus soaking
Cooking time: 12 minutes
Serves 4

1. Dissolve the tamarind in the water and strain through a fine sieve. Discard the pith.

2. Cut the halibut into thick chunks and leave to soak in the tamarind liquid until it is required for cooking.

3. Grind the lemon grass, onion, turmeric, chillies and shrimp paste together in a pestle and mortar, or combine in a blender.

4. Heat the oil in a wok or frying pan and fry the ground spices for 3 minutes over a moderate heat. Strain the tamarind liquid off the fish and add two-thirds of it to the pan.

5. Add the soy sauce, sugar, bruised lemon grass and tomato quarters to the pan. Bring to the boil.

6. Add the chunks of marinated fish and cook for 2 minutes until heated through. Check the seasoning and add the remaining tamarind liquid if necessary. Transfer to a heated serving dish and serve immediately.

Thai-style Shallow-fried Fish

Pla Too Tord

If flounder of good quality are not available, substitute sole. This dish depends on very fresh fish for success.

6 small flounder fillets
5 tablespoons corn oil
1 tablespoon lemon juice
salt
freshly ground black pepper
flour for coating
450 g (1 lb) bean sprouts
100 g (4 oz) quartered
*   mushrooms*
15 g ($\frac{1}{2}$ oz) Chinese leaves,
*   finely shredded*
100 g (4 oz) peeled cooked
*   prawns*
1 tablespoon light soy sauce

Preparation time: 15 minutes, plus marinating
Cooking time: 10–12 minutes
Serves 4

1. Cut the fish fillets into 1 cm ($\frac{1}{2}$ inch) wide strips and marinate in 1 tablespoon of the oil, lemon juice and salt and pepper to taste for 30 minutes.

2. Drain the fish strips and dust lightly with seasoned flour.

3. Heat 2 tablespoons of the oil in a wok. Add the fish and stir-fry over moderate heat for about 5 minutes. Remove the fish from the wok and keep warm.

4. Add the remaining oil to the wok. Stir in the bean sprouts and mushrooms and stir-fry for 2–3 minutes. Add the Chinese leaves and prawns. Stir in the soy sauce and heat through.

5. Gently fold in the fried fish. Adjust the seasoning if necessary. When the fish is heated through – about 3 minutes – transfer the fish and vegetables to a heated serving dish. Serve hot, garnished with lemon quarters.

Prawn Satay with Peanut Sauce

Gung Foi Satay

This Indonesian classic has become popular throughout the West. Satay (or saté) is basically spiced marinated meat or seafood on skewers, grilled and served with traditional peanut sauce. The name is thought to mean 'three pieces', from the number of chunks on each skewer.

24 large uncooked prawns, shelled
2 tablespoons coriander powder
1 tablespoon cumin powder
1 teaspoon turmeric powder
1 teaspoon chilli powder
½ onion, minced
1 tablespoon sugar
2 tablespoons salt
Peanut sauce:
2 stalks lemon grass
½ large onion, sliced
1 teaspoon chilli powder
1 teaspoon blachan (shrimp paste)
1 teaspoon salt
4 tablespoons peanut or hazelnut oil
1 tablespoon tamarind paste
250 ml (8 fl oz) water
1 tablespoon sugar
175 g (6 oz) peanuts, ground

Preparation time: 35 minutes, plus marinating
Cooking time: 4 minutes per skewer, and 7 minutes for the sauce
Serves 4

1. Slit each prawn down the back and remove the dark vein. Wash and dry.

2. Combine all the spice powders with the onion, sugar and salt and coat the prawns in the mixture. Set aside for 30 minutes for the prawns to absorb the flavours.

3. Meanwhile, make the Peanut sauce. Slice the lemon grass, using only 5 cm (2 inches) of the thick bulb end. Place in a blender with the sliced onion, chilli powder, shrimp paste and salt and purée to a fine consistency.

4. Heat the oil in a frying pan over a high heat. When it is smoking, add the purée, reduce the heat slightly and fry for 3 minutes.

5. Dissolve the tamarind paste in water and strain. Squeeze out and discard the pith. Add the juice to the pan with the sugar and ground peanuts and cook for 4 minutes over a low heat, stirring constantly to prevent lumps forming. Adjust the seasoning if necessary and transfer the sauce to a serving bowl.

6. Thread the prawns on to 8 bamboo shewers, 3 to each. Place the skewers through the tail and the thickest part of the prawns. Press any left-over spice mixture on to the prawns and grill over hot charcoal or under a preheated grill for 4 minutes, turning once. Serve immediately, with the Peanut sauce as a dip.

Prawn Sambal

Jheenga Sambal

The word 'sambal' is of Indian origin and refers to any chilli-hot dish in a thick spicy paste. It was taken to Malaysia by Indian workers.

300 g (11 oz) uncooked prawns
5 tablespoons sunflower oil
2 large onions, finely sliced
3 fresh red chillies
1 stalk lemon grass
2 garlic cloves
1 teaspoon blachan (shrimp paste)
6 candlenuts
2 tomatoes, quartered
2 teaspoons salt
1 teaspoon sugar
1 tablespoon lemon juice
120 ml (4 fl oz) water

Preparation time: 20 minutes
Cooking time: 8 minutes
Serves 4

1. Shell and clean the prawns and set aside until required.

2. Heat the oil in a wok or frying pan until it is smoking. Fry one of the sliced onions until it is soft.

3. Using a pestle and mortar or electric blender, grind together the red chillies, lemon grass, garlic, remaining onion, shrimp paste and candlenuts. Add this purée to the pan and combine with the softened onion.

4. Add the tomatoes and prawns and cook for 1 minute, stirring continuously. Do not overcook the prawns or they will be rubbery.

5. Add the salt, sugar, lemon juice and water and cook for a further 2 minutes. Transfer to a warmed platter and serve immediately, with boiled rice.

Crystal Prawns

This elegant Cantonese dish is quick to prepare and makes a delicious lunch dish or can be served as a starter.

225 g (8 oz) uncooked prawns, peeled and deveined
2 egg whites
1 tablespoon Chinese wine or dry sherry
a pinch of sugar
1 teaspoon salt
a pinch of freshly ground white pepper
50 g (2 oz) cornflour
600 ml (1 pint) sunflower oil
1 × 2.5 cm (1 inch) piece fresh root ginger, finely chopped
2 spring onions, finely chopped
25 g (1 oz) frozen peas, lightly boiled and drained
1 tablespoon chicken stock
a few drops of sesame oil

Preparation time: 10 minutes
Cooking time: 5 minutes
Serves 4

1. Place the prawns in a bowl with egg whites, 1 teaspoon Chinese wine, the sugar, ½ teaspoon salt, the white pepper and 40 g (1½ oz) cornflour and combine well.

2. Heat the oil in a wok. Add the prawns and stir-fry gently for about 2 minutes. Remove from the oil and drain on paper towels

3. Pour off most of the oil, leaving enough to coat the bottom of the wok. Reheat the wok and add the chopped ginger and spring onions. Stir-fry briefly, then add the remaining salt, peas, wine, white pepper, stock and cornflour.

4. Replace the prawns in the wok and heat through in the sauce. Transfer to a serving dish and sprinkle with sesame oil.

Prawn satay with peanut sauce (top);
Prawn sambal

When cooking Salt-grilled fish (top) it is important to preserve the original shape so that it can be elegantly presented. Salmon with sake lees (bottom) is a delicious dinner party dish, needing only a simple accompaniment of boiled rice.

Salt-grilled Fish

Sakana no Shioyaki

This Japanese method of preparing protein-rich fish is surprisingly simple – the fat in the skin of the fish oozes out during cooking and the salt creates moisture so that the flesh is deliciously moist. Hot steamed rice and green tea make good accompaniments.

1 × 750 g (1½ lb) mackerel or red snapper
salt
a few lemon wedges, to garnish
shoyu (Japanese soy sauce) (optional)

Preparation time: 15 minutes, plus standing
Cooking time: 10 minutes
Serves 4

1. Remove the scales from the fish, leaving the skin intact. Clean the fish thoroughly and remove the head, if wished, then sprinkle lightly inside and out with salt. Leave to stand for about 30 minutes.

2. Make 3 diagonal slashes on the surface of the fish. Grill under a preheated grill for about 5 minutes on each side, until the fish flakes easily when tested with a fork; do not overcook.

3. Serve hot with lemon wedges. Hand shoyu separately, if liked.

Fish Teriyaki

Tara no Teriyaki

In Japanese cooking, *teriyaki* refers to a sweet soy-sauce-based glaze that is applied in the last stages of grilling (or pan-frying) to fish, chicken, beef or pork. *Teri* literally translates as 'gloss' and describes the sheen of the sauce that goes over the grilled (*yaki*) foods. Oily fish such as mackerel, tuna and salmon are best suited to this cooking method, but it works well with cod too.

4 fish steaks or whole mackerel, cleaned and filleted
Tare sauce:
2 tablespoons shoyu (Japanese soy sauce)
2 tablespoons mirin (sweet rice wine)
1 tablespoon sake
1 tablespoon sugar

Preparation time: 10 minutes
Cooking time: 25 minutes
Serves 4

1. Make the sauce first. Put the shoyu, mirin, sake and sugar in a small saucepan and boil for 1 minute. Remove the pan from the heat.

2. Thread each fish steak or mackerel on to 2 lightly greased metal skewers, then cook the fish under a preheated hot grill until lightly browned on both sides. Remove from the grill and brush with some of the tare sauce. Return to the heat and cook until the tare dries. Repeat with more sauce until it is all used up. Turn the skewers in the fish each time you remove them from the grill, to prevent them sticking to the fish.

3. Remove the skewers from the fish carefully, so that the fish retains a nice shape. Place the fish on warmed individual plates and serve immediately, with steamed vegetables as an accompaniment.

Salmon with Sake Lees

Shake no Kasuzuke

When fresh salmon is plentiful, this is an excellent way to preserve some for later use. This Japanese dish makes a quick entrée and will keep for several months in the refrigerator. The flavour of kasu goes well with salmon, but it is strongly flavoured and should therefore be eaten in small quantities – until you acquire a taste for it, that is!

4 fresh salmon steaks
1½ tablespoons salt
Marinade:
450 ml (¾ pint) kasu (rice wine lees)
225 g (8 oz) sugar
To garnish:
1 small lettuce, shredded
½ small daikon (Japanese radish), puréed

Preparation time: 20 minutes, plus salting (see method)
Cooking time: 7 minutes
Serves 4

1. Preparation for this dish should begin 11 days before serving. Put the salmon steaks in a bowl and sprinkle both sides with the salt. Cover with plastic wrap or foil and leave in the refrigerator for 4 days to allow the flesh of the salmon to become firm.

2. Drain the fish well, then pat dry with paper towels. Mix together the marinade ingredients and use to coat both sides of the salmon. Place in a dish, cover, and keep in the refrigerator for 7 days before serving.

3. Remove most of the marinade from the salmon. Place the steaks under a preheated grill and grill for about 7 minutes on one side only, until the fish flakes easily when tested with a fork. Take care not to overcook as the marinade causes the fish to char easily.

4. Serve hot, with small mounds of shredded lettuce and puréed daikon.

Fish in Japanese Cooking

While only a small portion of the country is suitable for farming, the waters around Japan are rich fishing grounds which are a major source of food. Fish dishes range from the superbly refined classic recipes to simple family fare such as plain fried plaice garnished with grated daikon. Braised fish with rice and a green vegetable is the basis of a quick, simple meal. Choose cod, haddock, salmon or hake, cut into steaks, and fry gently in oil with a chopped onion. Make a sauce from 2 tablespoons each of sake, water, sugar and shoyu and add to the pan. Cover and simmer for 10 minutes or until the fish flakes easily when tested with a fork.

Assorted Raw Fish

Sashimi

Sashimi is perhaps the queen of Japanese delicacies, a dish of beautifully sliced fresh, raw fish whose presentation is an artistic triumph. You can use tuna, salmon, lemon sole, Dover sole, sea bass, sea bream, mackerel, prawns, squid, cuttlefish, bonito, carp, trout or even salmon roe. Whichever you choose, it must be very fresh, and you need at least 3 different types to make an interesting main course.

750 g (1½ lb) mixed fresh fish
1 teaspoon wasabi powder
shoyu (Japanese soy sauce)
1 × 5 cm (2 inch) piece daikon,
peeled and shredded

Preparation time: 1 hour
Serves 4

1. Clean and fillet the fish. If using mackerel, remove the transparent skin from each fillet. Prepare the squid as for cooking (see page 54). Do not wash the fish after it has been filleted, or it will be too wet and not have a good texture for serving raw. Pat it dry with paper towels.

2. Slice the fish with a very sharp knife (see page 52). Flat fish needs to be paper thin; sea bream and bass 1 cm (½ inch) thick. Tuna needs to be cut into bite-sized pieces 5 mm–1 cm (¼–½ inch) thick. Skin squid, octopus and cuttlefish, then cut into strips 5 cm (2 inches) long and 5 mm (¼ inch) wide.

3. Put the wasabi powder in an egg cup, add 1 teaspoon cold water and stir; the consistency should be firm, but not lumpy. Keep the egg cup well covered until serving time in order to preserve the pungency of the wasabi. Pour the shoyu into individual shallow dishes.

4. To serve, arrange the different fish decoratively on a large serving platter or board and garnish with the shredded daikon. Mould the wasabi into a small mound and place on the serving platter. Guests should mix a little of the wasabi with shoyu, then dip a slice of fish into this 'sauce' before eating. Boiled rice is eaten between mouthfuls of sashimi to cool down the palate – the combination of wasabi and shoyu is quite hot and salty.

Paper-wrapped Fish

Wrapping small pieces of food in paper before deep-frying is a popular cooking method in the western Chinese province of Szechuan. While the paper seals in flavour, it prevents the food absorbing too much oil.

450 g (1 lb) fish fillets (sole, plaice, bream)
1 teaspoon salt
1 teaspoon pale dry sherry
1 tablespoon oil
1 tablespoon shredded fresh root ginger
1 tablespoon shredded spring onion
oil for deep frying
spring onion tassels, to garnish (see page 61)

Preparation time: 15 minutes
Cooking time: 10 minutes
Serves 4

Left: Assorted raw fish
Below: Paper-wrapped fish

1. Cut each fish fillet into 2.5 cm (1 inch) squares, about 5 mm ($\frac{1}{4}$ inch) thick. Sprinkle with the salt and sherry and leave to marinate for 10 minutes.

2. Cut a 15 cm (6 inch) square piece of greaseproof paper or non-stick parchment for each piece of fish. Brush the squares of paper with oil. Place one slice of fish and two pieces of shredded ginger and spring onion on each oiled square. Fold into envelopes, tucking in the flaps to secure (see page 38).

3. Heat the oil in a wok to 180°C/350°F or until a cube of bread browns in 30 seconds. Deep-fry the wrapped fish for 3 minutes. Drain on paper towels, arrange on a serving plate and garnish with the spring onion tassels. The paper wrapping is opened by the guests.

Cantonese Lobster

This most luxurious of shellfish is a special occasion food in China. The way the lobster is presented in this recipe allows it to be eaten with the fingers.

1 lobster, about 1.5 kg (3 lb), alive if possible
5 tablespoons sunflower oil
4 slices root ginger, peeled and shredded
4 spring onions, cut into 2.5 cm (1 inch) lengths
$\frac{1}{2}$ teaspoon salt
150 ml ($\frac{1}{4}$ pint) chicken stock
1$\frac{1}{2}$ tablespoons soy sauce
2 tablespoons Chinese wine or dry sherry

Preparation time: 20 minutes
Cooking time: about 10 minutes
Serves 4

1. Kill the lobster (or ask the fishmonger to do this for you), clean it and chop through the shell into large bite-sized pieces. (See page 53.)

2. Heat the oil in a wok until it is smoking. Add the lobster pieces, cover and cook in the hot oil for 3 minutes. Lift out and drain on paper towels.

3. Add the ginger, spring onions and salt and stir in the hot oil for 1 minute. Add the stock, soy sauce and wine. Bring to the boil, stirring, then add the pieces of lobster. Turn them in the stock, and cover firmly. Leave to cook over high heat for 4 minutes, when the liquid should have reduced by about one-third.

4. Transfer the lobster pieces to a deep-sided serving dish, pour over the sauce and serve.

Fish in Vinegar Sauce

The cooking of the great metropolis of Shanghai in eastern China incorporates the best of the country's regional traditions. The sauce for this fish dish is richly flavoured and very smooth.

50 g (2 oz) lard
2–3 spring onions, white part only
450 g (1 lb) fish fillets (cod, halibut, snapper or John Dory), cut into chunks
2 tablespoons dry sherry
2 tablespoons soy sauce
150 ml (¼ pint) chicken stock or water
1 teaspoon finely chopped fresh ginger root
3 tablespoons wine vinegar
2 tablespoons sugar
2 teaspoons cornflour
1 teaspoon sesame oil

Preparation time: 5 minutes
Cooking time: 20 minutes
Serves 4

1. Melt the lard in a frying pan set over medium heat. Chop the spring onions into 2.5 cm (1 inch) pieces and add them to the pan. Fry until golden.

2. Add the fish pieces and sherry, and cook until almost all of the sherry has evaporated.

3. Add the soy sauce, stock or water, ginger and half the vinegar and sugar. Bring to the boil, reduce the heat, and simmer for 5 minutes.

4. Add the remaining vinegar and sugar. Mix the cornflour to a thin paste with 1 tablespoon water and add to the sauce, stirring constantly until it has thickened.

5. Transfer the fish in sauce to a heated platter and serve immediately, sprinkling the sesame seed oil on top.

Szechuan Crispy Whole Fish in Hot 'Tou Pan' Sauce

The attraction of this dish lies in the contrast of flavour between the rich spiciness of the sauce and the chunky flesh of the fish.

1 × 1 kg (2¼ lb) fish (carp, perch or pike)
3 slices root ginger, shredded and chopped
1 teaspoon salt
vegetable oil for deep-frying
3 tablespoons plain flour
3 spring onions, trimmed
4 tablespoons lard
2 rashers bacon, rinded and chopped
25 g (1 oz) Szechuan Ja-Chai pickle, chopped
25 g (1 oz) Chinese Snow Pickle, chopped (optional)
1 small green pepper, seeded and cut into strips
1 small red pepper, seeded and cut into strips
2 chilli peppers, seeded and shredded
1 tablespoon sugar
1 tablespoon yellow bean sauce
2 tablespoons dark soy sauce
2 tablespoons chicken stock
2 tablespoons dry sherry
1 tablespoon cornflour

Left: Szechuan crispy whole fish in hot 'tou pan' sauce

Preparation time: 20 minutes
Cooking time: 13–14 minutes
Serves 4–5

1. Scale and clean the fish. Mix the ginger with the salt and 1 tablespoon of the oil. Rub the fish inside and out with this mixture, then dust with 2 tablespoons of the flour.

2. Heat the oil in a deep-sided frying pan to 180°C/350°F or until a cube of bread browns in 30 seconds. Lower in the fish and deep-fry for 6–7 minutes. Remove the fish from the pan with a slotted spoon and drain on paper towels.

3. Cut the spring onions into 2.5 cm (1 inch) lengths.

4. Heat the lard in a wok or a frying pan. When it is hot, add the spring onions, bacon, pickles and all the peppers. Stir-fry over high heat for 2 minutes. Add the sugar, sauces, stock and sherry and stir-fry for a further 1½ minutes.

5. Mix the cornflour with 4 tablespoons of cold water to make a thin paste. Slowly pour the blended cornflour into the sauce, stirring constantly until it is thickened.

6. Lower the fish into the sauce and cook for 2 minutes on either side, basting as you cook. Reduce the heat to low and cook for 1 minute more.

7. Transfer the whole fish to a heated serving dish. Pour the sauce and vegetables over it and serve immediately.

Whole Fish in Garlic and Chilli Sauce

Ganshao Yu

In China, fish weighing less than 1 kg (2¼ lb) are often cooked whole, head and tail intact, and served right at the end of a banquet. The reason for this is partly because the word for fish is *yu*, pronounced the same as the Chinese character for 'to spare'; the Chinese like to think that there is always something on the table to spare.

1 large or 2 small grey mullet, carp or sea bass
3 tablespoons vegetable oil
1 garlic clove, crushed or finely chopped
2 slices fresh root ginger, peeled and finely chopped
2 tablespoons chilli bean paste
2 tablespoons Chinese wine or dry sherry
1 tablespoon soy sauce
1 teaspoon sugar
1 tablespoon vinegar
a little stock or water, if necessary
2 teaspoons cornflour
2 spring onions, finely shredded, to garnish

Preparation time: about 20 minutes
Cooking time: 15 minutes
Serves 4

1. Scale and clean the fish. Using a sharp knife, slash both sides of the fish diagonally as deep as the bone, at about 2 cm (¾ inch) intervals.

2. Heat the oil in a hot wok until it is smoking. Add the fish and fry for 3–4 minutes, turning it over once. Push the fish to one side, add the garlic, ginger, chilli bean paste, wine or sherry and soy sauce and stir until these ingredients are mixed to a smooth paste.

3. Push the fish back to the centre of the wok, add the sugar and vinegar and a little stock to moisten, if necessary. Cook for 2–3 minutes, turning the fish over once more.

4. Mix the cornflour with 1 tablespoon cold water to make a smooth paste. Stir this into the sauce and cook, stirring, until it has thickened.

5. Transfer the fish to a warmed serving dish and spoon over the sauce. Serve hot, garnished with shredded spring onions.

Fish with Bean Curd in Hot and Sour Sauce

Bean curd is a distinctive ingredient in Chinese cuisine. Not only is it very nourishing, but it is valued for its capacity to absorb true flavours.

450 g (1 lb) fish fillets (cod, halibut, snapper or John Dory), cut into 5 × 2.5 cm (2 × 1 inch) pieces
3 tablespoons soy sauce
4 tablespoons corn oil
2-3 spring onions, finely chopped
2-3 slices fresh root ginger, finely chopped
1 garlic clove, crushed
2 cakes bean curd, each cut into 12 cubes
1 teaspoon salt
2 tablespoons dry sherry
1 teaspoon sugar
1 tablespoon chilli sauce
2 tablespoons white wine vinegar
120 ml (4 fl oz) water
freshly chopped parsley, to garnish

Preparation time: 5 minutes, plus marinating
Cooking time: 20 minutes
Serves 4

1. Place the pieces of fish in a shallow dish, sprinkle with 1 tablespoon of the soy sauce and leave to marinate for 30 minutes, turning them over once.

2. Heat 3 tablespoons of the oil in a wok or frying pan set over medium heat. Add the fish pieces and cook until they are golden on all sides. Remove the fish from the pan with a slotted spoon and set aside to keep warm.

3. Heat the remaining oil in the pan. Add the spring onions, ginger and garlic and fry for a few seconds. Add the bean curd cubes, and return the fish pieces to the pan. Season with salt and add the sherry, sugar, remaining soy sauce, the chilli sauce, vinegar and water. Bring to the boil, reduce the heat and simmer for 10 minutes.

4. Transfer the fish, bean curd and sauce to a hot platter and serve immediately, garnished with chopped parsley.

Cantonese Red-cooked Fish

Ching Hong Shao Yu

Red cooking is a unique Chinese method. The soy sauce imparts a rich flavour and a reddish-brown colour to the food. In this Cantonese recipe strong-flavoured fish is substituted for the usual meat. As well as mackerel, carp, sea bass or mullet can be used.

750 g (1½ lb) mackerel, cleaned
1 tablespoon dark soy sauce
3 tablespoons vegetable oil
15 g (½ oz) wood ears, soaked for 20 minutes, and drained
50 g (2 oz) canned bamboo shoots, drained and sliced
3 spring onions, shredded
3 slices root ginger, shredded
2 teaspoons cornflour
1 tablespoon water
Sauce:
2 tablespoons dark soy sauce
2 tablespoons Chinese wine or dry sherry
2 teaspoons sugar
4 tablespoons beef stock
To garnish:
shredded spring onion
sliced cucumber

Preparation time: 10 minutes, plus marinating and soaking
Cooking time: 15 minutes
Serves 4-6

1. Make diagonal cuts down both sides of the fish. Rub with the soy sauce and leave to marinate for 15 minutes.

2. While the fish is marinating, combine the ingredients for the sauce.

3. Heat the oil in a wok until it smokes. Place the fish in the wok and fry on both sides until it is golden.

4. Add the sauce, wood ears and bamboo shoots, reduce the heat and continue cooking gently for about 10 minutes.

5. Add the spring onions and ginger, and continue to cook until the sauce has reduced by half. Blend the cornflour with the water to make a thin paste. Stir into the sauce to thicken slightly. Turn the fish over once and cook for 1 minute.

6. Transfer the fish to a heated platter, pour over the sauce and serve immediately, garnished with shreds of spring onion and a slice of cucumber.

Yellow river carp

Yellow River Carp

Zaolui Lay Yu

Each region of China boasts a number of recipes for carp, a large sweet fish that makes a splendid celebration dish. This stylish recipe is from Peking.

1 × 900 g (2 lb) carp
2 teaspoons salt
1½ tablespoons plain flour
1½ tablespoons cornflour
5 tablespoons water
600 ml (1 pint) vegetable oil
2 tablespoons lard
Sauce:
2 tablespoons sugar
4 tablespoons wine vinegar
1 tablespoon soy sauce

2 tablespoons Chinese wine or dry sherry
6 tablespoons water
1 tablespoon cornflour
To garnish:
spring onions tassels (see page 61)
white radish flower (see page 62)

Preparation time: 15 minutes
Cooking time: about 10 minutes
Serves 6–8

1. Scale and clean the carp. Rub the fish inside and out with salt. Using a sharp knife, score it on both sides with shallow criss-cross cuts.

2. Blend the flour and cornflour with the water to make a batter. Turn the fish in the batter until it is well coated on both sides.

3. Heat the oil in a wok until it is smoking. Place the fish in a wire basket and lower it into the oil. Deep-fry for 7–8 minutes. Remove, drain and keep hot.

4. Melt the lard in a small saucepan set over medium heat. Add all the sauce ingredients and stir together for 2 minutes until the sauce becomes thick and translucent.

5. To serve, transfer the carp to a heated serving dish and pour over the sauce. Garnish with spring onion tassels and a radish flower.

Scallop Fu-Yung

This Sechuan dish exploits the brief cooking time needed for scallops and tender chicken breasts to produce a delicate and delicious flavour.

1 tablespoon dry sherry
1 teaspoon salt
2 tablespoons cornflour
225 g (8 oz) fresh scallops, cut into 5 mm (¼ inch) slices
225 g (8 oz) chicken breast meat, cut into 5 mm (¼ inch) slices
9 tablespoons vegetable oil
5 egg whites
250 ml (8 fl oz) chicken stock
a large pinch of white pepper
To garnish:
2 tablespoons chopped cooked ham
2 tablespoons chopped fresh parsley

Preparation time: 5 minutes
Cooking time: 5 minutes
Serves 4

1. In a bowl mix together the sherry, ½ teaspoon of the salt and 1 tablespoon of the cornflour, to make a smooth paste. Add the sliced scallops and chicken breast meat and turn to coat in the mixture.

2. Heat 4 tablespoons of the oil in a wok. Add the scallops and chicken and stir-fry for 1 minute. Remove the wok from the heat.

3. Whisk the egg whites until they stand in stiff peaks. Fold in the remaining cornflour and salt, then the stock, pepper, scallops and chicken.

4. Heat the remaining oil in the wok. Add the egg white mixture and stir-fry until it is firm. Transfer to a heated platter and serve immediately, sprinkled with the chopped ham and parsley.

Ginger and Spring Onion Crab

Crabs are so widely used in Chinese cooking that there are a number of restaurants in Peking serving nothing else. Each diner is given a little hammer to crack open the shells. As this dish has to be eaten with the fingers, provide finger bowls and plenty of napkins.

1 × 1.25 kg (2¾ lb) crab, boiled and cleaned (see page 54)
3 tablespoons sherry
3 tablespoons soy sauce
2 tablespoons cornflour
4 tablespoons vegetable oil
4 slices root ginger, peeled and finely chopped
4 spring onions, finely chopped
1 teaspoon salt
2 teaspoons sugar

Preparation time: 20 minutes
Cooking time: 7 minutes
Serves 4

1. Chop the crab through the shell into large bite-sized pieces. Place the pieces in a bowl and sprinkle over 2 tablespoons of sherry and 2 tablespoons of soy sauce. Dust with the cornflour and turn the crab until all the pieces are well coated.

2. Heat the oil in a wok until it is smoking. Add the crab and fry for about 1 minute.

3. Add the ginger, spring onions, salt, sugar and remaining sherry and soy sauce. Stir-fry on high heat for about 3 minutes, stirring all the time. Add a little water if the mixture becomes very dry.

4. Transfer the crab pieces to a warm platter, pour the sauce over and serve immediately, with an accompaniment of lightly cooked broccoli.

Sweet and Sour Fish

In Cantonese food fruit juices are often used in savoury dishes, particularly in sweet and sour recipes like this delicious and quickly prepared fish composition.

450 g (1 lb) white fish fillets (cod, haddock, halibut), cut into 4 cm (1½ inch) slices
5 tablespoons cornflour, plus 1 teaspoon
1 egg
1 tablespoon cold water
600 ml (1 pint) vegetable oil
2 slices fresh root ginger, finely chopped
2 spring onions, finely chopped
50 g (2 oz) frozen peas
1 carrot, cut into rings
50 g (2 oz) canned bamboo shoots, drained and diced
2 tablespoons tomato ketchup
2 tablespoons wine vinegar
2 tablespoons orange juice
2 tablespoons sugar
1 tablespoon salt
2 tablespoons chicken stock

Preparation time: 15 minutes
Cooking time: 15 minutes
Serves 4

1. Dust the strips of fish with a little cornflour. Mix 4 tablespoons of cornflour with the egg and cold water to form a smooth batter.

2. Heat the oil in a wok to 180°C/350°F or until a cube of bread browns in 30 seconds. Dip the fish in the batter and deep-fry piece by piece for about 2 minutes, or until golden brown. Lift the fish out of the oil with a slotted spoon and drain on paper towels. Set the fish aside to keep warm.

3. Pour off all but 1 tablespoon of oil from the wok. Add the ginger, spring onions, peas, carrot and bamboo shoots. Stir-fry for 1 minute.

4. In a bowl mix together the tomato ketchup, vinegar, orange juice, sugar and salt. Add the mixture to the wok and stir all together.

5. Blend 1 teaspoon of cornflour with the chicken stock to form a thin paste. Add this to the wok. Bring to the boil, stirring constantly until the sauce thickens and becomes translucent.

6. Return the pieces of fish to the sauce, turn to coat and cook for 30 seconds. Transfer to a heated platter and serve immediately.

Variation: In Szechuan the fish is cooked in the sauce, which has crushed garlic, Chinese wine and chilli sauce added to give a spicier flavour. Since the fish is cooked for longer, larger pieces can be used.

Deep-fried Spiced Fish

It is interesting to compare this dish from western China with the Indian recipe for Baked Spiced Fish on page 58. This version is more suitable for firm white fish such as cod or halibut, or fine fish like Dover sole.

Deep-fried spiced fish

1 × 750 g (1½ lb) whole fish
1 teaspoon grated root ginger
3 spring onions, chopped
2 teaspoons salt
2 tablespoons dry sherry
vegetable oil for deep-frying
1 teaspoon ground Szechuan
   peppercorns
2 tablespoons sesame oil
To garnish:
lemon slices
parsley sprigs

Preparation time: 10 minutes, plus marinating
Cooking time: 8 minutes
Serves 4

1. Clean and scale the fish. Using a sharp knife, score both sides of the fish with shallow diagonal cuts.

2. Place the ginger, spring onions, 1 teaspoon of the salt and the sherry in a shallow oval dish. Mix lightly and add the fish. Cover with a sheet of greaseproof paper and leave to marinate for 30 minutes, turning the fish once.

3. Heat the oil in a wok or frying pan to 180°C/350°F or until a cube of bread browns in 30 seconds. Lower the fish into the hot oil and deep-fry for 7–8 minutes or until golden brown. Lift the fish from the oil with a slotted spoon and drain on paper towels. Place on a heated serving platter and sprinkle over the ground peppercorns and the remaining salt.

4. Heat the sesame oil briefly in a small saucepan or ladle and quickly pour it over the fish. Serve immediately, garnished with slices of lemon and sprigs of parsley.

POULTRY

*Because chicken lends itself so well to stir-frying and grilling, it is used
in many Oriental recipes, in combination with crunchy vegetables
and subtle spices. China has evolved some mouth-watering
ways with duck and from the Mughal rulers of India, who loved hunting
local game, come some splendid recipes for pheasant, partridge and quail.*

Mixed Grill

Teppanyaki

In Japanese, *teppan* means
'iron', and *yaki* means 'to fry' or
'to grill'. Any combination of
poultry, seafood or meat can be
used with vegetables in season
for this dish. As illustrated,
vegetables such as mild onions,
bean sprouts, sliced green or
red peppers, mangetout, French
beans, courgettes and
mushrooms are all suitable.
Traditionally, a heavy iron
griddle is used at the table, but
an electric frying pan may be
used instead.

*4 boned chicken breasts, cut
    into chunks or 4 sirloin or
    fillet steaks*
8 cooked, unpeeled prawns
*2 medium courgettes, sliced
    into julienne strips*
2 medium onions, finely sliced
225 g (8 oz) fresh bean sprouts
225 g (8 oz) button mushrooms
1 tablespoon vegetable oil
Ponzu (tart sauce):
*120 ml (4 fl oz) shoyu
    (Japanese soy sauce)*
*120 ml (4 fl oz) lime or lemon
    juice*
*4 tablespoons mirin (sweet rice
    wine)*
**Karashi jyoyu (mustard
    sauce):**
2 teaspoons dry mustard
2 teaspoons hot water
*3 tablespoons shoyu (Japanese
    soy sauce)*
2 tablespoons rice vinegar
1 teaspoon sesame seed oil

Preparation time: 20 minutes
Cooking time: see method
Serves 4

1. Arrange the chicken or beef,
prawns and vegetables
artistically on a large serving
plate.

2. To make the ponzu sauce,
mix together all the ingredients
and pour into individual dishes.

3. To make the karashi jyoyu
sauce, mix the mustard and
water to a paste, then add the
remaining ingredients. Pour into
individual dishes.

4. Heat a griddle or electric
frying pan at the table. Add the
oil, then some of the chicken
and prawns. As the meat
becomes tender, add a few
vegetables to the pan and cook
until they are tender but crisp.

5. Serve the chicken, prawns
and vegetables as they are ready,
letting the guests dip them into
their sauces while more
teppanyaki is cooking.

Braised Marinated Duck

Kamo no Tsukeyaki

Duck is used relatively little in Japanese cookery because of the high fat content. Most recipes, like this one, use a 'one-pot' cooking method in order to blend the flavour of the bird with vegetables.

1 × 2.5–2.75 kg (5–6 lb) duck, jointed
120 ml (4 fl oz) shoyu (Japanese soy sauce)
450 ml (¾ pint) sake
1 teaspoon grated fresh root ginger
salt
pepper
2 tablespoons vegetable oil
1 large onion, sliced
225 g (8 oz) mushrooms, sliced

Preparation time: 25 minutes, plus marinating
Cooking time: about 1¾ hours
Serves 4

1. Remove as much fat from the duck as possible. Mix together the shoyu, sake and ginger with salt and pepper to taste in a shallow dish. Add the pieces of duck and turn to coat them. Leave to marinate for 4 hours or overnight, turning the duck pieces occasionally.

2. Drain the duck pieces, reserving the marinade.

3. Heat the oil in a flameproof casserole over a medium heat. Add the duck and brown on all sides. Add the onion and mushrooms and cook for a further 5 minutes, stirring occasionally.

4. Pour off the fat from the casserole and add the reserved marinade. Bring to the boil, cover and simmer gently for 1½ hours or until the duck is very tender. Serve hot, accompanied by plain boiled rice and pickled vegetables.

Mixed grill

Chicken with Prawns and Vegetables

Umani

This quickly cooked Japanese dish would be an excellent choice for a lunch or supper.

4 dried shiitake mushrooms
4 uncooked langoustines
salt
175 ml (6 fl oz) Japanese Stock (see page 69)
3 tablespoons shoyu (Japanese soy sauce)
3 tablespoons sugar
24 mangetout
225 g (8 oz) boned chicken breast, diced
4 tablespoons sake
450 g (1 lb) fresh bamboo shoots

Preparation time: 15 minutes, plus soaking
Cooking time: 20 minutes
Serves 4

1. Soak the mushrooms in warm water for 25 minutes.

2. Drop the prawns into boiling salted water and simmer until they are deep pink. Drain well, then peel and devein.

3. Place the stock, shoyu, sugar and 1 teaspoon salt in a pan. Bring to the boil. Add the prawns. Simmer for 2 minutes. Drain, reserving the liquid.

4. Drop the mangetout into boiling salted water and simmer for 1 minute. Drain and add the mangetout to the reserved liquid. Simmer for 1 minute longer. Drain, reserving the liquid.

5. Add the chicken and sake to the reserved liquid, and simmer until the chicken is tender. Drain, reserving the liquid.

6. Drain the mushrooms, discard the stalks and slice the caps.

7. Add the bamboo shoots to the reserved liquid in a saucepan placed over moderate heat. Simmer until almost tender. Add the mushrooms to the pan and continue to simmer until both mushrooms and bamboo shoots are tender.

8. Return the prawns, mangetout and chicken to the pan and heat through. Divide the prawns, chicken and vegetables among 4 heated individual serving bowls, pour over any remaining liquid and serve immediately.

Chicken Deep-fried with Seaweed

Chicken Oharame

These little bundles of chicken are typically Japanese, delicate in flavour and a delight to the eye.

175 g (6 oz) boned chicken breast, skinned
1 tablespoon shoyu (Japanese soy sauce)
1 tablespoon sake
½ sheet of nori (dried lava paper), cut into 1 cm (½ inch) wide strips
½ egg white, lightly beaten
vegetable oil for deep-frying

Preparation time: 15 minutes, plus marinating
Cooking time: 8 minutes
Serves 4

1. Cut the chicken into strips measuring about 5 cm × 5 mm (2 × ¼ inch). Mix them with the shoyu and sake and leave to marinate for 1 hour.

2. Take 4 or 5 chicken strips in one hand. With the other hand, dip one end of a nori (seaweed) strip into the egg white and wrap it around the centre of the chicken strips.

3. Heat the oil in a wok or deep frying pan to 180°C/350°F or until a cube of bread browns in 30 seconds. Deep-fry the chicken bundles until they are cooked through but still tender. Lift out of the oil with a slotted spoon and drain on paper towels. Serve immediately.

Chicken Satay with Peanut Sauce

Sate Kuta-Kacang Tanah

In Bali, Indonesia, sunset is the time when the satay vendors do their best business with these tasty mouthfuls, cooked on bamboo skewers.

3 boneless chicken breasts, skinned and cut into bite-sized pieces
Marinade:
2 garlic cloves
¼ teaspoon salt
2 tablespoons light soy sauce
½ teaspoon brown sugar
1 tablespoon oil

Peanut sauce (see page 102)

Preparation time: 15 minutes, plus marinating
Cooking time: 8 minutes
Serves 4

1. Place the chicken cubes in a bowl. Soak 8–12 bamboo skewers in water to prevent them charring as the chicken cooks.

2. To make the marinade, crush the garlic with the salt and mix with the remaining ingredients. Pour over the chicken, cover and allow to stand at room temperature for 30 minutes, tossing the chicken once or twice.

3. Remove the skewers from the water and thread 4–5 pieces of chicken on each one, leaving a little space between the chicken so that it will cook evenly. Grill under a preheated grill or over hot coals, turning the skewers to brown the meat evenly and brushing it several times with the marinade. When the meat is tender, which should take about 8 minutes, place the skewers on individual plates and serve, handing the Peanut sauce separately.

Indonesian Spicy Chicken

This dish is quick and easy to prepare. Serve with prawn crackers, fried bananas and a selection of side dishes.

8 chicken pieces, skinned
juice of 1 lemon
3 tablespoons vegetable oil
300 ml (½ pint) water
Spice paste:
4 tablespoons desiccated coconut, soaked in 4 tablespoons hot water
2–4 red chillies, chopped
4 small onions, quartered
2 garlic cloves
4 candlenuts or Brazil nuts
1 teaspoon laos (optional)
1 cm (½ inch) piece fresh root ginger
1 teaspoon powdered lemon grass or grated lemon rind
1 teaspoon blachan (shrimp paste)
1 teaspoon sugar
1 teaspoon salt

Preparation time: 15 minutes, plus marinating
Cooking time: 45 minutes
Serves 4

1. Rub the chicken pieces all over with lemon juice and set aside for 20 minutes.

2. Put all the ingredients for the spice paste in a food processor or electric blender and work until smooth.

3. Heat the oil in a large frying pan and fry the paste, stirring, for 5 minutes.

4. Add the chicken pieces and fry for 5 minutes. Stir in the water and cook, uncovered, for 30 minutes or until the chicken is tender and the sauce has thickened.

5. Transfer to a warmed platter and serve hot.

Left: Chicken deep-fried with seaweed;
Chicken with prawns and vegetables
Below: Indonesian spicy chicken

Chicken with Cold-tossed Bean Sprouts

This cold, spicy chicken dish from Szechuan is often served at banquets in China, but also makes a particularly good lunch or picnic dish. The sauce gives the chicken an exotic flavour, but for a less peppery taste, the chilli oil can be omitted.

1 teaspoon wine vinegar
2 teaspoons sesame oil
1½ teaspoons sugar
a pinch of monosodium glutamate (optional)
225 g (8 oz) bean sprouts, blanched in boiling water and refreshed
2 cooked chicken breasts, cut into matchstick shreds
1½ tablespoons sesame paste or peanut butter
1 tablespoon soy sauce
1 teaspoon Worcestershire sauce
1 spring onion, finely chopped
1 slice fresh root ginger, peeled and finely chopped
1 garlic clove, crushed
1 tablespoon red chilli oil

Preparation time: 8 minutes
Serves 6

1. Mix together the vinegar, 1 teaspoon sesame oil, ½ teaspoon sugar and the monosodium glutamate, if using. Toss the bean sprouts in this moisture. Place on a serving dish and arrange the chicken meat on top.

2. In a bowl, mix together the sesame paste, soy sauce, remaining sugar and sesame oil, Worcestershire sauce, spring onion, ginger and garlic. Spoon this over the chicken and sprinkle the red chilli oil over. Serve cold.

Illustrated on page 159

Stewed Chicken with Lemon Grass

Thit Ga Ham Xa

This Vietnamese dish should be accompanied by a loaf of French bread.

1 × 1.5 kg (3 lb) chicken
5 tablespoons vegetable oil
2 shallots, sliced
6 garlic cloves, crushed
600–750 ml (1–1¼ pints) water
1 teaspoon salt
3 stems lemon grass, finely chopped
3 curry leaves or bay leaves
nuoc mam (fish gravy)
salt
freshly ground black pepper
2 tablespoons ground roasted peanuts

Preparation time: 10 minutes
Cooking time: about 1 hour
Serves 4

1. Bone the chicken (see page 57) and cut it into 12 portions.

2. Heat the oil in a large heavy-bottomed saucepan. Add the shallots and garlic and fry over moderate heat for 4–5 minutes or until golden brown. Add the chicken pieces and brown them on all sides.

3. Stir in the water, which should just cover the meat. Add the teaspoon of salt, lemon grass and curry leaves or bay leaves. Bring to the boil, reduce the heat and simmer for 45 minutes, stirring occasionally.

4. Season to taste with nuoc mam, salt and black pepper. Transfer to a heated serving dish and scatter ground peanuts on top. Serve immediately.

Right: Stewed chicken with lemon grass; Grilled skewers of chicken with five spices

Thai Chicken Ginger with Honey

The flavour of this dish is greatly improved if it is cooked the day before it is required, then reheated just before serving.

2 tablespoons dried Chinese mushrooms
5 spring onions, cut into 1 cm (½ inch) pieces
50 g (2 oz) fresh root ginger, shredded
2 tablespoons vegetable oil
3 chicken breasts, skinned, boned and cut into small pieces
3 chicken livers, chopped
1 onion, sliced
3 garlic cloves, chopped
2 tablespoons light soy sauce
1 tablespoon honey

Preparation time: 30 minutes, plus soaking
Cooking time: 15 minutes
Serves 4

1. Place the dried mushrooms in a bowl and cover with warm water. Leave to soak for 30 minutes. Put the spring onions in a bowl, cover with cold water and leave to soak.

2. Mix the ginger with a little cold water, then drain and squeeze. This reduces the hot taste a little. Rinse under cold running water and drain well.

3. Heat the oil in a wok over a medium heat. Stir-fry the chicken and liver pieces for 5 minutes. Remove from the wok with a slotted spoon and set aside.

4. Add the onion to the wok and fry gently until it is soft.

5. Drain the mushrooms, discard the stalks and slice the caps. Add to the wok with the garlic and stir-fry for 1 minute. Return the chicken and liver pieces to the wok.

6. Mix the soy sauce and honey together. Pour over the chicken and stir well. Add the ginger and stir-fry for 2–3 minutes. Add the drained spring onions. Transfer the mixture to a bowl, cover and leave overnight in the refrigerator.

7. Reheat to serve hot.

Grilled Skewers of Chicken with Five Spices

Ga Nuong Ngu Vi Thiong

This Vietnamese recipe for kebabs can also be used for lean pork fillet. Serve with plain boiled rice and a green salad.

1 × 1.5 kg (3 lb) tender young chicken
Marinade:
5 tablespoons vegetable oil
12 shallots, finely chopped
4 garlic cloves, crushed
200 ml ($\frac{1}{3}$ pint) sake or dry sherry
4 tablespoons soy sauce
1 teaspoon five-spice powder

Preparation time: 30 minutes, plus marinating
Cooking time: 35 minutes
Serves 4

1. Bone the chicken (see page 57) and cut the flesh into medium-sized pieces. Place in a shallow dish large enough to hold all the pieces in a single layer.

2. Make the marinade. Heat the oil in a small saucepan, add the shallots and garlic and cook for 2–3 minutes, until soft but not coloured. Stir in the remaining ingredients and bring to the boil. Reduce the heat and simmer, stirring occasionally, for 4–5 minutes.

3. Pour the marinade over the chicken and, using clean hands, gently press the pieces into the liquid to assist absorption. Leave to marinate for at least 30 minutes.

4. Drain the chicken pieces, retaining the marinade, and spread out on a wire rack to dry briefly. Thread the chicken pieces on to 8 metal skewers.

5. Arrange the chicken kebabs on an oiled grid over medium coals or under a preheated medium grill and brush liberally with the marinade. Cook for 15–20 minutes or until golden, turning frequently and brushing several times with the marinade. Serve hot.

Stir-fried Chicken with Lemon Grass and Chillies

Ga Xao Xa Ot

The aromatic flavour of lemon grass is a perfect foil for the chillies in this Vietnamese dish.

Oriental chicken

The chickens raised in South-east Asia yield relatively little meat, but the flavour is superb. In both Vietnam and Thailand chicken is extremely popular. Because the tender, delicate flesh blends so well with a whole range of flavourings, it is served in hundreds of different ways. The most popular cooking methods are frying, spit-roasting or barbecuing, and the birds are almost always jointed (see page 56). It is best to marinate chicken that is to be grilled, whether in a simple mixture of oil, lemon juice and herbs or a spicier version including garlic, coriander, peppercorns, lemon grass and chillies. Include a little nam pla (fish sauce) in chicken dishes to add a unique zest. Using a plain marinade gives you the opportunity to serve a flavourful sauce with the finished dish, such as Satay Sauce (page 208) or *Nam Prik*, the famed hot Thai sauce which is a traditional favourite. Every cook has an individual version, but the basic ingredients are dried shrimps, garlic, dried red chillies, sugar and nam pla, blended to a smooth consistency with lime juice. Tiny, fiery green chillies, finely chopped, are often included.

4 garlic cloves, chopped
100 g (4 oz) dried shallots
2 teaspoons Malaysian or Thai curry powder
1 teaspoon salt
2 pinches of freshly ground black pepper
1 teaspoon sugar
½ teaspoon monosodium glutamate (optional)
1 kg (2¼ lb) boneless chicken breast, cut in strips
3 stems lemon grass, chopped
2 red chillies, chopped
4 tablespoons vegetable oil
120 ml (4 fl oz) water
nuoc mam (fish gravy)
2 tablespoons freshly chopped coriander leaves, to garnish

Preparation time: 10 minutes, plus standing
Cooking time: 25 minutes
Serves 6

1. Using a mortar and pestle, grind 2 of the garlic cloves to a paste with the dried shallots, curry powder, salt, pepper, sugar and monosodium glutamate (if using).

2. Transfer the mixture to a large bowl, add the chicken strips and stir until well coated. Cover and set aside for 2 hours.

3. In a second bowl, combine the lemon grass and the chillies.

4. Heat the oil in a large frying pan, add the remaining garlic with the lemon grass and chillies and cook gently for 2–3 minutes.

5. Add the chicken strips and stir-fry for 5 minutes. Stir in the water and bring to the boil. Reduce the heat and simmer for 10–15 minutes or until the chicken is tender. Add nuoc mam to taste and sprinkle with additional pepper if liked.

6. Transfer to a heated platter and serve immediately, sprinkled with chopped coriander.

Stir-fried Chicken with Baby Corn Cobs and Chinese Mushrooms

Ga Xao Bap Non Va Nam Dong Co

This quickly prepared chicken dish is from Vietnam. Serve it with boiled rice.

25 g (1 oz) dried shiitake mushrooms
50 g (2 oz) baby corn cobs
5 tablespoons vegetable oil
2 garlic cloves, crushed
225 g (8 oz) boneless chicken breast, cut in strips
175 ml (6 fl oz) chicken stock
1 tablespoon nuoc mam (fish gravy)
⅓ teaspoon salt
⅓ teaspoon sugar
½ tablespoon cornflour
2 tablespoons water

Preparation time: 15 minutes, plus soaking
Cooking time: 30 minutes
Serves 4

1. Place the dried mushrooms in a bowl, add warm water to cover and soak for 15 minutes. Discard the stems and cut the caps into quarters.

2. Plunge the baby corn cobs in a saucepan of boiling unsalted water and cook for 5 minutes. Drain and refresh under cold running water. Drain again and set aside.

3. Heat the oil in a large frying pan or wok. Add the garlic and cook over moderate heat until golden. Add the chicken and stir-fry for 10 minutes. Lift out the chicken with a slotted spoon and set aside.

4. Add the mushrooms to the oil remaining in the pan, together with the baby corn cobs. Stir-fry for 1–2 minutes. Stir in the chicken stock and bring to the boil. Reduce the heat, return the chicken to the pan and season with nuoc mam, salt and sugar.

5. Simmer for 10 minutes or until the chicken is tender and the liquid is reduced by about half.

6. Combine the cornflour and water in a cup and mix to a creamy consistency. Add to the chicken mixture and cook, stirring constantly, until the sauce thickens. Transfer to a heated dish and serve immediately.

Right: Chicken in spicy sauce; Stir-fried chicken with baby corn cobs and Chinese mushrooms

Chicken in Spicy Sauce

Thit Ga Xao Cay

This Vietnamese recipe has more than a hint of French influence while retaining its Asian character.

1 × 1.5 kg (3 lb) tender young
   chicken
5 tablespoons vegetable oil
6 shallots or 1 large onion,
   thinly sliced
3 garlic cloves, crushed
6 tomatoes, seeded and chopped
4 teaspoons green peppercorns
2 bay leaves

250 ml (8 fl oz) water
about 1 tablespoon nuoc mam
   (fish gravy)
salt
about 1 teaspoon sugar
white pepper (optional)
1 cucumber, thinly sliced, to
   garnish

Preparation time: 25 minutes
Cooking time: 50 minutes
Serves 4

1. Bone the chicken (see page 57) and cut the flesh into cubes.

2. Heat the oil in a large heavy-bottomed saucepan. Add the shallots or onion and garlic and fry over moderate heat for 4–5 minutes or until golden brown. Add the chicken and fry, stirring frequently, for 10 minutes.

3. Stir in the tomatoes, peppercorns, bay leaves and water and bring to the boil. Reduce the heat and simmer for 30 minutes or until the sauce is thick.

4. Stir in the nuoc mam, salt and sugar to taste. Add a little ground white pepper if liked.

5. Transfer to a heated serving dish and garnish with sliced cucumber. Serve immediately.

Roast Pigeons

Bo Can Ro-ti

Though they are not as esteemed as duck, pigeons are widely used in Chinese cooking, usually braised or deep-fried. The marinade used in this Vietnamese recipe makes it possible to roast them without drying out. The rice alcohol used in the recipe is similar to Japanese sake.

4 oven-ready pigeons
175 ml (6 fl oz) rice alcohol or
    vodka
Marinade:
5 tablespoons vegetable oil
3 garlic cloves, crushed
½ onion, finely chopped
2 tablespoons soy sauce

2 teaspoons honey or golden
    syrup
⅓ teaspoon five-spice powder
a pinch of freshly ground black
    pepper
a pinch of monosodium
    glutamate (optional)
6 tablespoons water
Lemon dip:
2 lemons, cut in quarters
2 teaspoons salt
freshly ground black pepper

Preparation time: 30 minutes,
plus standing
Cooking time: 20 minutes
Oven: 230°C, 450°F, Gas Mark 8
Serves 4

1. Prepare the pigeons by rubbing them inside and out with rice alcohol or vodka. Place on a wire rack and set aside to dry.

2. Combine all the ingredients for the marinade and mix thoroughly. Paint the pigeons, inside and out, with this mixture and leave for about 1 hour to dry. Ideally, the birds should be hung in a cool, well-ventilated place, but they may be placed on a wire rack.

3. Arrange the pigeons on a rack in a roasting tin. Brush them liberally with the remaining marinade and roast in a preheated hot oven for 20 minutes.

4. Strip the flesh from the cooked pigeons and arrange on a warmed plate. Divide the lemon wedges among 4 dinner plates, and add ½ teaspoon salt and a pinch of pepper to each. Guests make their own dip by mixing the salt and pepper and moistening the mixture with a squeeze of lemon juice.

Hot and Spicy Quail

Chim Cut Ro-ti

In many countries of South-east Asia, quail is regarded as the prince of poultry. This Vietnamese recipe is ideal for a special barbecue. Serve with a selection of pickled vegetables.

4 oven-ready quail
3 tablespoons sesame seed oil for grilling
Marinade:
2 tablespoons vegetable oil
3 garlic cloves, crushed
4 spring onions, finely chopped
1 stem lemon grass, finely chopped
½ teaspoon cayenne pepper
5 drops of Worcestershire sauce
1 tablespoon nuoc mam (fish gravy)
1 teaspoon sugar
⅓ teaspoon salt
Lemon dip:
2 lemons, cut in quarters
2 teaspoons salt
freshly ground black pepper

Preparation time: 20 minutes, plus marinating
Cooking time: 15–20 minutes
Serves 4

Left: Roast pigeons; Hot and spicy quail

1. To prepare the quail, place them on a wooden board and, using a sharp kinife, split each of them down the spine. Splay the halves and flatten them with a cleaver.

2. Make the marinade. Heat the vegetable oil in a small saucepan, add the garlic, spring onions and lemon grass and cook over moderate heat for 2–3 minutes. Leave to cool. Stir in the cayenne pepper, Worcestershire sauce, nuoc mam, sugar and salt.

3. Arrange the quail in a shallow dish large enough to hold them all in a single layer. Pour the marinade over, cover the dish and marinate for 2 hours. Turn the quail over from time to time.

4. Drain the quail and thread them on to skewers. Arrange on an oiled grid over medium coals or under a preheated moderate grill and brush liberally with sesame oil. Grill for 15–20 minutes or until cooked, turning frequently and brushing with more oil as necessary.

5. Serve immediately, with lemon dip (see Roast Pigeons, left).

Symbols of Plenty

In China quails are regarded as symbolic of abundance. Inexpensive, a pair of these little game birds makes a substantial course for one. As the meat is on the dry side, it should be marinated as in the two recipes on this page, or braised in a flavourful sauce after being nicely browned in lard. To prepare a sauce, fry a little ginger and spring onion in a large saucepan, add ginger wine, sesame oil and seasonings and enough water to cover the birds. Cover tightly and cook over a moderate heat for 45 minutes. When the quail are ready, reduce the cooking liquid to serve as a rich gravy.

The Maharajah's Stuffed Quail

The combination of the tandoori marinade, the sweet but spicy glaze and the rice stuffing make this Indian recipe for quail fit for a prince.

4 oven-ready quails
275 ml (9 fl oz) (1 quantity) Tandoori Marinade (see page 45)
125 g (4 oz) Basmati or long-grain rice
Glaze:
4 tablespoons clear honey
1 tablespoon Worcestershire sauce
parsley sprigs, to garnish

Preparation time: 30 minutes, plus marinating
Cooking time: 15 minutes
Oven: 160°C, 325°F, Gas Mark 3
Serves 4

1. The quails can be boned if you wish (see page 57) but this is not necessary. Wash and dry the quails, wiping the cavity thoroughly with a clean tea towel or paper towels.

2. Make up the tandoori marinade in a large bowl. Place the quail in a deep dish and coat them liberally with the marinade. Cover and leave to stand in the refrigerator for up to 24 hours.

3. Cook the rice in plenty of boiling salted water for 10 minutes. Drain thoroughly, and allow to cool.

4. To make the stuffing, mix a little marinade with the rice to make it easy to mould. For each bird, take 1 tablespoon of rice and shape it into a ball. Place into the cavity of each quail. Alternatively, if you have boned the quail fold the bird around the rice ball, tucking in the skin and meat snugly so that the quail assumes its original shape.

5. Place the stuffed quails, breast side up, in a roasting tin. Place in a preheated moderate oven and bake for 15 minutes.

6. After 10 minutes' cooking time, heat the honey and Worcestershire sauce in a small saucepan to make the glaze. Pour the glaze over the quails and return them to the oven for 5 minutes.

7. Serve on individual plates, garnished with a sprig of parsley, accompanied by rice and salad.

Coconut Chicken

This delicious but mildly spiced chicken dish is typical of Malaysian cooking.

6 tablespoons sunflower oil
1 teaspoon black mustard seeds
1 teaspoon sesame seeds
1 teaspoon poppy seeds
½ teaspoon black cumin seeds
750 g (1½ lb) boneless, skinless chicken breast, diced
2–6 garlic cloves, finely chopped
300 ml (½ pint) milk
50 ml (2 fl oz) natural yoghurt
2 tablespoons desiccated coconut
1 tablespoon freshly chopped coriander
salt
To garnish:
20 unsalted cashew nuts, fried until golden
coriander sprigs

Preparation time: 15 minutes
Cooking time: 20 minutes
Serves 4

1. Heat the oil in a frying pan or wok and stir-fry the spice seeds for 1 minute. Add the diced chicken and stir-fry for about 5 minutes, turning the pieces frequently until they are white all over.

2. Add the garlic, milk, yoghurt and coconut to the pan. Simmer for 5 minutes, stirring from time to time.

3. Strew the chopped coriander over the chicken. Stir lightly and continue to simmer for a further 5–10 minutes, until the chicken is tender. Adjust the seasoning if necessary.

4. Transfer to a heated dish and serve immediately, garnished with fried cashews and sprigs of coriander.

Chicken Jalfrezi

Most Indian recipes for chicken involve jointing the bird before cooking. Here, tender breast meat is diced for quick stir-frying.

6 tablespoons concentrated butter or ghee
1 teaspoon white cumin seeds
1 teaspoon black mustard seeds
2–6 garlic cloves, chopped finely
5 cm (2 inch) piece fresh root ginger, sliced finely
1 large onion, sliced thinly
750 g (1½ lb) boneless, skinless chicken breast, diced
1 tablespoon Mild Curry Paste (see page 15)
½ red pepper, chopped
½ green pepper, chopped
2 tomatoes, skinned and chopped
1 tablespoon freshly chopped coriander leaves

Preparation time: 25 minutes
Cooking time: 25 minutes
Serves 4

1. Heat the butter or ghee in a large frying pan or wok. Stir-fry the cumin seeds and mustard seeds for 1 minute. Add the garlic (quantity according to taste) and stir-fry for 1 minute more.

2. Add the ginger and stir-fry for 2 minutes. Add the sliced onion and stir-fry until golden – about 5 minutes.

3. Place the chicken pieces in the pan and stir-fry to combine with the other ingredients for about 5 minutes.

4. Add the curry paste, red and green pepper, tomatoes and chopped coriander leaves with 1–2 tablespoons of water. Stir-fry for a further 10 minutes, until the ingredients are blended and heated through. Transfer to a heated platter and serve immediately.

Baked Spicy Quail

This Indian way with quail makes an unusual dinner party dish served with pilau rice, spiced okra and dry-fried spinach.

4 oven-ready quails
Marinade:
142 ml (5.2 fl oz) carton natural yoghurt
2 garlic cloves, chopped finely
75 g (3 oz) finely chopped onion
2 tablespoons Mild Curry Paste (see page 15)
2 teaspoons garam masala (see page 16)
½ teaspoon salt
Basting liquid:
125 ml (4 fl oz) white wine
125 ml (4 fl oz) double cream
2 teaspoons brown sugar
1 tablespoon Mild Curry Paste (see page 15)
sprigs of watercress, to garnish

Preparation time: 20 minutes, plus marinating
Cooking time: 15 minutes
Oven: 160°C, 325°F, Gas Mark 3
Serves 4

1. Combine the marinade ingredients in a large bowl and set aside for the flavours to blend.

2. Wash the quails, and wipe the cavity thoroughly with a clean tea towel or paper towels. Place the quails in a deep dish and coat them liberally with the marinade. Cover and leave to stand in the refrigerator for up to 24 hours.

3. Place the quails in a roasting tin and bake in a preheated moderate oven for 15 minutes.

4. While the quails are cooking, prepare the basting liquid. In a small saucepan, heat the wine to boiling point. Reduce the heat and stir in the cream, sugar and curry paste. Continue to stir for 2–3 minutes to dissolve the

sugar and blend the mixtures. After the quails have been cooking for 10 minutes, pour the hot basting liquid over them and return them to the oven for 5 minutes.

5. To serve, transfer the quails to individual dishes and pour over the basting liquid. Serve hot, garnished with sprigs of watercress.

Chicken jalfrezi (top) is a speedily prepared Indian stir-fry perfect for suppertime. If you like it hot, replace the peppers with finely chopped fresh green chillies. Coconut chicken (bottom) is equally quick to prepare but deliciously mild and aromatic.

Jaipuri partridge

Sri Lankan Duck

This full-flavoured casserole of duck is tender and spicy.

4 duck breasts, each weighing about 225 g (8 oz)
Spices (roast and ground) (see page 20):
2 teaspoons coriander seeds
1 teaspoon ground cinnamon
1 teaspoon white cumin seeds
1 teaspoon fennel seeds
8 green cardamoms
6 cloves

3 tablespoons concentrated butter or ghee
1 teaspoon white cumin seeds
1 teaspoon panch phoran (optional)
300 ml (½ pint) Curry Purée (see page 15)
3½ oz (100 g) desiccated coconut or creamed coconut block
1 teaspoon vinegar
1 tablespoon brown sugar
salt
sprigs of flat-leaved parsley, to garnish

Preparation time: 20 minutes
Cooking time: 55 minutes
Oven: 190°C, 375°F, Gas Mark 5
Serves 4

1. Using a sharp knife, remove the skin and fat from the duck breasts and cut the flesh into cubes.

2. Add a little water to the roast and ground spices to make a paste. Heat the butter or ghee in a frying pan and stir-fry the cumin seeds and panch phoran (if using) for 1 minute. Add the curry purée and stir-fry for 5 minutes. Add the spice paste and stir-fry for 2–3 minutes more.

3. Combine this mixture with the cubes of duck in a casserole and bake in a preheated moderately hot oven for 45 minutes, adding the coconut, vinegar, sugar and salt to taste after 20 minutes.

4. To serve, spoon off any excess oil and garnish with parsley sprigs.

Jaipuri Partridge or Pheasant

The Indian aristocracy are keen hunters and have evolved a number of excellent recipes, like this, for presenting game.

4 small partridge, total weight about 1.5 kg (3 lb) or 2 small pheasants of same total weight
450 ml (¾ pint) game stock or water
4 carrots, shredded
6 shallots or pickling onions
4 tablespoons sunflower or mustard blend oil
2 garlic cloves, finely chopped
5 cm (2 inch) piece fresh root ginger, chopped
1 onion, chopped
1 tablespoon Mild Curry Paste (see page 15)
2 tablespoons ground almonds
2 tablespoons desiccated coconut
Spices:
6 green cardamoms
6 cloves
10 cm (4 inch) piece cinnamon stick or cassia bark
1 teaspoon white cumin seeds
½ teaspoon fennel seeds
½ teaspoon fenugreek seeds
4 bay leaves
½ teaspoon Aromatic Salt (see page 12)
Scrambled egg:
25 g (1 oz) butter
3 eggs
1 teaspoon garlic powder
1 teaspoon Mild Curry Powder (see page 14)
1 tablespoon hazelnuts
1 tablespoon pistachio nuts
½ teaspoon Aromatic Salt
dill sprigs, to garnish

Preparation time: 25 minutes
Cooking time: 55 minutes
Serves 4

1. Skin the birds and wipe them inside and out with a clean damp cloth. Cut them into quarters with a cleaver and/ or a heavy sharp knife.

2. Bring the stock or water to the boil in a 3.5 litre (5 pint) saucepan with the spices. Place the carrots, shallots or pickling onions and pieces of meat into the pan. Simmer for 20 minutes, so that the meat is half cooked and the liquid slightly reduced. Strain off the liquid and reserve. Leave the meat aside until it is cool enough to handle.

3. Meanwhile, heat the oil in a large frying pan or wok and stir-fry the garlic for 1 minute. Add the ginger and stir-fry for 2 minutes more. Add the onion and stir-fry for another 5 minutes. Stir in the curry paste and the reserved liquid and bring the mixture to simmering point.

4. Remove the flesh of the partridge or pheasant from the bones (leaving the leg meat on the bone if preferred). Place the meat and the contents of the frying pan or wok into the saucepan. Bring back to simmering point and continue to cook for about 20 more minutes, so that the meat is tender and the liquid reduces further. It should be fairly dry, but not sticking to the pan.

5. Stir in the almonds and coconut and increase the heat briefly so that the meat is heated through. Take care that the consistency remains fairly dry without sticking to the pan.

6. Transfer the meat in its sauce to a heated serving dish and keep it warm while preparing the eggs.

7. Melt the butter in a pan. Beat the eggs in a bowl with the garlic and curry powder, nuts and salt. Pour this mixture into the pan and cook over a moderate heat, stirring all the time. When the eggs are just cooked but still soft, spoon them over the meat. Garnish with dill and serve at once.

Duck Pasanda

'Pasanda' means 'beaten meat'. In this recipe from northern India pieces of skinned duck breast are beaten, marinated overnight in red wine then simmered in curry sauce to produce a dish of great distinction.

4 duck breasts, each weighing about 225 g (8 oz)
125 ml (4 fl oz) red wine
3 tablespoons concentrated butter or ghee
300 ml (½ pint) Curry Purée (see page 15)
1 tablespoon Mild Curry Paste (see page 15)
1½ teaspoons Tandoori Masala (see page 44)
about 200 ml (7 fl oz) milk
2 teaspoons garam masala (see page 16)
2 tablespoons desiccated coconut or coconut powder
75 ml (3 fl oz) single cream
1 tablespoon chopped coriander
salt

Preparation time: 15 minutes, plus marinating
Cooking time: 40–45 minutes
Serves 4

1. Carefully remove the skin and fat from the duck breasts with a sharp knife. Halve each breast along the long side to give 8 pieces. Place the pieces between sheets of greaseproof paper and beat them flat, increasing their original size by half and making them about 5 mm (¼ inch) thick. Place the pieces in a shallow dish and cover them with the red wine. Leave to marinate for a minimum of 2 hours, or overnight.

2. To make the sauce, heat the butter or ghee in a frying pan or wok and stir-fry the curry purée for 5 minutes. Add the curry paste and tandoori masala and stir-fry for a further 3–4 minutes. As soon as these ingredients have blended, add about half the milk with the wine from the marinade in order to make a fairly liquid consistency.

3. Bring the sauce up to simmering point and place the duck pasandas in the pan, making sure they are covered with the sauce. Reduce the heat and let the duck simmer gently for 20 minutes, stirring from time to time to ensure it is not sticking to the pan. Do not cook the duck too quickly or the pieces will toughen.

4. Add the garam masala, coconut, cream and coriander and mix them in well. Continue to simmer for 10 minutes or so, adding the remaining milk a little at a time as required. Keeping the liquid balance correct is extremely important: by gradually reducing the sauce you should finally achieve a thickish creamy consistency, but while the duck is still cooking the sauce must be relatively liquid.

5. Adjust the seasoning if necessary and transfer to a heated dish to serve.

Steamed or Double-boiled Chicken with Chinese Cabbage

This method of cooking is preferred in China because it produces a very pure, true flavour, from which it follows that the chicken must be of very good quality and preferably free-range. Serve with plain boiled rice.

1 × 1.5 kg (3½ lb) chicken
2 teaspoons salt
6–8 dried shiitake mushrooms
750 g (1½ lb) Chinese cabbage
5 slices fresh root ginger
2 chicken stock cubes

Preparation time: 10 minutes
Cooking time: 2 hours 15 minutes
Serves 4–6

1. Bring a large saucepan of water to the boil. Add the salt and immerse the chicken in the water. Skim off all scum that rises to the surface and boil for 5–6 minutes. Drain the chicken thoroughly.

2. Soak the mushrooms in boiling water and leave to stand for 20 minutes. Drain and discard the stems. Cut the cabbage into 5 cm (2 inch) thick slices.

3. Place the mushrooms and ginger in a large, deep, heatproof bowl. Put the chicken on top of the vegetables and pour in just enough water to cover it. Cover the top of the bowl tightly with a piece of kitchen foil. Place the bowl in a very large saucepan containing about 5 cm (2 inches) of water, which should not come more than half-way up the sides of the bowl. Bring the water to the boil, then let it simmer for 1 hour.

4. Lift out the chicken and place the sliced cabbage in the bottom of the bowl. Sprinkle the cabbage with the crumbled stock cubes and replace the chicken. Cover the bowl again tightly with foil. Bring the water back to the boil and simmer gently for another hour.

Tropical Sweet and Sour Chicken

Sweet and sour meat and poultry dishes in the tropics tend to be fiery with chillies to whip up appetites made sluggish by the humidity. Those of us who live in temperate zones can reduce or even omit the chilli, according to taste.

225 g (8 oz) boneless chicken breast, skinned and cut into bite-sized pieces
1 egg, lightly beaten
3 tablespoons cornflour
400 ml (14 fl oz) vegetable oil for deep-frying
6 garlic cloves, sliced
½ onion, sliced
10 pineapple cubes
2 red chillies, cored, deseeded and sliced
1 tomato, quartered
Sauce:
1 tablespoon malt vinegar
1 tablespoon sugar
2 tablespoons tomato sauce
½ teaspoon salt
4 tablespoons pineapple juice
100 ml (3½ fl oz) water

Preparation time: 15 minutes
Cooking time: 15 minutes
Serves 4

1. Coat the pieces of chicken with the beaten egg. Toss the pieces lightly in cornflour.

2. Heat the oil in a wok or frying pan to 180°C/350°F or until a cube of bread browns in 30 seconds. Deep-fry the chicken for about 4 minutes until it is golden brown. Remove the chicken from the pan with a slotted spoon and drain on paper towels.

3. Pour off all but 3 tablespoons of oil from the pan. Reheat, and fry the garlic and onion till light brown. Add the pineapple, chillies and tomato and stir-fry for 1 minute.

4. Combine all the sauce ingredients in a bowl and add to the pan. Stir briefly and return the chicken to the pan. Continue to cook for 1–2 minutes until the sauce has thickened and nicely glazed. Transfer to a heated serving dish and serve immediately.

Chicken with Chilli Sauce

This hot dish from western China involves both deep-frying and stir-frying. Serve with plain boiled rice and sambals or pickled vegetables.

1 × 1.25 kg (2½ lb) roasting chicken, jointed (see page 56)
1 tablespoon cornflour
a pinch of salt
1 egg white
12 canned water chestnuts, drained
15 g (½ oz) fresh ginger root, peeled and grated
1 garlic clove, finely chopped
1 teaspoon chilli sauce
3 tablespoons Chinese wine or dry sherry

2 tablespoons tomato ketchup
2 tablespoons malt vinegar
2 tablespoons soy sauce
2 teaspoons Barbados sugar
vegetable oil for deep frying
2 tablespoons sesame oil

Preparation time: 20 minutes
Cooking time: 15 minutes
Serves 4

1. Take all the chicken meat from the bones. Discard the skin and cut the flesh into 2 cm (¾ inch) pieces.

2. Combine the cornflour with the salt and egg white in a large bowl. Add the chicken pieces and toss them to coat.

3. To make the sauce, cut the water chestnuts in half and mix them with the ginger, garlic, chilli sauce, wine or sherry, ketchup, vinegar, soy sauce and sugar.

4. Heat the oil in a wok or deep frying pan to 180°C/350°F or until a cube of bread browns in 30 seconds. Deep-fry the chicken pieces for about 2½ minutes or until they are golden brown. Lift out of the oil with a slotted spoon and drain on paper towels. Set aside and keep warm.

5. Heat the sesame oil in a wok or large frying pan set over high heat. Add the sauce, stirring constantly, and bring to the boil. Add the chicken pieces to the pan and stir to coat them with the sauce and heat through, about 1 minute. Transfer to a heated platter to serve.

*Steamed or double-boiled chicken with
Chinese cabbage; Tropical sweet and
sour chicken*

Peppered Smoked Chicken

There are many Chinese dishes that involve cross-cooking, like this one in which the chicken is first steamed for tenderness and then smoked in dry heat to crisp up the skin and give a delicious aromatic flavour to the meat.

2 tablespoons Szechuan or
  black peppercorns
1 × 1.5 kg (3¼ lb) roasting
  chicken
1 tablespoon salt
3 tablespoons dark brown
  sugar
2 tablespoons Chinese tea leaves
  or pine needles
1 teaspoon ground ginger
2 tablespoons sesame oil

Preparation time: 15 minutes
Cooking time: 1 hour 25 minutes
Serves 4

1. Place the peppercorns in a dry pan and cook over medium heat for 3 minutes. Crush them coarsely with a pestle and mortar. Rub the crushed peppercorns into the chicken skin and inside the cavity.

2. Place the chicken in a steamer over gently boiling water. Cover and steam for 1 hour. Lift out the chicken and allow to cool.

3. Line a large, heavy flameproof casserole with aluminium foil. Mix together the salt, sugar, tea leaves or pine needles and ginger and place in the casserole. Set a wire rack inside and place the chicken on it. Bring the sides of the foil up over the chicken and fold to seal. Put on the lid.

4. Set the casserole on a moderate heat for 15 minutes. Turn off the heat and leave to stand for 5 minutes.

5. To serve, joint the chicken and arrange on a heated serving plate. Brush with sesame oil and serve hot.

Drunken Chicken

This dish from Peking is ideal for a dinner party as it is prepared 2–3 days in advance. Serve with noodles and a selection of vegetable dishes.

1.2 litres (2 pints) water
1½ tablespoons salt
2 medium onions, sliced
4 slices fresh root ginger, peeled
1 × 1.25 kg (3 lb) chicken,
  trussed
600 ml (1 pint) Chinese wine
  or dry sherry
To garnish:
spring onion tassels (see page 61)
radish roses (see page 61)

Preparation time: 5 minutes, plus soaking
Cooking time: 20 minutes
Serves 4–6

1. Bring the water, salt, onions and ginger to the boil in a large pan. Simmer for 5 minutes, then put in the chicken. Bring back to the boil and simmer, covered, for 15 minutes. Turn off the heat and leave the chicken to soak in the cooling liquid for at least 3 hours.

2. Remove the chicken and place it in a stoneware jar or a casserole with a tight-fitting lid. Pour over the sherry or wine, completely immersing the chicken, and leave to soak for at least 48 hours. Turn the chicken every 12 hours.

3. To serve, drain off the sherry and untruss the chicken. Using a cleaver, chop it into bite-sized pieces. Arrange the pieces in the shape of a chicken on a bed of crisp lettuce. Garnish with spring onion tassels and radish roses.

Right: Fried eight-piece chicken; Stewed chicken with chestnuts

Cantonese Crystal Chicken

This gleaming dish is a wonderful set piece for a dinner party or buffet table.

1 × 1.5 kg (3½ lb) roasting
  chicken
4 spring onions
15 g (½ oz) fresh ginger root,
  peeled and chopped
½ teaspoon salt
2 tablespoons soy sauce
100 g (4 oz) lean cooked ham,
  sliced thinly
25 g (1 oz) gelatine
To garnish:
1 red pepper, cored, seeded and
  sliced into strips
1 green pepper, cored, seeded
  and sliced into strips

Preparation time: 25 minutes, plus cooling
Cooking time: 1 hour 20 minutes
Serves 4

1. Truss the chicken and put it into a saucepan or flameproof casserole. Cut 2 of the spring onions into 5 cm (2 inch) lengths, and add to the casserole with the chopped ginger. Pour in cold water to just cover the chicken legs. Set the pan on a moderate heat and bring the water to the boil.

2. Add the salt and soy sauce to the casserole. Cover and simmer for 1 hour or until the chicken is tender. Lift out the chicken and let it cool completely. Strain and reserve the stock.

3. When the chicken is cool, divide it into 24 pieces, discarding all the bones. Cut the ham into small squares and layer the ham and chicken in an oiled oval dish.

4. Soak the gelatine in 4 tablespoons of the reserved stock. Heat the remaining stock to just below boiling point. Reduce the heat, add the gelatine and stir until it has completely dissolved. Remove the pan from the heat. When the stock is cold, pour it slowly over the layered chicken and ham. Leave in a cool place for 3 hours for the jelly to set.

5. To serve, turn the jelly on to a flat serving plate. Garnish with strips of red and green pepper and the rest of the spring onion.

Fried Eight-piece Chicken

Shao Ba Kuai

1 × 1.25 kg (2½ lb) spring chicken
2–3 spring onions, chopped finely
2–3 slices fresh root ginger, chopped finely
2 tablespoons dry sherry
1 tablespoon sugar
3 tablespoons soy sauce
3 tablespoons cornflour
100 g (4 oz) lard
1 teaspoon sesame seed oil
chopped parsley, to garnish

Preparation time: 25 minutes
Cooking time: 25 minutes
Serves 4

1. Joint the chicken: cut the legs, wings and breasts from the bird and cut each breast in half (use the chicken carcass to make stock).

2. Mix the spring onions and ginger with 1 tablespoon of the sherry, 1 teaspoon of the sugar and 1 tablespoon of the soy sauce. Add the chicken pieces and leave to marinate for 3 minutes.

3. Coat each piece of chicken with cornflour. Melt the lard in a deep frying pan over a moderate heat. Add the chicken pieces and fry until they are golden.

4. Pour off the excess lard and add the remaining sherry, sugar, and soy sauce to the chicken. Bring to the boil, stirring.

5. Transfer the chicken pieces in sauce to a heated platter. Sprinkle over the sesame seed oil and serve immediately, garnished with parsley.

Stewed Chicken with Chestnuts

Hongsheo Lizi Ji

The aesthetics of Chinese cooking demand that the pieces of chicken be the same size as the chestnuts and browned to the same appealing colour.

1 × 1 kg (2¼ lb) chicken
6 tablespoons soy sauce
1 tablespoon dry sherry
2 tablespoons vegetable oil
2 slices fresh root ginger, chopped
4 spring onions, chopped
450 g (1 lb) chestnuts, peeled and skinned
450 ml (¾ pint) water
1 tablespoon sugar

Preparation time: 30 minutes, plus marinating
Cooking time: about 1 hour
Serves 4

1. Bone the chicken and cut the flesh into 3.5 cm (1½ inch) pieces.

2. Mix together the soy sauce and sherry in a dish and add the chicken pieces. Leave to marinate for 15 minutes.

3. Heat the oil in a large pan set over moderate heat. Add the chicken mixture, the ginger and half of the spring onions; stir-fry until the chicken is golden.

4. Add the chestnuts, water and sugar. Bring to the boil, cover and simmer for 40 minutes or until tender.

5. To serve, transfer to a warmed dish and garnish with the remaining spring onions.

Boneless Duck with Eight Precious Stuffing

This Cantonese classic is perfect for a dinner party as it is so easy to serve. If you do not wish to bone the duck yourself, ask the butcher to do it for you.

1 duck gizzard (optional)
2 tablespoons vegetable oil
4 spring onions, finely chopped
2 slices root ginger, peeled and finely chopped
4 dried Chinese mushrooms, soaked for 20 minutes, drained, stemmed and diced
20 dried lotus seeds, soaked overnight, drained and diced
15 g ($\frac{1}{2}$ oz) dried shrimps, soaked for 20 minutes, drained and chopped
100 g (4 oz) cooked ham, diced
8 dried chestnuts, soaked overnight, simmered until soft and chopped
2 tablespoons Chinese wine or dry sherry
2 tablespoons light soy sauce
$\frac{1}{2}$ teaspoon salt
freshly ground black pepper
450 g (1 lb) glutinous or pudding rice, cooked
1 duck, about 1.5 kg ($3\frac{1}{2}$ lb), boned (see page 57)
2 tablespoons dark soy sauce

Preparation time: 20 minutes, plus soaking
Cooking time: about 1 hour 15 minutes
Oven: 190°C, 375°F, Gas Mark 5
Serves 6–8

1. Boil the duck gizzard, if using, for 10 minutes, then drain and dice.

2. Heat the oil in a wok until it is smoking and add half of the spring onions and the ginger. Stir together for a few seconds, then add the mushrooms, duck gizzard, lotus seeds, shrimps, diced ham, chestnuts, wine, light soy sauce, salt and pepper. Mix together well. Remove the pan from the heat, add the rice and mix again.

3. Pack this mixture into the duck and reform the shape. Do not stuff it too full. Close up the tail and neck openings with a needle and thread.

4. Wipe the duck dry and brush it with the dark soy sauce. Place on a wire tray over a roasting tin and roast in a preheated moderately hot oven for $1\frac{1}{4}$ hours or until the juices run clear.

5. To serve, make a long central cut down the breast and sprinkle with the remaining spring onions.

East River Salt-buried Chicken

This Chinese way of cooking poultry is easy to do. Surprisingly, the flesh does not taste salty and the skin is dry, crisp and brown. The salt can be kept and re-used if fresh salt is added to it. Serve with rice or noodles and crispy seaweed.

1 × 1.5–1.75 kg (3–4 lb) chicken
$1\frac{1}{2}$ tablespoons Rose Dew liqueur or fruit-flavoured brandy
$1\frac{1}{2}$ tablespoons soy sauce
4 slices root ginger, shredded
1 large onion, finely sliced
1 tablespoon whole five-spice mixture
2.75–3 kg (6–7 lb) coarse sea salt

Preparation time: 15 minutes, plus marinating
Cooking time: about $1\frac{1}{2}$ hours
Oven: 180°C, 350°F, Gas Mark 4
Serves 4

1. Rub the chicken inside and out with a mixture of the Rose Dew liqueur and the soy sauce. Mix together the ginger, onion and five-spice and place inside the chicken. Leave to stand on a wire rack in a cool, well-ventilated place for 2–3 hours.

2. Place the salt in a deep flameproof casserole dish and warm it through in the oven, stirring it once or twice to ensure that it is evenly heated through. Make a well in the salt and bury the chicken, covering it completely. Cover the casserole and place it over a low flame for 10 minutes. Transfer to a preheated moderate oven and cook for $1\frac{1}{2}$ hours.

3. To serve, lift the chicken out of the casserole and brush it free of salt. Chop it through the bone into 20–24 pieces of the size called in China 'double mahjong' and arrange on a warm platter. Serve hot.

Jellied Duckling

In this Cantonese recipe, the duck is boiled twice to reduce the fat content, leaving the meat tender. The enriched cooking liquid sets to a delicious jelly.

1 × 2 kg ($4\frac{1}{2}$ lb) oven-ready duckling
500 g ($1\frac{1}{4}$ lb) belly pork
225 g (8 oz) pork skin
250 ml (8 fl oz) soy sauce
1 tablespoon salt
150 ml ($\frac{1}{4}$ pint) dry sherry
3 tablespoons sugar
1 teaspoon five-spice powder
3 spring onions
4 slices fresh root ginger
watercress leaves, to garnish

Preparation time: 15 minutes, plus setting
Cooking time: about $4\frac{1}{2}$ hours
Serves 6–8

1. Place the duckling in a large pan with the belly pork and the pork skin. Cover with water and bring to the boil. Boil for 2–3 minutes, then pour off the water.

2. Rinse the duckling, pork and pork skin under cold running water and put them back in the pan. Cover with fresh water. Add the soy sauce, salt, sherry, sugar, five-spice powder, spring onions and ginger. Cover the pan and bring to the boil. Reduce the heat to low and simmer for about 4 hours.

3. Lift the duckling out of the cooking liquid, drain and place on a large plate. Carefully bone the duckling, leaving the skin on. Arrange the meat in a deep oval dish.

4. Strain the stock, discarding the pork, pork skin and flavourings. Strain again through a fine-mesh sieve. Pour the strained stock carefully over the pieces of duck. Place the dish in the refrigerator to chill until the stock sets into a jelly.

5. To serve, invert the jellied duckling on to a platter and garnish with watercress leaves.

Right: Jellied duckling

Peking Duck

This Chinese dish is justifiably one of the most popular in the world. Each mouthful is an incomparable combination of crunchy vegetables, crispy skin and tender meat with piquant sauces, wrapped together in one roll.

*1 × 1.75–2 kg (4–4½ lb) oven-
  ready duck*
1 tablespoon brown sugar
1 teaspoon salt
300 ml (½ pint) warm water
Mandarin pancakes:
450 g (1 lb) plain flour
300 ml (½ pint) boiling water
1 teaspoon vegetable oil
a little sesame seed oil
To serve:
1 small cucumber
10 spring onions
Sauce:
4 tablespoons vegetable oil
*8 tablespoons yellow bean
  sauce*
4 tablespoons sugar
1 teaspoon sesame oil

Preparation time: about 50 minutes, plus drying overnight and cooling
Cooking time: 2 hours
Oven: 200°C, 400°F, Gas Mark 6
Serves 4

1. Immerse the duck in a pan of boiling water for 1 minute. Drain thoroughly and hang up to dry in a well-ventilated room overnight.

2. Dissolve the sugar and salt in the warm water and rub the duck all over with this mixture. Hang it up to dry thoroughly once more until the coating is dry – about 2 hours.

3. Place the duck on a rack over a roasting pan to catch the fat and bake in a preheated oven for 1¼ hours. Do not open the oven door while the duck is cooking.

4. Make the sauce. Heat the oil in a small saucepan. Add the yellow bean sauce and stir over a low heat for 2 minutes. Add the sugar and sesame oil and stir for a further 1½ minutes. Leave to cool for 20–30 minutes. Transfer to individual bowls to serve.

5. Cut the cucumber into strips 5 cm (2 inches) long. Cut the spring onions into pieces the same size.

6. Make the pancakes. Sift the flour into a mixing bowl. Gradually add the boiling water and vegetable oil, stirring all the time to make a firm dough. Knead the dough into a roll 5 cm (2 inches) in diameter. Cut into 1 cm (½ inch) slices and form each piece into a small ball. Flatten each ball with the palm of the hand into a round flat disc on a board or work surface. Brush one side of each pancake with sesame seed oil and sandwich the pancakes together in pairs. Using a small rolling-pin, roll the sandwich into a pancake about 10–13 cm (4–5 inches) in diameter. Repeat until all the dough has been used.

7. Heat a dry frying pan over a moderate heat. When it is very hot, fry the 'sandwiches' one at a time. Turn them as soon as air bubbles appear on the surface. Cook the other side until little brown spots appear underneath. Remove from the pan and peel the two layers apart very gently. Fold each one in half and place them on a warmed serving dish, covered with foil to prevent them drying out. (If they get cold, they can easily be reheated in a steamer).

8. The carving of the duck is usually carried out at the table. Using a small sharp knife, first remove all the skin in small strips and place on a warmed serving dish. Next peel off the meat in small strips and arrange in a second warmed serving dish. Each guest takes a pancake, brushes it with sauce, and places a strip of cucumber, a piece of spring onion and a piece of duck meat and skin in the centre. To close the pancake, fold over one edge and roll it up.

Duck on Skewers

Kao Chuan Ya

Filleted duck breasts are meaty and tender and convenient to use for kebabs and barbecues. This Chinese recipe makes either 8 small or 4 large skewers. If cooking on the larger, metal skewers, remove the pieces of duck after cooking and skewer one or two pieces on to wooden cocktail sticks to serve.

*4 duck breasts, boned and
  skinned*
Marinade:
2 tablespoons brown sugar
1 teaspoon salt
4 tablespoons soy sauce
1 tablespoon sesame seed oil
*1 cm (½ inch) piece fresh root
  ginger, peeled and finely
  chopped*
1 teaspoon sesame seeds

Preparation time: 20 minutes, plus marinating
Cooking time: 8–12 minutes
Serves 4

1. Cut the duck breasts into 32 small pieces. In a large bowl, mix together the ingredients for the marinade, and stir in the pieces of duck. Cover and leave to marinate for 3–4 hours in a cool place, or overnight in the refrigerator. Spoon the marinade over the duck several times so that the pieces become evenly coated.

2. Remove the duck with a slotted spoon and thread on to 8 bamboo skewers or 4 large metal skewers. Place on the grid

of a moderately hot barbecue and cook the small skewers for 8–10 minutes, the large ones for 10–12 minutes. Turn the skewers several times during cooking and baste with the remaining marinade.

3. The duck may be served hot or cold, on or off the skewers.

Peking duck, with piquant sauce and slivers of cucumber and spring onions encased in a thin pancake, is one of the world's most popular classic dishes.

MEAT

Despite the restrictions of various dietary laws, Oriental cooks have devised numerous tempting meat dishes, particularly with large proportions of vegetables – a combination both delicious and healthy. Often stir-fried, meat is also steamed, poached or grilled. Oven-baked Spiced Leg of Lamb is a meltingly tender recipe from India.

Japanese 'Roast' Beef

Wafu Roast Beef

Wafu Roast Beef is traditionally served with finely chopped spring onions and grated fresh root ginger. Each person mixes a little spring onion and ginger with some of the sauce, then dips a slice of meat into it before eating. If you prefer, mustard can be substituted for the ginger and spring onion. (Japanese mustard is very hot).

750 g (1½ lb) sirloin of beef
1 garlic clove, peeled and sliced
100 ml (3½ fl oz) shoyu
    (Japanese soy sauce)
100 ml (3½ fl oz) sake (rice
    wine)
1½ teaspoons sugar
parsley sprigs, to garnish
To serve:
2 spring onions, trimmed and
    finely chopped
2.5 cm (1 inch) fresh root
    ginger, peeled and grated

Preparation time: 10 minutes
Cooking time: 15–20 minutes
Serves 4

1. Put the beef in a deep saucepan with the garlic, shoyu, sake and sugar. Put an otoshi-buta (small wooden lid) or small upturned plate on top of the joint, cover the pan with a lid, place over high heat and bring to the boil. Lower the heat and simmer for 10 minutes, shaking the saucepan occasionally so that the meat does not stick.

2. Transfer the meat to a board, cut in half and check the extent of the cooking. If the meat is too rare for your liking, return it to the saucepan and cook for a further few minutes. When the meat is cooked, remove the saucepan from the heat. Leave the meat to cool in the liquid, covered with the lid.

3. Slice the meat thinly, and arrange the slices on individual plates. Garnish with parsley sprigs. Serve cold, with the cooking liquid from the meat served in individual bowls, and the prepared spring onions and ginger.

Beef with Vegetables

Sukiyaki

Most Japanese families have special sukiyaki pans to cook this popular dish at the table, but a heavy-based frying pan and a portable cooking stove will do the job just as well. Sukiyaki is very informal – the host or hostess cooks the first amount of meat and vegetables at the table, adding flavouring ingredients to his or her taste. After the first cooking it is every man for himself, and ingredients are selected, cooked and

Japanese 'roast' beef; Beef with vegetables

flavoured according to individual tastes. Bowls of plain boiled rice are served to each guest to be eaten alongside the sukiyaki.

450 g (1 lb) sirloin or topside of beef
4 heads of Chinese leaves
1 bunch watercress
2 thin leeks, white parts only
8 button mushrooms
100 g (4 oz) firm tofu (bean curd)
200 g (7 oz) shirataki (yam noodles), or fine vermicelli
1 small piece of beef fat (suet)
Japanese Stock (see page 69)
shoyu (Japanese soy sauce)
mirin (sweet rice wine)
sake (rice wine)
sugar
4 eggs

Preparation time: 20 minutes, plus freezing and chilling
Cooking time: see method
Serves 4

1. Freeze the meat for 45 minutes, leave for 10 minutes on a board, then cut into wafer-thin slices with a very sharp knife. Arrange the meat on a platter. Cover and chill in the refrigerator.

2. Wash the Chinese leaves. Cut them in half lengthways, then into 5 cm (2 inch) lengths. Wash and trim the watercress. Slice the leeks diagonally. Wipe and trim the mushrooms. Cut the tofu into 4 cm (1½ inch) cubes. Cook the shirataki (if using) in boiling water for 3 minutes, then drain. If using vermicelli, soak it in boiling water for 10 minutes, then drain. Arrange the vegetables, tofu and noodles on a platter.

3. Place a cast-iron frying pan on a portable cooking stove in the centre of the dining table. Surround with the platters of raw ingredients and with jugs of stock, shoyu, mirin and sake, and a pot of sugar.

4. Melt a little beef fat in the pan, then add a few slices of meat and cook until lightly browned. Add a selection of the other raw ingredients, then pour in stock, soy sauce, mirin, sake and sugar to taste. Each diner beats an egg lightly in his or her bowl, takes a selection of the cooked ingredients and mixes them with the egg.

Raw Beef

Yukhwe, or raw beef, is a Japanese dish rather like steak tartare, and usually served as a starter. Top-quality sirloin steak is used. Buy 225 g (8 oz) in a piece and freeze it for 45 minutes before slicing into fine shreds with a very sharp knife. Leave to thaw completely, then mix with a little crushed garlic, sesame oil, sesame seeds, sugar, salt and white pepper. Shred the flesh of a pear and a seeded cucumber, and arrange in separate piles on 4 plates. Spoon the meat mixture over the pear and cucumber and top with the yolk of a fresh egg.

Grilled Ginger Pork

Shoga-yaki

An easy and economical dish from Japan, which is none-the-less delicious enough to be served at dinner parties. Serve with French beans and plain boiled rice.

2× 175–225 g (7–8 oz) pork
    fillets
5 cm (2 inch) piece fresh root
    ginger, peeled and grated
4 tablespoons shoyu (Japanese
    soy sauce)
grated daikon (white radish),
    to garnish

Preparation time: 5 minutes, plus marinating
Cooking time: 30–35 minutes
Serves 4

1. Put the pork fillets in a shallow dish. Add the grated ginger and shoyu. Leave to marinate in a cold place for at least 30 minutes.

2. Wrap each fillet in foil, seal the edges and reserve any marinade in the dish. Place under a preheated hot grill for 5 minutes, then turn the grill down to low and continue cooking for a further 20–25 minutes, or until the pork is thoroughly cooked.

3. Unwrap the pork and cut each fillet into 1 cm ($\frac{1}{2}$ inch) slices. Place on warmed individual plates. Pour the meat juices from the foil into a small saucepan and add any reserved marinade. If there is not enough sauce add a few spoonfuls of water and shoyu to taste. Bring to the boil and simmer for about 5 minutes, then pour over the meat. Serve hot.

Pork with Shredded White Cabbage

Tonkatsu

This deep-fried breaded pork is a popular family supper or lunch dish in Japan. It is simple, economical and filling, yet also extremely delicious.

750 g (1$\frac{1}{2}$ lb) pork fillet
salt
freshly ground black pepper
plain flour for coating
2 eggs, lightly beaten
about 100 g (4 oz) dried white
    breadcrumbs
10 cm (4 inch) wedge hard
    white cabbage
vegetable oil for deep-frying
Tonkatsu sauce:
shoyu (Japanese soy sauce)
sake
Worcestershire sauce
Japanese mustard

Preparation time: 15 minutes
Cooking time: about 20 minutes
Serves 4

1. Cut the pork fillet crossways into 1 cm ($\frac{1}{2}$ inch) slices. Sprinkle lightly with salt and pepper. Dust with flour, shaking off any excess. Dip each pork slice into the beaten eggs, then coat in the breadcrumbs. Press lightly so that the breadcrumbs adhere to the meat.

2. Separate the cabbage leaves, then cut each one in half, discarding the thick and tough central stalks. Pile the leaves on top of each other, then cut into fine shreds. Arrange one quarter of the shredded cabbage on each of 4 individual plates so that half of the plate is covered.

3. To make the Tonkatsu sauce, combine all the ingredients in a bowl or jug, adjusting the quantities to taste. Pour into 4 individual bowls.

4. Heat the oil in a deep-fat frier or deep frying pan to 180°C/350°F or until a cube of bread browns in 30 seconds. Gently slide in the pork pieces one at a time. Deep-fry in batches for 3–5 minutes until golden brown. Remove with a slotted spoon and drain on a wire rack. When all the pork has been cooked, arrange the slices on the plates with the cabbage. Serve immediately, with the Tonkatsu sauce for dipping.

Simmered Pork

Long, slow simmering is a favourite Oriental cooking method for cheaper cuts of meat (see Clear Simmered Beef, page 31). In one of the classic Japanese recipes a small 450 g (1 lb) piece of belly pork is first briefly marinated in sake, then simmered in stock or water for 1 hour. At the next stage the meat is cut into quarters, and simmered for a further 30 minutes in 450 ml ($\frac{3}{4}$ pint) of the cooking liquid to which 2 tablespoons each of mirin (sweet rice wine) and sugar have been added. Finally, 4 tablespoons shoyu and 25 g (1 oz) dried bonito flakes are added and the cooking continued for 2 hours. The pork is extremely tender and is best served with plain rice and pickled vegetables.

Left: Grilled ginger pork

Meat with Miso

Niku no Miso-yaki

Akamiso (Japanese red soy bean paste) gives meat an entirely different flavour. Served with hot steamed rice and salad, this dish makes a quick family meal.

750 g (1½ lb) beef flank steak, in one piece
4 tablespoons akamiso
2 tablespoons shoyu (Japanese soy sauce)
1½ tablespoons sugar
1 teaspoon freshly grated root ginger
1 spring onion, chopped
2 tablespoons vegetable oil
toasted sesame seeds, to garnish

Preparation time: 25 minutes, plus marinating
Cooking time: 2 minutes
Serves 4

1. Cut the meat lengthways through the middle, then cut into thin slices across the grain. Place the slices in a bowl with the akamiso, shoyu, sugar, ginger and spring onion. Mix well, then leave to marinate for 10 minutes.

2. Place a frying pan over high heat. Add the oil, then the meat and marinade. Stir-fry for about 2 minutes. Serve hot, sprinkled with toasted sesame seeds.

Above: Meat with miso; Vinegared cucumber (page 161)

Grilled Beef with Lemon Grass

Thit Bo Xao Xa Ot

In Asia, dishes which are assembled at table by the guests themselves are very popular and great fun to do. This Vietnamese version is centred round tender steak with a symphony of vegetables enhanced with herbs.

50 g (2 oz) rice vermicelli
3 garlic cloves, crushed
1 stem lemon grass, finely
  chopped
2 teaspoons salt
1 teaspoon sugar
½ teaspoon monosodium
  glutamate (optional)
6 tablespoons vegetable oil
450 g (1 lb) fillet steak, thinly
  sliced
12 sheets banh trang (rice
  paper)
1 iceberg lettuce, shredded
½ cucumber, sliced
2 tablespoons pickled carrot or
  radish
1 tablespoon chopped fresh mint
1 tablespoon chopped fresh
  coriander
nuoc mam giam (see page 92)
2 spring onions, finely chopped
2 tablespoons ground roasted
  peanuts

Preparation time: 15 minutes,
plus marinating
Cooking time: 8–10 minutes
Serves 4

1. Bring a large saucepan of water to the boil, add the vermicelli and cook for 2–3 minutes or until tender. Drain in a colander, rinse well and drain again.

2. Combine the garlic, lemon grass, salt, sugar, monosodium glutamate (if using) and half the oil in a shallow dish large enough to hold all the meat in a single layer. Add the beef and mix well. Cover and marinate for 30 minutes.

3. Meanwhile, prepare the banh trang by dipping the sheets in water. Shake off excess water, roll the banh trang loosely and arrange on a large serving platter, with the lettuce, cucumber, pickled carrot or radish, mint and coriander.

4. Place the rice vermicelli in a small bowl, and fill another bowl with nuoc mam giam. Set aside.

5. Drain the beef slices. Arrange them on an oiled baking sheet over medium coals or under a preheated low to medium grill. Cook for 2 to 3 minutes on each side, or to taste.

6. Heat the remaining oil in a small saucepan. Place the spring onions in a small heatproof bowl, carefully add the hot oil and mix gently.

7. Arrange the grilled beef slices on a heated platter and brush with the aromatic oil. Sprinkle with ground roasted peanuts.

8. Guests make their own banh trang rolls, using a slice of beef and selection of vegetables and vermicelli as the filling for each roll, and dipping the filled rolls in the Nuoc mam giam sauce.

Stir-fried Beef with Oyster Sauce

Thit Bo Xao Dau Hao

This Vietnamese recipe combines tender steak with rich, dark oyster sauce for a delicious supper dish.

4–6 tablespoons vegetable oil
300 g (11 oz) rump steak,
  sliced thinly
225 g (8 oz) mangetout,
  trimmed
2 garlic cloves, crushed
120 ml (4 fl oz) chicken stock
3 tablespoons oyster sauce
2 teaspoons cornflour
2 tablespoons water

Preparation time: 10 minutes
Cooking time: 12–15 minutes
Serves 4

1. Heat 4 tablespoons of the oil in a large frying pan. Add the beef and cook for 2 to 3 minutes until it is sealed on all sides. With a slotted spoon, transfer the beef slices to a large plate and reserve.

2. Add the mangetout to the oil remaining in the pan and stir-fry for 2 to 3 minutes. Remove with a slotted spoon and add to the meat.

Grilled beef with lemon grass; Grilled beef in vine leaves

Grilled Beef in Vine Leaves

Thit Bo Nuong La Nho

3. Pour the remaining oil into the pan if necessary and, when hot, add the garlic. Cook over moderate heat until golden, then return the beef and mangetout to the pan with the stock and oyster sauce. Stir-fry for 5 minutes.

4. Meanwhile, combine the cornflour and water in a cup and mix to a cream. Add to the mixture and cook, stirring constantly, until the mixture thickens. Serve immediately.

This Vietnamese way with stuffed vine leaves is ideal for a barbecue.

300 g (11 oz) minced steak
3 shallots, finely chopped
4 garlic cloves, crushed
½ teaspoon freshly ground black
 pepper
½ teaspoon monosodium
 glutamate (optional)
225 g (8 oz) fresh or drained
 canned vine leaves
oil for grilling
nuoc mam giam (see page 92)

Preparation time: 15 minutes, plus standing
Cooking time: 10 minutes
Serves 4

1. Mix the minced steak with the shallots, garlic, pepper and monosodium glutamate (if using) in a large bowl, using clean hands to press and mould the mixture together. Set aside for 30 minutes.

2. Meanwhile, place the vine leaves in a large heatproof bowl. Add boiling water to cover. Allow to stand for 1 minute, then drain. Keep the leaves in the bowl but cover it tightly with cling film so they do not dry out.

3. Place a vine leaf, shiny side down, on the work surface. Trim the stalk. Place a little of the filling in the centre, then turn in the sides to enclose it. Roll up sausage-fashion. Repeat with the remaining leaves.

4. Arrange the vine leaf parcels on an oiled grid over medium coals or under a preheated moderate grill, and brush liberally with oil. Cook for 10 minutes, turning occasionally and brushing with oil as necessary. Serve hot with Nuoc mam giam sauce.

Pork and Lettuce Parcels

Thit Heo Cuon Hanh Huong

These pretty parcels, tied with spring onion green, are a popular summer speciality in Vietnam.

1 bunch spring onions, green tops only
450 g (1 lb) lean belly of pork
3 slices root ginger, peeled
1 lettuce, separated into leaves
½ cucumber, sliced
2 tablespoons freshly chopped mint
2 tablespoons freshly chopped coriander
nuoc mam giam (see page 92) to serve

Preparation time: 15 minutes, plus standing
Cooking time: 45–60 minutes
Serves 4

1. Place the spring onion tops in a heatproof bowl, pour boiling water over and allow to stand for 1 minute. Drain and reserve.

2. Combine the pork and ginger in a large saucepan. Add water to cover. Bring to the boil, reduce the heat and simmer for 45 minutes to 1 hour or until the pork is tender. Drain the pork. When it is cool enough to handle, cut it in thin 3 mm (⅛ inch) strips. Allow to cool completely.

3. Blanch the lettuce leaves by dipping them in boiling water to make them pliable. Spread out a lettuce leaf on a wooden board or clean work surface. Top with a couple of pork shreds, 1 or 2 cucumber slices and a little mint and coriander. Fold to a neat parcel and secure with a length of spring onion green, tying it in a neat bow.

4. Arrange the parcels on a serving platter with a bowl of nuoc mam giam in the centre as a dip. Serve cold.

Spiced Lamb Kebabs

Tikka Kebab

A fine northern Indian delicacy, *Tikka Kebab* can be found over charcoal barbecues at virtually every street corner. Ideally they should be cooked on a griddle over charcoal, but satisfactory results can be obtained by grilling.

450 g (1 lb) boneless shoulder or leg of lamb
juice of 1 lemon
150 ml (¼ pint) natural yoghurt
4 small onions, quartered
3 garlic cloves, chopped
½ teaspoon turmeric
1 tablespoon vinegar
½ teaspoon salt
1 teaspoon freshly ground black pepper
1 green pepper, cored, seeded and cut into squares
1 lemon, quartered, to garnish

Preparation time: 10 minutes, plus marinating
Cooking time: about 10 minutes
Serves 4

1. Cut the lamb into 2.5 cm (1 inch) cubes, being careful to trim away excess fat and gristle. Put the lamb in a bowl and sprinkle with the lemon juice.

2. Put the yoghurt, half the onion, the garlic, turmeric, vinegar, salt and pepper in a blender or food processor and purée until the mixture is evenly blended. Pour over the lamb and stir well. Cover and leave to marinate in the refrigerator overnight.

3. To cook, thread the cubes of marinated meat on to kebab skewers, alternating with the green pepper and remaining onion quarters. Barbecue the kebabs over medium coals or cook under a preheated grill, turning them frequently, until tender – about 10 minutes.

4. Serve hot, garnished with lemon quarters, and accompanied by Naan (see page 196) and salad.

Caramel Pork

Thit Heo Kho

The sweet sauce of this Vietnamese dish complements the pork while the daikon adds a sharp contrast. Serve with boiled rice.

50 g (2 oz) sugar
water (see method)
450 g (1 lb) leg of pork, cut into large cubes
3 daikon (white radishes), peeled and thinly sliced
½ onion, chopped
5 tablespoons nuoc mam (fish gravy)
½ teaspoon freshly ground black pepper

Preparation time: 5 minutes
Cooking time: 1–1¼ hours
Serves 4

1. Place the sugar in a large heavy-bottomed saucepan and heat gently until it begins to smell burnt. Stir in 2 tablespoons of water (take care as the mixture may 'spit').

2. Add the pork and the radishes and top up with sufficient water to cover the meat. Add the daikon, onion and nuoc mam with pepper. Bring to the boil, then reduce the heat and simmer for 45 minutes to 1 hour, or until the pork is cooked and the liquid is reduced to one-third of its original quality.

3. To serve, transfer to a heated serving dish.

Pork figures large in Vietnamese cuisine, along with chicken and beef. Caramel pork (top) is braised until tender in a sweet but tangy sauce. Pork and lettuce parcels (bottom), flavoured with fresh herbs, are excellent for picnics.

Spiced Minced Beef

Dum Ka Keema

In the central Indian state of Andhra Pradesh, where this dish comes from, it is sometimes cooked as a meat loaf that can be sliced and taken on picnics. Peas are often added at the last minute for added colour.

3 tablespoons ghee
2 large onions, sliced
2 garlic cloves, sliced
1 teaspoon turmeric
2 teaspoons chilli powder
½ teaspoon ground coriander
½ teaspoon cumin seeds
1 teaspoon salt
1 teaspoon freshly ground black
    pepper
450 g (1 lb) minced beef

Preparation time: 10 minutes
Cooking time: about 20 minutes
Serves 4

1. Melt the ghee in a pan set over a moderate heat. Add the onions and garlic and fry gently until soft. Add the turmeric, chilli, coriander and cumin, season with salt and pepper and fry for a further 3 minutes, stirring constantly.

2. Add the beef and fry, stirring, until the meat is cooked and the curry is dry. Transfer to a heated serving dish and serve hot with a bowl of natural yoghurt.

Curried lamb with yoghurt and tomatoes

Curried Lamb with Yoghurt and Tomatoes

Rogan Josh

This classic dish from Kashmir in northern India gets its name from its rich, red appearance, contributed by the ground chillies and paprika pepper. To make it less fiery, omit the ground chillies and substitute more paprika powder.

2 tablespoons ghee or
    concentrated butter
675 g (1½ lb) lean lamb, cut
    into 2.5 cm (1 inch) cubes
4 bay leaves
2 brown cardamoms
6 cloves
6 black peppercorns
1 teaspoon black cumin seeds
2 × 2.5 cm (1 inch) pieces
    cinnamon stick
1 tablespoon salt
600 ml (1 pint) hot water

Vegetable mixture:
2 tablespoons ghee or
    concentrated butter
1 onion, chopped
4 green cardamoms
4 tablespoons tomato purée
1 × 142 ml (5 fl oz) carton
    natural yoghurt
Paste:
1 onion, chopped
6 garlic cloves
1 tablespoon coriander seeds,
    roasted
25 g (1 oz) root ginger, crushed
1 teaspoon red chilli powder
1 teaspoon turmeric powder
1 teaspoon paprika pepper
To serve:
1 teaspoon garam masala
    (page 16)

Preparation time: 20 minutes
Cooking time: 2½ hours
Serves 6

1. Melt the ghee or butter in a saucepan. Fry the pieces of lamb, bay leaves, brown cardamoms, cloves, peppercorns, cumin seeds and cinnamon pieces gently for 15 minutes, stirring so that the meat is coloured evenly. Transfer the meat and spice mixture to a plate.

2. To make the vegetable mixture, melt the ghee in the saucepan and fry the onion and green cardamoms until they are golden. Stir in the tomato purée. Add the yoghurt a tablespoon at a time, combining each addition with the onion mixture.

3. Grind the ingredients for the paste together to give a smooth consistency. Add the paste to the vegetables and cook, stirring continuously, for 5 minutes.

4. Return the lamb and spices to the pan and stir all together well. Add the salt and water. Cover and simmer for 2½ hours, or until the meat is tender. Serve hot, sprinkled with the garam masala and accompanied by plain boiled rice.

Vinegared Pork

Shikar Vindaloo

Vindaloo is thought to mean 'with wine (or vinegar) and garlic'. This very hot dish comes from the south-western part of India occupied by the Portuguese, and it is only Indian Christians who eat pork.

2 teaspoons chopped fresh
   ginger
½ teaspoon cardamom seeds
½ teaspoon ground cloves
1 tablespoon ground coriander
2 teaspoons turmeric
4 teaspoons chilli powder
1 teaspoon ground cumin seeds
1 teaspoon salt
½ teaspoon freshly ground black
   pepper
150 ml (¼ pint) vinegar
450 g (1 lb) boned pork, cut
   into 4 cm (1½ inch) cubes
3 tablespoons ghee or
   concentrated butter
5 garlic cloves, sliced

Preparation time: 30 minutes, plus marinating
Cooking time: about 1 hour 15 minutes
Serves 4

1. Mix the ginger, all the spices and seasonings with 2 teaspoons of vinegar to make a thick paste. Rub this into the pieces of pork and leave to marinate for 30 minutes.

2. Melt the ghee or butter in a heavy-based saucepan set over a moderate heat. Fry the sliced garlic for 1–2 minutes, stirring constantly. Add the pork to the pan and cover with the remaining vinegar.

3. Bring the liquid to the boil. Reduce the heat, cover the pan and simmer for about 1 hour or until the meat is tender. Serve hot with chappattis.

The Maharajah's Royal Venison Curry

The strong flavour of venison here combines with curry spices to give a rich and magnificent dish.

675 g (1½ lb) venison, diced
300 ml (½ pint) red wine
4 tablespoons vegetable oil
300 ml (½ pint) Curry Purée (see page 15)
2 tablespoons Mild Curry Paste (see page 15)
1 × 425 g (14 oz) can tomatoes, strained and juice retained
1 red pepper, chopped finely
1 tablespoon garam masala (see page 16)
2 tablespoons dried fenugreek leaves
salt
Spices (roast and ground):
1 teaspoon fennel seeds
8 green cardamoms
1 teaspoon fenugreek seeds
1 teaspoon black mustard seeds
2 teaspoons white cumin seeds
freshly chopped parsley, to garnish

Preparation time: 20 minutes, plus marinating
Cooking time: 1 hour 20 minutes
Oven: 190°C, 375°F, Gas Mark 5
Serves 4

1. Wash the meat in two or three changes of cold water, drain and pat dry with paper towels. Place in a 3 litre (5 pint) casserole with the wine and spices. Cover and marinate for 6–24 hours.

2. Heat the oil in a large frying pan or wok. Stir-fry the curry purée for 5 minutes. Blend in the curry paste. Add this mixture to the venison in the casserole and stir to combine. Place in a preheated oven and bake for 20 minutes.

3. Remove the casserole from the oven and add the tomatoes, pepper, garam masala and fenugreek leaves and salt to taste, with a little water or juice from the canned tomatoes to moisten, if necessary. Replace the casserole in the oven and continue to cook for 55 minutes. Check half-way through the cooking time to ensure that the meat is not becoming dry. If necessary, add a little more water or tomato juice.

4. Serve hot, with a little freshly chopped parsley sprinkled on top.

Burmese Pork and Bean Sprout Curry

The combination of meat with piquant fish sauce shows the influence of Chinese cooking in this recipe, producing a combination of delicious complementary flavours in a single dish.

575 g (1¼ lb) pork fillet, diced
4 tablespoons ghee or concentrated butter
300 ml (½ pint) Curry Purée (see page 15)
1 tablespoon Mild Curry Paste (see page 15)
4 tablespoons nuoc mam (fish sauce) or puréed anchovies
1–6 fresh green chillies, cored, deseeded and chopped
1 tablespoon mild mango or brinjal pickle, chopped
1 tablespoon vinegar
100 g (4 oz) bean sprouts
flesh of ½ fresh coconut plus milk of 1 coconut or 2 tablespoons desiccated coconut
1 tablespoon tomato purée
2 teaspoons garam masala (see page 16)

Preparation time: 20 minutes
Cooking time: 1 hour 10 minutes
Oven: 190°C, 375°F, Gas Mark 5
Serves 4

1. Place the pork in a 3 litre (5 pint) lidded casserole.

2. Heat the ghee or butter in a large frying pan or wok set over a moderate heat. Add the curry purée and stir-fry for 5 minutes. Add the curry paste, fish sauce or puréed anchovies, chillies to taste, mango or brinjal pickle and vinegar. Continue to stir-fry for 1–2 minutes to blend. Add this mixture to the pork.

3. Place the casserole in a preheated moderately hot oven and bake for 1 hour. After 20 minutes, check to see if the pork is getting too dry, and add a little water if necessary. Return the casserole to the oven.

4. Wash the bean sprouts in several changes of water. Blanch them in boiling water, drain and rinse. Drain again.

5. After 40 minutes' cooking time, add the bean sprouts, coconut flesh and milk or desiccated coconut, tomato purée and garam masala to the casserole. Return to the oven for the remainder of the cooking time.

6. Before serving, spoon off excess oil from the casserole. Serve hot.

A long tradition of hunting in India has produced a number of marvellous recipes for game such as The Maharajah's royal venison curry (top). Burmese pork and bean sprout curry (bottom) strikes a perfect balance between the flavour of the tender meat and the rich sauce.

Spiced Leg of Lamb

Raan masaledar

There are a number of recipes for a whole leg of lamb emanating from northern India, where they are so tender when cooked that they can be served with a spoon.

1 × 3 kg (7 lb) leg of lamb
3 lemons
2 teaspoons salt
10 garlic cloves, peeled
2 × 7.5 cm (3 inch) pieces fresh root ginger, peeled
1 teaspoon freshly ground black pepper
5 cm (2 inch) piece cinnamon stick
10 cloves
seeds of 20 cardamoms
2 tablespoons clear honey
600 ml (1 pint) natural yoghurt
50 g (2 oz) shelled pistachios
100 g (4 oz) blanched almonds
2 teaspoons chilli powder
1 teaspoon turmeric

Preparation time: 40 minutes, plus marinating
Cooking time: 2 hours 20 minutes
Oven: 230°C, 450°F, Gas Mark 8; then 180°C, 350°F, Gas Mark 4; then 220°C, 425°F, Gas Mark 7
Serves 8

1. Ask your butcher to cut the protruding leg bone as close to the meat as possible. Remove all the fat and the white parchment next to the flesh. Make deep slashes in the lamb with a sharp knife. Place it in an ovenproof dish or casserole with a tight-fitting lid.

2. Cut two of the lemons in half, and rub the cut surfaces over the lamb, squeezing the juice into the slashes in the meat. Sprinkle with the salt and set aside.

3. Purée the garlic and ginger to a paste in a blender or food processor. Add the pepper, and rub this mixture evenly into the meat. Cover and marinate for 8 hours.

4. Crush the cinnamon, cloves and cardamom seeds in a mortar and pestle. Put the honey in a blender or food processor with the yoghurt, pistachios, almonds, chilli powder and turmeric. Blend or process until well mixed together, then sprinkle in the crushed cinnamon, cloves and cardamoms. Pour this mixture evenly over the lamb, cover and marinate for a further 8 hours.

5. Place the covered lamb dish in a preheated hot oven and cook for 10 minutes. Reduce the temperature to moderate and cook for a further 2 hours, basting the meat every 15 minutes or so. Remove the lid of the dish, increase the oven temperature and cook for a further 10 minutes.

6. This dish can be served hot, straight from the oven, but it is more traditional to let it cool for an hour first.

Spiced leg of lamb; Potatoes in yoghurt (page 204); Spiced semolina dessert (page 218)

Lamb with Spinach

Saag gosht

This recipe from Andhra Pradesh in central India can also be used for beef. If you use lamb, serve aubergines as an accompaniment.

450 g (1 lb) spinach
4 tablespoons ghee or concentrated butter
300 ml (½ pint) Curry Purée (see page 15)
4 tomatoes, skinned and chopped
2 tablespoons Mild Curry Paste (see page 15)
450 g (1 lb) lean lamb, diced
1 tablespoon garam masala (see page 16)
1 tablespoon dried fenugreek leaves
salt

Preparation time: 15 minutes
Cooking time: 1 hour 10 minutes
Oven: 190°C, 375°F, Gas Mark 5
Serves 4

1. Prepare the spinach. If it is fresh, wash the leaves thoroughly and chop them roughly. If it is frozen, choose the leaf spinach rather than the chopped variety and defrost it completely. Drain very well. If using canned spinach, strain off the excess liquid.

2. Heat the butter or ghee in a large frying pan or wok set over a moderate heat. Stir-fry the curry purée for 5 minutes. Add the tomatoes, spinach and curry paste. Simmer for 5 minutes, stirring occasionally, until the ingredients have blended.

3. Add the lamb to the pan, mixing it in well. Transfer the mixture to a heavy-lidded casserole and bake in a preheated moderately hot oven for 20 minutes. Add the garam masala, fenugreek and salt to taste, with a little water to moisten if necessary. Return to the oven and cook for a further 40 minutes.

4. To serve, spoon off any excess oil from the casserole. Serve hot.

Lamb with Dal and Vegetables

Dhansak

In this dish from Maharashtra the vegetables can be varied according to preference and availability: always include aubergine, courgette and spinach, with green and red pepper, tomatoes, potatoes, peas or okra.

125 g (4 oz) red lentils
2–3 tablespoons vegetable oil
1 medium aubergine, sliced
2 courgettes, sliced
225 g (8 oz) fresh spinach, washed, drained and chopped
4 tablespoons concentrated butter or ghee
300 ml (½ pint) Curry Purée (see page 15)
2 tablespoons Mild Curry Paste (see page 15)
450 g (1 lb) lean lamb, diced
1 tablespoon freshly chopped coriander leaves
1 tablespoon brown sugar
1 tablespoon garam masala (see page 16)
salt
parsley sprigs, to garnish

Preparation time: 20 minutes, plus soaking
Cooking time: 2 hours
Oven temperature: 190°C, 375°F, Gas Mark 5
Serves 4

1. Sift through the lentils for grit. Soak them in twice their volume of water for 1–2 hours.

2. Prepare the vegetables. Heat the oil in a heavy saucepan set over a moderate heat and fry the aubergines until golden on both sides. Add the courgettes and stir-fry for 5 minutes. Add the spinach and stir-fry for 1 minute. Reduce the heat, cover the pan and cook for 5 minutes.

3. Strain the lentils and cook them in an equal volume of boiling water for 20–30 minutes. Drain and keep hot.

4. Heat the butter or ghee in a frying pan. Stir-fry the curry purée for 5 minutes. Add the curry paste and stir in the cooked vegetables. Transfer this mixture to a heavy lidded casserole. Stir in the diced lamb and bake in a preheated oven for 20 minutes.

5. Remove the casserole and add the chopped coriander, sugar, garam masala, drained lentils and salt to taste with a little water to moisten if necessary. Return the casserole to the oven and cook for a further 40 minutes. If, at the end of the cooking time, there is an excess of oil, spoon it off before serving.

6. Serve hot, garnished with sprigs of parsley.

Indian cookery includes a range of delicious recipes for lamb (since Hindus cannot eat beef and pork is forbidden to Muslims). Lamb with spinach (top) contrasts the sweetness of the meat with the slight bitterness of spinach. Lamb with dal and vegetables (bottom) is a rich and filling composite dish. The proportion of meat to lentils can be reduced if you wish and a great variety of seasonal vegetables can be used.

Savoury Beef Curry

Methi Gosht

Cubes of beef cooked with
dried fenugreek leaves
produces a rich but sharp curry.

4 tablespoons ghee or
  concentrated butter
300 ml (½ pint) Curry Purée
  (see page 15)
2 tablespoons Mild Curry Paste
  (see page 15)
675 g (1½ lb) stewing beef, diced
4 tomatoes, chopped
4 tablespoons dried fenugreek
  leaves
1 tablespoon garam masala
  (see page 16)
salt
2 tablespoons freshly chopped
  parsley, to garnish

Preparation time: 10 minutes
Cooking time: about 1 hour
Oven: 190°C, 375°F, Gas Mark 5
Serves 4

1. Heat the ghee or butter in a
wok or large frying pan and stir-
fry the curry purée over
moderate heat for 5 minutes.
Stir the curry paste in well to
blend, and add the diced beef.
Stir-fry for about 5 minutes
more to seal the meat.

2. Transfer the meat and sauce
to a heavy, lidded casserole and
bake in a preheated oven for 20
minutes. Stir in the tomatoes,
fenugreek leaves, garam masala
and salt to taste, with a little
water to moisten if necessary.
Return the casserole to the oven
and continue cooking for a
further 25 minutes.

3. Before serving, spoon off any
excess oil from the surface of
the curry. Serve hot, garnished
with chopped parsley.

Beef Pasanda

Beating the steaks before
marinating means that as well as
being imbued with spicy
flavours the meat is meltingly
tender and can be cooked very
quickly.

675 g (1½ lb) lean beef, rump,
  fillet or topside
150 ml (¼ pint) red wine
2 teaspoons garam masala (see
  page 16)
1 teaspoon ground mace
½ teaspoon ground cinnamon
4 tablespoons vegetable oil
300 ml (½ pint) Curry Purée
  (see page 15)
1 tablespoon Mild Curry Paste
  (see page 15)
175 ml (6 fl oz) milk
2 tablespoons ground almonds
2 tablespoons desiccated
  coconut
salt
4 tablespoons double cream
  (optional)
To garnish:
parsley sprigs
chopped pistachio nuts

Preparation time: 15 minutes,
plus marinating
Cooking time: about 20
minutes
Serves 4

1. Slice the beef into 4 steaks.
Beat them with the back of a
wooden spoon until they are
5 mm (¼ inch) thick. Cut each
steak in half to give 8 pieces
in all.

2. Marinate the steaks in the
wine and spices (garam masala,
mace and cinnamon) for up to
24 hours.

3. Heat the oil in a frying pan or
wok and stir-fry the curry purée
for 5 minutes over moderate
heat. Add the curry paste and
mix well.

4. Lift the steaks out of the
marinade and add them to the
pan 2 at a time. Fry the steaks
quickly to seal – allow about 20
seconds on each side. When all
the steaks are in the pan and
have browned, add the milk,
ground almonds, desiccated
coconut and salt. Stir in the
marinade. Simmer for 10
minutes, until the meat is
cooked.

5. Transfer to a heated dish and
pour on the cream, if liked.
Serve with rice and garnished
with parsley sprigs and chopped
pistachios.

Mongolian Hot Pot

Also known as 'Mohammedan Fire Kettle', this classic dish originated in Mongolia but achieved fame in Peking. The fire kettle has a large funnel rising from the centre of the cooking pot and the foods are cooked in the 'moat' surrounding the funnel (see page 30). The cooking liquid should be good Chinese stock, but consommé, beef stock or chicken stock can be used.

1 kg (2¼ lb) piece frozen lamb
  fillet
1 kg (2¼ lb) Chinese cabbage
450 g (1 lb) fresh spinach
2 cakes bean curd, thinly sliced
50 g (2 oz) cellophane noodles
2.25 litres (4 pints) Chinese
  Clear Stock (see page 68)
Sauces and dips:
6 tablespoons finely chopped
  spring onion
2 tablespoons freshly chopped
  Chinese parsley
6 tablespoons soy sauce
6 tablespoons sesame paste
2 tablespoons pale dry sherry
2 tablespoons sugar
2 tablespoons hot chilli or
  Tabasco sauce
2 tablespoons sesame oil
1 tablespoon salted or
  fermented bean curd

Preparation time: 35–40
minutes, plus thawing
Cooking time: see method
Serves 6

1. Allow the lamb to defrost slightly, but while it is still partially frozen, cut it into paper-thin slices. Arrange the slices on a serving platter and allow to thaw.

2. Shred the cabbage and cut away the thicker parts of the spinach. Wash and dry the green vegetables and place in serving dishes. Arrange the bean curd and noodles on another dish.

3. Put the sauce and dip ingredients in individual bowls, so that each person can prepare his own sauce.

4. If using a fire kettle and charcoal, fill the moat with stock before starting the fire. When the stock is boiling furiously, add about a quarter of the prepared vegetables and the noodles. Within 1–2 minutes it will reboil. Each person picks up a piece of meat with bamboo chopsticks (do not use plastic ones) and dips it into the boiling liquid. As soon as the colour of the meat changes, it is done. He then retrieves it, together with some vegetables and noodles, dips them in the sauce he has mixed on his own plate and eats them while piping hot.

5. More vegetables are added as required. As the meal progresses, the flavour of the stock becomes richer. When all the meat has been eaten, the remainder of the vegetables, bean curd and noodles are added to the soup. Boil vigorously for 3–4 minutes, then ladle into individual bowls and serve as soup to end the meal.

Opposite: Beef pasanda
Left: Mongolian hot pot

Ham with Lotus Seeds in Honey Sauce

In China lotus seeds are added to festival dishes, since they are a symbol of fertility – their name, *lien jee*, is phonetically the same as the words meaning 'continuation of birth of sons'.

1 × 5 cm (2 inch) thick slice of ham, weight about 1–1.25 kg (2–2½ lb)
3 tablespoons soft brown sugar
a pinch of ground cinnamon
6 tablespoons water
100 g (4 oz) lotus seeds
Honey sauce:
3 tablespoons clear honey
1½ tablespoons sugar
2 teaspoons cornflour
3 tablespoons water

Preparation time: 20 minutes
Cooking time: about 2¾ hours
Serves 6

1. Place the ham on a heatproof dish. Put into a steamer and steam steadily for 1 hour. Cut the ham into 8 pieces and reassemble them into the original shape.

2. Heat the brown sugar, cinnamon and water in a small saucepan over a gentle heat until the sugar is dissolved. Add the lotus seeds and cook, stirring, for 2 minutes.

3. Spoon the lotus seeds in syrup over the ham. Return the dish to the steamer and steam steadily for a further 1½ hours.

4. To make the Honey sauce, place all the ingredients in a small saucepan set over a gentle heat and cook, stirring continuously, until thickened. Pour the sauce over the lotus seeds on top of the ham. Serve hot; the ham should be tender enough to be broken into small bite-sized pieces with chopsticks.

Red, White and Green Kidney

This Chinese dish derives its descriptive name from the pink of the ham, the white of the chicken and the green of the vegetables accompanying the kidney.

2 eggs, beaten
3 tablespoons cornflour
salt
225 g (8 oz) cooked chicken breast meat, finely chopped
175 g (6 oz) cooked ham, minced
2–3 spring onions, finely chopped
4 × 100 g (4 oz) pig's kidneys, cored
225 g (8 oz) Brussels sprouts
25 g (1 oz) lard
150 ml (¼ pint) Chinese Clear Stock (see page 68)
1 tablespoon water

Preparation time: 15 minutes
Cooking time: 35 minutes
Serves 8

1. Beat the eggs with 2 tablespoons of the cornflour and a little salt.

2. Mix together the chopped chicken meat, the ham and spring onions.

3. Cut each kidney into 8 slices. Dip each slice into the egg mixture, then coat with a little of the chicken and ham mixture. Arrange in rows on a well-greased heatproof plate. Steam for 30 minutes.

4. While the kidneys are steaming, prepare the Brussels sprouts. Melt the lard in a saucepan over a moderate heat. Add the sprouts and stir-fry with a little salt and about half the stock until they are just tender. Arrange the sprouts around the cooked kidney slices and keep hot.

5. Heat the remaining stock in a clean saucepan. Mix the remaining cornflour with a tablespoon of water to make a thin paste. Stir into the stock and continue to cook, stirring, until it has thickened. Check the seasoning. Pour the sauce over the kidney and serve hot.

Lion's Head Meatballs

See Jee Tao

These generously proportioned meatballs are often served in China on a bed of spinach, with noodles arranged on top like a lion's mane.

1 kg (2¼ lb) minced pork
4 tablespoons soy sauce
1 tablespoon Chinese wine or dry sherry
1½ tablespoons sugar
1 cm (½ inch) piece fresh root ginger, peeled and chopped finely
½ teaspoon finely ground black pepper
1 tablespoon sesame oil
vegetable oil for deep frying
500 ml (18 fl oz) cold water
1 tablespoon cornflour

Preparation time: 20 minutes
Cooking time: about 3½ hours
Serves 4–6

1. In a bowl mix together the pork, 1 tablespoon soy sauce, wine, ½ tablespoon sugar, the ginger, pepper and sesame oil until everything is thoroughly blended. Beat the mixture well, and form it into 4 meatballs.

2. In a wok, heat the oil for deep-frying. When it is hot, but not smoking, lower the meatballs in batches of two and deep-fry until they are brown all over. Lift out of the oil with a slotted spoon and set aside to keep warm.

3. Place the water in a saucepan large enough to hold the meatballs in a single layer. Bring the water to the boil, and gently lower the meatballs into the pan. Sprinkle over the remaining soy sauce and sugar. Cover, reduce the heat and simmer gently for about 3 hours, checking from time to time to see that the liquid has not all evaporated.

4. After 3 hours, lift out the meatballs, drain and place on a serving dish. Keep them warm while you prepare the sauce.

5. Combine the cornflour with water to make a thin paste. Stir into the cooking liquid over a moderate heat until it has thickened. Pour the sauce over the meatballs and serve with bowls of plain rice.

Twice-cooked Pork with Chilli Bean Sauce

Hui Gou Rou

To be authentic, the cut of meat used is the belly of pork, known as 'five-flower' pork in China because the alternate layers of fat and meat form a pretty pink and white pattern when viewed in cross-section.

Above: Twice-cooked pork with chilli bean sauce

350 g (12 oz) belly pork in one piece, not too lean
100 g (4 oz) bamboo shoots
100 g (4 oz) celery sticks
3 tablespoons vegetable oil
2 spring onions, cut in pieces
1 garlic clove, finely chopped
2 tablespoons Chinese wine or dry sherry
1 tablespoon soy sauce
1 tablespoon chilli bean sauce

Preparation time: 10 minutes, plus cooling
Cooking time: 30–35 minutes
Serves 4

1. Place the whole piece of pork in a saucepan of boiling water and cook for 25–30 minutes. Remove the meat and leave to cool. When it is cool, cut it across the grain (see page 29) into thin slices about 5 × 2.5 cm (2 × 1 inches) in size.

2. Cut the bamboo shoots and celery into chunks about the same size as the pork.

3. Heat the oil in a hot wok until it is smoking. Add the spring onions and garlic to flavour the oil, then add the vegetables and stir-fry for a few seconds.

4. Add the pork pieces to the wok, then the wine or sherry, soy and chilli bean sauces. Stir-fry for 1–2 minutes, transfer to a heated platter and serve immediately, with deep-fried rice noodles.

Aubergine and Pork in Hot Sauce

Yuxiang Qiezi

Aubergines can absorb a great deal of oil, making them too soft and indigestible. The cooking method in this recipe ensures that they retain texture while being flavoured with the delicious spicy sauce, a perfect accompaniment to the shredded pork.

175 g (6 oz) fillet of pork, shredded
2 spring onions, chopped finely
1 slice fresh root ginger, peeled and chopped finely
1 garlic clove, chopped finely
1 tablespoon soy sauce
2 teaspoons Chinese wine or sherry
1½ teaspoons cornflour
225 g (8 oz) aubergine, sliced
salt
300 ml (½ pint) vegetable oil for deep-frying
1 tablespoon chilli sauce
3–4 tablespoons chicken stock or water
chopped spring onion, to garnish

Preparation time: 15 minutes, plus marinating
Cooking time: 15–20 minutes
Serves 4

1. Place the pork in a bowl with the spring onions, ginger, garlic, soy sauce, wine and cornflour. Mix well and leave to marinate for about 20 minutes.

2. Dust the aubergine slices with salt and leave to stand for 10 minutes to 'sweat'. Rinse in cold water, pat dry with paper towels, and cut each slice into quarters.

3. Heat the oil in a wok to 180°C/350°F or until a cube of bread browns in 30 seconds. Reduce the heat, add the aubergine and deep-fry for about 1½ minutes. Remove the aubergine from the oil with a slotted spoon and drain on paper towels.

4. Pour off all but 1 tablespoon of oil from the wok. Add the pork and stir-fry for about 1 minute. Add the aubergine and chilli sauce and cook for about 1½ minutes, then moisten with the stock or water. Simmer, stirring occasionally, until the liquid has almost completely evaporated.

5. Transfer to a heated serving dish and serve hot, garnished with chopped spring onion.

Aubergine and pork in hot sauce; Stir fried liver with spinach

Stir-fried Liver with Spinach

The amount of pork eaten in China probably outweighs all other meats several times over, and there are as many economical dishes like this as elaborate recipes for banquets.

350 g (12 oz) pig's liver, cut into thin triangular slices
2 tablespoons cornflour
4 tablespoons vegetable oil
450 g (1 lb) fresh spinach leaves, washed and drained thoroughly
1 teaspoon salt
2 slices fresh root ginger, peeled
1 tablespoon soy sauce
1 tablespoon Chinese wine or dry sherry
shredded spring onion, to garnish

Preparation time: 15 minutes
Cooking time: 3 minutes
Serves 3–4

1. Blanch the pieces of liver for a few seconds in boiling water. Drain, and coat the slices with the cornflour.

2. Heat 2 tablespoons of the oil in a wok set over a moderate heat and stir-fry the spinach and salt for 2 minutes. Remove the spinach and arrange it around the edge of a warmed serving dish. Keep hot.

3. Heat the remaining oil in the wok until it is very hot. Add the ginger, liver, soy sauce and wine. Stir well and cook for 1 minute, so that the liver is still tender.

4. Pour the contents of the wok into the centre of the spinach, garnish with shredded spring onion and serve immediately.

Fried Buns Stuffed with Pork, Prawns and Vegetables

These savoury stuffed buns are often eaten in China on a picnic or while travelling. They are perfect for a supper dish accompanied by a choice of vegetables.

1 tablespoon dried yeast
100 ml (3½ fl oz) warm water
a pinch of sugar
450 g (1 lb) plain flour
Filling:
225 g (8 oz) minced pork
100 g (4 oz) peeled prawns, finely chopped
200 g (7 oz) Chinese cabbage, finely shredded
2 spring onions, chopped finely
2 cm (1 inch) piece root ginger, peeled and finely chopped
a few drops of sesame oil
a pinch of monosodium glutamate (optional)
1 tablespoon soy sauce
a pinch of freshly ground white pepper
100 ml (3½ fl oz) vegetable oil
To garnish:
watercress leaves
parsley sprigs

Preparation time: 10 minutes, plus proving and rising
Cooking time: 10 minutes
Serves 4–5

1. To make the dough, mix the yeast with 2 tablespoons of the warm water and the pinch of sugar. Leave in a warm place until it becomes frothy.

2. Sift the flour into a bowl, add the yeast mixture and the remaining warm water. Knead together to form a soft dough. Continue kneading for about 10 minutes or until the dough becomes smooth and elastic. Place in a bowl and cover with a piece of cling film. Put the bowl in a warm place and leave until the dough has doubled its bulk (about 1 hour).

3. To make the filling, mix together the pork, prawns, Chinese cabbage, spring onions, ginger, sesame oil, monosodium glutamate (if using), soy sauce and white pepper in a bowl.

4. When the dough has doubled its bulk, knead it well on a floured board, then return it to the bowl and leave it to rise again. When it has again doubled in size, knead it for the third time and roll it into a long sausage shape. Cut the dough into about 35 pieces and roll each small piece into a ball.

5. Using a rolling pin, roll each ball into a flat circle. Place about 2 teaspoons of filling on a circle of dough and bring up the edges to form a flower. Twist the edges together to seal. Prepare all the circles of dough in this way.

6. Heat a wok and place all the prepared buns in it. Pour in about 350 ml (12 fl oz) water and simmer for about 6 minutes. Pour off the water. Add the vegetable oil to the wok and fry the buns for 3–4 minutes or until the bottoms are golden brown.

7. Remove the buns from the wok with a slotted spoon and drain on paper towels. Arrange on a warm serving platter and serve immediately, garnished with watercress and parsley.

Braised Pork with Pumpkin

This Chinese recipe is a delicious winter dish in which the sweetness of the pumpkin complements the pork perfectly.

2 tablespoons dry sherry
5 tablespoons soy sauce
350 g (12 oz) belly pork, rind removed
3 tablespoons vegetable oil
500 g (1¼ lb) pumpkin, peeled, seeded and cut into 5 cm (2 inch) cubes
300 ml (½ pint) Chinese Clear Stock (see page 68)
2 teaspoons sugar

Preparation time: 10 minutes
Cooking time: 20 minutes
Serves 4

1. Mix together half the sherry and 1 tablespoon of the soy sauce in a bowl. Cut the pork into small pieces 1 cm (½ inch) thick and place in the bowl. Turn to coat thoroughly.

2. Heat the oil in a wok or frying pan over a moderate heat. Add the pork pieces and stir-fry until they are browned all over. Add the pieces of pumpkin and stir well.

3. Add the stock, sugar and remaining sherry and soy sauce. Bring to the boil and simmer for 15 minutes or until the pumpkin is tender. Transfer to a heated serving dish and serve immediately.

Szechuan Hot-fried Crispy Shredded Beef

Many Szechuan dishes have a more 'chewy' texture than elsewhere in China – this is achieved by frying food until it is quite dry, even crusty, then tossing it in a sauce, giving a highly concentrated flavour.

4 eggs
½ teaspoon salt
100 g (4 oz) cornflour
450 g (1 lb) topside of beef, cut into matchstick strips
600 ml (1 pint) vegetable oil
3 medium carrots, scraped and cut into matchstick strips
2 spring onions, cut into 2.5 cm (1 inch) sections
2 fresh chillies, cored, seeded and shredded
3 garlic cloves, crushed
6 teaspoons sugar
2 tablespoons soy sauce
4 tablespoons wine vinegar

Preparation time: 20 minutes
Cooking time: 10 minutes
Serves 4–6

1. Mix together the eggs, salt and cornflour and toss the beef in this mixture until it is all well coated.

2. Heat the oil in a wok to 180°C/350°F or until a cube of bread browns in 30 seconds. Stir-fry the beef for 1½ minutes or until it is crispy. Remove the beef from the oil with a slotted spoon and drain on paper towels.

3. Reheat the oil and deep-fry the carrots for 1½ minutes. Remove and drain on paper towels.

4. Pour off most of the oil, leaving about 1½ tablespoons in the bottom of the wok. Reheat, then add the spring onions, chillies and garlic. Stir-fry together for about 30 seconds over the heat then add the sugar, soy sauce and vinegar.

5. Return the meat and carrots to the sauce. Toss them together over the heat briefly. Transfer to a heated platter and serve immediately.

Ants Climbing Trees

Mayi Shangshu

The creativeness of Chinese cooking extends to the naming of dishes. This one is thought to look like ants (the little pieces of meat) scrambling over the branches of a tree (the entangled noodles).

225 g (8 oz) fillet of pork, minced
2 tablespoons soy sauce
1 tablespoon sugar
1 teaspoon cornflour
½ teaspoon chilli sauce or Tabasco
3 tablespoons vegetable oil
1 small red chilli, seeded and chopped
2 spring onions, chopped
75 g (3 oz) cellophane noodles, soaked in water for 30 minutes and drained
120 ml (4 fl oz) chicken stock or water
shredded spring onion, to garnish

Preparation time: 10 minutes, plus marinating
Cooking time: 20–25 minutes
Serves 4

1. Put the pork in a bowl with the soy sauce, sugar, cornflour and chilli sauce. Mix well and leave to marinate for about 20 minutes.

2. Heat the oil in a wok set over a moderate heat and stir-fry the chilli and spring onions for a few seconds. Add the pork mixture and stir-fry until the pork changes colour.

3. Add the noodles to the wok and blend in well.

4. Add the stock or water and continue cooking, stirring frequently, until all the liquid has been absorbed.

5. Transfer to a heated platter and serve hot, garnished with shredded spring onion.

Right: Chicken with cold-tossed bean sprouts (page 118); Szechuan dan dan noodles (page 186); Oxtail noodles with parsley, coriander and spring onions

Oxtail Noodles with Parsley, Coriander and Spring Onion

This Szechuan dish makes a wonderfully hearty and satisfying winter meal.

1.8 kg (4 lb) oxtail, cut up
450 g (1 lb) rice stick noodles
600 ml (1 pint) beef stock
1 chicken stock cube
4 tablespoons soy sauce
freshly ground black pepper
3 tablespoons hoisin sauce
2 tablespoons yellow bean paste
1 tablespoon sugar
6 tablespoons Chinese wine or
  dry sherry
5 spring onions, finely chopped
1½ tablespoons cornflour
5 tablespoons water

To garnish:
4 tablespoons chopped parsley
3 tablespoons chopped
  coriander leaves

Preparation time: 15 minutes
Cooking time: about 4 hours
Oven: 180°C, 350°F, Gas Mark 4
Serves 6

1. Parboil the oxtail in boiling water for 5–6 minutes and drain. Cook the noodles in boiling water for 5 minutes then drain.

2. Heat the stock in a casserole. Add the crumbled stock cube, soy sauce, pepper (to taste), hoisin sauce, yellow bean paste, sugar and half the wine. Bring to the boil and add the oxtail. Stir until the oxtail is well coated with sauce. Cover and cook in a preheated oven for 3½ hours, stirring every half hour and adding more stock when necessary.

3. Place the drained noodles in a wok. Sprinkle them evenly with the chopped spring onion. Pour the gravy from the casserole over the noodles and spring onion. Stir lightly over a moderate heat for 3 minutes, until the noodles are heated.

4. Pour the noodles into a large serving dish. Sprinkle the remainder of the wine over the oxtail in the casserole. Blend the cornflour and water to make a thin paste and stir into the casserole. Turn the oxtail over a few times, until a glossy sauce has formed.

5. Arrange the oxtail on top of the noodles in the serving dish. Spoon over any remaining sauce. Sprinkle with chopped parsley and coriander and serve hot.

VEGETABLES

At any Oriental meal, a selection of vegetables is a must, chosen for freshness and colour and cooked to preserve maximum flavour and texture. These recipes will transform your ideas about the humble cabbage or potato, and demonstrate how to use ingredients such as bean curd and seaweed that are highly valued in the East.

Vegetable Tempura

Kaki-age

In Japanese cuisine, it is important that the cooking medium, whether hot oil or charcoal, should give no inappropriate flavours to the food. Choose a very pure light oil such as safflower for deep-frying.

½ *medium carrot*
50 g (2 oz) French beans
2 potatoes, peeled
1 egg
50 g (2 oz) plain flour, sifted, plus extra for sprinkling
oil for deep-frying
To serve:
Tentsuyu sauce (see below)
1 × 2.5 cm (1 inch) piece fresh root ginger, peeled and grated
1 × 5 cm (2 inch) piece daikon (Japanese radish), peeled and grated

Preparation time: 30 minutes
Cooking time: 2 minutes
Serves 4

1. Peel the carrot and shred it finely into 5 cm (2 inch) lengths. Slice the French beans in half lengthways, and cut into 5 cm (2 inch) lengths. Cut the potatoes into matchstick strips.

2. To make the batter, put the egg in a bowl and stir in 50 ml (2 fl oz) ice-cold water. Add the flour all at once and mix to a lumpy batter: using 2 pairs of hashi (chopsticks) to do this would give the right texture (see page 37).

3. Put some of the prepared vegetables in a ladle and sprinkle them with a little flour. Add 1 or 2 tablespoons of the batter and mix well in the ladle.

4. Heat the oil in a deep-fat frier or deep frying pan to about 160°C/325°F or until a cube of bread browns in 45 seconds. Deep-fry the vegetables, a ladleful at a time, for about 2 minutes until they are golden and crisp. Remove from the hot oil with a perforated spoon and drain on paper towels.

5. To serve, pour the Tentsuyu sauce into 4 small bowls. Put the grated ginger and daikon in separate bowls. Fold a large paper towel in half and place on a bamboo dish or serving platter. Arrange the vegetables on the paper and serve immediately, with the bowls of sauce, ginger and daikon. Each diner should mix grated ginger and daikon to taste with some of the sauce, then dip the vegetables into the sauce before eating.

Tentsuyu Sauce

200 ml (7 fl oz) Japanese Stock (see page 69)
50 ml (2 fl oz) shoyu (Japanese soy sauce)
50 ml (2 fl oz) mirin (sweet rice wine)

Preparation time: 1 minute
Cooking time: 5 minutes
Serves 4

1. Bring the stock to the boil in a small saucepan with the shoyu and mirin. Transfer to 4 small bowls and serve.

Perfect Tempura

Batter for tempura should be made as soon as possible before use. Do not allow it to stand as you might for Western-style battered foods. Before dredging the foods lightly with flour, dry them on paper towels. The consistency of the batter may be modified slightly to make it thicker, by using a little less iced water, or more if you prefer a thin coating of batter.

The deep-frying technique used for tempura can also be used for foods with coatings other than batter. Try, for example, somen (fine egg noodles) chopped into 5 mm (¼ inch) lengths; crushed harusame; crushed nuts such as cashews or walnuts, finely sliced almonds, or sesame seeds; seaweed – nori, wakame or konbu – cut into very thin strips and crushed rice crackers are also used.

Many different vegetables are also excellent for deep-frying.

Right: Vegetable tempura with Tentsuyu sauce

Vinegared Cucumber

Sunomono

This classic Japanese salad may be served as an hors d'oeuvre or as an accompaniment.

1 large or 2 small cucumbers
1 teaspoon salt
15 g ($\frac{1}{2}$ oz) wakame (dried
young seaweed)
2.5–4 cm (1–1$\frac{1}{2}$ inch) piece
fresh root ginger
Saubaizu sauce:
3 tablespoons rice vinegar
1 tablespoon shoyu (Japanese
soy sauce)
1 tablespoon sugar
$\frac{1}{4}$–$\frac{1}{2}$ teaspoon salt

Preparation time: 10 minutes, plus soaking
Serves 4

1. Halve the cucumber(s) lengthways; remove the seeds with a sharp-edged teaspoon. Slice the cucumber very thinly and sprinkle with the salt. Using your hands, squeeze the cucumber slices a few times, then rinse under cold running water in a bamboo strainer or sieve.

2. Put the wakame in a bowl and cover with cold water. Leave to soak for 5–10 minutes, or until it becomes fully expanded and soft. Drain in a sieve, rinse with boiling water, then rinse under cold running water. Drain well and squeeze out any excess water with your hands. Cut the wakame into 2.5 cm (1 inch) lengths, if it is not already chopped.

3. Peel and shred the ginger, then place in a bowl of ice-cold water to crisp up.

4. Put all the ingredients for the sauce in a bowl, mix well together, then add the sliced cucumber and wakame. Toss well.

5. Transfer the salad to individual salad bowls, shaping it into neat mounds. Drain the shredded ginger and sprinkle over the top. Serve cold.

Illustrated on page 139

Tree Oyster Mushrooms

Shimeji

The shimeji has been cultivated in Japan for years as a fresh fungus 'vegetable' and is now becoming more widely available. It has a slight shellfish flavour.

225 g (8 oz) fresh shimeji (tree oyster mushrooms)
1½ teaspoons butter
1 garlic clove, crushed
1 teaspoon sake (rice wine)
3 tablespoons chicken stock
salt
freshly ground black pepper

Preparation time: 5 minutes
Cooking time: 3 minutes
Serves 4

1. Tear the shimeji into bite-sized pieces.

2. Melt the butter in a frying pan over low heat. Add the garlic and stir-fry for 30 seconds. Add the shimeji and sake. Stir-fry for 1 minute, then add the chicken stock and season with salt and pepper. Serve immediately.

Tree oyster mushrooms; Cabbage pickles; Mustard-pickled aubergine

Cabbage Pickles

Nappa no Tsukemono

This recipe, using brine, is one of the simplest ways of preserving vegetables for the pickles so popular in Japan.

1 large head Chinese cabbage
3 tablespoons coarse salt
4 tablespoons seedless raisins or stoned prunes
250 ml (8 fl oz) water
3 dried chillies

Preparation time: 5 minutes, plus marinating
Storage time: 1 week in brine, if kept in the refrigerator
Serves 4–6

1. Cut the Chinese cabbage into quarters and place in a glass bowl. Sprinkle the layers with the salt. Add the raisins or prunes, water and chillies and stir well until the salt has dissolved.

2. Place a saucer on top of the cabbage, put a heavy weight on top and leave to marinate for 12 hours.

3. Discard the raisins or prunes and wash the cabbage quickly. Squeeze out the excess moisture and slice the cabbage into bite-size pieces. Serve cold.

Spiced Okra

Bhindi Masaledar

In the East and Middle East okra are prized not only for their delicious flavour, but for the rich texture they give to dishes like this Indian recipe.

450 g (1 lb) okra, trimmed
50 ml (2 fl oz) sunflower oil
1 teaspoon fenugreek seeds
1 tablespoon ground coriander
1 teaspoon turmeric
1 teaspoon chilli powder
salt
5–6 sprigs fresh coriander, chopped, to garnish

Preparation time: 5 minutes
Cooking time: 25 minutes
Serves 4

1. Cut the okra into 2.5 cm (1 inch) rings.

2. Heat the oil in a wok and fry the fenugreek seeds until they are browned. Add the okra, ground coriander, turmeric, chilli powder and salt and toss to mix thoroughly.

3. Cook, uncovered, over a low heat for about 20 minutes, tossing frequently until the okra is tender and dry.

4. Serve hot, sprinkled with freshly chopped coriander leaves.

Mustard-pickled Aubergine

Nasu no Karashi

The clean sharp flavour of this pickle is typically Japanese, but goes well with many South-east Asian dishes.

*1 medium aubergine, or 6
  small Japanese elongated
  aubergines*
750 ml (1¼ pints) water
1 tablespoon salt
Dressing:
1 teaspoon dry mustard
*3 tablespoons shoyu (Japanese
  soy sauce)*
*3 tablespoons mirin (sweet rice
  wine)*
3 tablespoons sugar

Preparation time: 15 minutes,
plus standing and chilling
Serves 4

1. Cut the aubergine crossways into slices about 3 mm (⅛ inch) thick. Cut the slices into quarters. Soak in the water, with the salt added, for 1 hour.

2. Make the dressing. Put all the ingredients in a bowl and stir well to combine.

3. Drain the aubergine and pat dry with paper towels. Arrange the pieces carefully in a glass serving bowl and pour the dressing over evenly and slowly.

4. Cover the bowl with cling film and chill in the refrigerator for several hours or overnight before serving, to allow the flavours to develop.

Curried Okra and Potatoes

Bhindi aur Aloo ki Bhaji

While this recipe is from India, okra are well known across the tropical world and are used in the Caribbean as well as in Asia. Use very fresh, tender pods for the best results.

450 g (1 lb) okra, trimmed
4 tablespoons sunflower oil
1 teaspoon black mustard seeds
1 medium onion, sliced
    lengthways
225 g (8 oz) potatoes, peeled
    and cut into 2.5 cm (1 inch)
    cubes
1 teaspoon salt
1 teaspoon turmeric
1 teaspoon chilli powder
1 tablespoon ground coriander
2 tomatoes, chopped
4 sprigs of fresh coriander,
    chopped, to garnish

Preparation time: 20 minutes
Cooking time: about 40 minutes
Serves 4

1. Cut each okra in half and cut each piece into 4 lengthways. Set aside.

2. Heat the oil in a wok and fry the mustard seeds until they begin to pop. Add the onion and stir-fry for 2–3 minutes.

3. Reduce the heat and carefully add the okra and potatoes. then the salt, turmeric, chilli powder and ground coriander. Toss the ingredients well. Cover and cook for about 25 minutes, tossing the vegetables every few minutes.

4. Stir in the chopped tomatoes, toss well and cook for a further 10–15 minutes. Serve hot, sprinkled with freshly chopped coriander.

Dry-fried Spinach

Tali Saag

Spinach is a much-prized vegetable in India. As it is very delicate, both in structure and in taste, a particularly gentle spicing is used.

3 tablespoons ghee or
    concentrated butter
1 small onion, sliced
1 teaspoon garam masala (see
    page 16)
1 teaspoon salt
900 g (2 lb) leaf spinach, well
    washed

Preparation time: 10 minutes
Cooking time: about 15 minutes
Serves 4

1. Melt the ghee in a heavy pan, add the onion and fry gently until it is soft. Add the garam masala and salt and fry for a further 3 minutes, stirring constantly.

2. Add the spinach and cook for about 5 minutes, covered, shaking the pan constantly. Serve hot.

Right: Spiced aubergines and tomatoes; Stir-fried spinach; Spiced potatoes and cauliflower

Spiced Aubergines and Tomatoes

Baigan Tamatar

The aubergine is a popular vegetable in Indian cuisine. It should be shiny, purple and firm when at its peak. This version goes well with tandoori dishes.

6 tablespoons ghee
1 large onion, sliced
2 garlic cloves, sliced
1 teaspoon ground coriander
1 × 2.5 cm (1 inch) piece
    cinnamon stick
1 teaspoon chilli powder
1 teaspoon salt
1 teaspoon freshly ground black
    pepper
450 g (1 lb) aubergines,
    chopped into 2.5 cm (1 inch)
    pieces
450 g (1 lb) tomatoes, chopped
    into 2.5 cm (1 inch) pieces
3 tablespoons tomato purée
250 ml (8 fl oz) water

Preparation time: 20 minutes
Cooking time: 35 minutes
Serves 4

1. Melt the ghee in a heavy pan, add the onion and garlic and fry gently until soft. Add the coriander, cinnamon and chilli powder and season with salt and pepper. Fry for 3 minutes, stirring constantly.

2. Add the aubergines, tomatoes and tomato purée and toss gently to coat with the spice mixture.

3. Stir in the water and bring to the boil. Reduce the heat and simmer for 25–30 minutes, until the aubergines are tender and the sauce is quite thick. Increase the heat to boil off any excess liquid, if necessary. Serve hot.

Spiced Potatoes and Cauliflower

Aloo gobi

Aloo gobi is a good example of the way in which Indian cuisine can adapt itself to use vegetables which are not indigenous. Potatoes and cauliflower are now available in India, grown in the more temperate zones.

*4 tablespoons ghee or
    concentrated butter*
*900 g (2 lb) potatoes, cut into
    2.5 cm (1 inch) cubes*
2 large onions, sliced
4 garlic cloves, sliced
2 teaspoons chilli powder
1 teaspoon turmeric
1 teaspoon ground coriander
2 teaspoons salt
*½ teaspoon freshly ground black
    pepper*
1.2 litres (2 pints) water
450 g (1 lb) cauliflower florets
175 g (6 oz) peas
*2 teaspoons garam masala (see
    page 16)*

Preparation time: 15 minutes
Cooking time: about 35 minutes
Serves 4

1. Melt the ghee in a heavy pan. Add the potatoes and fry gently for exactly 1 minute. Remove from the pan with a slotted spoon and set aside.

2. Add the onions and garlic to the pan and fry gently until soft. Add the chilli powder, turmeric and ground coriander and season with salt and pepper. Fry for a further 3 minutes, stirring constantly.

3. Return the potatoes to the pan, add the water and bring to the boil. Reduce the heat and simmer for 10 minutes.

4. Add the cauliflower and peas. Simmer for a further 15 minutes until the vegetables are tender and the sauce is thick.

5. Increase the heat to boil off any excess liquid, if necessary. Stir in the garam masala and serve hot.

Rajma Lobia Curry

This Indian dish combines red kidney beans (rajma) and black-eyed bean (lobia) in a spicy curry base. To save time, canned beans may be used, with their liquid, instead of the dried beans.

225 g (8 oz) red kidney beans
225 g (8 oz) black-eyed beans
3 tablespoons sunflower oil
40 g (1½ oz) fresh root ginger, thinly sliced
1 onion, chopped
2 teaspoons garam masala (see page 16)
1 teaspoon ground coriander
1 teaspoon ground cumin
½ teaspoon chilli powder
300 ml (½ pint) tomato juice
salt
3–4 tablespoons lemon or lime juice
chervil sprigs, to garnish

Preparation time: 15 minutes, plus soaking overnight
Cooking time: about 50 minutes
Serves 4

1. Rinse the kidney beans in cold water and drain. Place them in a bowl with twice their volume of cold water and leave to soak overnight. Next day rinse the beans in cold water 3 or 4 times. Follow the same procedure of rinsing and soaking for the black-eyed beans, keeping them separate from the kidney beans.

2. Take two saucepans and place 1.2 litres (2 pints) of water in each. Bring each to the boil. Put the kidney beans in one pan and the black-eyed beans in the other and boil them both rapidly for 45 minutes.

3. After about 30 minutes, heat the oil in a wok or large frying pan and stir-fry the ginger for 1 minute. Add the onion and continue to stir-fry for 3–4 minutes.

4. Quickly mix the garam masala, coriander, cumin and chilli powder with enough water to make a paste. Add the paste to the wok and stir it in for 2–3 minutes.

5. Add the tomato juice and cook until it comes to simmering point.

6. As soon as the beans are tender and completely cooked, strain them and add them to the pan. Season with salt to taste.

7. Just before serving, stir in the fresh lemon or lime juice. Serve hot, garnished with sprigs of chervil.

Chick Peas and Lentils with Cumin Seeds

Tarka Channa Dhal

The Indians have discovered that certain spices, amongst them coriander and cumin, make pulses easier to digest as well as good to eat.

50 g (2 oz) chick peas
175 g (6 oz) red lentils
2 tablespoons sunflower oil
2 teaspoons white cumin seeds
2 teaspoons black mustard seeds
2–4 garlic cloves, finely chopped
1 large onion, thinly sliced
1 tablespoon Mild Curry Paste (see page 15)
salt
parsley sprigs, to garnish

Preparation time: 10 minutes, plus soaking
Cooking time: 1 hour
Serves 4

1. Rinse the chick peas and lentils separately 2 or 3 times. Still keeping them separate, soak them in plenty of cold water overnight to allow them to swell and soften.

2. Drain the chick peas. Boil 1.2 litres (2 pints) of water in a saucepan and boil the chick peas vigorously for 45 minutes.

3. Drain the red lentils and in another pan bring 450 ml (¾ pint) water to the boil. Add the lentils and bring the water back to simmering point, stirring from time to time. Cover the pan and leave to simmer for 20 minutes. Stir the lentils to prevent them sticking to the pan. Add a little water, if necessary, and continue to simmer.

4. Heat the oil in a wok or large frying pan. Stir-fry the cumin seeds and mustard seeds for 1 minute. Add the garlic and stir-fry for 1 minute more. Add the onion and stir-fry for 5 minutes more. Blend in the curry paste.

5. Taste the chick peas and lentils to make sure they are cooked. Strain the chick peas and add them to the lentils.

6. Add the fried mixture to the pulses and season with salt to taste. Serve hot, garnished with parsley sprigs.

Dhal; Rajma lobia curry; Chick peas and lentils with cumin seeds

Dhal

Pulses such as dried beans, split peas and lentils are staple foods in India. This simple recipe can be used for any kind of lentils.

250 g (8 oz) red lentils
300 ml (½ pint) water
1 teaspoon garlic powder
1 teaspoon ground cumin
1 teaspoon garam masala (see page 16)
a knob of ghee or concentrated butter
salt
parsley sprigs, to garnish

Preparation time: 5 minutes, plus standing
Cooking time: about 35 minutes
Serves 4

1. Rinse the lentils 2 or 3 times in cold water. Place them in a bowl with at least three times their volume of water and leave to stand for 2–3 hours or overnight if necessary. Strain and rinse them again.

2. Bring the measured water to the boil. Add the lentils, stirring occasionally until they reach simmering point. Cover the saucepan and cook for 20 minutes. The lentils should have absorbed the water, but will not yet be cooked.

3. Add the garlic powder, ground cumin and garam masala and simmer the dhal for 10–15 minutes more, stirring occasionally to prevent it sticking. Stir in the ghee or butter and season with salt to taste. Serve immediately, garnished with parsley sprigs.

Vietnamese Green Salad

Rau Tron

This salad is a refreshing and attractive accompaniment to any spicy dish.

1 large lettuce
mint leaves
coriander leaves
1 cucumber

Preparation time: 10 minutes
Serves 4

1. Separate the lettuce leaves, wash and pat dry with paper towels or a clean tea towel. Pile them in the centre of a serving dish.

2. Arrange the mint and coriander leaves in separate piles around the lettuce.

3. Peel the cucumber in thin strips to give an attractively variegated finish. Cut the cucumber in half lengthways and scoop out all the seeds. Slice into thin, half-moon-shaped slices. Place the slices in an overlapping circle around the edge of the dish. Serve immediately.

Illustrated on pages 100–101

Indian Salad

Salat

Indian salads are invariably chopped and mixed with various spices, some of them quite hot. Although this recipe calls for the inclusion of chopped fresh green chillies, it is not too hot, and you can omit the chillies if you wish.

1 lettuce or head of Chinese leaves
1 teaspoon salt
1 teaspoon freshly ground black pepper
1 teaspoon chilli powder
4 tomatoes
½ cucumber
2 sticks celery
1 large onion
2 teaspoons coriander seeds
juice of 1 lemon
2 fresh green or red chillies (optional)
½ teaspoon paprika

Preparation time: 20 minutes
Serves: 8–10

1. Separate the lettuce leaves or Chinese leaves. Wash and pat dry with paper towels or a clean tea towel. Mix together the salt, pepper and chilli powder. Pile one leaf on top of another, sprinkling each one with a little of the spice mixture. When you have 5 or 6 leaves together, cut them crossways into 2.5 cm (1 inch) shreds.

2. Put the shredded spiced lettuce leaves in a large salad bowl. Chop the tomatoes and cucumber and celery, add them to the lettuce and toss gently.

3. Slice half of the onion into thin rings and coarsely chop the other half. Mix the chopped onion with the lettuce, tomatoes, cucumber and celery.

4. Dry-fry the coriander seeds in a heavy-based frying pan and crush them coarsely in a mortar and pestle. Mix the crushed seeds into the mixed salad and sprinkle with lemon juice.

5. Arrange the onion rings over the top of the salad. Top and tail the chillies (if using), core and remove the seeds. Chop the chillies into 5 mm (¼ inch) pieces and sprinkle on top.

6. Chill the salad in the refrigerator and sprinkle with the paprika before serving.

Crispy Bean Curd with Tomato Sauce

Dau Hu Rau Voi Sot Ca Chua

This Vietnamese dish combines nourishing bean curd with a colourful sauce that is full of flavour.

oil for deep frying
6 pieces bean curd, halved then cut into small triangles
3 large tomatoes, skinned, seeded and finely chopped
150 ml (¼ pint) chicken stock
1 tablespoon nuoc mam (fish gravy)
a pinch of salt
⅓ teaspoon sugar
2 spring onion tops, cut into fine strips

Preparation time: 15 minutes
Cooking time: 40–45 minutes
Serves 4

Left: Crispy bean curd with tomato sauce; Stir-fried mixed vegetables

1. Heat the oil in a deep-fat fryer or wok, add the bean curd and fry until it is golden brown. Remove from the oil with a slotted spoon and set aside.

2. Place the tomatoes in a medium saucepan with the chicken stock, nuoc mam, salt and sugar. Bring to the boil, reduce the heat and simmer for 15–20 minutes.

3. Add the bean curd and simmer for 10–15 minutes more. The sauce should be quite thick and tasty. Serve immediately, with strips of spring onion arranged on top.

Stir-fried Mixed Vegetables

Rau Xao

Vietnamese vegetable cooking is full of contrasts, and in this stir-fry there is a variety of colours and textures.

25 g (1 oz) wood ears (dry weight), soaked in warm water for 15 minutes
2 carrots, finely sliced
1 × 100 g (4 oz) piece bamboo shoot, thinly sliced
1 Chinese cabbage, stems only, diced
100 g (4 oz) green beans, halved
4 tablespoons sunflower oil
2 garlic cloves, crushed
2–3 slices fresh root ginger, peeled and cut in slivers
100 g (4 oz) bean sprouts
½ teaspoon salt
freshly ground black pepper
½ teaspoon monosodium glutamate (optional)
1 teaspoon cornflour
1 tablespoon water

Preparation time: 25 minutes
Cooking time: 20 minutes
Serves 4

1. Drain the wood ears thoroughly and chop them roughly. Set aside.

2. Bring a large saucepan of water to the boil. Add the carrots and cook for 10 minutes. Add the bamboo shoot, Chinese cabbage and green beans and cook for 5 minutes more. Drain thoroughly and reserve.

3. Heat the oil in a wok or large frying pan, add the garlic and ginger and stir-fry for 2 minutes. Add the bean sprouts and stir-fry for 30 seconds.

4. Stir in all the reserved vegetables, including the wood ears, and season with salt, pepper and monosodium glutamate (if using). Stir-fry for 1–2 minutes more. The vegetables should remain crisp.

5. Mix the cornflour with the water to make a thin paste. Add to the wok and stir constantly to bind the vegetables together. Serve immediately.

Indonesian Vegetable Curry

This curry could be used either as a main dish or as an accompaniment for other dishes in a meal.

Spice paste:
2–6 garlic cloves
1 large onion, finely chopped
1 × 2.5 cm (1 inch) piece fresh root ginger
1 red pepper, chopped
2–6 fresh red chillies, chopped
10 unsalted cashew nuts or candlenuts
1 teaspoon pepper
1 teaspoon turmeric

Curry:
4 tablespoons sunflower oil
3–4 tablespoons fresh lemon juice
300 g (10 oz) aubergines, chopped
300 g (10 oz) courgettes, sliced
1 head of Chinese leaves, bottom half only, chopped
1 tablespoon brown sugar
salt

Preparation time: 5 minutes
Cooking time: 12–16 minutes
Serves 4

1. Put all the ingredients for the spice paste into a liquidizer and blend to a fairly stiff consistency, using as little water as possible.

2. Heat the oil for the curry in a large frying pan or wok. Add the paste and stir-fry for 5 minutes, adding the lemon juice gradually, so that it is incorporated smoothly. Stir in enough water to give the sauce a pouring consistency.

3. Add the aubergines, courgettes and Chinese leaves to the sauce. Simmer for 5–10 minutes, until the aubergines are tender. Stir in the brown sugar and season to taste with salt. Serve at once.

Thai Vegetable Curry

Krung Gaeng Keo Wan

The green curries of Thailand are among the hottest in South-east Asia, usually including ginger and pepper as well as the ingredients listed in this milder version.

Fragrant water:
175 ml (6 fl oz) water
4 tablespoons thinly pared lemon rind
Green purée:
1 green pepper
1–6 green chillies
1 bunch watercress
2 tablespoons chopped coriander
4 spinach leaves
2–4 garlic cloves
1 × 5 cm (2 inch) piece fresh root ginger
Curry:
4 tablespoons sunflower oil
2 puréed anchovies
2 tablespoons desiccated coconut
1 × 175 g (6 oz) can water chestnuts
475 g (15 oz) baby sweetcorn cobs
175 g (6 oz) bamboo shoots, sliced
To garnish:
lime wedges
basil sprigs

Preparation time: 10 minutes
Cooking time: about 15 minutes
Serves 4

1. Place the water and lemon rind in a saucepan and boil for 1 minute. Remove from the heat and set aside to allow the flavour to infuse.

2. Put the ingredients for the green purée in a liquidizer and process until smooth, adding a little water if necessary.

3. Heat the oil in a large frying pan or wok and stir-fry the green purée for 5–6 minutes.

4. Strain the fragrant water and add to it the puréed anchovies and coconut mixed to a runny paste with water. Combine the fragrant water mixture with the green purée in the frying pan or wok and mix together until smooth.

5. Add the water chestnuts, baby sweetcorn cobs and bamboo shoots. If canned vegetables are being used, add some of their liquid to the pan – enough to make the curry runny but not watery. Simmer the vegetables for 5–6 minutes.

6. Serve the curry hot, garnished with lime wedges and sprigs of basil.

Festive Vegetable Achar

This spicy pickle came to South-east Asia with merchants from North India centuries ago and was readily adopted by the migrant people who had already evolved a spicy cuisine from the best of Chinese, Malay and Indonesian cooking. It is prepared in great vats for serving during Chinese New Year.

5 cabbage leaves
1 cucumber
3 carrots, trimmed
1 head cauliflower
1.5 litres (2½ pints) vinegar
20 shallots, peeled and chopped
2 tablespoons shredded ginger
1 thumb-size piece fresh turmeric
3 red chillies, cored, seeded and chopped
2 teaspoons shrimp paste
5 candlenuts
1 large onion, chopped
6 tablespoons sunflower oil
200 g (7 oz) peanuts
3 tablespoons sugar
4 tablespoons sesame seeds

Preparation time: 45 minutes
Cooking time: 8 minutes
Serves 4

1. Cut the cabbage into strips measuring about 5 × 1 cm (2 × ½ inch). Remove the pith from the cucumber and cut it into similar strips. Cut the carrots into pieces the same size and separate the cauliflower into small florets.

2. Bring the vinegar to the boil in a saucepan and drop handfuls of the cabbage, cucumber, carrots, cauliflower and shallots into the boiling liquid to scald for 1 minute. Lift out with a slotted spoon and drain well.

3. Grind together in a mortar or blender the ginger, turmeric, chillies, shrimp paste, candlenuts and onion to make a paste.

4. Heat the oil in a wok or frying pan and fry the ground mixture for 5 minutes. Place in a glass or enamel (not metal) bowl and mix in the vegetables thoroughly. Refrigerate for at least 1 day, preferably more. To serve, mix in the peanuts and sugar and sprinkle the sesame seeds over the top.

Spicy Long Beans with Fish Cake

Long or runner beans are symbolic in China of longevity, and are used in a number of ways. Here they are combined with fish cakes, readily available in Chinese supermarkets.

8 long or runner beans
1 block fish cake
3 tablespoons sunflower oil
2 garlic cloves, crushed
1 tablespoon chilli bean paste
150 ml (¼ pint) water
1 teaspoon salt

Preparation time: 10 minutes
Cooking time: 10 minutes
Serves 4

1. Cut the beans into 5 cm (2 inch) lengths, wash and drain. Slice the fish cake into lengths of roughly the same thickness as the beans.

2. Heat the oil in a wok or frying pan and fry the garlic till light brown. Add the chilli bean paste and cook the mixture, stirring all the time, for 1 minute.

3. Add the long beans and cook, stirring well, for 2–3 minutes. Add the fish cake and water. Cook over high heat, stirring well, for 1–2 minutes. Add salt to taste and serve immediately.

Spicy long beans with fish cake (top) is a good example of the way this vegetable, a favourite in China, is used in combination with other ingredients.

Festive vegetable achar (below) is a wonderful melange of pickles that fits well into almost any menu.

Bean Sprout Salad

Chinese salads are rarely based on raw vegetables. They are usually composed of vegetables which are blanched, refreshed in cold water and mixed in a dressing.

450 g (1 lb) fresh bean sprouts
1 teaspoon salt
2.25 litres (4 pints) water
Dressing:
2 tablespoons soy sauce
1 tablespoon vinegar
1 tablespoon sesame oil
50 g (2 oz) cooked ham or
    chicken, finely sliced, to
    garnish

Preparation time: 10–15 minutes, plus standing
Serves 4

1. Wash and rinse the bean sprouts in a basin of cold water, discarding the husks and other small pieces that float to the surface (it is not necessary to top and tail each sprout).

2. Bring the water, with the salt added, to the boil, and add the bean sprouts. Cook for 2 minutes only. Drain in a colander, rinse under cold water until cool, and drain again.

3. Mix together the ingredients for the dressing. Place the sprouts in a serving bowl and pour over the dressing, tossing to combine. Let it stand for 10–20 minutes.

4. Serve garnished with finely sliced ham or chicken.

Braised Aubergines

While there are a number of Chinese recipes combining vegetables with a proportion of meat, there are many which are purely vegetarian, such as this, deriving from the cooking of monasteries and temples.

275 g (10 oz) aubergines
600 ml (1 pint) oil for deep-
    frying
2 tablespoons soy sauce
1 tablespoon sugar
2 tablespoons Chinese Clear
    Stock (see page 68) or water
1 teaspoon sesame oil

Preparation time: 10 minutes
Cooking time:
Serves 4

1. Discard the stalks of the aubergines and cut the flesh into diamond-shaped chunks.

2. Heat the oil in a wok or saucepan to 160°C/325°F or until a cube of bread browns in 45 seconds. Deep-fry the aubergine chunks in batches until they are golden. Remove from the hot oil with a perforated spoon and drain on paper towels.

3. Pour off the excess oil, leaving about 1 tablespoon in the wok. Return the aubergines to the pan. Add the soy sauce, sugar and the stock or water. Cook for about 2 minutes over a fairly high heat, adding more stock or water if necessary and stirring occasionally.

4. When the liquid has been almost completely absorbed, add the sesame oil, stir once and serve.

Fried Lettuce

Stir-frying is the most commonly used method of cooking vegetables in China. This recipe for lettuce intensifies its greenness while retaining firmness of texture.

1 large cos lettuce
2–3 tablespoons sunflower oil
1 teaspoon salt
1 teaspoon sugar

Preparation time: 5 minutes
Serves 4

1. Discard the tough outer leaves of the lettuce and wash the remainder well. Shake off the excess water and tear the larger leaves into 2 or 3 pieces.

2. Heat the oil in a wok or large saucepan and add the salt. Throw in the lettuce leaves and stir vigorously as though tossing a salad. Add the sugar and continue to stir-fry.

3. As soon as the leaves begin to wilt, quickly transfer them to a serving dish and serve.

Aubergines in Fragrant Sauce
Yuziang Qiezi

The aubergine is a native of tropical Asia, where the most common types are smaller and longer than the shiny purple globes we are used to in the West. The flavour is the same, however – delicious.

225 g (8 oz) aubergines
100 g (4 oz) pork fillet
600 ml (1 pint) oil for deep-
    frying
2 spring onions, finely chopped
1 slice fresh ginger root, peeled
    and finely chopped
1 garlic clove, peeled and finely
    chopped
1 tablespoon soy sauce
1 tablespoon medium sherry
1 tablespoon chilli sauce
2 tablespoons cornflour
1 tablespoon water

Preparation time: 20 minutes
Cooking time: 7–9 minutes
Serves 4

1. Peel the aubergines, then cut them into strips about the size of potato chips. Cut the pork into thin matchstick strips.

2. Heat the oil in a wok or saucepan to 160°C/325°F or until a cube of bread browns in 45 seconds and deep-fry the aubergine pieces for 1–2 minutes. Remove from the oil with a perforated spoon and drain on paper towels.

3. Pour off the excess oil from the wok or saucepan, leaving about 1 tablespoon. Quickly stir-fry the spring onions, ginger and garlic. Add the pork and stir-fry for 2 minutes.

4. Add the soy sauce, sherry and chilli sauce and blend well. Add the aubergine and cook together for 1–2 minutes.

5. Combine the cornflour with the water to make a thin paste and pour it into the wok or saucepan. Cook, stirring, until the sauce thickens, and serve hot.

Chinese Cabbage and Mushrooms

Fried lettuce; Chinese cabbage and mushrooms

This Chinese recipe is a good winter dish and makes a suitable accompaniment for pork dishes.

6–8 dried shiitake mushrooms, soaked in warm water for 20–30 minutes
450 g (1 lb) Chinese cabbage leaves
3 tablespoons sunflower oil
1 teaspoon salt
1 teaspoon sugar
1 tablespoon soy sauce
1 teaspoon sesame oil

Preparation time: 15 minutes
Cooking time: 8 minutes
Serves 4

1. Drain the mushrooms, reserving the liquid, and discard the stalks. Cut the caps in half or quarters if large. Cut the cabbage leaves into 2.5 cm (1 inch) squares.

2. Heat the oil in a wok or frying pan and stir-fry the cabbage and the mushrooms until soft. Add the salt, sugar and soy sauce and cook for a further 1½ minutes.

3. Stir in a little of the reserved mushroom liquid, add the sesame oil, and serve.

Celery Salad

This fresh, crisp Chinese salad goes well with any pork dish.

1 celery stick
1 small green pepper, cored and seeded
1 teaspoon salt
2.25 litres (4 pints) water
Dressing:
2 tablespoons soy sauce
1 tablespoon vinegar
1 tablespoon sesame oil
1 slice fresh ginger, peeled and finely shredded, to garnish

Preparation time: 15–20 minutes
Serves 4

1. Thinly slice the celery diagonally. Thinly slice the green pepper. Place them both in a pan of boiling, salted water for 1–2 minutes only. Drain into a colander and rinse well under cold water. Drain thoroughly.

2. For the dressing, mix together the soy sauce, vinegar, and sesame oil.

3. Place the celery and green pepper in a serving dish and pour over the dressing. Toss well. Serve garnished with finely shredded ginger.

Stir-fried Bean Sprouts and Green Beans

Above: Braised bean curd; Stir-fried bean sprouts and green beans; Sweet and sour cucumber
Far right: Four precious vegetables

Douya Chao Caidou

For this light and pretty Chinese dish, only fresh bean sprouts should be used. Canned bean sprouts do not have the necessary crunchy texture.

450 g (1 lb) fresh bean sprouts
225 g (8 oz) dwarf French beans
3–4 tablespoons sunflower oil
1 spring onion, finely chopped
1 teaspoon salt
1 teaspoon sugar
1 teaspoon sesame oil

Preparation time: 10 minutes
Cooking time: 2 minutes
Serves 4

1. Wash and rinse the bean sprouts in a basin of cold water, discarding the husks and other small pieces that float to the surface. (It is not necessary to top and tail each sprout). Drain well. Top, tail and halve the French beans.

2. Heat the oil in a wok until it is smoking. Add the spring onion to flavour the oil, then add the beans and stir a few times.

3. Add the bean sprouts and stir-fry for 30 seconds. Add the salt and sugar and stir-fry for 1 minute more.

4. Serve hot, sprinkled with sesame oil.

Sweet and Sour Cucumber

Tangcu Huanggua

This Chinese side dish could happily accompany any South-east Asian recipe. Choose a dark green and slender cucumber, for better flavour and firmness.

1 cucumber
1 teaspoon salt
2 tablespoons caster sugar
2 tablespoons vinegar
1 tablespoon sesame oil
strips of red and yellow pepper, to garnish

Preparation time: 5 minutes, plus marinating
Serves 4

1. Cut the cucumber in half lengthways, but do not peel it. Cut each half lengthways into 3 long strips and cut these into 2.5 cm (1 inch) lengths. Place the pieces in a bowl, add the salt, sugar and vinegar and leave to marinate for 10–15 minutes.

2. To serve, place the cucumber strips in a serving bowl, add the sesame oil and mix well. Garnish with the red and yellow pepper strips, and serve chilled.

Braised Bean Curd

Lu doufu

The soy bean is central to Chinese cooking for the range of products it offers. Bean curd is a tremendously valuable food, providing protein, oil, roughage, vitamins and salt. After cooking, the texture is like a honeycomb, and a crunchy garnish is essential.

450 g (1 lb) firm bean curd
300 ml (½ pint) vegetable stock
2 spring onions, trimmed
5 cm (1 inch) piece fresh root
*   ginger, peeled*
3 tablespoons soy sauce
2 tablespoons Chinese wine or
*   dry sherry*
1 tablespoon sugar
To garnish:
shredded spring onions
carrot flowers (see page 62)

Preparation time: 10 minutes, plus cooling
Cooking time: 40 minutes
Serves 4

1. Put the bean curd in a saucepan, cover with cold water and bring to the boil. Cover the pan with a lid and cook over high heat for 10 minutes.

2. Meanwhile, put the stock in a separate saucepan with the spring onions and ginger. Bring to the boil and simmer gently for 5 minutes, to flavour the stock.

3. Drain the bean curd and add it to the stock with the soy sauce, Chinese wine or sherry and sugar. Bring the liquid back to the boil, cover and simmer gently for 30 minutes. Turn off the heat and leave the bean curd in the cooking liquid until it is completely cold.

4. To serve, remove the bean curd from the liquid with a perforated spoon. Cut into slices and arrange on a serving plate. Garnish with shredded spring onions and carrot flowers, and serve cold.

Crispy 'Seaweed'

There are various types of seaweed used in Chinese cooking, but this dish is actually greens prepared to resemble 'hair vegetable seaweed', which is not itself very flavoursome.

900 g (2 lb) spring greens,
*   shaved into very fine shreds*
600 ml (1 pint) sunflower oil
1½ teaspoons caster sugar
½ teaspoon salt
a pinch of monosodium
*   glutamate (optional)*
50 g (2 oz) flaked almonds

Preparation time: 20 minutes, plus draining
Cooking time: 2½ minutes
Serves 4

1. Wash the spring green shavings and dry them thoroughly by spreading them out on paper towels and draining for about 30 minutes (they must be completely dry).

2. Heat the oil in a wok until it is smoking. Remove it from the heat and immediately throw in the spring green shavings. Stir and return the wok to the heat. Stir-fry for 2½ minutes. Remove and drain.

3. Arrange the 'seaweed' on a serving dish. Sprinkle evenly with the sugar, salt, monosodium glutamate (if used) and almonds. Serve hot.

Four Precious Vegetables

Speed in cooking is the essence of this Cantonese recipe, in which freshness of flavour, brightness of colour and crispness of texture combine. Substitute mangetout, peas or French beans for the broccoli florets if you wish.

4 tablespoons sunflower oil
100 g (4 oz) canned bamboo
*   shoots, drained and cut into*
*   2.5 cm (1 inch) pieces*
100 g (4 oz) carrots, peeled
*   and sliced into thin rings*
100 g (4 oz) fresh mushrooms,
*   left whole if small or*
*   quartered*
100 g (4 oz) broccoli florets
1 teaspoon salt
1 teaspoon sugar
1 teaspoon sesame oil

Preparation time: 10 minutes
Cooking time: 3–4 minutes
Serves 4–6

1. Heat the oil in a wok set over a moderate heat. Add the bamboo shoots and carrots and stir-fry for 1–2 minutes.

2. Add the mushrooms and broccoli florets, sprinkle with salt and sugar and stir-fry together for about 1½ minutes.

3. Sprinkle with sesame oil and serve hot or cold.

Braised Cabbage in Soy Sauce

This is probably the most widely cooked vegetable in all China. It combines freshness with savouriness and is therefore an ideal accompaniment for rice or fried rice dishes.

1.25 kg (2½ lb) Savoy cabbage
3½ tablespoons vegetable oil
3 slices root ginger, peeled and roughly shredded
1 garlic clove, peeled and finely chopped
1 tablespoon sugar
2 tablespoons light soy sauce
1½ chicken stock cubes
4 tablespoons chicken stock
2 tablespoons dry sherry
2 tablespoons butter

Preparation time: 10–15 minutes
Cooking time: 15 minutes
Serves 4–5

1. Cut the stem from the cabbage. Cut the cabbage from the top downwards into 4–6 segments, then cut each segment into 3 pieces.

2. Heat the oil in a large saucepan set over moderate heat. Add the ginger and stir-fry for 30 seconds. Add the garlic and continue to stir-fry for a further 30 seconds.

3. Add the cabbage, increase the heat and turn the cabbage in the flavoured oil. Sprinkle with sugar, then add the soy sauce, crumbled stock cubes, stock and sherry. Turn the cabbage pieces around in the sauce, until they are evenly covered.

4. Add the butter and continue to turn the cabbage for 15 seconds. Cover the pan and reduce the heat to very low. Simmer gently for 10 minutes. Turn the cabbage over once more and cook very gently for a further 2 minutes. Serve hot.

Chinese Cabbage with White Fu-Yung Sauce

Because this dish is given a feeling of purity by its combination of the pale green of the Chinese cabbage and the whiteness of the sauce, it is often served as a contrast to richer, dark meat dishes.

675 g (1½ lb) Chinese cabbage
1 tablespoon dried shrimps
1 chicken stock cube
300 ml (½ pint) chicken stock
Fu-Yung sauce:
2 egg whites
2 tablespoons cornflour
1 teaspoon salt
3–4 tablespoons milk
1 tablespoon cream or
    1 tablespoon butter
2 tablespoons minced chicken breast meat

Preparation time: about 10 minutes, plus soaking
Cooking time: 15 minutes
Serves 4–5

1. Cut the cabbage into 7.5 × 5 cm (3 × 2 inch) pieces. Soak the dried shrimps in boiling water for 10 minutes, then drain. Add the shrimps and crumbled stock cube to the stock in a large saucepan or deep frying-pan with a lid. Bring to the boil, stir and simmer for 1 minute.

2. Add the cabbage to the pan. Stir and mix the shrimps gently with the cabbage. Cover the pan and simmer gently for 8 minutes, stirring once or twice. Drain, reserving the cooking liquid.

3. To make the sauce, beat the egg whites with a fork for 1 minute, then add the cornflour and salt and beat for a further 30 seconds. Add the milk, cream, butter and minced chicken. Pour in the reserved stock. Stir well to mix and pour into a small saucepan. Cook, stirring, over a moderate heat for 2–3 minutes, until thickened.

4. Arrange the cabbage attractively in a deep serving dish. Pour the sauce evenly over, and serve hot.

White Braised Cabbage

This recipe is from the north of China, and with any meat or chicken dish and a serving of rice or noodles would make a very satisfying meal.

2 tablespoons sunflower oil
1 large Chinese cabbage, cut roughly into 8 pieces
1 teaspoon salt
2 slices fresh root ginger, peeled
25 g (1 oz) dried shrimps, soaked for 20 minutes and drained
250 ml (8 fl oz) chicken stock
a pinch of monosodium glutamate (optional)
1 tablespoon cornflour
2 tablespoons white wine

Preparation time: 5 minutes, plus soaking
Cooking time: 20 minutes
Serves 4

1. Heat the oil in a pan set over a moderate heat and add the cabbage pieces. Sprinkle with salt. Turn the cabbage to coat it with the oil and add the ginger, dried shrimps and half the chicken stock. Cover and simmer gently for 15 minutes.

2. Mix together the monosodium glutamate, if used, cornflour and remaining stock and pour over the cabbage pieces. Add the wine and turn the cabbage carefully so that it is coated in sauce but not broken up. Simmer for 5 minutes.

3. Carefully lift out the cabbage pieces and arrange them on a serving dish, retaining their original shape as far as possible. Pour over the sauce and serve.

*Braised cabbage in soy sauce; Chinese
cabbage in white fu-yung sauce*

RICE, EGGS AND NOODLES

Where rice – the single most important element in Oriental cooking – is not grown, noodles made from wheat flour form the staple diet. As this chapter shows, both can be used as the basis of some satisfying composite dishes. Eggs are often served as a snack, but the recipes in this chapter are substantial enough for lunch or supper.

Chilled Noodles

Hiyashi Somen

In the long stifling months of summer in Japan this cooling meal is very popular.

450 g (1 lb) somen (fine dried noodles)
8–12 large, headless uncooked prawns, defrosted if frozen
4–5 dried shiitake mushrooms, soaked in warm water for 20 minutes
2 tablespoons shoyu (Japanese soy sauce)
2 tablespoons mirin (sweet rice wine)
1 tablespoon sugar
2 small tomatoes, quartered
225 g (8 oz) boiled ham, finely shredded
½ cucumber, finely shredded
Sauce:
1 × 15 cm (6 inch) square konbu (dried kelp)
25 g (1 oz) katsuo-bushi (dried bonito flakes)
65 ml (2½ fl oz) shoyu (Japanese soy sauce)
65 ml (2½ fl oz) mirin (sweet rice wine)
1 × 2.5 cm (1 inch) piece fresh root ginger, peeled and grated
2 shiso leaves or spring onions, finely chopped

Preparation time: 25 minutes, plus chilling
Cooking time: 30 minutes
Serves 4

1. Bring a large saucepan of water to the boil and plunge the somen into the water. Cook, uncovered, over a moderate heat for 8–10 minutes until they are tender but still retain bite. Drain the somen in a colander and rinse them under cold running water to remove starch.

2. Place the somen in a large glass bowl and cover with fresh cold water. Add a few ice cubes, then place the bowl in the refrigerator while preparing the remaining ingredients.

3. Wash and shell the prawns, retaining the shell on the end of the tail. Remove the black vein from the back of the prawns. Plunge the prawns into a saucepan of boiling water for 2 minutes, then drain thoroughly and rinse under cold running water until cool. Drain on paper towels and chill in the refrigerator until it is time to serve.

4. Drain the mushrooms and reserve 300 ml (½ pint) of the soaking liquid (if there is not enough, make up the quantity with water). Squeeze the mushrooms dry, discard the hard stalks, then shred the caps finely. Place them in a saucepan with the shoyu, mirin and sugar and cook over moderate heat until all the liquid has been absorbed. Remove the pan from the heat and set aside.

5. To make the sauce, pour the reserved soaking liquid from the mushrooms into a saucepan. Add the konbu, katsuo-bushi, shoyu and mirin and bring to the boil, taking out the konbu just before the liquid reaches boiling point. Cook for 5 minutes, then strain through a fine sieve lined with muslin or cheesecloth. Leave the sauce to cool, then chill in the refrigerator.

6. To serve, garnish the somen in the cold water with quartered tomatoes. Arrange the ham, cucumber, mushrooms and chilled prawns in a serving dish. Divide the cold sauce equally among 4 individual bowls and stir in the grated ginger and chopped shiso leaves or spring onions. Each diner puts a little of the ham, cucumber, mushrooms and prawns into his or her bowl of sauce, then takes some cold somen with hashi (chopsticks) and dips this into the sauce before eating.

Noodles

The generic term for noodles in Japan is *menrui*; those eaten in the north are made of buckwheat, for example soba, and those in the south from wheat flour, such as udon and somen. If a recipe calls for udon, you can almost always use soba if you prefer them.

Noodles are eaten as the Italians eat pasta – al dente – and they must be consumed quickly before the hot broth makes them too soft. This entails a good deal of noisy slurping, perfectly acceptable to the Japanese in this instance, and the best evidence of enjoyment. Noodles are popular for lunch with busy workers. 'Fast food' they may be, but noodle dishes are nutritious as well as filling and tasty. They are often served in egg soup based on good Japanese stock flavoured with shoyu and mirin. The beaten eggs are stirred into the hot soup and stirred until they cook in threads.

To reheat cooked noodles, place them in a colander and plunge into a saucepan of boiling water until heated through. Lift out of the water and shake the colander to prevent the strands sticking together.

Noodles with Broth

Tsukimi Udon

There are many varieties of noodle in Japan. Udon are the traditional thick, white type and the egg on top of this dish is like the full moon – hence the meaning of the title, 'seeing the moon noodles'.

450 g (1 lb) udon (thick dried noodles)
900 ml (1½ pints) Japanese Stock (see page 69)
1 tablespoon sugar
1½ teaspoon salt
1 tablespoon shoyu (Japanese soy sauce)
4 eggs
To garnish:
2 spring onions, thinly sliced
1 × 13 cm (5 inch) square piece of nori (dried lava paper), toasted and finely shredded

Preparation time: 10 minutes
Cooking time: 30 minutes
Serves 4

1. Bring a large pan of water to the boil. Add the noodles, stirring constantly, and bring back to the boil. Add 250 ml (8 fl oz) cold water and bring back to the boil again. Cook for 10–12 minutes until the noodles are al dente. Drain the noodles in a colander, rinse under cold running water to remove the starch and drain again.

2. Put the stock, sugar, salt and shoyu in a large pan and stir well. Bring to the boil over high heat, then add the noodles. Bring back to the boil, stirring constantly, and cook until the noodles are heated through.

3. Pour the noodles in broth into 4 warmed individual bowls. Break 1 egg into each bowl. Cover the bowls with lids, and the heat from the noodles will cook the eggs in 3–4 minutes or according to taste. Garnish with spring onions and nori shreds and serve hot.

Above: Steamed pink rice with beans (page 187); Chilled noodles; Noodles with broth

Chilli Noodles

Mee Goreng

This dish is often presented as Indian in South-east Asia, but it is in fact plagiarized from the Chinese by Indonesian and Malaysian restaurants which have given the recipe extra spice.

150 g (6 oz) dry wheat noodles
4 tablespoons sunflower oil
4 shallots, sliced
75 g (3 oz) minced lamb
1 teaspoon chilli powder
75 g (3 oz) beansprouts

1 boiled potato, diced
1 tomato, chopped
2 eggs
2 teaspoons salt
1 tablespoon tomato sauce

Preparation time: 10 minutes
Cooking time: 12 minutes
Serves 4

1. Bring a large saucepan of water to the boil and cook the noodles for 3 minutes. Drain well and set aside.

2. Heat the oil in a wok or frying pan over a moderate heat and fry the shallots till light brown.

3. Add the minced lamb and fry for 1 minute until it takes colour. Add the chilli powder, beansprouts, noodles, potato and tomato. Cook, stirring, over a high heat for 2 minutes.

4. Push the mixture to one side of the wok and crack the eggs into the pan. Cook for 1 minute, then cut them up with the ladle or stirring spoon. Add the salt and tomato sauce to the eggs.

5. Stir all the ingredients together and cook for 1 minute more. Sprinkle in a few drops of water if the mixture becomes too dry.

6. Transfer the Chilli noodles to a warmed serving dish and serve at once.

Singapore Noodles

The original version of this dish is a rich mixture of noodles, beansprouts, boiled pork, squid, prawns, egg and rich meat stock, though it can be modified to suit your taste. Use chicken breast instead of pork, for instance. If squid is not to your taste, leave it out. What is important is the stock.

Left: Singapore noodles (top); Mee Goreng

2 rounds dry noodles
500 ml (18 fl oz) water
100 g (4 oz) lean pork, cut into 5 cm (2 inch) strips
75 g (3 oz) uncooked shelled prawns
75 g (3 oz) squid, cleaned and sliced (see page 54)
4 tablespoons sunflower oil
2 garlic cloves, crushed
75 g (3 oz) beansprouts
1 tablespoon light soy sauce
1 tablespoon dark soy sauce
½ teaspoon freshly ground black pepper
1 bunch fresh chives, chopped
2 eggs

Preparation time: 15 minutes
Cooking time: 17 minutes
Serves 4

1. Boil the noodles in plenty of water for 2 minutes and drain. Bring the measured water to the boil in a saucepan and cook the pork, prawns and squid together for 5 minutes. Drain and reserve the cooking water for stock.

2. Heat the oil in a wok or frying pan and fry the garlic until light brown. Add the beansprouts and noodles and cook, stirring, for 2 minutes over a high heat.

3. Add the pork, prawns and squid, the soy sauces, pepper and chives and stir-fry for 1 minute more.

4. Push the mixture to one side of the pan and crack in the eggs. Cook for 1 minute and add the reserved stock. Bring to the boil and cook for 2 minutes, stirring the mixture well.

5. Turn the noodles on to a warmed plate and serve at once. Serve sliced chillies and lemon juice in a side dish.

Vegetarian Chow Mein

There is a strong tradition of vegetarianism in China deriving from Buddhism, but the recipes are far from ascetic. This one is particularly rich in flavour.

6 medium dried shiitake mushrooms, soaked in warm water for 20–30 minutes
450 g (1 lb) Chinese noodles (or spaghettini)
175 (6 oz) soy-braised bamboo shoots
4 tablespoons sunflower oil
4 slices fresh root ginger, shredded
2 garlic cloves, crushed
150 g (5 oz) Chinese cabbage, shredded
75 g (3 oz) hot Szechuan pickle (Ja-Chai), shredded
1 tablespoon chilli bean sauce

1½ tablespoons hoisin sauce
2 tablespoons light soy sauce
25 g (1 oz) butter
150 g (5 oz) mangetout, finely sliced
150 g (5 oz) bean sprouts
2 spring onions, cut into 1.5 cm (1 inch) lengths
1 small red pepper, cored, seeded and shredded
100 g (4 oz) firm button mushrooms, thinly sliced
1 teaspoon salt
1 tablespoon dark soy sauce
1 teaspoon sesame oil
1 tablespoon brandy

Preparation time: 25 minutes, plus soaking
Cooking time: 15 minutes (20 minutes with spaghettini)
Serves 4

1. Drain the shiitake mushrooms, reserving the liquid. Discard the stalks and shred the caps finely.

2. Cook the noodles in boiling water for 5 minutes (10 minutes for spaghettini). Turn off the heat and leave the pasta to stand in the hot water for 3 minutes (or 5 minutes for spaghettini). Drain and rinse in cold water. Set aside.

3. Cut the soy-braised bamboo shoots into matchstick shreds.

4. Heat half the oil in a wok or frying pan. When it is hot, add the ginger, garlic, dried mushrooms, shredded cabbage, shredded pickle and shredded bamboo shoots. Stir-fry for 2½ minutes over a high heat. Add the hot bean sauce and hoisin sauce. Stir-fry for 1 minute more.

5. Turn the noodles into the pan. Turn and toss them with the ingredients in the pan, then sprinkle with light soy sauce and half the mushroom liquid. Heat through thoroughly, turning a few times. Remove the wok from the heat.

6. Heat the remaining oil with the butter in another wok or frying pan. When the butter has melted, add the mangetout and stir-fry over a moderate heat for 1 minute. Turn the heat up high and add the bean sprouts, spring onions, red pepper and button mushrooms. Sprinkle with the salt and dark soy sauce, sesame oil and brandy. Continue to stir and turn the ingredients in the pan for 1 minute.

7. Transfer the hot noodle mixture to a heated serving dish. Heat the vegetable mixture for 30 seconds over a high heat. Pour over the noodles and serve.

Chow Mein (Fried Noodles)

Chao Mian

This is the most famous of Chinese noodle dishes, and while it is the ancient forerunner of Italian pasta with sauce, demonstrates the more complex cooking procedures of the East.

450 g (1 lb) egg noodles (or spaghettini)
salt
4 tablespoons sunflower oil
1 medium onion, thinly sliced
100 g (4 oz) cooked meat (pork, chicken or ham), cut into thin shreds
100 g (4 oz) mangetout or French beans, trimmed
100 g (4 oz) fresh bean sprouts
2–3 spring onions, finely shredded
2 tablespoons light soy sauce
1 tablespoon sesame seed oil or chilli sauce

Preparation time: 5 minutes
Cooking time: 15–20 minutes
Serves 4

1. Cook the noodles or spaghettini in a large saucepan of boiling, salted water according to the instructions on the packet. Drain and rinse under cold running water until cool; set aside.

2. Heat about 3 tablespoons of the oil in a hot wok. Add the onion, meat, mangetout or beans and the bean sprouts and stir-fry for about 1 minute. Add 1 teaspoon of salt and stir a few times more, then remove from the wok with a perforated spoon and keep hot.

3. Heat the remaining oil in the wok and add the spring onions and noodles, with about half of the meat and vegetable mixture. Add the soy sauce and stir-fry for 1–2 minutes or until heated through.

4. Transfer the mixture from the wok to a warmed large serving dish, then pour the remaining meat and vegetable mixture on top as a dressing. Sprinkle with sesame seed oil or chilli sauce (or both, if preferred). Serve immediately.

Noodles in Soup

Tang Mian

In China, noodles are more commonly served in soup than fried (as in Chow Mein). There is little difference in the ingredients, but in this recipe peeled prawns have been used instead of strips of cooked meat.

225 g (8 oz) peeled prawns
salt
1 teaspoon cornflour
1 tablespoon cold water
100 g (4 oz) bamboo shoots or button mushrooms
100 g (4 oz) spinach leaves, Chinese leaves or cos lettuce, well washed and patted dry
350 g (12 oz) egg noodles (or spaghettini)
600 ml (1 pint) well-flavoured chicken stock
2 tablespoons light soy sauce
3 tablespoons sunflower oil
2 spring onions, thinly shredded
2 tablespoons Chinese wine or dry sherry
1–2 teaspoons sesame oil (optional)

Preparation time: 20 minutes
Cooking time: about 20 minutes
Serves 4

1. Place the prawns in a bowl with a pinch of salt.

2. Mix the cornflour to a smooth paste with the cold water and stir into the prawns.

3. Finely shred the bamboo shoots or mushrooms and the green leaves.

4. Cook the noodles or spaghettini in a large saucepan of boiling salted water according to the instructions on the packet. Drain, and place in a warmed large serving bowl or 4 individual bowls. Bring the stock to the boil and pour it over the cooked noodles, with about half of the soy sauce. Keep hot.

5. Heat the oil in a hot wok. Add the shredded spring onions to flavour the oil, then add the prawn mixture and the shredded vegetables. Stir a few times, add 1½ teaspoons salt, the remaining soy sauce and the wine or sherry. Cook for about 1–2 minutes, stirring constantly.

6. Pour the mixture over the noodles and sprinkle with sesame oil, if using. Serve hot.

Right: Chow mein; Special-fried rice (page 191); Noodles in soup

Soft Noodles with Crab Meat Sauce

The crab meat sauce lifts plain boiled noodles well out of the ordinary in this recipe from China.

150 g (5 oz) egg noodles
a pinch of salt
2 tablespoons sunflower oil
1 small can crab meat (about 100 g (4 oz) drained weight)
100 g (4 oz) spinach or cabbage leaves, cut into shreds
1 teaspoon light soy sauce
250 ml (8 fl oz) Chinese Clear Stock (see page 68)
1 spring onion, finely chopped, to garnish

Preparation time: 15–20 minutes
Cooking time: about 20 minutes
Serves 2

1. Cook the noodles in a large saucepan of boiling, salted water according to the instructions on the packet. Drain well and keep warm in a serving dish.

2. Heat the oil in a hot wok and stir-fry the crab meat and green leaves for 4–5 minutes. Add the soy sauce and stock and cook, stirring, for 5 minutes or until heated through.

3. Pour the hot sauce over the noodles, garnish with chopped spring onion and serve immediately.

Boiled Noodles

300 g (11 oz) egg noodles
200 g (7 oz) chicken breast
meat, cut into matchstick
strips
2 teaspoons cornflour
8 dried shiitake mushrooms,
soaked in warm water for
20–30 minutes
225 g (8 oz) spinach leaves,
well washed
225 g (8 oz) bamboo shoots
1 litre (1¾ pints) Chinese Clear
Stock (see page 68)
4 spring onions, finely chopped
2 slices fresh root ginger, peeled
and finely chopped
8 tablespoons sunflower oil

Sauce:
8 tablespoons soy sauce
4 tablespoons sherry
2 tablespoons salt
2 teaspoons sugar

Preparation time: 20 minutes
Cooking time: about 20
minutes
Serves 4

1. Cook the noodles in a large saucepan of boiling water for 5 minutes until soft but not sticky. Drain through a sieve and place in a large heated bowl to keep warm.

2. Mix the shredded chicken with the cornflour. Drain the mushrooms, discard the stems and cut the caps into thin shreds.

3. Drain the spinach and dry the leaves on paper towels. Cut into thin strips. Cut the bamboo shoots in thin strips.

4. Bring the stock to the boil and pour it over the cooked noodles.

5. Heat the oil in a hot wok and stir-fry the chicken for 1 minute.

Add the ingredients one by one, in the following order, stir-frying each addition for 1 minute: first the bamboo shoots, then the mushrooms, spinach, spring onions and finally the ginger.

6. To make the sauce, combine the soy sauce, sherry, salt and sugar. Add to the wok and continue to stir-fry for 1–2 minutes. Pour this mixture over the noodles in stock and serve.

Fried Noodles with Bean Sprouts

Mi Xao Gia

Noodles are used widely in
Vietnamese cooking, very often
for snacks or light meals.

4 bundles dried egg noodles
4 tablespoons sunflower oil
200 g (7 oz) fresh bean sprouts
2 tablespoons chopped spring
  onions
sugar
soy sauce
salt
2–3 drops sesame oil

Preparation time: 5 minutes,
plus standing and drying
Cooking time: 15–20 minutes
Serves 4

1. Place the bundles of noodles
in a large saucepan with a pinch
of salt, and pour over boiling
water to cover. Allow to stand
for 5 minutes. Bring the liquid
back to the boil and cook the
noodles, stirring constantly, for
4–5 minutes or until tender but

still firm to the bite. Drain in a
colander, rinse with cold water
and drain again. Leave to dry for
15 minutes before proceeding.

2. Heat the oil in a large frying
pan (preferably non-stick) and
add the bean sprouts. Stir-fry for
2–3 minutes.

3. Add the onions and noodles,
increase the heat to high and
stir-fry until all the liquid has
evaporated. Remove from the
heat and season to taste with
sugar, soy sauce and salt.
Sprinkle with a few drops of
sesame oil and serve
immediately.

Rice Vermicelli with Barbecued Pork

Bun Thit Heo Nuong

Rice vermicelli is a hallmark of authentic Vietnamese cookery. It is widely used as an accompaniment and as the basis for soups and other savoury dishes, but requires delicate handling for satisfactory results.

50 g (2 oz) rice vermicelli
2 garlic cloves, crushed
2 spring onions, roughly chopped
1 teaspoon black jack (see Fish au Caramel, page 94)
$\frac{1}{2}$ teaspoon salt
$\frac{1}{2}$ teaspoon freshly ground black pepper
300 g (11 oz) pork belly, sliced and cut into squares
1 iceberg lettuce, shredded
$\frac{1}{2}$ cucumber, sliced
2 tablespoons pickled carrots or gherkins
1 tablespoon fresh mint leaves
1 tablespoon freshly chopped coriander leaves
8 tablespoons nuoc mam giam, or to taste (see page 92)

Preparation time: 30 minutes, plus marinating
Cooking time: about 25 minutes
Serves 4

Left: Fried noodles with bean sprouts; Rice vermicelli with barbecued pork

1. Bring a large saucepan of salted water to the boil. Add the rice vermicelli and boil, stirring constantly, for 3–5 minutes or until the vermicelli is tender but still firm to the bite. Drain the vermicelli in a colander and rinse under cold running water to remove excess starch. Drain once again thoroughly. Set aside.

2. Combine the garlic, spring onions and black jack in a shallow dish large enough to hold all the thin squares of pork in a single layer. Add salt and pepper and the pork. Mix well, cover and set aside to marinate for at least 30 minutes, preferably 2 hours.

3. Prepare the lettuce, cucumber, pickled vegetables, mint and coriander leaves and divide between 4 individual bowls. Top each portion of vegetables with cooked vermicelli. Set aside.

4. Place the marinated pork squares on a baking sheet and cook over medium coals or under a preheated moderate grill for 15–20 minutes, turning once during the cooking period.

5. Divide the barbecued pork slices between the bowls and top each with 2 tablespoons nuoc mam giam, or to taste. Each guest mixes the contents of his or her bowl thoroughly before beginning to eat.

Rice Stick Noodles with Mixed Seafood

A typically Chinese mixture, this recipe combines vegetables and seafoods to make a delicately flavoured main meal dish.

450 g (1 lb) rice stick noodles
4 large dried shiitake mushrooms, soaked in warm water for 20 minutes
3–4 tablespoons sunflower oil
2 onions, thinly sliced
3 slices fresh root ginger, peeled and shredded
3 rashers bacon, shredded
1$\frac{1}{2}$ tablespoons dried shrimps, soaked for 15 minutes and drained
4–5 tablespoons fresh or canned clams
6 tablespoons chicken or vegetable stock
3 tablespoons light soy sauce
1 teaspoon salt
25 g (1 oz) lard
100–225 g (4–8 oz) broccoli, separated into florets
4–5 tablespoons peeled prawns
100 g (4 oz) fresh squid, shredded
2 tablespoons Chinese wine or dry sherry

Preparation time: 10 minutes
Cooking time: 30 minutes
Serves 4–6

1. Bring a large saucepan of water to the boil and cook the noodles for 7–8 minutes. Drain well and rinse under cold running water. Drain again and set aside.

2. Drain the mushrooms, discard the stems and shred the caps.

3. Heat the oil in a wok set over moderate heat. Add the onions, ginger, bacon, mushrooms, dried shrimps and clams and stir-fry for 3 minutes.

4. Add half the stock, 2 tablespoons of the soy sauce and the salt to the ingredients in the wok. Continue to stir-fry for a further 1$\frac{1}{2}$ minutes.

5. Add the noodles to the wok and mix well. Increase the heat to high and cook, stirring, for a further 3–4 minutes. Remove the wok from the heat.

6. Melt the lard in a clean frying pan. Add the broccoli florets and stir-fry over high heat for 2 minutes. Add the remaining stock and soy sauce, the fresh prawns and squid. Stir-fry for 2 minutes. Sprinkle in the wine or sherry and remove from the heat. Keep hot.

7. Return the wok containing the noodle mixture to the heat and stir-fry for 30 seconds until it is heated through. Transfer to a warmed serving dish and pour the broccoli and fish mixture on top. Serve immediately.

Three-colour Rice

Three-colour Rice, or *Sanshoku Gohan*, is actually white: the colour in this Japanese dish comes from its three toppings.

The rice is Vinegared Rice (page 23). The three colours are: first, pink from fish flakes prepared as for Rolled Rice with Nori (page 80); second, golden brown, from minced chicken poached in stock flavoured with mirin and shoyu; and, third, bright yellow, from scrambled eggs flavoured with salt, sugar and sake.

Each bowl of rice is served with a spoonful of one of these flavourings on top and garnished with a slice of lemon or a whole cooked prawn. The pale colours look exquisite against the pure white rice.

Burmese White Cabbage and Noodle Curry

The egg noodles in this recipe make it quite a substantial dish, suitable for a main course.

450 g (1 lb) white cabbage
3 tablespoons sunflower oil
2–4 garlic cloves, thinly sliced
1 teaspoon sesame seeds
1 teaspoon turmeric
1 tablespoon chopped coriander
6 spring onions, finely chopped
1–4 fresh green chillies, seeded and finely chopped
1 red pepper, seeded and thinly sliced
200 g (7 oz) egg noodles
2 tablespoons nam pla (fish sauce), or puréed anchovies
fresh coconut, shredded, or desiccated coconut, to garnish (optional)

Preparation time: 10 minutes
Cooking time: 15 minutes
Serves 4

1. Shred the cabbage in a food processor, or slice very finely by hand.

2. Heat the oil in a large frying pan or wok, add the garlic and stir-fry for 1 minute. Add the sesame seeds and turmeric and fry for 1 more minute. Add the coriander, spring onions, chillies and red pepper and bring the mixture to simmering point.

3. Meanwhile, bring a large saucepan of water to the boil and put the noodles in it. When the water comes back to simmering point, remove the pan from the heat and leave to stand for 8 minutes.

4. Add the fish sauce or puréed anchovies and sliced cabbage to the frying pan or wok and cook briskly until the cabbage is cooked but still retains some bite.

5. Strain the noodles and add them to the vegetable mixture. Serve, garnished with coconut if liked.

Right: Noodles with sesame paste sauce

Szechuan Dan Dan Noodles

Hot pickle and chilli oil give this recipe the hot, tangy flavour characteristic of Szechuan cooking.

450 g (1 lb) rice stick noodles
3 tablespoons sunflower oil
1½ tablespoons dried shrimps, soaked for 20 minutes, drained and chopped
6 dried shiitake mushrooms, soaked for 20 minutes
50 g (2 oz) Szechuan hot pickle, chopped
2 garlic cloves, crushed
3 teaspoons minced fresh root ginger
225 g (8 oz) minced pork
1½ tablespoons light soy sauce
1 tablespoon red chilli oil or chilli sauce
2 spring onions, finely chopped
600 ml (1 pint) chicken stock
salt
freshly ground black pepper

Preparation time: 15 minutes
Cooking time: 10 minutes
Serves 6

1. Blanch the noodles in boiling water for 2 minutes. Drain, rinse in hot water and keep warm.

2. Drain the mushrooms, discard the stems and shred the caps. Heat the oil in a wok over a high heat and add the mushrooms, shrimps, pickle, garlic and ginger. Stir-fry for 30 seconds. Add the pork to the wok and stir-fry with the other ingredients for 4 minutes.

3. Combine the soy sauce with the red chilli oil, spring onions and 150 ml (¼ pint) of the stock. Add this liquid to the wok. Season with salt and pepper, and simmer for 5 minutes.

4. Add the remaining stock to the pan and bring to the boil. Divide the noodles among 6 individual bowls and pour the sauce on top. Serve immediately.

Illustrated on page 159

Japanese Fried Rice

Itame Gohan

Always an important ingredient in any meal containing it, rice is also used very imaginatively in Japanese cooking.

1 tablespoon sunflower oil
1 medium onion, finely chopped
1 small green pepper, cored, seeded and finely chopped
1 small garlic clove, crushed
575 g (1¼ lb) steamed rice (see page 22)
1 egg, beaten
2 tablespoons shoyu (Japanese soy sauce)

Preparation time: 5 minutes
Cooking time: about 10 minutes
Serves 6

1. Heat the oil in a frying pan set over a moderate heat. Add the onion, green pepper and garlic and fry until softened.

2. Stir in the rice and heat through, stirring occasionally.

3. Add the egg and shoyu to the pan and cook, stirring for 2–3 minutes, or until the egg has just set – do not overcook.

Noodles with Sesame Paste Sauce

Dan Dan Mian

Most Chinese noodles, like those in this recipe, are made from wheat flour, though rice flour and pea starch flour noodles are also used.

450 g (1 lb) fresh noodles
900 ml (1½ pints) Chinese Clear Stock (see page 68)
Sauce:
2 tablespoons sesame seed paste
4 tablespoons water
4 tablespoons chopped spring onions
1 teaspoon crushed garlic
1 tablespoon soy sauce
2 tablespoons red wine vinegar
2 teaspoons hot pepper oil
1 teaspoon salt

Preparation time: 10 minutes
Cooking time: 10 minutes
Serves 4

1. Cook the noodles in plenty of boiling salted water until just tender. Bring the stock to the boil in another saucepan.

2. To make the sauce, mix the sesame seed paste with the water until evenly combined. Blend in the spring onions, garlic, soy sauce, vinegar, hot pepper oil and salt.

3. When the noodles are cooked, drain them well. Divide the boiling stock between 4 individual soup bowls, add the cooked noodles and top with the sauce. Each person tosses the contents of his bowl before eating.

Steamed Pink Rice with Beans

Sekihan

This pale pink rice is a Japanese celebration dish, prepared for special occasions such as birthdays. For the colour to be achieved, preparation must be started the day before the dish is required.

200 g (7 oz) azuki beans
750 g (1¾ lb) glutinous rice
goma jio (made with 1 teaspoon black sesame seeds and 2 teaspoons salt, (see page 16)

Preparation time: 25 minutes, plus standing
Cooking time: about 2 hours
Serves 8–10

1. Pick over and wash the azuki beans. Put them in a pan and cover with cold water. Bring to the boil, then drain; cover with fresh cold water and bring to the boil again. Reduce the heat, cover with a lid and simmer gently for about 40 minutes, adding more water to keep the beans covered during cooking. Drain and reserve the cooking liquid.

2. Wash the rice thoroughly. Drain and place in a bowl. Cover the rice with the reserved azuki liquid and leave to stand overnight to allow the rice to acquire a pinkish colour.

3. Drain the rice and reserve the liquid. Mix the rice and azuki beans together, taking care not to crush the beans. Line a steamer plate or other heatproof plate with a piece of cheesecloth. Bring the water in the steamer to the boil, then spread the rice and bean mixture on the cloth, patting it smooth and making a few vent holes in it with the handle of a wooden spoon. Steam over high heat for about 50 minutes or until the rice is cooked, basting every 12 minutes with the reserved azuki liquid.

4. Divide into individual serving bowls and sprinkle with goma jio. Serve hot or warm.

Illustrated on page 179

Rice for Breakfast

A savoury rice dish often eaten for breakfast in China is Rice Congee, which is a kind of thick soup or gruel. Served hot, it is easy to digest and makes a nourishing start to the day. Pudding rice must be used to get the necessary soft texture.

For six people only 100 g (4 oz) pudding rice is necessary. After washing, the rice is added to a saucepan containing 1.75 litres (3 pints) of good chicken stock at a rolling boil. The heat is reduced to low and the stock and rice left to simmer for 2 hours, during which time the grains of rice soften and plump up. Seasoning may be added at this point. Just before serving, 100 g (4 oz) finely minced chicken breast, coated lightly with beaten egg white, is stirred into the liquid. The chicken cooks very quickly in the hot soup, which is served with minced ham and spring onions scattered on top.

Lamb with Rice

Katchi Biriyani

In this classic recipe from central India, the meat and rice are cooked separately, then layered, thus ensuring that the rice is cooked to perfection.

75 g (3 oz) ghee or
*   concentrated butter*
1 onion, sliced
1 bay leaf
1 × 1 cm (½ inch) stick
*   cinnamon*
4 small green cardamoms
6 cloves
450 g (1 lb) shoulder of lamb off
*   the bone, cubed*
2 teaspoons ground ginger
2 garlic cloves, crushed
½ teaspoon ground turmeric
2 teaspoons ground coriander
2 teaspoons ground cumin
150 ml (¼ pint) natural yoghurt
1 teaspoon salt
1 teaspoon chilli powder
450 ml (¾ pint) water
Rice:
675 g (1½ lb) rice
2.25–2.75 litres (4–5 pints)
*   water*
2 teaspoons salt
1 bay leaf
1 × 1 cm (½ inch) stick
*   cinnamon*
1 teaspoon black cumin seeds

To finish:
1 small onion, sliced and fried
3–4 sprigs coriander leaves,
*   chopped*
2 green chillies, seeded and
*   very finely chopped*
freshly ground black pepper
4 small green cardamoms,
*   ground*
juice of 2 lemons
a pinch of ground saffron
*   dissolved in water*
3 tablespoons milk
25 g (1 oz) ghee or
*   concentrated butter, melted*

Preparation time: 40 minutes
Cooking time: 2 hours
Serves 4–6

1. Melt the ghee or butter in a large pan set over a moderate heat and fry the onion until golden. Add the bay leaf, cinnamon, cardamoms and cloves. Fry for 1 minute. Add the lamb, ginger, garlic, turmeric, coriander, cumin, yoghurt, salt and chilli powder and stir well. Cover and cook until dry.

2. Increase the heat and fry until the oil separates from the mixture. Add the water and continue cooking for 40–50 minutes or until the lamb is tender. There should be about 3 tablespoons of thick sauce.

3. While the meat is cooking, prepare the rice. Place the rice in a large saucepan and add the water, salt, bay leaf, cinnamon stick and the black cumin seeds. Bring to the boil and cook the rice until it is almost tender. Remove from the heat and drain thoroughly.

4. Put a thin layer of rice in the base of a clean, heavy-based pan. Spread over a layer of cooked meat, without the sauce, followed by layers of fried onion, chopped coriander leaves and chilli. Repeat the layers once or twice, retaining a little fried onion and chopped coriander, and finishing with a layer of rice. Sprinkle the surface with the reserved fried onion and coriander leaves, freshly ground black pepper to taste, the ground cardamoms and lemon juice.

5. With the handle of a wooden spoon, make three or four holes in the rice to allow the steam to rise. Pour the saffron, the remaining sauce, milk and butter at random over the surface. Place the pan on a moderate heat, and as soon as any steam is visible, reduce the heat, cover the pan and cook very gently for 5 minutes.

6. To serve, use a wide spoon and from one edge scoop out and mix a portion of the rice and meat together.

Variation: Prepare the meat mixture as in step 1 but do not cook. Cook the rice for 7–8 minutes only. Place all the meat in a large casserole and spread the rice evenly on top. Sprinkle with the fried onions, chopped coriander, chilli, lemon juice and milk. Make holes in the rice and pour the saffron over the surface. Cook in a preheated moderate oven, 160°C, 325°F, Gas Mark 3, for 50–60 minutes. Before serving, mix the cooked rice and meat together.

Pilau Rice

A pilau is a dish of rice cooked with other ingredients, in this case aromatic spices, ground almonds and coconut. The name is of Middle Eastern origin, and the dish probably came to India with the Persians.

300 g (10 oz) Basmati rice
1.8 litres (3 pints) water
1 tablespoon concentrated
*   butter or ghee*
½ teaspoon fennel seeds
½ teaspoon black cumin seeds
4 green cardamoms
4 whole cloves

2 star anise
1 × 2.5 cm (1 inch) piece
*   cinnamon stick or cassia*
*   bark*
1 tablespoon ground almonds
1 tablespoon desiccated coconut
*   or coconut powder*
20 saffron strands (optional)

Preparation time: 10 minutes, plus soaking
Cooking time: 15 minutes
Serves 4

1. Leave the rice to soak for about 30 minutes in cold water. Bring the measured water to the boil in a large saucepan. Rinse the rice two or three times in cold water, finally in hot water, and tip it into the boiling water. Put on the lid, cook for 1 minute and stir. Replace the lid and cook for 6 minutes. Test the rice – it should be almost cooked. Simmer for 1–2 minutes then strain off all the excess water. The rice can be left to go cold or used at once.

2. Heat the ghee or butter in a large frying pan or wok and fry the fennel and cumin seeds, cardamoms, cloves, star anise and cinnamon for 1 minute. Add the rice and stir-fry until it has reached serving temperature.

3. Add the ground almonds, coconut and saffron, if using, to the rice. Transfer to a lidded serving bowl and keep it warm until ready to serve. Before serving fluff up the rice with a fork to allow steam to escape.

Lime Rice

This delicious rice recipe is perfect with the fish curries of India and South-east Asia.

300 g (10 oz) Basmati rice
600 ml (1 pint) water
2 tablespoons sunflower or mustard blend oil
2 tablespoons unsalted cashew nuts
1 teaspoon black mustard seeds
1 teaspoon sesame seeds
1 teaspoon crushed dried curry leaves (optional)

½ teaspoon turmeric
½ teaspoon mango powder (optional)
the flesh of ¼ coconut, grated, or 1 tablespoon desiccated coconut
3–4 tablespoons lime juice

Preparation time: 10 minutes, plus soaking
Cooking time: 15–20 minutes
Oven temperature: 110°C, 225°F, Gas Mark ¼
Serves 4

1. Leave the rice to soak for about 30 minutes in cold water. In a 3-litre (5 pint) flameproof lidded casserole bring the measured water to the boil. Rinse the rice two or three times in cold water, then finally in hot water. Tip the rice into the casserole and stir from time to time until the water returns to the boil. Place the lid on the casserole and turn the heat down to low. Let the rice cook for 8 minutes.

2. Meanwhile, heat the oil in a frying pan over moderate heat and fry the cashew nuts for 2 minutes. Add the mustard and sesame seeds, curry leaves (if using), turmeric and mango powder (if using) and fry for 1 minute. Stir the oil, nuts and spices into the cooked rice.

3. Add the coconut and lime juice and put the covered casserole into a preheated cool oven for a minimum of 30 minutes. It can be kept warm for 1–2 hours without spoiling. Just before serving, fluff up the rice with a fork to allow any steam to escape.

Pilau rice (top); Lime rice

Savoury Rice with Lentils

Kitcheri

This Indian dish has become truly international, inspired by the seafood kitcheris or kedgerees of the Keralonese coasts. The following is a basic recipe with lentils. Variations often include smoked haddock, poached and flaked, and a garnish of quartered hard-boiled eggs.

350 g (12 oz) Basmati or Patna rice
100 g (4 oz) green lentils
4 tablespoons ghee or concentrated butter
1 large onion, sliced
2 garlic cloves, sliced
1½ teaspoons turmeric
10 cloves
6 cardamom pods
1 × 7.5 cm (3 inch) piece cinnamon stick
salt
1 teaspoon freshly ground black pepper
900 ml (1½ pints) boiling water

Preparation time: 15 minutes, plus soaking
Cooking time: about 50 minutes
Serves 4

1. Wash the rice and lentils thoroughly. Place them together in a bowl and cover with cold water. Leave to soak for 2 hours. Drain well.

2. Melt the ghee or butter in a large heavy-based pan. Add the onion and garlic and fry gently until soft. Add the spices and seasonings and fry for a further 3 minutes, stirring constantly.

3. Add the rice and lentils to the pan and toss for 5 minutes until every grain is coated. Add the measured water and bring it back to the boil. Reduce the heat, cover with a tight-fitting lid and simmer for 20–30 minutes until the rice and lentils are cooked, but not mushy.

4. Before serving, remove the lid from the pan and boil off any excess liquid, turning the rice and lentils over constantly to prevent them sticking to the bottom of the pan.

Savoury rice with lentils, perfect for vegetarians and highly nutritious, makes a filling lunch or supper dish.

Saffron Rice

Kesari Chawal

In India this gloriously coloured rice is often served at festivals as the golden colour is thought to bring joy and happiness. While turmeric can be used to colour the rice instead of saffron, it cannot imitate saffron's delicate flavour.

175 g (6 oz) ghee or
    concentrated butter
2 large onions, sliced
350 g (10 oz) Basmati or
    Patna rice
1 teaspoon cloves
4 cardamoms
1 teaspoon salt
1 teaspoon freshly ground black
    pepper
½ teaspoon saffron threads,
    soaked in 1 tablespoon
    boiling water for 30 minutes
750 ml (1¼ pints) boiling water
varak (silver leaf) (optional),
    to garnish

1. Melt the ghee in a large, heavy-based saucepan, add the onions and fry gently for 4–5 minutes until soft.

2. Wash the rice thoroughly two or three times in cold water and drain. Add the rice to the pan with the cloves, cardamoms, salt and pepper and fry for 3 minutes, stirring frequently.

3. Add the saffron with its liquid to the pan and stir well to mix.

4. Add the measured water to the pan and bring back to the boil. Reduce the heat and simmer for 15–20 minutes, covered, until the rice is cooked. Drain well. Serve hot, garnished with varak, if liked.

Illustrated on page 197

Preparation time: 10 minutes
Cooking time: 30 minutes
Serves 4

Special-fried Rice

Chao Fan

In China this is served as a meal or a snack in its own right. To make a less substantial dish, simply stir-fry cold cooked rice in a little oil, adding beaten eggs, a few finely chopped spring onions and a pinch of salt.

2–3 eggs
2 spring onions, finely chopped
2 teaspoons salt
3 tablespoons vegetable oil
100 g (4 oz) peeled prawns
100 g (4 oz) cooked meat
    (chicken, pork or ham), cut
    into small cubes
4 tablespoons fresh or frozen
    peas, cooked
1 tablespoon light soy sauce
350–450 g (12oz–1lb) cold
    cooked rice

Preparation time: 5 minutes
Cooking time: about 8 minutes
Serves 4

1. Lightly beat the eggs with about 1 teaspoon of the spring onions and a pinch of salt.

2. Heat about 1 tablespoon of the oil in a hot wok, add the eggs and scramble until set. Remove and set aside in a bowl.

3. Heat the remaining oil in the wok. Add the prawns, meat and peas and stir-fry for 30 seconds. Add the soy sauce and continue to stir-fry for 2–3 minutes.

4. Add the rice and scrambled eggs with the remaining spring onions and salt. Stir to separate each grain of rice. Serve hot.

Illustrated on page 183

Indonesian Savoury Rice

Nasi Goreng

This generous and delicious rice dish is probably the best known Indonesian recipe.

4 medium onions, chopped
2 large garlic cloves, chopped
1 × 2.5 cm (1 inch) piece fresh
    root ginger, peeled and
    chopped
2 red chillies, coarsely chopped
1 teaspoon blachan (shrimp
    paste)
85 ml (3 fl oz) sunflower oil
3 eggs, lightly beaten
100 g (4 oz) large uncooked
    prawns, peeled and deveined
225 g (8 oz) cooked chicken,
    diced
450 g (1 lb) cold, cooked long-
    grain rice

2 tablespoons light soy sauce
2 tablespoons lemon juice
1 teaspoon demerara sugar
salt
freshly ground black pepper
50 g (2 oz) cooked ham, cut
    into thin strips
To serve:
50 g (2 oz) salted peanuts,
    coarsely chopped
2 tomatoes, thinly sliced
1 small onion, thinly sliced

Preparation time: 15 minutes
Cooking time: 25 minutes
Serves 4

1. Place the onions, garlic, ginger, chillies and blachan in a food processor or electric blender and blend to a purée. Set aside.

2. Heat 2 tablespoons of the oil in a medium frying pan set over moderate heat. Add the eggs and allow them to set like a thin omelette. Cook until it is golden and set. Do not stir. Remove from the pan and cut into thin strips. Set the egg strips aside and keep warm.

3. Heat the remaining oil in a wok or large frying pan over a moderate to high heat. Add the onion purée and cook for 5–10

minutes, stirring constantly, until golden brown. Add the prawns and stir-fry until they turn pink.

4. Add the chicken, rice, soy sauce, lemon juice and demerara sugar. Season to taste with salt and pepper. Cook, stirring constantly, until the mixture is heated through and the rice is coated.

5. Transfer the rice mixture to a heated platter and garnish with the ham and egg strips. Serve immediately, handing the peanuts, tomatoes and onion slices separately.

Vietnamese Special-fried Rice

Com Chien Thap Cam

While rice is usually served in Vietnam as an accompaniment to fish or meat, this dish is a meal in itself and popular at lunchtime.

2 Chinese sausages
2 eggs
2 tablespoons water
6 tablespoons sunflower oil
1 shallot, finely chopped
50 g (2 oz) ham, diced
25 g (1 oz) shrimps
225 g (8 oz) plain boiled rice (uncooked weight)
2 tablespoons soy sauce
½ teaspoon sugar
½ teaspoon salt
a pinch of monosodium glutamate (optional)

Preparation time: 10 minutes
Cooking time: 25 minutes
Serves 4

1. Place the Chinese sausages in the top of a steamer over boiling water. Steam for 15 minutes, then allow to cool slightly. Slice the sausages thinly and set aside.

2. Beat the eggs with the water in a small bowl. Heat 1 tablespoon of oil in a small frying pan. Add the egg mixture and swirl the pan to cover the base evenly. Reduce the heat. Using a spatula or round-bladed knife, lift the sides of the omelette to allow any uncooked egg to flow underneath. As soon as the omelette is cooked, flip it on to a plate. When it is cool, cut it into strips.

3. Heat the remaining oil in a large frying pan (a non-stick pan works best). Add the shallot and fry over moderate heat for 2 minutes, stirring all the time. Add the ham, shrimps, rice, soy sauce, sugar, salt and monosodium glutamate, if used, and the sausage slices and omelette strips. Cook, stirring, for 2–3 minutes. Serve immediately.

Right: Fried rice with eggs; Vietnamese special-fried rice

Crispy Rice and Chilli Prawns

The piquant flavour of this rice dish is typical of the Chinese province of Szechuan. Serve as a supper dish or as part of a dinner party menu.

50 g (2 oz) cornflour
1 egg white
2 tablespoons Chinese wine or dry sherry
½ teaspoon freshly ground white pepper
225 g (8 oz) uncooked prawns, peeled and deveined
600 ml (1 pint) sunflower oil
2 fresh green chillies, seeded and finely chopped
2 slices fresh root ginger, peeled and finely chopped
2 spring onions, finely chopped
250 ml (8 fl oz) chicken stock
25 g (1 oz) canned bamboo shoots, drained and finely sliced
25 g (1 oz) frozen peas, thawed
25 g (1 oz) cooked ham, finely shredded
2 teaspoons tomato purée
1 teaspoon sugar
1 teaspoon vinegar
2 teaspoons salt
1 tablespoon water
225 g (8 oz) crispy rice (see page 23)

Preparation time: 10 minutes
Cooking time: 15 minutes
Serves 4

1. Mix all but 2 tablespoons of the cornflour with the egg white, wine and white pepper. Toss the prawns in this mixture until they are thoroughly coated.

2. Heat the oil in a wok to 180°C/350°F, or until a cube of bread browns in 30 seconds. Add the prawns and stir-fry for 1 minute over a high heat until the prawns change colour. Lift the prawns out of the oil with a perforated spoon and drain on paper towels. Set aside and keep warm.

3. Heat 1 tablespoon of oil in another wok or saucepan. Add the chillies, ginger and spring onions. Stir together over moderate heat for 30 seconds then add the chicken stock, bamboo shoots, peas, ham, tomato purée, sugar, vinegar, salt and prawns.

4. Blend the remaining cornflour with 1 tablespoon water to make a thin paste. Stir into the mixture to thicken the sauce and cook, stirring frequently, for 8–10 minutes over moderate heat.

5. Replace the wok with the oil over the heat. When the oil is smoking, add the rice, which should be quite dry. The rice will immediately puff up and rise to the top. Remove the rice from the oil with a perforated spoon and drain on paper towels. Transfer the rice to a deep bowl and pour over the prawns in sauce. Serve immediately.

Fried Rice with Egg

Com Chien Trung

This very simple Vietnamese recipe can be served as an accompaniment to a main course or as a quick snack.

2 eggs
2 tablespoons water
6 tablespoons sunflower oil
2 spring onions, finely chopped
225 g (8 oz) plain boiled rice (uncooked weight)
2 tablespoons soy sauce
½ teaspoon salt
½ teaspoon sugar
a pinch of monosodium glutamate (optional)

Preparation time: 5 minutes
Cooking time: 10 minutes
Serves 4

1. Beat the eggs with the water in a small bowl. Heat 1 tablespoon of the oil in a small frying pan, add the egg mixture and swirl to cover the base of the pan. Reduce the heat. Using a spatula, lift the sides of the omelette to allow any uncooked egg to flow underneath. As soon as the omelette is cooked, slip it on to a plate. When it is cool, cut it into strips.

2. Heat the remaining oil in a large frying pan (a non-stick pan works best). Add the spring onions and stir-fry for 2 minutes over moderate heat.

3. Add the rice and omelette strips. Stir in the soy sauce, salt, sugar and monosodium glutamate, if using. Cook, stirring, for 2–3 minutes until the mixture is dry. Serve immediately.

Ekoori

This dish from the Parsees of Bombay on the west coast of India turns the conventional scrambled egg into a deliciously spiced food.

a knob of ghee or concentrated butter
1 teaspoon white cumin seeds
1 teaspoon sesame seeds
½ teaspoon turmeric
1 garlic clove, chopped finely
6 eggs, lightly beaten
Aromatic Salt (see page 12)
garam masala (see page 16), to garnish

Preparation time: 5 minutes
Cooking time: 5 minutes
Serves 4

1. Heat the ghee or butter in a small heavy saucepan. Stir-fry the cumin, sesame seeds and turmeric for 1 minute. Add the garlic and stir-fry for 1 minute more.

2. Add the eggs to the pan and keep stirring over a low to moderate heat until the eggs have reached the texture you prefer. Sprinkle with aromatic salt to taste.

3. Transfer to heated individual plates and serve immediately, garnished with garam masala and accompanied by Chappati (see page 199) or Puri (see page 198).

Emerald Fried Rice

This beautiful rice dish can be served with any meat or fish dish as part of an elegant dinner party menu.

225 g (8 oz) spring greens, finely shredded
2 teaspoons salt
5 tablespoons sunflower oil
3 eggs, lightly beaten
2 spring onions, finely chopped
450 g (1 lb) cooked rice
a pinch of monosodium glutamate (optional)
75 g (3 oz) cooked ham, finely shredded

Preparation time: 15 minutes, plus soaking
Cooking time: 3–4 minutes
Serves 4–6

1. Sprinkle the shredded spring greens with 1 teaspoon salt and leave to stand for 10 minutes. Squeeze out the liquid and chop the greens finely.

2. Heat 1 tablespoon of oil in a frying pan or crêpe pan. Pour in the beaten egg and allow it to spread thinly over the bottom of the pan. When the omelette is golden brown on the underside, turn it over with a palette knife and cook the other side gently. Remove the omelette from the pan and cut it into fine strips.

3. Heat another tablespoon of oil in the frying pan and add the finely chopped greens. Stir-fry for about 30 seconds then remove the greens from the pan.

4. Heat the remaining oil in a wok until it is smoking. Add the spring onions, then the rice, and toss well together until the rice is heated through. Add the remaining salt with the monosodium glutamate, if using, the greens, omelette strips and ham. Toss all the ingredients together for 1 minute and serve hot.

Indian Omelette

This omelette is delicious in its own right but can also be served with other dishes. This recipe makes enough for 2 people; for 4, make a second omelette, keeping the first one warm.

2 teaspoons freshly chopped coriander
2 teaspoons freshly chopped parsley
1 teaspoon snipped chives
1 teaspoon chopped mixed herbs
1–3 fresh green chillies, seeded and finely chopped (optional)
4 eggs
1 tablespoon ghee or concentrated butter
To garnish:
Aromatic Salt (see page 12)
garam masala (see page 16)
Mild Curry Powder (see page 14)
parsley sprigs

Preparation time: 5 minutes, plus standing
Cooking time: 2–3 minutes
Serves 2

1. Combine the coriander, parsley, chives, and mixed herbs with the chillies, if using.

2. Break the eggs into a large bowl and gently whisk them with a fork, mixing in the herbs. Let this mixture stand for 30 minutes.

3. Place a 25 cm (10 inch) frying pan over a moderate heat. When the pan is hot, put in the ghee or butter. Let it melt and swirl it around to cover the surface of the pan. Give the egg mixture a final stir and tip it into the pan, swirling it around to cover the whole pan. Spread it out with the fork. Shake the pan to prevent the omelette from sticking. When it is set enough for your taste (it should not be overcooked) fold each side to the centre and cut it in half widthways.

4. Transfer to heated plates and sprinkle aromatic salt, garam masala and curry powder on top. Garnish with a sprig of parsley and serve.

*Quail's egg curry; Indian omelette;
Ekoori, served with Deep-fried
wholewheat bread (page 198)*

Quail's Egg Curry

This Indian dish could use hen's
eggs, if quail's eggs are not
available; use 1 hen's egg for
every 3 quail's eggs. Have the
eggs at room temperature
before you begin to cook.

24 quail's eggs
2 tablespoons sunflower oil
300 ml (½ pint) Curry Purée
  (see page 15)
2 tablespoons Mild Curry Paste
  (see page 15)
1 × 425 g (14 oz) can chopped
  tomatoes
1 tablespoon dried fenugreek
  leaves
2 teaspoons dried mint
1 tablespoon desiccated coconut
  or coconut powder
2 tablespoons single cream
1 tablespoon garam masala
  (see page 16)
salt
mint sprigs, to garnish

Preparation time: 30 minutes
Cooking time: 15 minutes
Serves 4

1. Prick the blunt end of each
egg with a pin, just piercing the
shell into the sac of air. (This
will prevent the eggs from
cracking when placed in boiling
water.) Boil 1.2 litres (2 pints)
water in a large saucepan.
Carefully lower the eggs into the
boiling water and let them boil
for a total of 4 minutes.

2. Remove the pan from the
heat and immediately run cold
water into it to cool the eggs
and stop them cooking further.
Shell the eggs and let them
stand in cold water while
making the curry sauce.

3. Heat the oil in a large frying
pan or wok set over a moderate
heat and stir-fry the curry purée
for 5 minutes. Add the curry
paste, tomatoes, fenugreek and
mint. Bring the mixture to
simmering point, and stir in the
coconut, cream and garam
masala. Season with salt to taste,
and add water, if necessary, to
obtain a creamy consistency.

4. Bring the sauce gently back to
simmering point and carefully
add the eggs. Let the curry cook
for 5 minutes to heat the eggs
through. Serve immediately,
garnished with mint sprigs.

BREADS AND PANCAKES

There is a great variety of breads made in the different regions of India, and they can be served with any dish, traditionally used to scoop up thick sauces. Try them all to find your favourite. Savoury fritters and pancakes are ideal for snacks, and make a quick but satisfying meal served with light dishes and salads.

Poppadoms

Poppadoms are not easy to make and there is a wide variety imported from India, none of which is expensive; but if you would like to try making your own, this recipe is quick and straightforward.

450 g (1 lb) red lentils or urhad (lentil flour)
4½ teaspoons salt
1 tablespoon baking powder
250 ml (8 fl oz) tepid water
about 50 g (2 oz) ghee or concentrated butter
2 teaspoons black peppercorns
vegetable oil for frying

Preparation time: 1 hour, plus drying
Cooking time: 10 seconds (per 2)
Oven: 180°C, 350°F, Gas Mark 4
Makes about 20

1. If using lentils, grind them into a fine flour in a blender or food processor. Sift the lentil flour, salt and baking powder into a bowl and gradually add the tepid water to form a very firm dough.

2. Warm the ghee until it has melted. Knead the dough for at least 20 minutes, sprinkling it with enough melted ghee to prevent it sticking to the bowl. Crush the peppercorns, sprinkle them over the dough, then knead them in until evenly distributed.

3. Break the dough into about 20 pieces the size of golf balls. Roll out each piece very thinly, until about 15 cm (6 inches) in diameter. Stack them on top of each other, separating each one with a sheet of greaseproof paper, then dry them out in a preheated moderate oven for 2–2½ hours. Store in an airtight tin: they will keep for several weeks.

4. To cook the poppadoms, pour oil into a deep, heavy-based frying pan to a depth of 2.5 cm (1 inch). Heat the oil until it is very hot (a small piece of poppadom will immediately start to sizzle and float to the surface when dropped into the pan). Fry the poppadoms two at a time in the hot oil, rotating them for 5–10 seconds as they cook, using a combination of slotted spoon and fish slice. Turn them over and fry for a further 5–10 seconds.

5. Lift the cooked poppadoms out of the frying pan, allowing excess oil to drain back, then stack them upright (as in a toast rack) in a warm place until well drained. Ideally, poppadoms should be served within 1 hour of frying, but they can be kept crisp, or be re-crisped, in a hot oven.

Leavened Bread with Poppy Seeds

Naan

Naan is traditionally cooked on the walls of a clay oven (tandoor). Rolled-out dough is slapped on the inside of the oven wall near the top where it cooks very quickly in the fierce heat. Special irons are used, one with a flat end to scrape the naan from the wall and one with a hook to remove it from the oven.

450 g (1 lb) strong plain white flour
1 teaspoon baking powder
1 teaspoon salt
2 eggs, beaten
300 ml (½ pint) milk
1 tablespoon honey
50 g (2 oz) ghee or concentrated butter
2 tablespoons poppy seeds

Preparation time: 30 minutes
Cooking time: about 10 minutes, if baking; 3 minutes under a grill
Oven: 220°C/425°F, Gas Mark 7
Makes 6

1. Sift the flour, baking powder and salt into a bowl. Add the eggs and mix well. Warm the milk and honey gently in a saucepan until the honey has melted, then add gradually to the flour and egg mixture to form a dough. Knead well for 5–10 minutes.

2. Warm the ghee until it has melted. Divide the dough into 6 equal pieces. Brush one with a little of the ghee and knead again. Form into an oval shape about 1 cm (½ inch) thick. Pick up some of the poppy seeds with moistened hands and press them into the dough. Repeat with the remaining pieces of dough and melted ghee to make 6 naan altogether.

3. Arrange the naan on baking sheets and bake in a preheated hot oven for about 10 minutes, until the bread is puffed, golden and slightly scorched. Alternatively, cook under an extremely hot grill for 1½ minutes one each side. Serve immediately.

Right, clockwise from top left: Poppadoms; Saffron rice (page 191); Leavened bread with poppy seeds; Fried unleavened bread; Lentil sauce with hot topping (page 206)

Fried Unleavened Bread

Paratha

Paratha is a very easy Indian bread to make. They can be served as an accompaniment just as they are, but to make a more filling meal, stuff the breads with a mixture of potatoes and peas or spinach.

450 g (1 lb) ata (chapatti flour) or wholemeal flour
1 teaspoon salt
600 ml (1 pint) water
225 g (8 oz) ghee or concentrated butter

Preparation time: 30 minutes, plus resting
Cooking time: about 8 minutes
Makes 4–6

1. Sift the flour and salt into a bowl. Gradually add the water and mix to a firm dough. Knead the dough for at least 10 minutes, until it glistens and does not stick to the bowl. Cover the bowl with a wet cloth and leave in a cool place for 4 hours.

2. Warm the ghee until it has melted. Divide the dough into 4–6 balls and roll each one out on a floured board to a circle about 5 mm ($\frac{1}{4}$ inch) thick. Using a pastry brush, generously brush some of the melted ghee over the surface of a circle of dough. Starting at one side, roll the dough up to form a sausage shape. Take one end of the sausage and wrap it round to form a spiral. Roll this spiral out to a circle 5 mm ($\frac{1}{4}$ inch) thick. Brush with more melted ghee and repeat the process 4 times.

3. Finally, roll out the dough until slightly less than 5 mm ($\frac{1}{4}$ inch) thick. Repeat with the remaining dough to make 4–6 parathas altogether. Melt the remaining ghee in a heavy-based frying pan until fairly hot. Fry the parathas until golden brown and crisp on both sides, turning once. Drain and serve immediately.

Illustrated on page 198

Deep-fried Wholewheat Bread

Puri

A traditional Indian breakfast will often include *puris*, eaten simply with plenty of chutney. Many people send to the bazaar for them rather than cook them at home, as they are more easily prepared in bulk. Serve piping hot.

175 g (6 oz) ata (chapatti flour)
½ teaspoon salt
150 ml (¼ pint) water
50 g (2 oz) ghee or concentrated butter, melted vegetable oil for deep-frying

Preparation time: 15 minutes, plus standing
Cooking time: 2 minutes each
Makes 8–10

1. Sift the flour and salt into a bowl. Gradually add the water and mix to a firm dough. Add the ghee or butter and knead it in well. Cover and leave to rest for 30 minutes.

2. Divide the dough into 8–10 pieces, about 2.5 cm (1 inch) in diameter, then form them into balls. Roll them out on a lightly floured surface to rounds, just less than 3mm (⅛ inch) thick.

3. Heat the oil in a large, heavy-based pan until it is moderately hot or until a puri immediately starts to sizzle when placed in the oil and starts to float near to the surface. Deep-fry the puris one at a time for about 1½ minutes or until they puff up and float to the surface, spooning oil over them as they fry. Remove from the pan with a perforated spoon, drain on paper towels and keep hot in the oven while deep-frying the remaining puris. Serve hot.

Unleavened Bread

Chapatti

Of all Indian breads, *chapatti* are the easiest to make. They are, in fact, flat pancakes made with a wholemeal flour called ata, sometimes also called chapatti flour. This flour is available at Indian food shops, but if you are unable to find it, ordinary plain wholemeal flour can be used equally successfully.

350 g (12 oz) ata (chapatti flour) or wholemeal flour
¾ teaspoon salt
about 300 ml (½ pint) water

Preparation time: 10 minutes
Cooking time: 6–8 minutes each
Makes 8–10

1. Sift the flour and salt into a bowl, then gradually add the cold water and mix to a firm dough.

2. Turn the dough out on to a lightly floured surface and knead well until it is smooth and elastic. Break the dough into 8–10 pieces and form each piece into a ball. Roll out each ball of dough to a thickness of 3 mm (⅛ inch).

3. Dust an ungreased, heavy-based frying pan or griddle (preferably cast iron) with a little chapatti or wholemeal flour. Place the pan over the heat until very hot, then add a chapatti and cook for 3–4 minutes until blisters appear on the surface. Turn the chapatti over and cook for a further 3–4 minutes.

4. Remove the chapatti from the pan with tongs, then place under a preheated hot grill for a few seconds until black blisters appear and the chapatti swells up. Wrap immediately in a warm teatowel (to keep in the moisture) and place in a basket while cooking the remaining chapattis. Serve warm.

Left: Deep-fried wholewheat bread; Fried chick pea flour bread; Fried unleavened bread (page 197)

Note: If you wrap the chapattis in a teatowel after cooking, you can make them an hour or two in advance.

Chick Pea Fritters

Pakoras

These Indian fritters may be served as a snack at any time of day, and are particularly good with drinks before dinner. The batter is so good that it is sometimes deep-fried and served on its own, without vegetables.

150 g (5 oz) besan (chick pea flour)
½ teaspoon chilli powder
½ teaspoon salt
150 ml (¼ pint) natural yoghurt
1 teaspoon lemon juice
350 g (12 oz) chopped mixed vegetables: cauliflower, green peppers, peas, carrots, for example
vegetable oil for deep-frying

Preparation time: 10 minutes, plus standing
Cooking time: 5 minutes each
Serves 4

1. Sift the flour into a bowl, rubbing any lumps through the sieve with the back of a wooden spoon. Add the chilli powder and salt and mix well. Stir in the yoghurt and lemon juice gradually. Cover and leave in a cool place for 2 hours until the batter is thick; it should be much thicker than a pancake batter.

2. Heat the oil in a deep pan until a little of the batter, dropped into the oil, sizzles and rises to the surface. Coat spoonfuls of the mixed vegetables completely in batter and gently slide into the oil. Cook one at a time until nicely golden. Lift out of the oil with a perforated spoon and drain on paper towels. Keep warm until all the vegetables and batter have been used. Serve warm.

Note: Pakoras will keep in an airtight container for 3 days. Reheat under the grill before serving.

Fried Chick Pea Flour Bread

Besani Roti

This Indian fried bread has an irresistible flavour. Chick pea flour is more aromatic than ordinary wheat flour but less starchy. While it is difficult to knead to a smooth dough, this is essential for a good result.

225 g (8 oz) besan (chick pea flour)
1 teaspoon salt
200 ml (⅓ pint) water
100 g (4 oz) ghee
175 g (6 oz) butter, melted

Preparation time: 20 minutes
Cooking time: 6 minutes each
Makes 4–6

1. Sift the flour into a bowl, rubbing the lumps through the sieve with the back of a wooden spoon. Stir in the salt. Gradually add the water and mix to a firm dough. Knead in the ghee and work until smooth.

2. Divide the dough into 4–6 pieces, each about 7.5 cm (3 inches) in diameter, then form into balls. Roll out on a lightly floured surface to a 5 mm (¼ inch) thickness.

3. Spread a little of the melted butter over the bottom of a heavy-based frying pan, then cook the rotis one at a time, over a low heat, for about 3 minutes on each side. Transfer to an ovenproof plate and keep warm in the oven while cooking the remainder. Serve hot, brushed with the remaining melted butter.

Onion Pancakes

In northern China these savoury pancakes are either served alone or as an accompaniment to meat and poultry dishes. Using lard improves both texture and flavour.

450 g (1 lb) plain flour
250 ml (8 fl oz) boiling water
300 ml (½ pint) cold boiled
    water
450 g (1 lb) onions, finely
    chopped
5 tablespoons lard or vegetable
    oil
1½ tablespoons salt

Preparation time: 20 minutes, plus resting
Cooking time: 4 minutes
Makes 10

1. Sift the flour into a bowl. Pour in the boiling water, stirring all the time to form a stiff dough. Add the cold water to the dough and when it is cool enough to handle, knead until smooth. Cover the dough with a clean teatowel and leave it to rest for 30 minutes.

2. Roll the dough into a long sausage shape and cut it into 10 pieces. Roll each piece into a ball, then flatten each ball with a rolling pin into a small pancake about 7.5 cm (3–4 inches) in diameter. Sprinkle each pancake with the chopped onion and salt. Fold the edges of the pancake into the middle and then roll it out into a pancake again.

3. Heat 2 tablespoons of lard in a frying pan and fry the pancakes in batches for 2 minutes on each side or until golden brown, adding more lard as necessary. Keep the pancakes warm until all the dough has been used and serve immediately.

Pork and Spring Onion Pancakes

In northern China where wheat is the staple food, pancakes are often made to accompany the meal.

225 g (8 oz) plain flour
150 ml (¼ pint) boiling water
2 teaspoons sunflower oil
1½ tablespoons sesame oil
Filling:
100 g (4 oz) cooked pork
6 spring onions
1 tablespoon salt
2 tablespoons Chinese wine or
    dry sherry
1 tablespoon sesame oil
sunflower oil for shallow frying

Preparation time: 20 minutes, plus resting
Cooking time: 5 minutes
Makes 12

1. Sift the flour into a mixing bowl and make a well in the centre. Mix together the water and oil and gradually stir the liquid into the flour using chopsticks or a wooden spoon. Turn the dough on to a floured work surface and knead until firm. Let the dough rest for 10 minutes.

2. Divide the dough into 3 and roll each piece into a long, flat oval shape.

3. Combine the pork and spring onions with the salt, wine and sesame oil. Scatter about 1 tablespoon of this mixture over each pancake. Fold the two long sides of each pancake into the centre and then fold each one in half lengthways. Form into a round, flat coil and tuck in the end. Roll the coil flat.

4. Heat about 2 tablespoons of oil in a frying pan set over moderate heat. Fry a pancake for about 5 minutes, turning it once, until brown on both sides. Remove the pancake from the pan and keep warm while frying the remainder, adding more oil to the pan as necessary. Serve hot.

Savoury Pancakes

Dosas

In India there are a number of savoury pancakes made with different flours. They are often served simply with chutney but can be filled with a cooked vegetable or mixture of vegetables (potatoes are the most popular) and rolled up to make a satisfying snack.

150 g (5 oz) urhad dal (small
    lentils)
50 g (2 oz) Basmati or Patna
    rice
600 ml (1 pint) water
½ teaspoon bicarbonate of soda
1 teaspoon chilli powder
½ teaspoon salt
vegetable oil for shallow-frying

Preparation time: 15 minutes, plus soaking
Cooking time: 5 minutes each
Makes 12–15

1. Wash the dal and rice thoroughly, drain and place in a bowl with the measured water. Leave to soak overnight.

2. Place the dal, rice and water in a liquidizer and blend until smooth. Add the bicarbonate of soda, chilli powder and salt and stir well.

3. In a cold, heavy-based frying pan, pour enough batter to just cover the bottom. Place the pan over the heat. When the batter is just starting to set, pour about 1 tablespoon of oil around the edge of the dosa, then shake the pan to spread the oil. Fry the dosa for about 1 minute, or until it is golden underneath. Do not turn the dosa over. Remove from the pan and roll up. Repeat until all the batter has been used. Serve hot, enclosing a filling if liked.

Indonesian spicy beef crêpes

Indonesian Spicy Beef Crêpes

These flavoursome filled pancakes can be served as snacks or as part of a more complex dinner menu.

150 g (5 oz) plain flour
120 ml (4 fl oz) milk, at room temperature
120 ml (4 fl oz) water
2 eggs, at room temperature, lightly beaten
salt
2–3 tablespoons ghee or concentrated butter
Filling:
2 teaspoons sunflower oil
350 g (12 oz) lean minced beef
50 g (2 oz) peas
1 garlic clove, crushed
1 teaspoon finely chopped fresh root ginger
½ teaspoon sugar
½ teaspoon freshly ground black pepper
¼ teaspoon freshly grated nutmeg

a pinch of chilli powder
salt
2 teaspoons cornflour
1 tablespoon water
85 ml (3 fl oz) ghee or concentrated butter
To garnish:
six 1 × 13 cm (½ × 5 inch) thin ribbons of blanched spring onion
six 1 × 13 cm (½ × 5 inch) thin ribbons of blanched carrots

Preparation time: 10 minutes, plus standing
Cooking time: 20 minutes
Makes 12

1. To make the crêpes, combine the flour, milk, water, eggs and salt in a medium bowl and mix until smooth. Cover and stand at room temperature for 1 hour.

2. Heat 1 tablespoon of the ghee in a 15 cm (6 inch) non-stick frying pan over moderate to low heat. Ladle 3 tablespoons of the batter into the pan, tilting the pan until the bottom is covered with a thin layer of batter. Cook for 1 minute until the underside is light brown, shaking the pan frequently to prevent sticking. Turn the crêpe out on to a paper towel and cover with waxed paper. Repeat with the remaining batter to give 12 crêpes.

3. To make the filling, heat the sunflower oil in a large frying pan over moderate to high heat. Add the beef, peas, garlic, ginger, sugar, pepper, nutmeg, chilli powder and salt. Stir-fry for 4 minutes, until the beef is almost cooked through. Remove the pan from the heat and pour away excess fat.

Dissolve the cornflour in the water to make a thin paste and stir into the beef mixture.

4. Arrange 2 tablespoons of the filling in the centre of the cooked side of each crêpe. Fold the bottom edge over the filling. Fold the sides over slightly, then roll up each crêpe to enclose the filling.

5. Heat the butter in a large frying pan over a moderate heat. Add the filled crêpes, in batches if necessary, seam side down. Cook on both sides for about 4 minutes until brown and crisp.

6. To serve, tie half the crêpes around the centre with spring onion strips, and the other half with carrot strips. Serve immediately.

SAUCES, CHUTNEYS AND ACCOMPANIMENTS

No Chinese or Indian meal would be complete without an accompaniment of colourful little dishes of pickles and chutneys, made from fruit or vegetables and adding zest to the main dish.

Cucumber Raita

Raita is an important accompaniment to many Indian foods, its delicious coolness providing the perfect antidote to hot curries. Its essential ingredient is yoghurt, to which may be added other 'cool' foods, such as cucumber, as in this recipe, or tomatoes and even fruits like bananas.

100 g (4 oz) cucumber, thinly sliced
salt
2× 150 g (5 oz) cartons natural yoghurt
50 g (2 oz) spring onions, thinly sliced
1 green chilli, seeded and finely chopped
coriander leaves, to garnish

Preparation time: 5 minutes, plus draining
Serves 4

1. Put the cucumber into a colander, sprinkle with salt and leave to drain for 30 minutes. Dry thoroughly.

2. Mix the yoghurt with salt to taste and fold in the cucumber, spring onions and chill until required. Garnish with coriander leaves to serve.

Illustrated on page 84

Mint Raita

This raita is the customary accompaniment for Indian tandoori dishes.

2 tablespoons finely chopped mint leaves
6 tablespoons natural yoghurt
1 tablespoon double cream
1 teaspoon garam masala (see page 16)
mint sprigs, to garnish

Preparation time: 5 minutes
Serves 4–6

1. Mix the mint with the yogurt, cream and garam masala. Place the raita in a serving bowl.

2. Chill briefly before serving garnished with mint sprigs.

Fresh Chilli

This very hot chutney is not for the novice curry eater. It keeps well and the amount given in this recipe should be sufficient for several meals.

225 g (8 oz) fresh green chillies, seeded and chopped
250 ml (8 fl oz) malt vinegar

Preparation time: 5 minutes
Makes approx. 250 g (8 oz)

1. Place the chillies in a blender or food processor with the vinegar and work to a purée.

2. Place the purée in a sterilized jar. Top up the jar with vinegar to prevent a mould from forming. Cover the jar tightly.

3. The chutney will change from bright to dark green in colour after 1–2 weeks but will keep indefinitely.

Onion Salad

Cachumber

This onion salad is often served with curries in India, adding a fresh taste to the meal and also providing a good source of Vitamin C.

1 onion, chopped
225 g (8 oz) tomatoes, skinned and chopped
1–2 green chillies, seeded and chopped
1–2 tablespoons vinegar
salt

Preparation time: 10 minutes, plus chilling
Serves 4

1. Put the onion, tomatoes and chillies in a serving dish. Pour over the vinegar, making sure the mixture does not become too liquid. Add salt to taste.

2. Chill the salad before serving.

Clockwise from top left: Cucumber raita; Onion salad; Mint raita; Fresh chilli

Mango Chutney

Unlike other Indian chutney recipes in this chapter, this mango chutney does not need to be made fresh daily, but will keep for several months. It is among the most popular of Indian chutneys and is often varied by the use of other fruits – apples instead of mangoes, for instance, or a mixture of apples, pears, peaches, plums and sultanas.

900 g (2 lb) very firm mangoes
450 g (1 lb) sugar
600 ml (1 pint) vinegar
1 × 5 cm (2 inch) piece ginger
4 garlic cloves
½-1 tablespoon chilli powder
1 tablespoon mustard seeds
2 tablespoons salt
100 g (4 oz) raisins or sultanas

Preparation time: 10 minutes
Cooking time: 50 minutes
Makes about 1.25 kg (2½ lb)

1. Peel the mangoes and cut into small pieces; set aside.

2. Place the sugar and all but 1 tablespoon of the vinegar in a pan and simmer for 10 minutes.

3. Place the ginger, garlic and remaining vinegar in an electric blender or food processor and work to a paste. Add to the pan and cook for 10 minutes, stirring.

4. Add the mango and remaining ingredients and cook, uncovered, for about 25 minutes, stirring as the chutney thickens.

5. Pour into hot sterilized jars, cover with waxed discs, then seal with cellophane covers and label. The chutney will keep for several months.

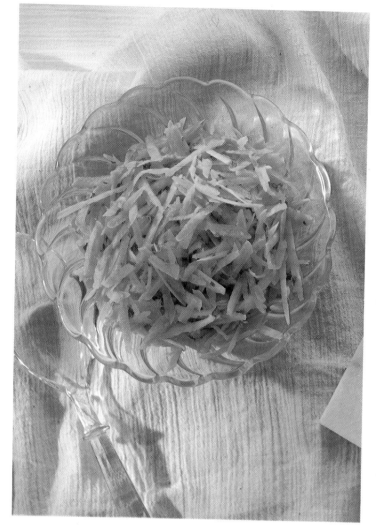

Coriander Chutney

Chutney is an important part of most Indian meals. It is served with curry and as an accompaniment to plain boiled rice. In India it is usually made fresh daily.

1 bunch coriander leaves
1 green chilli
100 g (4 oz) fresh, grated or desiccated coconut
3 garlic cloves
2 onions, sliced
1 × 2.5 cm (1 inch) piece of fresh root ginger
½ teaspoon ground cumin
juice of ¼ lime
1 teaspoon sugar

Preparation time: 10 minutes
Serves 4

1. Wash and dry the coriander leaves. Pass all the ingredients except the lime juice and sugar through a mincer or blender.

2. Mix the lime juice with the sugar and combine with the other ingredients.

Carrot Salad

This is a refreshing and colourful salad to serve with Indian curry dishes.

100 g (4 oz) carrots, grated
25 g (1 oz) grated onion
½ tablespoon grated root ginger
1 tablespoon finely chopped mint
½ teaspoon salt
½ teaspoon sugar
1 tablespoon lemon juice

Preparation time: 5 minutes, plus chilling
Serves 4

1. Mix all the ingredients together, cover and chill for 1–2 hours before serving.

Potatoes in Yoghurt

Aloo Raita

This excellent way with potatoes is a fine example of how Indian cooking can be adapted to use in authentic style vegetables not native to the country. Use a firm variety of potato that will not disintegrate when cooked.

225 g (8 oz) potatoes, peeled
salt
750 ml (1¼ pints) natural yoghurt
1 teaspoon cumin seeds
¼ teaspoon chilli powder
freshly ground black pepper
chopped coriander leaves, to garnish

Preparation time: 10 minutes
Cooking time: 20 minutes
Serves 4

1. Cook the potatoes in boiling salted water until just tender. Drain and cool, then dice them.

2. Whisk the yoghurt in a bowl with the cumin seeds, chilli powder and salt and pepper to taste. Chill.

3. Mix the potatoes into the yoghurt mixture just before serving, garnished with chopped coriander leaves.

Illustrated on pages 148–149

Spicy Onion Sauce

Another hot and spicy sauce from India – this time based on onions and garlic.

100 g (4 oz) ghee
1 large onion, peeled and sliced
2 garlic cloves, peeled and
*   sliced*
1 teaspoon ground coriander
1 teaspoon turmeric
1 teaspoon chilli powder
½ teaspon salt
1 teaspoon freshly ground black
*   pepper*
300 ml (½ pint) water
1 teaspoon garam masala (see
*   page 16)*

Preparation time: 5 minutes
Cooking time: 30 minutes
Makes approx. 450 ml (¾ pint)

1. Melt the ghee in a heavy-based saucepan. Add the onion and garlic and fry gently for 4–5 minutes until soft but not brown. Stir in the coriander, turmeric, chilli, salt and pepper, blending well. Add the water and bring to the boil, reduce the heat and simmer for 10 minutes, stirring frequently.

2. Add the garam masala and simmer for a further 5 minutes before serving. Use hot as required.

Far left: Carrot salad
Right: Crunchy pickled cucumber

Crunchy Pickled Cucumber or Cabbage

Pickles are a regular accompaniment to rich fish or meat dishes in the cuisine of Szechuan in China.

4 teaspoons salt
4 dried chillies, seeded and
*   shredded*
3 tablespoons gin
2 medium cucumbers or 1
*   large hard white cabbage,*
*   thinly sliced*
600 ml (1 pint) malt vinegar

Preparation time: 10 minutes, plus marinating

1. Sprinkle the salt, chillies and gin over the cucumber. Leave to season for 2 hours.

2. Place the mixture in jars and pour in the vinegar. Let it stand for 3 days, turning or shaking once a day.

Spiced Fruit and Vegetables

Its unusual combination of ingredients makes this dish an interesting accompaniment for Indian main dishes.

1 tablespoon sunflower oil
1 onion, chopped
4 celery stalks, chopped
1 tablespoon curry powder
1 tablespoon flour
300 ml ($\frac{1}{2}$ pint) vegetable stock
   or water
1 × 2.5 cm (1 inch) piece of
   fresh root ginger, finely
   chopped, or 1 teaspoon
   ground ginger
juice and grated rind of 1
   lemon
1 × 400 g (14 oz) can apricot
   halves, drained
2 bananas, peeled and thickly
   sliced
450 g (1 lb) cooking apples,
   peeled, cored and quartered
100 g (4 oz) raisins
150 ml ($\frac{1}{4}$ pint) soured cream

Preparation time: 5 minutes
Cooking time: 25 minutes
Serves 6

1. Heat the oil in a heavy-based saucepan over a moderate heat. Fry the onion and celery in the oil until golden. Stir in the curry powder and flour and cook gently for 2–3 minutes, stirring constantly.

2. Mix the stock or water with the ginger and gradually stir into the pan. Add the lemon juice, rind, apricots, bananas, apples and raisins. Stir well and cook, covered, over low heat until the fruit is tender.

3. Just before serving, stir in the soured cream.

Hot Tomato Chutney

This chutney goes well with curries, and is also good with cold roast meats. Make it when tomatoes are in full season. The raisins and sultanas in this recipe could be replaced by dried apricots, which should be soaked overnight.

900 g (2 lb) tomatoes,
   quartered
120 ml (4 fl oz) malt vinegar
225 g (8 oz) sugar
100 g (4 oz) raisins
100 g (4 oz) sultanas
25 g (1 oz) blanched almonds,
   sliced
4 garlic cloves, finely sliced
25 g (1 oz) fresh root ginger,
   peeled and finely chopped
1 tablespoon chilli powder
$\frac{1}{2}$ tablespoon salt

Preparation time: 10 minutes
Cooking time: 1 hour
Makes approx. 1.5 kg (3 lb)

1. Put the tomatoes and vinegar into a large saucepan and heat gently until the juice starts to run. Add the sugar and bring slowly to the boil. Simmer for 5 minutes.

2. Add the remaining ingredients and simmer for 30 minutes or until the mixture has thickened.

3. Leave until cold, then pour into sterilized jars and cover with a wax disc and a screw-topped lid. Store in a cool place.

Lentil Sauce with Hot Topping

Tarka Dal

Dal, or lentil sauce, is a staple dish found throughout the Indian sub-continent. This version of the dish is given added piquancy by its topping, with its unusual combination of garlic and lovage seeds.

450 g (1 lb) red lentils
50 g (2 oz) ghee
1 medium onion, thinly sliced
1 garlic clove, thinly sliced
1$\frac{1}{2}$ teaspoons turmeric
$\frac{1}{2}$ teaspoon salt
1 teaspoon freshly ground black
   pepper
1 litre (1$\frac{3}{4}$ pints) water
4 fresh green chillies, cored and
   seeded

Topping (Tarka):
2 tablespoons sesame oil
4 garlic cloves, thinly sliced
1 small onion, thinly sliced
1 teaspoon lovage seeds

Preparation time: 12–15 minutes
Cooking time: about 30 minutes
Oven: 180°C, 350°F, Gas Mark 4
Serves 4

1. Wash the lentils well in cold water. Drain and pick out any stones or discoloured lentils. Melt the ghee in a large, heavy-based saucepan, add the onion and garlic and fry gently for 4–5 minutes until soft. Sprinkle in the turmeric, salt and pepper, then add the lentils, stirring well so that they become well coated.

2. Pour in the water, bring to the boil, then add the whole prepared chillies. Boil for about 20 minutes, stirring from time to time, until the lentils have turned into a yellow sauce, the consistency of a thick custard. (It may be necessary to add more water during cooking,

depending on the absorbency of the lentils.) Pour the sauce into a warmed serving dish, cover and keep hot in a preheated moderate oven.

3. To make the tarka, heat the oil in a frying pan until smoking. Add the garlic and onion, fry quickly until the garlic blackens, then throw in the lovage seeds. Fry for a further 10 seconds, then pour over the lentil sauce. Serve hot.

Illustrated on page 197

Hot tomato chutney (left); Brinjal pickle

Brinjal Pickle

This pickle is for those who like their relishes hot. The amount of chillies in it could be reduced though the pickle would lose its characteristic bite. It keeps well in a cool place.

900 g (2 lb) aubergines
1 tablespoon salt
300 ml ($\frac{1}{2}$ pint) hot water
100 g (4 oz) tamarind
50 g (2 oz) cumin seeds
25 g (1 oz) dried red chillies
50 g (2 oz) fresh root ginger,
  peeled and chopped
50 g (2 oz) garlic
300 ml ($\frac{1}{2}$ pint) malt vinegar
150 ml ($\frac{1}{4}$ pint) sunflower oil
2 teaspoons mustard seeds
225 g (8 oz) sugar

Preparation time: 25 minutes, plus soaking
Cooking time: 45 minutes
Makes approx. 1.5 kg (3 lb)

1. Thinly slice the aubergines, sprinkle with the salt and leave in a colander for 30 minutes to drain. Pour the hot water on to the tamarind and leave to soak for 20 minutes. Press through a fine sieve and set aside.

2. Put the cumin, chillies, ginger, garlic and 2 tablespoons of the vinegar into a food processor or electric blender and work to a paste.

3. Heat the oil in a large saucepan and fry the mustard seeds until they begin to

splutter. Quickly add the spice paste and fry, stirring, for 2 minutes. Add the aubergine, tamarind water, remaining vinegar and the sugar and stir well. Bring to the boil, then simmer for 30 to 35 minutes, until the mixture is thick and pulpy.

4. Leave until cold; pour into sterilized jars and cover with a disc of waxpaper and a screw-topped lid. Store in a cool place.

Apricot Chutney

Khubani ki chutney

This cooked chutney will keep for some time in airtight jars. A typical Indian chutney, it can be served with many snacks or main dishes, according to personal taste.

225 g (8 oz) dried apricots, soaked overnight
150 ml ($\frac{1}{4}$ pint) vinegar
250 g (9 oz) sugar
25 g (1 oz) fresh ginger root, peeled and crushed
4 garlic cloves, crushed (optional)
about 1 teaspoon chilli powder
a pinch of salt

Preparation time: 10 minutes, plus soaking overnight
Cooking time: about 55 minutes
Serves 4

1. Place the apricots and the soaking liquid with enough water to cover in a saucepan. Simmer until tender then beat or blend to a smooth consistency.

2. In a separate pan place the vinegar, sugar, crushed ginger and garlic, chilli powder and salt. Heat gently, stirring, until the sugar has dissolved, then increase the heat until a syrup is formed.

3. Stir the apricots into the syrup and simmer gently for about 10 minutes to the desired thickness. Allow to cool and bottle in airtight jars with vinegar-proof tops.

Satay Sauce

Peanuts are a distinctive ingredient in Indonesian cooking and this peanut-based sauce is a popular and widely used accompaniment for satay dishes.

2 onions
1–2 tablespoons peanut oil
75 g (3 oz) roasted peanuts
$\frac{1}{2}$ teaspoon chilli powder
150 ml (1$\frac{1}{4}$ pint) warm water
1 teaspoon brown sugar
salt
1 tablespoon soy sauce
juice of $\frac{1}{2}$ lime or lemon

Preparation time: 10 minutes
Cooking time: 15 minutes
Serves 4

1. Slice 1 of the onions. Heat the oil in a wok or frying pan over a moderate heat and fry the onion until soft and transparent.

2. Chop the second onion finely, put it in a mortar with the peanuts and chilli powder and pound to a paste or blend in a liquidizer.

3. Add the paste to the fried onion and fry together for 3 minutes, stirring well. Gradually dilute with the water and stir in the sugar. Cook for a few minutes to concentrate the sauce to the consistency of single cream.

4. Season with salt to taste, add the soy sauce and lime or lemon juice, stir and use for basting or serving with all satay dishes.

Shantung Sauce

This sauce from northern China goes well with chicken and rice dishes.

2 garlic cloves, finely chopped
2 chillies, finely chopped
2 spring onions, finely chopped
1 teaspoon sugar
1 teaspoon sesame oil
2$\frac{1}{2}$ tablespoons chicken stock
$\frac{1}{2}$ teaspoon salt
pinch monosodium glutamate (optional)
3 teaspoons dry sherry
2 teaspoons wine vinegar
$\frac{1}{2}$ tablespoon red chilli oil

Preparation time: 10 minutes
Cooking time: 1–2 minutes

1. Heat a wok or frying pan, then add the garlic, chillies, spring onions, sugar and sesame oil. Stir-fry for 1 minute, then add the chicken stock, salt, monosodium glutamate (if using), sherry, vinegar and chilli oil. Stir over medium heat until boiling, then simmer briefly, until thickened slightly.

Tomato Sauce

This versatile sauce from eastern China is excellent poured over simply cooked white fish and may also be used as a dip.

1 tablespoon sunflower oil
1 onion, diced
3 canned pineapple rings, diced
1 green pepper, cored, seeded and diced
3 tablespoons sugar
3 tablespoons wine vinegar
6 tablespoons water
3 tablespoons tomato purée
1 tablespoon Chinese wine or dry sherry
2 teaspoons cornflour
a pinch of salt
1 teaspoon sesame oil

Preparation time: 15 minutes
Cooking time: about 10 minutes

1. Heat the oil in a wok or frying pan.

2. Add the onion, pineapple, and green pepper to the wok and stir-fry together for about 30 seconds. Mix together the sugar, vinegar, water, tomato purée, wine, cornflour, salt and sesame oil, and add to the vegetables.

3. Bring to the boil, stirring. If the sauce becomes too thick add a little more water.

Achar

Tomato Sambal

Side dishes, or sambals, are
essential features of Indonesian
meals. Often quite fiery like this
Tomato Sambal, they are used
to balance the often mild taste
of the main dish.

2–3 tablespoons peanut oil
3 garlic cloves, crushed
about ½ teaspoon tamarind pod,
  crushed
1 small onion, chopped
2 fresh red chillies, seeded and
  shredded
450 g (1 lb) tomatoes, peeled
  and sliced
1–2 leeks, washed and sliced
salt
1 tablespoon brown sugar
150 ml (¼ pint) coconut milk
  (see page 14)

Preparation time: 15 minutes
Cooking time: 18–20 minutes
Serves 4

1. Heat the oil in a wok or frying
pan over moderate heat and fry
the garlic, tamarind and onion
for 3–4 minutes.

2. Add the chillies and tomatoes
to the pan and stir-fry for 2
minutes. Add the leeks and stir-
fry for 2 minutes more. Sprinkle
over the salt and sugar.

3. Gradually blend the coconut
milk into the mixture. Reduce
the heat and simmer gently for
10 minutes. Serve hot.

Achar

This Malaysian pickle will keep
for several months in the
refrigerator, provided it is stored
in clean, sterilized jars and
tightly sealed.

600 ml (1 pint) pickling
  vinegar
3 carrots, cut into 2.5 × 5 cm
  (1 × 2 inch) sticks
1 cucumber, unpeeled, cut into
  2.5 × 5 cm (1 × 2 inch) sticks
225 g (8 oz) cauliflower florets
300 g (10 oz) salted peanuts,
  ground
300 g (10 oz) sesame seeds,
  toasted
225 g (8 oz) demerara sugar
3 fresh red chillies, seeded and
  finely chopped
3 fresh green chillies, seeded
  and finely chopped
175 ml (6 fl oz) sunflower oil
5 garlic cloves, finely chopped
2 teaspoons ground turmeric
salt

Preparation time: 10 minutes
Cooking time: 12–13 minutes
**Makes about 1.2 litres (2
pints)**

1. Bring the vinegar to the boil
in a large saucepan over a
moderate heat. Add the carrots
and blanch for 1 minute. Using
a small slotted spoon, remove
the carrots from the vinegar,
shaking off any excess. Place in
a large bowl.

2. Blanch the cucumber and
cauliflower in the same way and
transfer to the bowl. Save the
vinegar for other uses.

3. Add the peanuts, sesame
seeds, sugar and chillies to the
vegetables and toss well to coat.
Cover and set aside.

4. Heat the oil in a large frying
pan over a moderate heat. Add
the garlic, turmeric and salt to
taste and cook for 2–3 minutes,
stirring constantly. Remove from
the heat and let cool completely.

5. Pour the garlic oil mixture
over the vegetables and toss
well to coat. Cover and chill
overnight before serving.

DESSERTS AND SWEETS

Everyday meals in the East usually end with fresh fruit, of which an abundance is available in many regions. Desserts are often reserved for festivals, whether plain cakes or wickedly sweet Indian puddings. The ethereally light desserts served at Japanese banquets are an elegant way to end any meal, especially if you have delicate porcelain bowls.

Steamed Sponge Cake

This very light and airy cake is traditionally eaten during the Chinese spring festival. Serve it with China tea.

6 eggs, separated
100 g (4 oz) caster sugar
3 tablespoons water
100 g (4 oz) flour
½ teaspoon baking powder
1 teaspoon vanilla essence
1 teaspoon lemon essence
oil for greasing

Preparation time: 25 minutes
Cooking time: 30–40 minutes
Serves 4–6

1. Line a 20 cm (8 inch) cake tin with oiled greaseproof paper. Put a rack or trivet in a wok or large saucepan. Pour in water to just below it. Bring to the boil.

2. Whisk the egg yolks with the sugar and water until they are very light and fluffy. Sift in the flour and baking powder and beat until they are well blended in. Stir in the vanilla and lemon essences. Stiffly whip the egg whites and fold into the mixture.

3. Pour the batter into the prepared tin. Put the tin into the wok or saucepan. Cover with a lid or greased foil and steam the cake for 30–40 minutes until it is firm to the touch and has shrunk slightly from the sides of the tin. Top up with boiling water during the cooking period if necessary. Turn on to a wire rack to cool.

Peking Toffee Apples

These apple pieces, encased in crisp, fine toffee, make a delicious dessert, popular in Chinese restaurants in many parts of the world.

100 g (4 oz) plain flour
1 egg
100 ml (3½ fl oz) water, plus 2 tablespoons
4 crisp apples, peeled, cored and cut into fat slices
600 ml (1 pint) sunflower oil, plus 1 tablespoon
6 tablespoons sugar
3 tablespoons golden syrup

Preparation time: 15 minutes
Cooking time: 20 minutes
Serves 4

1. Mix together the flour, egg and 100 ml (3½ fl oz) of the water to make a batter. Dip each piece of apple into the batter.

2. In a wok or deep frying pan heat 600 ml (1 pint) of the oil to 180°C/350°F or until a cube of bread browns in 30 seconds. Deep-fry the apple pieces for 2 minutes, then remove and drain on paper towels.

3. In another pan, heat together the sugar, and the remaining oil and water. Dissolve the sugar over a gentle heat, then simmer for 5 minutes, stirring constantly. Add the golden syrup and boil until the hard crack stage is reached (151°C/304°F) or until it forms brittle threads when dropped into iced water. Put in the fried apples and turn to coat each piece.

4. Remove the apple pieces with a slotted spoon and drop into iced water. Remove immediately and serve.

Deep-fried Sweet Potato Balls

These crisply fried titbits, coated in crunchy sesame seeds, are a product of Cantonese cooking, from the south of China.

450 g (1 lb) sweet potatoes
100 g (4 oz) glutinous rice flour
50 g (2 oz) brown sugar
50 g (2 oz) sesame seeds
oil for deep frying

Preparation time: 20 minutes
Cooking time: about 30 minutes
Serves 4

1. Put the potatoes in a saucepan, cover with water and bring to the boil. Reduce the heat and simmer for 15–20 minutes or until the potatoes are tender. Drain and peel. Mash the potatoes, then beat in the glutinous rice flour and sugar.

2. With dampened hands, form the mixture into walnut-sized balls. Roll each ball in sesame seeds until well coated.

3. Heat the oil to 160°C/325°F, or until a cube of bread browns in 45 seconds. Deep-fry the potato balls until golden brown. Drain on paper towels.

4. Serve hot.

Right: Rice-stuffed pears; Peking toffee apples

Rice-stuffed Pears

Vary this Chinese dessert by coring the pears and leaving them whole. The rice stuffing is then pushed down the core. Whole pears would take a few minutes longer to cook than halved ones.

225 g (8 oz) flaked rice
25 g (1 oz) almonds, skinned and roughly chopped
1 × 100 g (4 oz) can lotus seeds, drained and roughly chopped

6 red and green glacé cherries, finely chopped
50 ml (2 fl oz) sunflower oil
2 tablespoons sugar
4 pears, peeled, halved and cored
Sauce:
1 tablespoon sugar
100 ml (3½ fl oz) water
25 g (1 oz) cornflour
1–2 drops pink food colouring (optional)

Preparation time: 10 minutes
Cooking time: 40 minutes
Serves 4

1. Place the flaked rice in a bowl, cover with water and steam for 30 minutes.

2. Mix together the cooked rice, almonds, lotus seeds, cherries, oil and sugar.

3. To make the sauce, dissolve the sugar in the water. Blend the cornflour with the food colouring (if using) and add this to the sugar and water. Bring to the boil to form a sauce.

4. Stuff the rice mixture into the pear halves. Place the stuffed pear halves in a steamer basket and steam for about 15 minutes.

5. Serve the stuffed pears with the sauce poured over.

Lychee Sorbet

Lichi Bian Choz Ling

The familiar lychee from China takes on an unusual role in this recipe, imparting its exotic and delicate flavour to a very refreshing sorbet.

1 × 450 g (1 lb) can lychees
100 g (4 oz) granulated sugar
2 tablespoons lemon or lime juice
2 egg whites
thinly pared rind of 1 lime, to decorate

Preparation time: 30 minutes, plus freezing
Cooking time: 20 minutes
Serves 6

1. Drain the juice from the lychees into a measuring jug and make up to 300 ml ($\frac{1}{2}$ pint) with cold water. Pour this liquid into a saucepan and stir in the sugar. Heat gently until the sugar has dissolved, then bring to the boil. Simmer gently, without stirring, for 10 minutes, then remove from the heat. Set aside and allow to cool slightly.

2. Purée the lychees in a blender or food processor or press through a sieve. Mix the purée with the sugar syrup and lemon or lime juice. Pour the mixture into a shallow freezer container and place in the freezer for 1–2 hours, or until nearly frozen.

3. Whisk the egg whites in a clean, dry bowl until fairly stiff. Cut the frozen mixture into small pieces, then work in a blender or food processor to break down the crystals. Without allowing the mixture to melt, quickly fold in the whisked egg white until evenly incorporated, then pour into a slightly deeper freezer container. Return to the freezer for 2–3 hours or until firm.

4. Meanwhile, prepare the decoration. Plunge the lime rind into a saucepan of boiling water and blanch for 2 minutes. Drain, refresh under cold running water, then pat dry with paper towels and cut into thin strips.

5. To serve the sorbet, remove from the freezer 10 minutes before serving. Scoop the sorbet into individual glass dishes and sprinkle with the lime rind. Serve immediately.

Fruit Salad Ice Mountain

Hoa Qua Tuoi

This simple Vietnamese dessert is both refreshing and pleasing to the eye. For best results, the fruit and the syrup should be very cold when the dish is served.

Syrup:
225 g (8 oz) sugar
350 ml (12 fl oz) water

1 small watermelon
1 papaya
1 × 312 g (11 oz) can lychees
1 × 454 g (16 oz) can longans
1 × 454 g (16 oz) can jack fruit
3 bananas
100 g (4 oz) fresh dates
2 tablespoons seedless raisins
crushed ice
fresh mint leaves, to decorate

Preparation time: 20 minutes, plus cooling and chilling
Cooking time: 5 minutes
Serves 4

1. First make the syrup. Combine the sugar and water in a small heavy-bottomed saucepan. Bring to the boil, stirring constantly until the sugar has dissolved. Boil steadily, without stirring, for 2 minutes. Remove from the heat and set aside. When cool, refrigerate until required.

2. Prepare the fruit. Cut the watermelon in half, discard the seeds and cut the flesh into cubes or rounds. Transfer to a large bowl. Add the papaya, prepared in the same way. Drain the lychees, longans and jack fruit and cut the jack fruit into quarters. Slice the bananas. Stir all these fruits into the bowl together with the dates and raisins. Chill all the fruit in the refrigerator until required.

3. Just before serving, pile crushed ice in the centre of a large platter to make a miniature ice mountain. Decorate with the fruit salad, then decorate carefully with fresh mint leaves. Trickle cold syrup over the top of the mountain and serve with the remaining syrup in a small jug, and with cream, whipped if desired.

Almond Fruit Salad

Although a dessert course is almost unknown at everyday Chinese and Japanese meals, it is not unusual to serve fresh fruit at meals. The almond syrup in this dessert gives a deliciously oriental flavour to the fresh fruit of the salad.

4 dessert apples, cored
4 peaches, skinned and stoned
100 g (4 oz) strawberries
4 slices pineapple
100 g (4 oz) fresh lychees
Almond syrup:
1 tablespoon cornflour
2 tablespoons water
2 tablespoons ground almonds
450 ml ($\frac{3}{4}$ pint) water
3 tablespoons sugar

Preparation time: 20 minutes, plus cooling
Cooking time: 20 minutes
Serves 4–6

1. First, make the syrup. Blend the cornflour with the 2 tablespoons of water. Put the almonds, water, blended cornflour and sugar into a pan and mix well.

2. Gradually bring to the boil, stirring, then simmer for 10 minutes, stirring constantly. Remove from the heat and leave to cool, stirring occasionally to prevent a skin forming.

3. Slice the apples, peaches and strawberries; cut the pineapple into cubes and skin the lychees. Put all the fruit in a bowl and mix well. Spoon over the almond syrup and chill before serving.

Right: Fruit salad ice mountain

Agar Agar Jelly

Thach

This jelly is typical of Vietnamese desserts; it is light, refreshing and uses fruit.

10 g (¼ oz) agar agar strands
water (see method)
6 tablespoons sugar
5 drops banana essence
crushed ice
slices of starfruit (carambolas),
to decorate

Preparation time: 15 minutes, plus soaking and chilling
Cooking time: about 10 minutes
Serves 4

1. Place the agar agar strands in a bowl. Add cold water to cover and set aside for at least 1 hour.

2. Meanwhile, combine 5 tablespoons of the sugar with 250 ml (8 fl oz) water in a small saucepan. Bring to the boil, stirring until the sugar has dissolved. Boil steadily, without stirring, for 2 minutes, then add 3 drops of banana essence and set aside to cool.

3. Drain the agar agar strands and place them in a saucepan with 600 ml (1 pint) water. Bring to the boil, reduce the heat and simmer, stirring constantly until all the agar agar has dissolved. Stir in the remaining sugar and banana essence. Pour into a shallow baking tray and allow to cool, then refrigerate until quite firm.

4. When the agar agar jelly is solid, cut it into julienne (matchstick) strips. Half fill 4 tall serving glasses with jelly strips, top with crushed ice and add 2–3 teaspoons of the banana syrup to each glass. Mix well and decorate with slices of starfruit.

Banana and Pineapple Fritters

Chuoi Va Thom Chien Gion

Thick apple rings, or any other firm fruit, may be used in this Vietnamese recipe instead of the banana or pineapple. If tinned fruit is used, it must be well drained.

Batter:
50 g (2 oz) self-raising flour
150 g (5 oz) plain flour
¼ teaspoon baking powder
pinch of salt
1½–2 teaspoons vegetable oil
water (see method)
1 egg white, stiffly beaten

oil for deep-frying
4 bananas
4 pineapple rings, fresh or
*   canned*
icing sugar, sieved, to coat

Preparation time: 10 minutes
Cooking time: 15–20 minutes
Serves 4

1. Prepare the batter. Combine the flours, baking powder, salt and oil in a large bowl. Stir in enough water to form a smooth paste. Lightly fold in the stiffly beaten egg white.

2. Heat the oil in a deep-fat fryer.

3. Meanwhile, peel the bananas and cut them in half lengthways. Drain the pineapple rings on paper towels to remove excess juice or syrup.

4. Quickly dip the fruit into the batter and cook in batches in the hot oil until puffed and golden. Do not add too many fritters to the pan at any one time, or the temperature of the oil will fall and the results will be unsatisfactory.

5. Drain the cooked fritters on paper towels, sprinkle with sieved icing sugar and serve immediately, while they are still hot.

Eight Treasure Rice Pudding

This popular 'grand occasion' Chinese dessert takes its name from the eight different types of dried and candied fruits or nuts it traditionally contains.

350 g (12 oz) short-grain
*   pudding rice*
4 tablespoons caster sugar
50 g (2 oz) unsalted butter
100 g (4 oz) glacé cherries,
*   chopped*
50 g (2 oz) crystallized orange
*   peel, chopped*
25 g (1 oz) each angelica,
*   walnuts and whole blanched*
*   almonds, chopped*
50 g (2 oz) seedless raisins,
*   chopped*
5 tablespoons sweet bean paste

Sugar syrup:
300 ml (½ pint) water
50 g (2 oz) sugar
few drops of almond essence

Preparation time: 20 minutes
Cooking time: about 1¾ hours
Serves 6

1. Rinse the rice, drain and put it into a pan with enough water to cover. Bring to the boil, simmer for 15 minutes and drain. Stir in the sugar and half the butter.

2. Use the remaining butter to grease a 900 ml (1½ pint) pudding basin, and line it with a thin layer of rice. Press a little of each fruit and nut into this layer in a decorative pattern. Mix together the remaining rice, fruit and nuts. Spoon alternate layers of this mixture and bean paste into the basin, finishing with the rice mixture. Press down firmly.

3. Cover the basin with greaseproof paper and foil, making a pleat in the centre; secure with string. Steam for 1–1¼ hours.

4. To make the syrup, bring the water and sugar to the boil, stirring. Remove from the heat and add the almond essence.

5. Turn the pudding out on to a warmed serving dish and serve hot, with the sugar syrup.

Banana and pineapple fritters; Agar agar jelly

Banana Cake

Banh Chuoi

This Vietnamese version of China's steamed cake (see page 210) includes fruit, as do so many desserts and sweet dishes from Vietnam.

6 bananas
200 ml (7 fl oz) water
200 ml (7 fl oz) coconut milk
200 g (7 oz) plain flour
100 g (4 oz) sugar

Preparation time: 10 minutes, plus cooling
Cooking time: about 40 minutes
Serves 6

1. Peel the bananas and cut them into thick rounds. Put them into the saucepan with the water. Bring the water and bananas to the boil and simmer until the water has reduced to a quarter of its original volume. Set aside to cool.

2. Mix the coconut milk with the plain flour and the sugar. Add the reduced banana-and-water mixture to this, then stir all together thoroughly.

3. Pour the mixture into an earthenware container and steam it in the top part of a steamer for 30 minutes. Serve hot or cold, with single cream.

Sweet Peanut Cream

Peanut butter forms the basis for a sweet creamy dessert in this recipe from China.

50 g (2 oz) smooth peanut butter
1 litre (1¾ pints) milk or water
4 tablespoons sugar
4 teaspoons rice flour or cornflour, dissolved in 4 tablespoons water

Preparation time: 5 minutes
Cooking time: 15 minutes
Serves 4

1. Put the peanut butter into a saucepan and gradually stir in the milk or water to make a smooth paste. Add the sugar and bring to the boil, stirring constantly.

2. Add the dissolved rice flour or cornflour and cook, stirring, until the mixture thickens.

3. Transfer to a bowl and serve warm, as a dessert.

Almond Jelly with Lychees

Versions of this popular dessert may be found in eating houses throughout Kuala Lumpur and Penang in Malaysia. If agar-agar is not available, the recipe can be made with one sachet of gelatine instead.

600 ml (1 pint) water
3 teaspoons agar agar powder
100 g (4 oz) sugar
250 ml (8 fl oz) evaporated milk
½ teaspoon almond essence
1 × 450 g (1 lb) can lychees in syrup, chilled
6 maraschino cherries, to decorate

Preparation time: 10 minutes, plus chilling
Cooking time: about 10 minutes
Serves 6

1. Place the water in a saucepan and sprinkle the agar agar powder over the top. Bring slowly to the boil, then simmer for 5 minutes. Add the sugar and milk and heat gently, stirring all the time, until the sugar dissolves.

2. Add the almond essence drop by drop, to suit your taste.

3. Pour the jelly into a cake tin or mould, and chill for 1 hour or until it has set.

4. To serve, cut the jelly into squares or diamond shapes. Drain the lychees, reserving 1 cup of the syrup. Arrange the jelly pieces and lychees in 6 individual bowls, pour a little syrup over and decorate each serving with a cherry.

Tangerine Baskets

This attractive-looking sweet is traditionally served for Japan's charming Doll Festival, celebrated on 3 March.

4 tangerines
15 g (½ oz) gelatine
450 ml (¾ pint) water
75 g (3 oz) sugar

Preparation time: 15–20 minutes
Cooking time: 5 minutes
Serves 4

1. Cut each tangerine to make it look like a small basket with a handle: hold the tangerine stalk end up, make two parallel cuts 1 cm (½ inch) apart, on both sides of the top centre down one-third of the fruit. Then, cut horizontally on each side of the handle and remove the two pieces you have cut out.

2. Carefully extract all the pulp from the tangerine and squeeze out its juice into a small bowl. You should now have a small, empty basket. Repeat the procedure for the remaining tangerines.

3. Dissolve the gelatine in the water in a basin over a saucepan of hot water. Add the sugar and tangerine juice, leave until the jelly begins to set, then spoon it into the tangerine baskets and chill.

Apple 'gelatine'; Almond creams with apricot sauce

Apple 'Gelatine'

Ringo no Kanten

This is a fruit jelly dessert from Japan, using kanten (agar-agar) rather than gelatine.

2 blocks of kanten (agar-agar)
450 ml ($\frac{3}{4}$ pint) water
450 ml ($\frac{3}{4}$ pint) apple juice
a pinch of salt
$\frac{1}{2}$ lemon, thinly sliced
a pinch of dried peppermint leaves
prepared fruit in season, such as strawberries, melon, pears (optional)

Preparation time: 10 minutes, plus chilling
Cooking time: 10 minutes
Serves 6

1. Put the kanten into a saucepan, cover with the water and apple juice and add the salt, lemon slices and peppermint. Bring to the boil, stirring, and simmer until the kanten has completely dissolved.

2. Strain into a bowl. Allow to cool slightly, then add the fruit, if using. Pour into a decorative mould and chill until set.

Almond Creams with Apricot Sauce

Almond Cream no Anzu Sauce-soe

This is another of those deliciously creamy desserts with which the Japanese like to end a meal.

1 tablespoon gelatine, dissolved according to instructions on packet
100 g (4 oz) sugar
a pinch of salt
2 eggs, separated
300 ml ($\frac{1}{2}$ pint) milk
$\frac{1}{2}$ teaspoon almond essence
250 ml (8 fl oz) double cream
toasted flaked almonds, to decorate
Sauce:
350 ml (12 fl oz) apricot juice
100 g (4 oz) sugar
1 teaspoon lemon juice
75 g (3 oz) dried apricots, chopped

Preparation time: 20 minutes, plus cooling
Cooking time: 25–30 minutes
Serves 8

1. Place the gelatine, half the sugar, the salt, egg yolks and milk in a saucepan and heat gently, stirring until the gelatine has completely dissolved and the mixture is smooth. Remove from the heat and stir in the almond essence. Chill until the mixture is beginning to thicken.

2. Beat the egg whites until frothy, then gradually beat in the remaining sugar and continue beating until stiff and glossy. Whip the cream until thick. Fold the cream and egg whites into the egg yolk mixture. Divide between eight moulds each with a 150 ml ($\frac{1}{4}$ pint) capacity. Chill until set.

3. To make the sauce, place all the ingredients in a saucepan, cover and simmer for 20–25 minutes or until the apricots are tender. Chill.

4. To serve, pour the sauce over the almond creams and top with flaked almonds.

Indian Ice Cream with Pistachios

Pista Kulfi

This very rich ice cream is traditionally served from conical moulds.

300 ml ($\frac{1}{2}$ pint) double cream
300 ml ($\frac{1}{2}$ pint) milk
1 × 400 g (14 oz) can condensed milk
1 tablespoon clear honey
2 tablespoons chopped pistachios
2 teaspoons rose water
green food colouring (optional)

Preparation time: 15 minutes, plus cooling and chilling
Cooking time: 50 minutes
Serves 6–8

1. Heat the cream, milk, condensed milk and honey together in a heavy-based saucepan. Bring gently to the boil, stirring constantly, then simmer for 45 minutes over very low heat.

2. Remove the pan from the heat and sprinkle in the pistachios and rose water, then add a little food colouring, if using. Allow the mixture to cool.

3. Pour the mixture into a shallow 900 ml ($1\frac{1}{2}$ pint) freezer container or 6 to 8 *kulfi* moulds and freeze for 3 to 4 hours.

4. Remove from the freezer and leave at room temperature for 20 to 30 minutes to soften, before serving.

Peach 'Gelatine'

Momo no Kanten

This sweet recipe from Japan can be served with tea, or as a snack or a dessert. It may be made with unsweetened crushed pineapple, rather than the peach pulp, if preferred.

1 long kante (agar-agar)
450 ml (¾ pint) water
350 g (12 oz) sugar
120 ml (4 fl oz) fresh peach pulp
juice of ½ lemon
2 egg whites

Preparation time: 25 minutes, plus soaking
Cooking time: 10 minutes
Makes 24

1. Wash the kante under cold running water, then put in a pan, cover with the water and leave to soak for 20–30 minutes.

2. Bring to the boil over moderate heat until completely melted, then add the sugar and stir until dissolved. Strain through a very fine sieve, then stir in the peach pulp and lemon juice and leave to cool.

3. Beat the egg whites until stiff, then gradually fold in the cooled peach liquid. Pour into a shallow tin and chill in the refrigerator until set.

4. Cut into 2.5 cm (1 inch) squares or diamond shapes. Serve chilled.

Cream Cheese Balls in Syrup

Rasgullah

Another favourite Indian sweet, these cool-tasting cream cheese balls flavoured with rose water, help cool the palate after a hot curry.

paneer, made with 2.25 litres (4 pints) milk (see page 18, double quantity)
75 g (3 oz) blanched almonds, chopped
115g (4½ oz) semolina
12–15 cubes sugar
Syrup:
1 litre (1¾ pints) water
1 litre (1¾ pints) sugar
pinch of cream of tartar
½ teaspoon rose water

Preparation time: 15 minutes
Cooking time: 2½ hours
Makes 12–15

1. Stir the paneer to a smooth paste, then add the almonds and semolina. Knead well until smooth.

2. When the palm of the hand is greasy, mould the paste. Break the dough into 12–15 pieces, about the size of walnuts. Shape into balls, moulding each one around a cube of sugar.

3. To make the syrup, put all the ingredients, except the rose water, in a heavy pan and heat gently until the sugar has dissolved, stirring occasionally.

4. Bring to the boil, add the balls of dough, then lower the heat and simmer very gently for 2 hours.

5. Stir in the rose water, then serve hot or cold.

Caramelized Banana Slices

This is a popular way of serving fruit in Thailand, and Thai cooks apply the method to many fruits besides bananas, including apples, pears, oranges, tangerines and pineapples. Each guest should have a bowl of iced water for dipping the slices before eating them.

4 ripe firm bananas
lime or lemon juice
peanut oil for deep frying
6 tablespoons sugar
3 tablespoons water

Preparation time: 15 minutes
Cooking time: 30 minutes
Serves 4

1. Peel the bananas and slice them thinly lengthways. Sprinkle with lime or lemon juice and set aside while you heat the oil and prepare the caramel.

2. To make the syrup, slowly melt the sugar in the water over a low heat, then increase the heat and let the mixture boil until it turns a pale caramel colour – do not allow it to brown. to prevent the syrup over-cooking, as soon as it turns pale golden, remove the pan from the heat and stand it on a teatowel, dipped in cold water and wrung out.

3. Deep-fry the banana slices, a few at a time, in the heated oil for a few seconds. Remove with a slotted spoon to a heated metal dish. Continue until all the slices are fried and set out on the serving dish, which should be big enough to take them in a single layer.

4. Reheat the syrup and pour it over the banana slices in an even trickle so that it coats all the slices. Serve at once.

Spiced Semolina Dessert

Halwa

Just about every city in India has its own version of this famous sweetmeat. It is worth making at home, although traditionalists say the halwa-maker's art is inherited and cannot be learnt.

225 g (8 oz) semolina
4 tablespoons desiccated coconut
450 g (1 lb) sugar
1 tablespoon poppy seeds
seeds of 6 cardamoms
600 ml (1 pint) water
100 g (4 oz) ghee, melted

Preparation time: 10 minutes, plus cooling
Cooking time: 1 hour, 15 minutes
Serves 4

1. Put the semolina in a large, heavy-based saucepan with the coconut, sugar, poppy and cardamom seeds. Mix well then stir in the water. Bring to the boil, stirring constantly, then lower the heat and simmer for at least 1 hour until every ingredient is soft, stirring frequently.

2. Gradually add the ghee and mix well to incorporate.

3. Transfer the mixture to a shallow tray and spread evenly. Leave to cool, then cut into triangles or diamond shapes. Store in an airtight container in a cool place.

Illustrated on pages 148–149

Carrot Pudding

Gajjar Kheer

That sweet vegetable, the carrot, is used to great effect in this Indian pudding. It is a very rich pudding, so one serving each will be sufficient for most people.

450 g (1 lb) carrots, grated
225 g (8 oz) sugar
1.15 litres (2 pints) milk
6 cardamoms
1 tablespoon sultanas
1 tablespoon slivered almonds

Preparation time: 5 minutes
Cooking time: 1 hour
Serves 4

1. Put the carrots in a bowl and sprinkle with the sugar. Set aside.

2. Put the milk in a pan with the cardamoms. Bring to the boil and simmer for 45 minutes or until the milk is reduced by half. Add the carrots, then simmer until the mixture thickens.

3. Remove the pan from the heat and leave to cool slightly. Stir in the sultanas and almonds. Serve hot or cold.

Doughnut Spirals in Syrup

Jallebi

In many Indian cities you will encounter these deep-fried, pretzel-like sweets being sold on open stalls in the streets. Best eaten fresh and still warm, they are fried specially for their customers by the stall holders.

275 g (10 oz) plain flour
40 g (1½ oz) rice flour
pinch of baking powder
½ teaspoon salt
175 ml (6 fl oz) water
vegetable oil for deep-frying
Syrup:
1 litre (1¾ pints) water
1 litre (1¾ pints) sugar
pinch of cream of tartar
½ teaspoon rose water
*½ teaspoon yellow or red food
  colouring (optional)*

Preparation time: 15 minutes, plus chilling
Cooking time: about 20 minutes
Makes 20–24

1. Sift the flour, baking powder and salt into a bowl. Add the water gradually and beat to a smooth batter. Cover and chill overnight.

2. The next day, make the syrup: put the water, sugar and cream of tartar in a heavy pan and heat gently until the sugar has dissolved, stirring occasionally. Add the rose water and food colouring, if using.

3. Heat the oil in a deep pan until a little of the batter, dropped into the hot oil, sizzles and turns crisp.

4. Put the batter into a piping bag, fitted with a 2.5 cm (1 inch) plain nozzle. Pipe spirals, about 10 cm (4 inches) in diameter, into the hot oil. Deep-fry in batches for about 3 minutes until crisp, then remove from the pan with a slotted spoon and drain on paper towels.

5. Immerse the jallebi in the syrup for 30 seconds while still warm. Serve hot or cold.

Doughnut spirals in syrup; Cream cheese balls in syrup; Carrot pudding

Index

USEFUL ADDRESSES

These are suppliers of Oriental foodstuffs.

Asian Food Centre
544 Harrow Road
London W9
081-960-3731

Asian Stores
58 Westbourne Grove
London W2
071-727-5033

East-West Provisions
61a Woodstock Road
Oxford
0865-311288

Evergreen Stores
17 Goldhurst Terrace
London NW6
071-624-4983

Far East Supermarket
28 High Road
Willesden Green
London NW10
081-459-0977

Loon Fung Supermarket
42–44 Gerrard Street
London W1
071-437-1922

Loon Moon Supermarket
9a Gerrard Street
London W1
071-734-9940

See Woo Supermarket
18–20 Lisle Street
London WC2
071-439-8325

Win Yit Supermarket
96–98 Coventry Street
Birmingham 5
021-643-2851
and
45–47 Faulkner Street
Manchester
061-236-4152

ACKNOWLEDGMENTS

Special photography, Vernon Morgan: 1, 2–3, 4–5, 6–7, 20, 28, 29, 30, 31, 32, 33, 35 (except bottom, left), 36, 37, 38, 39 (except top), 40, 42, 44–45, 48, 59, 100–101, 133, 148–149.

Food prepared for photography by Allyson Birch and Kathy Man. *Stylist:* Marian Price.
All other photographs from the Octopus Group Picture Library.
Line drawings by Will Giles and Sandra Pond.